STRIVE FOR A 5

Preparing for the
AP® United States History Exam

Warren Hierl
Career Center, Winston-Salem, North Carolina

Louisa Bond Moffitt
Marist School, Atlanta, Georgia

Nancy Schick
Los Alamos High School, Los Alamos, New Mexico

AMERICA'S HISTORY
Eighth Edition

James A. Henretta
Eric Hinderaker
Rebecca Edwards
Robert O. Self

Bedford/St. Martin's   Boston ◆ New York

Manufactured in the United States of America.

6 7 8 9   20 19 18

For information, write: Bedford/St. Martin's, 75 Arlington Street, Boston, MA 02116 (617-399-4000)

ISBN 978-1-4576-2902-0

Acknowledgments

Text acknowledgments and copyrights appear at the back of the book on page 394, which constitute an extension of the copyright page. Art acknowledgments and copyrights appear on the same page as the art selections they cover. It is a violation of the law to reproduce these selections by any means whatsoever without the written permission of the copyright holder.

AP® is a trademark registered and/or owned by the College Board, which was not involved in the production of, and does not endorse, this product.

Brief Contents

Contents

SECTION 3
Practice Tests   299

Preface for Teachers

Strive for a 5: Preparing for the AP United States History Exam is a student prep guide, designed to provide students with a thorough review of the course material while practicing AP test-taking skills that will stand them in good stead for the AP U.S. History (APUSH) Exam. Designed to pair with *America's History*, Eighth Edition, by James A. Henretta, Eric Hinderaker, Rebecca Edwards, and Robert O. Self, *Strive for a 5* applies an AP-specific framework to the text's narrative and offers extended attention to the new AP U.S. History Exam format and strategies for taking the exam. Either assigned as a core component of the test preparation coursework or recommended to students as an independent review and practice tool, *Strive for a 5* is designed to familiarize students with the new APUSH exam format, thematically organize and review the key concepts, and provide level-appropriate practice questions and answer explanations. For students who are striving for a 5, there is no better preparation guide.

The College Board has revised the APUSH course and exam beginning in the 2014–2015 school year. The revised course and exam emphasize seven big ideas, or themes, in U.S. history, a newly revised course outline consisting of twenty-five key concepts within nine historical periods, with new foci on historical thinking skills and learning objectives. Students will find a fuller description of both the course and exam in the sections "Overview of the AP® U.S. History Course" on page 3 and "Familiarizing Yourself with the Exam" on page 6. Students will find ample and relevant practice of these skills within the pages of *Strive for a 5*.

Features of This Prep Guide

The **Introduction for Students, Section 1**, serves as an introduction to the new AP U.S. History course and exam, including an overview of the four question types, strategies for answering the questions, tips for successful historical writing, and a brief overview of some of the scoring changes for the exam. Students should also visit the College Board for the most up-to-date information about how the exams are scored. You and they will find this at the College Board site at apcentral.collegeboard.com. You will find rubrics for the document-based and long essay questions in the Appendix to *AP® United States History Course and Exam Description Including the Curriculum Framework, Updated Fall 2015*.

In the **Review of AP United States History in Section 2**, **period overviews** follow the AP nine-period structure and groups the chapter reviews with the appropriate AP period. The book is also organized into nine parts, and, at times, the periodization of the course and book overlap; at other times, the book and course deviate chronologically. When this happens, it is a perfect time to get students to practice the historical thinking skill of chronological reasoning. Each of the nine periods includes **Practice Questions**, including stimulus-based multiple-choice questions, short-answer questions, and either a practice document-based question (Periods 2, 4, 6, and 8) or a long essay question (Periods 3, 5, 7). Periods 1 and 9 do not include practice questions for the DBQ or the long essays because the new APUSH exam will never contain a DBQ or long essay on these two periods.

Two full-length AP-style practice exams in Section 3 conclude this book. With 55 stimulus-based multiple-choice questions, four short-answer questions, a DBQ, and two long essay questions, these practice exams offer students the chance to measure their progress and areas in which they need further review before the College Board exam. Each practice exam comes with model answers and explanations. Thus, students will become increasingly comfortable with the AP style while completing a comprehensive review of the textbook material.

About the Authors

Warren Hierl taught Advanced Placement U.S. History at the Career Center in Winston-Salem, North Carolina, for twenty-eight years. He has conducted more than ninety one-day Advanced Placement workshops, more than eight five-week-long Advanced Placement Summer Institutes throughout the Southeast, and more than seventy pre-AP workshops throughout the country. He was a member of the committee that wrote the original *Advanced Placement Social Studies Vertical Teams Guide* and, with Nancy Schick, the *Advanced Placement U.S. History Teachers Guide*. He has been a reader, a table leader, and an exam leader, and, for the past eight years, the question leader on the DBQ at the AP U.S. History reading.

Louisa Bond Moffitt holds a Ph.D. in U.S. History and has been teaching AP United States history at Marist School in Atlanta, Georgia, for more than twenty-eight years. She has been involved with the AP U.S. History reading for many years, serving as an exam leader and assistant chief reader for that exam. She is currently working as the question leader for the alternate AP U.S. History exam. In addition, she has been a member of the AP U.S. History test development committee, as well as several other test development committees. She has also coauthored a number of textbooks dealing with international relations built around conversations among former U.S. secretaries of state and defense. She has been active in the field of Middle East studies and has been recognized by the Middle East Studies Association for her work with both students and teachers. She is the chair of the History Department at Marist School and leads numerous AP U.S. workshops during the summers and throughout the school year.

Nancy Schick holds a B.A. in political science from Michigan State University and an M.A.T. from the University of Pittsburgh. She taught AP U.S. History and AP European History for nearly twenty years at Los Alamos High School in New Mexico. She has been a reader, table leader, and exam leader for AP U.S. history for many years and served four years on the AP U.S. History Development Committee. She has led over forty summer institutes and many workshops in several states and farther afield in Saipan and El Salvador. She has received grants from the National Endowment for the Humanities, the Gilder Lehrman Institute, the Goethe Institut, and the U.S. Institute of Peace. She was a Fulbright-Hays scholar in Southeast Asia, a Presidential Scholar Distinguished Teacher five times, and the 2005 New Mexico Teacher of the Year.

SECTION 1
Introduction for Students

Welcome to the AP U.S. History course, sometimes called APUSH. Your teacher is no doubt looking forward to teaching you not only the content of American history but also the concepts and historical skills. Although you may be concerned about the difficulty of the course and the AP exam at the end of the school year, you will be well on your way to success as you learn to think like a historian and see the course as an exciting challenge.

Many resources are available to help you. One is your textbook, another is this test preparation manual, and a third is the College Board Web site (apcentral.collegeboard.com), where you can find much more information about the course and the exam. If your textbook came with the adaptive learning system called LearningCurve, you can log in and watch your progress through the game-like review program. The questions in LearningCurve are not exactly like the AP questions you will see on the exam, but they do test your knowledge and reasoning skills in U.S. history.

Overview of the AP® U.S. History Course

The AP U.S. History course is a comprehensive history of the parts of North America that became the United States from just before European contact in 1492 to the present. This course examines many aspects of U.S. history: political, cultural, social, economic, and diplomatic. Your teacher and your textbook will help you to understand how these threads are woven together into a diverse and complex American tapestry.

You will also learn how to analyze and interpret primary source materials, connect issues of one time period with those of another, and write clearly and succinctly in order to support a thesis. As you "strive for a 5," the highest score on the AP exam, you will master the historical content, achieve the thematic learning objectives, and develop the critical thinking skills essential to both the AP U.S. History course and the exam.

Your teacher will explain how the APUSH course is structured. For more detail, go to apcentral.collegeboard.com, and find the curriculum framework for U.S. History under "Advances in AP." There you will find the course description for the revised course that begins in fall 2015 with the first exam administered in May 2016. This course is substantially different from the previous U.S. History course, which was taught until the 2013–2014 school year. Thus, using older test preparation guides and exams will not be as helpful and could mislead you about what to expect on the exam.

Briefly, the course is divided into nine historical periods, and there are seven themes that cut across all nine periods. The periods are:

Period 1: 1491–1607

Period 2: 1607–1754

Period 3: 1754–1800

Period 4: 1800–1848

Period 5: 1844–1877

Period 6: 1865–1898

Period 7: 1890–1945

Period 8: 1945–1980

Period 9: 1980–Present

The themes are:

American and National Identity

Work, Exchange, and Technology

Migration and Settlement

Politics and Power

America in the World

Geography and the Environment

Culture and Society

Each theme weaves through the more than five hundred years of U.S. history and is accompanied by a set of thematic learning objectives. In addition, each of the nine periods requires that you examine key concepts that are broken down into subconcepts and specific examples. This may sound complicated, but the curriculum framework that establishes this structure is designed to show you clearly just what it is that you are expected to know and to do.

In addition to the historical content, you will develop and practice historical thinking skills. There are nine skills divided into four types. For example, one skill type is Analyzing Historical Sources and Evidence, and one specific skill in that group is "Analyzing Evidence: Content and Sourcing." (This skill will be very important when you approach the document-based question on the exam.) The historical thinking skills are:

Skill Type I: Analyzing Historical Sources and Evidence

Skill 1: Analyzing Evidence: Content and Sourcing (Primary Sources)

Skill 2: Interpretation (Secondary Sources)

Skill Type II: Making Historical Connections

Skill 3: Comparison

Skill 4: Contextualization

Skill 5: Synthesis

Skill Type III: Chronological Reasoning

Skill 6: Causation

Skill 7: Patterns of Continuity and Change over Time

Skill 8: Periodization

Skill Type IV: Creating and Supporting a Historical Argument

Skill 9: Argumentation

In Section 1 of this test preparation guide, we suggest strategies for reviewing the course information and approaching each type of question on the exam. In Section 2, you will review the content of the AP U.S. History course and the textbook. Our goal is for you to build confidence by knowing what to expect from the exam and reviewing the most important elements of the APUSH course.

Preparing for the AP® U.S. History Exam

The African American author James Baldwin once observed, "American history is longer, larger, more various, more beautiful, and more terrible than anything anyone has ever said about it." You have begun your in-depth examination of the story of the United States, and perhaps you've already discovered some beautiful and terrible truths that were new to you. You are also learning how historians examine and write about the past: you too can learn how to "do" history.

Rigorous historical study of the nation is both challenging and rewarding. The AP Examination in May is your chance to demonstrate your mastery of U.S. history. Although the challenges of the course and test may feel overwhelming from time to time, with advance planning and consistent effort, you can enter the examination room with confidence. *Strive for a 5* will help you get there!

What's in This Book?

Preparation is the key to success in the AP U.S. History course. Your textbook, *America's History*, Eighth Edition, by James A. Henretta, Eric Hinderaker, Rebecca Edwards, and Robert O. Self, is an important resource, and—along with this *Strive for a 5*—you have the tools you need to earn a top score.

Section 1 (which you're reading right now) explains how to register for the exam and make a review plan for yourself. Here you will also find explanations of and guidelines for how to respond to the four types of questions on the AP Exam: multiple-choice questions, short-answer questions, document-based question, and long essay question.

Section 2 follows the organization of the AP U.S. History course and correlates course themes and key concepts with *America's History*, Eighth Edition. Both the course and *America's History* are divided into nine chronological periods, or parts. Within each period, you will find a period overview, a list of key terms, and questions to consider as you read and study. Also included are chapter summaries from *America's History*. Following the chapter summaries you will find a thematic timeline, followed by practice questions—multiple-choice, short-answer, and either a long essay or a document-based question. Each part also contains answers with explanations for multiple-choice questions as well as feedback on the short-answer, document-based, and long essay questions.

Section 3 consists of two full-length AP-style practice exams that require you to put all of your preparation into action. These are designed to follow the AP format and prepare you for the real thing. The answer keys for both practice tests are at the end of Section 3.

Registering for the Exam

Your teacher and school are probably facilitating your exam registration, but if not, make sure that you do not miss the registration deadline in late February. If you are taking this exam without having taken the course or if your school does not offer AP courses, or if you are unaffiliated with a school (for example, if you are home-schooled), check with the College Board to find the name of an AP coordinator for your area. If you are anxious about other registration issues, consult the College Board's Web site (www.collegeboard.com) and locate the AP home page. Here you can access a page for students and parents where you will find the *Bulletin for AP Students and Parents.*

Familiarizing Yourself with the Exam

If your teacher has not given you AP exam questions as practice, you should examine closely the two practice tests in this book. You can also go to the AP Web site (apcentral.collegeboard .com). Once there, search for information on the AP U.S. History Exam. You can download the College Board's *AP® United States History: Course and Exam Description Including the Curriculum Framework, Updated Fall 2015,* which includes information about the exam as well as sample questions. If you are using a test-prep guide or any other resources linked to AP U.S. History exams given before May 2015, remember that the new exam is much different.

The AP U.S. History Exam is 3 hours 15 minutes long and consists of two sections and four parts. The first section of the exam contains multiple-choice and short-answer questions. The multiple-choice part consists of fifty-five questions arranged into sets of two to five questions that focus on a single primary source, secondary source, map, or illustration (these are known as *stimulus questions*). The multiple-choice questions test your knowledge of the key concepts and learning objectives found in the *AP® United States History Course and Exam Description Including the Curriculum Framework, Updated Fall 2015*, as well as required content. You have 55 minutes to answer the multiple-choice questions.

The four short-answer questions focus on the themes and historical thinking skills required for the APUSH course. You will answer a key question in U.S. history, sometimes using stimuli such as a primary source or a secondary source. You have 50 minutes to answer the four short-answer questions.

The second section of the exam consists of two essay questions: a document-based question (DBQ) and a long essay question. The document-based question (55 minutes) tests your ability to analyze historical evidence and then to use that evidence to answer a historical question in a coherent, well-organized essay with a clear thesis, appropriate use of evidence, and a conclusion. You will have to analyze the evidence and support your thesis with specific, relevant historical evidence. For the long essay question (35 minutes), you have a choice between two questions. The long essay assesses your historical thinking skills and ability to analyze and synthesize significant events or issues in U.S. history. Questions are limited to the topics specifically mentioned in the curriculum framework's key concepts, but you must use historical examples to support your answer. These examples may come from the curriculum framework or from your text or your classroom discussions. We suggest more specific strategies for these question types later in this section.

Setting Up a Review Schedule

Your teacher has factored the testing date into his or her course planning; she or he may also offer review sessions that are specifically applicable to the AP test. Beyond what your teacher offers, be sure to set up your own review schedule, allowing time to review each of the nine parts of the textbook and nine periods of the course, take and then review the two practice tests, and review any concepts that seem challenging.

The spring term at any high school can be hectic. Adding AP exam preparation to your weekly schedule a few months prior to the exam, particularly if you are taking exams in more than one subject, is essential. Ideally, you should allow one week for reviewing each of the nine textbook parts, plus a week for taking and reviewing each of the practice tests. If you don't have time to go through the nine periods, at least take the practice tests to see what topics and skills you need to review. Cramming the night before the test is never a good idea. Your priority the evening before the test is to get a good night's sleep!

Successful Historical Writing

You will spend almost half of the time taking the AP exam on planning and writing the two essays. Framing and responding to analytical questions is an essential part of what historians do; in fact, the poet W. H. Auden once noted, "History is, strictly speaking, the study of questions." The essay questions on the AP exam have more than one correct approach. Whether you are writing an essay for your class or responding to the AP exam, start by thinking about how you will frame your argument and use your time.

Effective historical writing differs from simple expression of opinion: you must use evidence to back up your generalizations and support your arguments. Good historical essay writing starts with a clearly articulated thesis and should build on a coherent organization.

What does it mean to organize your ideas effectively? Try this exercise. The following sentences are in scrambled order. Read them carefully and figure out how you can order them for maximum clarity. *Hint: Which sentence establishes an idea that unifies all of the other information? That one should come first.*

(A) The southern terrain and climate lent itself to farming large tracts of land for cash crops.
(B) Over time, southern planters came to view themselves as akin to landed gentry and shaped a patriarchal social structure that reinforced their authority.
(C) Geographic, economic, and social factors all played a part in advancing the South's dependence on slavery.
(D) The most affordable means of tending to the plantations' cash crops was using slaves.
(E) Slavery was an integral part of southern colonial society.

Write the corresponding letters for each sentence on how you think they should be ordered here:

_____

Now that you've attempted to reorder the sentences, can you figure out what question was being asked?

Here is the question: How did economic, geographic, and social factors encourage the growth of slavery as an important part of the economy of the southern colonies between 1607 and 1775?

And here is how the paragraph can best be organized:

Slavery was an integral part of southern colonial society (E). Geographic, economic, and social factors all played a part in advancing the South's dependence on slavery (C). The southern terrain and climate lent itself to farming large tracts of land for cash crops (A). The most affordable means of tending to the plantations' cash crops was using slaves (D). Over time, southern planters came to view themselves as akin to landed gentry and shaped a patriarchal social structure that reinforced their authority (B).

Note the paragraph's underlying logic: the thesis, or topic sentence, addresses the three factors that influenced the southern development of slavery. Those three factors are then addressed in the order they are first mentioned in the first sentence. Chronology is suggested in the last sentence, which begins, "Over time . . ."

Besides ordering your information thoughtfully, you should structure your response in a way that responds precisely to the question posed. After you have read a long essay or document-based question, ask yourself: "What is the question asking?" "How many paragraphs should my response have?" "What should the first paragraph include?" Be strategic. Remember how many essays the AP exam readers have to read and evaluate in a very short period of time. Clarity and directness are essential qualities of successful responses.

First, draft your thesis. Your thesis should not be a restatement of the question; it should be your opinion *about* the question, backed up with the evidence supplied (in the case of the DBQ) and your own information. For example, if the essay is about the economy of the Chesapeake colonies in the colonial period, you will need to discuss tobacco. But the thesis would not be, "Tobacco was very important to the economy of the Chesapeake colonies." Rather, it should be something more like, "Tobacco cultivation created distinctive social, political, and cultural patterns in the Chesapeake colonies that persisted into the nineteenth century, particularly as slave labor became the primary means to grow and harvest tobacco."

Then think about how many paragraphs you will need, and sketch out an outline that includes the examples you will use as evidence to support your thesis. As you begin to write your supporting paragraphs, remember that sentences need to be clear and coherent, as do entire paragraphs. Each paragraph's topic sentence serves as the thesis for that paragraph; in addition, each paragraph should act as a building block toward proving the essay's main thesis. Keeping the essay's main thesis in mind throughout the writing process will ensure that the composition stays on topic.

Another key to excellent historical writing is narrative flow, which can be achieved by connecting each paragraph to the ones before and after by means of transitional words and phrases or a linking sentence. When you are reviewing and revising your own essays, ask yourself: "Does this paragraph logically follow from the preceding one?" "Does it add something significant to the thesis announced in the opening paragraph?" "Is the transition to the next paragraph smooth?" Paying attention to the transitions between your supporting paragraphs will set your writing apart.

Finally, an effective essay must have a conclusion that summarizes its main points and explains how those points interconnect. It is not the place to introduce new information. The conclusion should do more than merely restate the essay's original thesis; it is where you will validate your opinion. Avoid addressing the reader directly or using crutches like "in conclusion" or "in summary"; the content of the concluding paragraph alone should make its purpose clear.

Taking the AP®
U.S. History Exam

This section provides an outline of the test's four parts and offers some basic strategies for tackling AP questions successfully. All four types of questions are designed to test your mastery of both historical content and skills.

When starting the AP U.S. History course, many students ask, "Are we going to have to memorize dates?" Here is the answer from the College Board: "Although there is little to be gained by rote memorization of names and dates in an encyclopedic manner, a student must be able to draw upon a reservoir of systematic factual knowledge in order to exercise analytic skills intelligently." In other words, you're going to have to know your material. Although you are not required to memorize specific dates, the importance of having a firm grasp of chronology and context cannot be overestimated; these are essential to understanding history.

Strategies for the Multiple-Choice Section

The multiple-choice questions on the examination require skills beyond simple recognition and recall. All of these questions include a source such as a text source, map, photograph, chart, or cartoon that you must analyze before making an answer choice. There are between two and five questions for each source. Some compare topics across time periods. All of the questions require you to make the best choice among four possible answers, several of which may be plausible but not specific enough.

The most important advice we can give you is to read the source and the possible choices extremely carefully. Some of the questions will relate directly to the source you have read, but others will require you to recall information from the course content.

Tips for Answering Multiple-Choice Questions

+ Read each question carefully.
+ Read all possible answers and cross out those you believe are incorrect; narrowing your choices gives you the chance to make an educated guess.
+ Connect the specific information of the question to broader trends and themes.
+ Assess the source carefully and eliminate answers that go beyond the bounds of the evidence given.
+ Make a habit of checking your answer sheet frequently throughout the test to ensure that you are filling in the correct ovals—especially if you skip questions or leave some to come back to later.

The Short-Answer Questions

The short-answer questions focus on both historical content and skills. Each question will have three parts, so be sure to label your answers (a), (b), and (c). Some of the questions include a source, which might be text or a photograph or a map. Your answers must be expressed in complete sentences, not bullet points, but you do not need to write a formal essay with a thesis and conclusion. Many of the short-answer questions give you a choice of addressing differing aspects of the historical question; be sure you are not trying to answer ALL the topics when only one is required. Often the second section of the question leads from the first one, that is, you might be asked to describe an event or policy in the first part of the question and then explain why it was successful or not in the second part.

The Document-Based Question

The document-based question essay (DBQ) is the hallmark exercise of the AP U.S. History Exam. DBQs can be drawn from any historical period except Periods 1 and 9. The DBQ asks you to connect relevant evidence from multiple sources (generally five to seven documents) and use those connections to construct an analytical or interpretative essay response. In asking you to place the evidence in context and then use it to explain a cause or to substantiate a thesis, or both, the AP Exam is, in effect, asking you to perform the central creative act of the historian's craft. Remember that each DBQ will focus on one of these historical thinking skills: causation, change and continuity over time, comparison, interpretation, or periodization. The DBQ will also assess your ability to demonstrate the skills of historical argumentation, appropriate use of relevant historical evidence, contextualization, and synthesis.

When approaching the DBQ, do not immediately look at the documents. First, read the question very carefully. After making sure that you understand all of the terms in the prompt, brainstorm a list of relevant information. Try to frame an argument without using the documents, because solely relying on the documents rather than weaving both the documents and outside information into your essay can limit your score. Only after you have done this should you consider the documents and determine how you can best use them in your essay.

Frequently DBQ documents will contradict each other. This is an opportunity to begin sorting and categorizing the documents. For example, you might divide the documents into those supporting and those opposing a proposed policy. Another way to analyze documents might be by their author and his or her background, status in society, gender, job, motivation, or other factors. Is the document written by a man or a woman? By a wealthy industrialist or a factory worker? Thus, the documents themselves provide important keys needed to answer the question. You must use all or all but one of the documents to demonstrate your ability to weigh the relevance of evidence provided, sort through their complexities, and use those complexities in support of your thesis. For example, you might consider the intended audience of the document, its point of view, its format, and its limitations (what *doesn't* it say?).

The DBQ also requires the use of outside information that tests your ability to integrate your historical knowledge with the documents. If you can use information from the documents and connect it to your own knowledge, you will have a stronger essay.

In Section 2 of *Strive for a 5,* you will find a practice DBQ for four of the nine periods in the course. You will also find two additional practice DBQs in the two full-length practice tests in Section 3.

If you have written a research paper or prepared an evidence-based essay in class, you have already practiced the process of writing a DBQ. The purpose of the essay is to prove a point, using your own knowledge of history and the evidence put before you to arrive at a historical narrative or explanation.

Breaking the process down into multiple steps helps you master the process of answering DBQs. A strong DBQ response is well organized and establishes a thesis using the documents and outside information. With practice, you should be able to analyze and digest each document, determine its relevance, and use it in support of a thesis. The very best essays, like good historical writing, focus only on those elements of the documents that serve the thesis. Therefore, do not waste time and space extensively quoting or summarizing the documents.

What's the best way to cite the documents? Avoid saying "Document A says . . ." in an essay. Imagine that your essay can be read on its own, without that packet of documents attached. It's best to cite the source in the least disruptive manner possible so the essay flows well. Parenthetical citations can work, but it is smoothest to identify the quote within your own sentences, like this: "As Thomas Jefferson wrote in the Declaration of Independence in 1776, 'All men are created equal.'"

Tips for Answering Document-Based Questions

- ✦ Read the question carefully to determine exactly what is being asked of you.
- ✦ Determine how each document source relates to the question at hand.
- ✦ Find sentences in the document excerpts that contain key terms and ideas mentioned in the question.
- ✦ Determine the extent to which different document excerpts are similar or contradictory. Sort documents into several different categories to help analyze them.
- ✦ Analyze any maps or visual documents to determine their relevance to the topic.
- ✦ Be sure to include as many pertinent details as possible in support of your DBQ thesis, but don't feel compelled to include extraneous detail.
- ✦ Sophisticated essays often address ambiguities and contradictions in documents and other evidence. Don't be afraid to try to account for these contradictions.

The Long Essay Question

You will choose one of two long essay questions. These questions are included to measure your ability to think critically, recall pertinent information, and write a well-conceived essay that proves your thesis. As with the DBQ, you need to develop a thesis, that is, an argument *about* the topic. Because you do not have documents available, however, you need to provide the historical evidence yourself. Following the thesis, you need several paragraphs that put forward historical information to prove your point. Your conclusion should add to your original thesis and include the arguments stated in the intervening paragraphs. Following the general guidelines for historical writing in the previous section will help you to succeed on the free-response questions.

Tips for Answering Long Essay Questions

- ✦ Read the two questions and determine which one you can answer more successfully.
- ✦ Sketch out a brief outline, recording facts and examples that you remember and organizing them in a sensible way. Each section of the outline should generate a supporting paragraph for your essay. Remember to use clues from the question to structure your essay when possible.
- ✦ Develop a thesis that takes a clear stand on the question posed. Be sure to state the thesis in your introductory paragraph.
- ✦ Begin each supporting paragraph with a clear topic sentence.

- ✦ Consider transitions between paragraphs.
- ✦ Conclude by restating your thesis in a fresh way, perhaps by making a connection to another moment in American history.
- ✦ Keep in mind the volume of essays the exam readers must assess. Clarity and organization are key.
- ✦ Determine what historical thinking skills you must demonstrate in responding to the essay prompt.

Scoring the New AP® U.S. History Exam

The biggest change in scoring for the new APUSH exam is related to scoring the document-based question (DBQ). In the past, DBQs were graded holistically and on a 9-point scale. Now, you can earn a maximum of 7 points, each earned by satisfying a particular requirement. You can earn 1 point for your thesis, a maximum of 3 points for your use of documents, and 1 point for inclusion of relevant outside examples. You can receive 1 point for contextualization, where you must broaden your discussion to reference broader historical events. Finally, the last point to be earned is for synthesis. This is a sophisticated skill that you must demonstrate in this essay. You can earn this synthesis point for extending your thesis, accounting for contradictory information, or connecting your discussion to other historical periods or contexts. For the most up-to-date information on how the exams are scored, please visit the College Board site at apstudent .collegeboard.com. You will find rubrics for the document-based and long essay questions in the Appendix to *AP® United States History Course and Exam Description Including the Curriculum Framework, Updated Fall 2015*.

SECTION 2
A Review of
AP United States History

PERIOD 1
1491–1607

Overview

Period 1 focuses on the North American continent from 1491 until 1607, the years from just before the arrival of European explorers to the founding of the Jamestown colony by the British. These years include the initial contacts between American Indians and the earliest explorers, as well as the introduction of West African slaves to the Western Hemisphere.

The overview begins with an examination of the various native populations that migrated to and spread across North America—their origins and the different ways each group adapted to the conditions they faced in the regions they settled. The American Indian societies that developed shared some common characteristics, but all had to make unique adjustments to the environments they encountered. The result was the creation of societies of varying complexity.

Indians living in present-day Mexico and the American Southwest relied on the cultivation of maize, with the addition of a mix of foraging and hunting to sustain their communities. Settlement of the western Great Plains was limited until the arrival of horses with the Spanish made possible a nomadic lifestyle based on hunting. Those who settled in the Northeast and Southeast relied on both agriculture and hunting, practices that led to more permanent towns and villages.

The arrival of European explorers in the fifteenth and sixteenth centuries brought significant changes to both the Eastern and Western Hemispheres. The introduction of trade goods and agricultural products, as well as diseases on both side of the Atlantic, set off a series of changes that had a lasting impact on the entire world. Called the Columbian Exchange, this series of contacts and interactions initiated demographic, social, and economic changes that reshaped the history of all the regions involved. Areas where the Spanish and Portuguese explored saw the emergence of a racially mixed population, one made even more diverse by the introduction of West African slaves. The Spanish justified slavery by labeling it the *encomienda* system, arguing that offering conversion to Christianity offset the disadvantages of being enslaved. The introduction of horses, pigs, and cattle further altered the economy and lifestyles of those who lived in the Western Hemisphere.

European rivalries led to intense competition for control of the Western Hemisphere. The desire for wealth, the wish to extend political power, and the determination to spread Christianity fueled these rivalries. European nations experienced growth in both population and wealth, furthering the shift from a feudal economy to more modern capitalism. Changes in technology and better business organization also boosted international trade, leading to more rapid changes for the economies of all involved.

Colonization led to significant changes in how Europeans, American Indians, and West Africans viewed each other. Europeans tended to judge all peoples by European standards and saw anyone different from themselves as backward and in need of "civilization." This belief in white superiority led to the justification and extensive use of slavery and other methods of control, such as forced conversion to Christianity. In spite of these hardships, both American Indians and West Africans managed to adapt to the harsh conditions they faced while still finding ways to maintain cultural and linguistic aspects of their distinct heritages, as well as some measures of autonomy in their daily lives.

Key Terms

Be sure that you understand the meaning of these terms and their relevance in U.S. history.

Animism
Capitalism
Civic humanism
Columbian Exchange
Cultural autonomy
Demographic change

Encomienda system
Feudalism
Predestination
Primogeniture
Social diversification
Social issues

Questions to Consider

As you study Period 1, keep the following thematic questions in mind.

American and National Identity

✦ In what ways did American Indians and Africans struggle to maintain their identity and autonomy in the face of Europeans' attempts to subjugate them?

Work, Exchange, and Technology

✦ Why did the economies of native societies differ so much?
✦ What advantages and disadvantages accrued to both European and native societies as a result of the Columbian Exchange?
✦ What impact did technological advancements have on Portuguese and Spanish exploration to the New World?

Migration and Settlement

✦ What forces resulted in the emergence of diverse native societies in both North and South America?
✦ Why were Europeans able to develop and maintain an extensive slave trade?
✦ Why did African slaves replace Indian labor in Spanish New World colonies?
✦ In what ways did the Spanish presence in the Western Hemisphere shape native social, economic, and political development?

Politics and Power

✦ In what ways was European colonization of the New World promoted by national conflicts in Europe?
✦ What factors led American Indian societies to resist the European domination and influence?
✦ What shape did Indian resistance take, and how successful was it?

America in the World

- ✦ How did economic and political rivalries in Europe affect the forms of colonization in North America?
- ✦ What effects did Spanish and Portuguese colonists have on the American Indian population?
- ✦ What effects did the Columbian Exchange have in Europe, Africa, and the Americas?

Geography and the Environment

- ✦ How did different Indian societies confront the environmental challenges?
- ✦ How did the varied environments in North and South America shape the emergence of vastly different economic, social, and political development among American Indian societies?

Culture and Society

- ✦ What religious and social beliefs promoted Spanish and Portuguese colonization in the New World?
- ✦ In what ways did overseas expansion change how Europeans viewed Africans and American Indians?
- ✦ How and why did Africans and American Indians both adapt some aspects of European culture and resist European attempts to change their values and beliefs?

America's History Chapter Summaries

(required AP® content in bold)

Chapter 1
Colliding Worlds, 1450–1600

Chapter 1 discusses the earliest inhabitants of the Western Hemisphere, their migration from Asia, and the different societies that developed as they adapted to new surroundings. The chapter also looks at Western Europe and West and Central Africa on the eve of first contact. It then examines the earliest explorations of the Spanish and the Portuguese into Africa and the Americas.

The first Americans migrated across a land bridge from Siberia in far eastern Asia across the Bering Strait into what today is Alaska. Over time, Native Americans spread across the Americas and adapted to a **variety of environments and developed unique political, economic, language, and social structures**. Mesoamerica was home to the Aztec Empire, and the Andes region was dominated by the Incas. Both societies were led by priests and warrior-kings who managed large, agriculturally based populations with complex political and religious systems. While nothing on the scale of the Aztecs and Incas developed north of Mexico, **maize cultivation spread from Mexico into the Rio Grande Valley and beyond** (ex: Cahokia, Pueblos). **Along the Atlantic coast, native peoples practiced both agriculture and hunting-gathering**. Indians living on the **edges of the Western Plains established a more mobile lifestyle**.

By the late 1400s, European explorers began to arrive in the Americas by sea, **seeking to expand their empires**. The Spanish and the Portuguese were the first to "discover" the Americas as they looked for sea routes to Asia. The Spanish conquistadors began to systematically conquer native empires in Mesoamerica and Peru, **destroying civilizations and introducing diseases that killed millions**. The Indians of Mesoamerica and South America were better organized and able to offer some resistance to European conquerors, while those of North America were weaker lineage-based societies that were more easily subjugated.

Europe in the mid-1400s was largely a land of peasants farming manorial land. Hierarchy authority rested in the hands of the monarchs, the nobility, and the Church, although all of these institutions were on the verge of change with the arrival of the Renaissance. **New technologies made exploration and trade easier**. The power of the merchant class grew as **Europeans became aware of the immense riches to be found in Asia and other parts of the world**. The Portuguese were the first to branch out toward Africa in search of a lucrative gold trade. It was through this trade that the **Portuguese adopted the system of acquiring African slaves**. As their African trade networks expanded, other European countries also looked for ways to both exploit Africa and find a quicker route to the Far East. **Trade in African slaves soon became a lucrative international business** that would have a lasting impact on four continents.

The Spanish soon replaced the Portuguese as the leading empire builders, sending expeditions around Africa as well as across the Atlantic. Native tribes in the West Indies as well as in Mesoamerica fell at the hands of Spanish conquistadors. Many of those who survived the initial onslaught later **died of epidemic European diseases** (ex: smallpox, measles). Paying little attention to Indian culture and traditions, the **Spanish justified their conquests, seeing themselves as bearers of "civilization."** The Spanish created their own bureaucratic empire in the New World, establishing institutions such as **Catholic Church to convert native peoples** and the Spanish legal code and organizing **Indians into their labor force in a system known as the *encomienda*. The Spanish justified the subjugation of Africans and American Indians by claiming superiority and offering them the opportunity to become Christians.**

Chapter 2
American Experiments, 1521–1700

Chapter 2 spans both Periods 1 and 2 of the AP United States History course. The chapter explores the three types of distinctive colonies that emerged in the Americas: the Spanish colonies in Mexico and Peru that relied on the wealth and labor of Indian peoples, the plantation colonies of the tropics and subtropics where slave labor worked to product sugar and other crops, and the colonies where Europeans sought to establish societies similar to the ones they knew in Europe. All of these colonial endeavors brought disease, displacement, or subjugation to native people, but there were **significant differences in the Europeans' approaches to colonization.**

The Spanish came to the New World in search of gold and silver, relying on conquistadors to establish military control and then sending priests to work for the **conversion of native people to Catholicism.** Many Spanish soldiers eventually took Indian wives, leading to the **creation of a society that included large numbers of mixed-race people.** The Spanish used the *encomienda* system to commandeer Indian lands and labor. **Some Indian groups resisted Spanish control and attempted to retain some of their cultural traditions.** When **African slaves replaced native labor, they too managed to retain much of their own cultures.**

The **Columbian Exchange** is the term given to the movement of peoples, diseases, plants, and animals among societies on both sides of the Atlantic Ocean. Beginning with the Spanish and the Portuguese, **epidemic diseases from the Old World**, such as smallpox, influences, measles, and yellow fever, decimated Native American populations. The exchange of **new crops and livestock** transformed the American landscape.

The plantation colonies that emerged first in Brazil saw **the introduction of plantation-based African slave labor to the Americas who replaced Native Americans** , who had succumbed in large numbers to disease. Later **plantation societies emerged in the Caribbean**, based on a single crop: sugar. In the colony of Virginia, established at Jamestown in 1607, tobacco cultivation based on the plantation model emerged as the dominant economic system. At first, planters used indentured servants from England, but as the **supply of indentured servants dwindled, the colony came to rely on slaves imported from Africa.** Slavery as an institution became more rigid and harsher, and a **slave's status became permanent and hereditary.** Although they had few rights, **slaves managed to find ways to resist their bondage.** Continuing **competition for land led to conflicts between Indians and settlers as well as conflicts among the settlers themselves** (ex: Bacon's Rebellion).

The Dutch colony of New Netherland and the French colony of New France both began as fur trading enterprises. French and Dutch trappers and traders often **intermarried with American Indians, building trade alliances in order to obtain valuable furs.** In New France, Jesuit missionaries made concerted efforts to convert Native Americans to Catholicism, allowing some incorporation of native traditions into Catholic rituals.

The British colonies in New England, settled by Separatists and Puritans, established **closely knit communities that stressed family and religious principles. They founded small villages and towns and organized their economy around farming and commerce.** They also brought with them British forms of government, establishing the first representative assemblies in the New World. As the Puritan population grew and settlements expanded, they came into **direct conflict with American Indians** (ex: Puritan-Pequot War, Metacom's War).

Thematic Timeline

THEME	REQUIRED CONTENT	SUPPORTING EXAMPLES
AMERICAN AND NATIONAL IDENTITY	• Though both Indians and Africans in the New World adapted to European language and culture, they were able to maintain elements of their own culture and values.	**Pre-Columbian, up to 1492** • Algonquians and other tribes form a strong tribal identity. **Events in Europe, 1400–1607** • Europeans begin to develop a national rather than a local identity (fifteenth century). • The Spanish base their "Spanish-ness" on Catholicism and then expel or forcibly convert Jews and Muslims (1492). **Western Hemisphere, 1492–1607** • Indians and Africans attempt to maintain their traditional identities even when controlled by the Spanish.
WORK, EXCHANGE, TECHNOLOGY	• Maize cultivation was pivotal to the economic development of North American Indians. • The transatlantic slave trade was initiated by the Portuguese and Spanish who worked with some Africans to acquire slave labor. • The Spanish developed the *encomienda* system, first using Indian labor and then slaves from Africa.	**Pre-Columbian, up to 1492** • Domestication of crops in Mexico and Peru (6000 B.C.). • Incas establish their capital at Cuzco, a complex road system, and administrative centers (fourteenth and fifteenth centuries). • Maize grown in Mississippi Valley (1000 A.D.). • Division of labor in native societies is often based on gender. **Events in Europe, 1400–1607** • New navigational instruments and better shipbuilding methods enable Europeans to enter an era of exploration. • As overseas trade expands, Europeans, especially the Portuguese and Spanish, realize the economic value of slaves captured in Africa. Slavery had become a central element of the trans-Saharan trade network. **Western Hemisphere, 1492–1607** • Horses brought from Europe transform life on the Great Plains and make the Comanches and Sioux formidable tribes. • The Columbian Exchange brings new technologies, food, and diseases to both the New World and Europe. Smallpox and other European diseases decimate Indian communities. • The discovery of gold and silver vastly increases the importance of Spanish possessions in the New World, but the ensuing inflation eventually contributes to the collapse of the Spanish economy and its empire. • In the 1530s, Portuguese establish sugar plantations in Brazil and eventually replace native American labor with African slaves.

THEME	REQUIRED CONTENT	SUPPORTING EXAMPLES
MIGRATION AND SETTLEMENT	• American Indians migrated throughout North America and developed diverse and complex societies. • Indian societies that depended on a combination of agriculture and haunting tended to live in permanent villages. • The Columbian Exchange brought significant changes to native peoples in the Western Hemisphere and to Europeans living in the New World and in Europe.	**Pre-Columbian, up to 1492** • Three separate migrations of Asians to the Americas (13,000 B.C.–3000 B.C.). • Diverse and complex societies develop in the eastern woodlands of North America, notably the Algonquin and Iroquois. • Other complex Indian societies such as the Utes and Shoshones develop in the Great Basin. **Western Hemisphere, 1492–1607** • Portuguese sailors find routes to Africa and India, establishing trading posts. • The Spanish and then the Portuguese look west to the Atlantic. • Columbus sails to the New World (1492) and in four voyages brings 1,000 Spanish men with him. • Ponce de Leon arrives in what is now Florida (1513). • Pedro Cabral sails to what is to become Brazil (1500). • After the arrival of Europeans, the Indian population greatly declines. • In Mesoamerica, the Indian population declines from 20 million in 1500 to 3 million in 1650. • Disease is the primary reason for the decline of native populations. Warfare is the other key reason. • African slaves are bought to New World in huge numbers.
POLITICS AND POWER	• Native people and Africans attempted to maintain their autonomy despite European efforts to control them.	**Pre-Columbian, up to 1492** • In Cahokia in the Mississippi River Valley, Indians develop a sophisticated governmental structure (1000). • Native tribes in North America establish a variety of political systems—for example, chiefdoms (Powhatan Indians) and local leadership (Delaware Indians). • Warfare is common among native peoples, fought for geopolitical reasons as well as a rite of passage and a method to resolve conflicts between families. • Aztecs and Incas establish great empires in, respectively, Mexico and Peru (fourteenth century). • Powerful chiefdoms compete for control of what will become New England.

THEME	REQUIRED CONTENT	SUPPORTING EXAMPLES
POLITICS AND POWER (*continued*)		**Events in Europe, 1400–1607** • Until the fifteenth century, European monarchs are weak, with power centered in the church, the nobility, and the village. Feudalism is the dominant system. • In the fifteenth century, powerful monarchies begin to emerge, and feudalism ends. • Prince Henry the Navigator promotes Portuguese exploration (mid-fifteenth century). • Ferdinand and Isabella begin their reign in Spain and foster exploration and nationalism. • Dutch Calvinists revolt against Spanish rule, winning their independence in 1581. • The Protestant Reformation exacerbates the rivalry between Spain and England, resulting in the defeat of the Spanish Armada (1588). • As England prospers, the foundations of mercantilism are established. **Western Hemisphere, 1492–1607** • The Iroquois Confederacy is formed by union of the Five Nations (c. 1500). • The Spanish bring key institutions with them to the New World—town councils, legal code, and the Catholic Church—in attempts to maintain centralized control over Spanish possessions in North and South America. • Cortez defeats the Aztecs (1521). • Pizarro conquers the Incas (1535).
AMERICA IN THE WORLD	• The arrival of Europeans in the fifteenth and sixteenth centuries led to demographic and social change. • The Spanish and Portuguese conquests led to epidemics, racial mixing, and a caste system. • The Spanish introduced new crops and domesticated animals to the Western Hemisphere, leading to significant economic, political, and social change. • Spanish and Portuguese explorers had little understanding of the native peoples living in the Americas.	• The Columbian Exchange has significant consequences in the Americas, Europe, and Africa.

THEME	REQUIRED CONTENT	SUPPORTING EXAMPLES
GEOGRAPHY AND THE ENVIRONMENT	• Native Americans and Europeans who came to the New World adapted to varied environments and also transformed these environments. • Due to a scarcity of natural resources, American Indian societies in the Plains and Great Basin were largely mobile.	**Pre-Columbian, up to 1492** • The Algonquin tribe uses waterways to develop a mobile society. • The Anasazi grow maize by the first century A.D. • Pueblo cultures form farming communities, despite the challenges of an arid climate (600). • By 1000, Pueblo peoples build irrigation systems, allowing them to form large settlements. • In the years following 1159, Chaco Canyon and other large southwestern Indian settlements are abandoned due to drought and depleted soil. **Western Hemisphere, 1492–1607** • The ending of large-scale burning of new farmland may have long-term environmental consequences. • The Columbian Exchange had a huge impact on the ecology of both Europe and the Americas.
CULTURE AND SOCIETY	• In addition to seeking wealth and power, Europeans came to the New World to spread Christianity. • European exploration and settlement of the Western Hemisphere contributed to the end of feudalism in Western Europe. • European exploration and contact with Indians fostered debate over the definition of *civilized* and the treatment of native peoples.	**Pre-Columbian, up to 1492** • Pacific coast Indian tribes such as the Chinook and Tlingit develop clearly defined social hierarchies. • In many Indian societies where kinship forms the basis of the community, the leaders are often the best hunters. • Most Indians are animists. • Women often hold power due to the importance of fertility in Indian culture. • Indians appeal to the spirits for aid in warfare. **Events in Europe, 1400–1607** • Nationalism and the accompanying drive to explore help bring about the end of feudalism. • The Renaissance reaches its peak (mid-fifteenth century). • The Protestant Reformation begins (1517). • Henry VIII of England establishes the Church of England (1534). • Catholic Reformation and the founding of the Jesuits increase missionary zeal (mid-sixteenth century). **Western Hemisphere, 1492–1607** • The Iroquois develop a matriarchal society. • Spanish missionaries convert Indians in the West and Southwest to Catholicism, but Catholicism adapts to a new environment in Indian communities.

Period 1 Practice Questions

Multiple-Choice Questions

Questions 1–3 refer to the map below.

Native American Peoples, 1492

1. American Indian culture had a different view of landownership than did Europeans in that they thought
   - (A) land should be owned by individual members of the society.
   - (B) tribal ownership of land was perpetual and exclusive.
   - (C) they owned the use of the land but not the land itself.
   - (D) all land was open to settlement by all people at any time.

GO ON TO THE NEXT PAGE.

2. American Indian cultures

   (A)   established a common written language.

   (B)   established trade networks and communication over relatively large areas.

   (C)   had peaceful relationships with each other that included voluntary emigration.

   (D)   formed major alliances to combat attempts by Europeans to encroach on their lands.

3. Which of the following is true about American Indian cultures prior to contact with Europeans?

   (A)   They experienced frequent epidemic diseases.

   (B)   They had developed wheeled vehicles pulled by livestock.

   (C)   They exchanged goods with African societies.

   (D)   They were engaged in frequent conflicts with other American Indian groups.

Questions 4–7 refer to the map below.

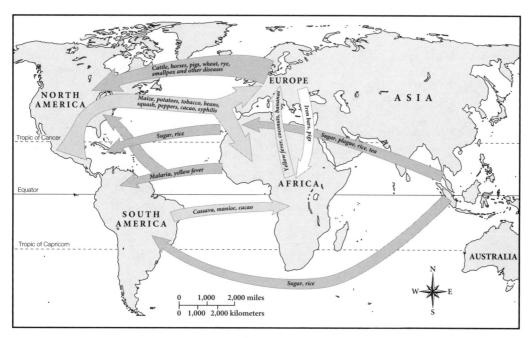

The Columbian Exchange

4. The primary positive benefit of the Columbian Exchange was

   (A)   the exchange of food products between Europe and the Western Hemisphere.

   (B)   the introduction of horses into Europe.

   (C)   the introduction of cattle into Europe.

   (D)   the exchange of architectural design techniques between the two continents.

5. The primary negative consequence of the Columbian exchange was the exchange of

   (A)   food products that led to debilitating illnesses for both American Indians and Europeans.

   (B)   concepts of autocratic governments that delayed the development of democracy.

   (C)   epidemic diseases introduced from Europe into the Americas.

   (D)   modern methods of warfare introduced to Europeans by American Indians.

GO ON TO THE NEXT PAGE.

6. Prior to European contact, North American Indians were
   - (A) dominated by the Plains Indians, who possessed horses.
   - (B) dominated by the eastern woodland tribes, who possessed firearms.
   - (C) dependent on imports of foodstuffs from Mexican tribes for survival.
   - (D) distinct societies with different economies and lifestyles.

7. As the Spanish explored North America prior to 1600, they discovered
   - (A) a Northwest Passage (an all-water route) to Asia.
   - (B) massive storehouses of precious metals among American Indian tribes.
   - (C) little of interest to keep them pushing north to Canada.
   - (D) evidence that Europeans had significant contact with American Indians prior to 1492.

END OF MULTIPLE-CHOICE SECTION

Short-Answer Question

Answer a, b, and c.

a)   Identify one key way in which the French and American Indians interacted economically in the Western Hemisphere prior to 1650.

b)   Identify one key way in which the Spanish and American Indians interacted economically in the Western Hemisphere prior to 1650.

c)   Provide one piece of evidence to suggest how the interaction shaped relationships between and French and American Indians or the Spanish and American Indians.

END OF SHORT-ANSWER SECTION

Answer Key to Period 1 Practice Questions

Multiple-Choice Questions

1.

Answer	Learning Objectives	Historical Thinking Skills	Key Concepts in the Curriculum Framework
C	CUL-4.0	Contextualization	1.1

Explanation: American Indian conception of landownership differed greatly from European perspectives. American Indians' conceptions were not exclusive or permanent. Tribes might defend lands as their own, but once they abandoned the land or were forced off it, they retained no title to it.

2.

Answer	Learning Objectives	Historical Thinking Skills	Key Concepts in the Curriculum Framework
B	WOR-1.0	Analyzing Evidence: Content and Sourcing	1.1

Explanation: While trade and communication networks were established over relatively large areas, a common written language was not a characteristic of American Indian culture. There were frequent hostilities between tribes both before and after European contact. The failure of American Indians to unite to defend their lands from white encroachment diluted their strength.

3.

Answer	Learning Objectives	Historical Thinking Skills	Key Concepts in the Curriculum Framework
D	WOR-1.0	Periodization	1.1

Explanation: Natives of the Western Hemisphere engaged in frequent warfare with each other prior to contact with Europeans. Once Europeans arrived, they were able to take advantage of lingering hostilities among tribes. Precontact North America was free from epidemic diseases for a variety of reasons; the American Indians had no domesticated livestock, and they had no contact with Africa.

4.

Answer	Learning Objectives	Historical Thinking Skills	Key Concepts in the Curriculum Framework
A	WXT-2.0	Causation	1.2

Explanation: The exchange of foodstuffs between the Western Hemisphere and Europe greatly expanded the possibility of supporting a larger worldwide population. Horses and cattle were introduced from Europe to the Americas, not vice versa. Although the exchange of design techniques was important, it was not beneficial in the way that the exchange of food products was.

5.

Answer	Learning Objectives	Historical Thinking Skills	Key Concepts in the Curriculum Framework
C	WXT-2.0	Causation	1.2

Explanation: The spread of microbes across the Atlantic to native populations who had no immunity to epidemic diseases cost many more lives than conflicts between Europeans and American Indians. The exchange of food products was positive overall for both European and American diets. There is little evidence to suggest that the Columbian Exchange delayed the development of democracy, and American Indians did not introduce Europeans to modern methods of warfare.

6.

Answer	Learning Objectives	Historical Thinking Skills	Key Concepts in the Curriculum Framework
D	GEO-1.0	Analyzing Evidence: Content and Sourcing	1.1

Explanation: Distinct American Indian cultures emerged and varied from hunter-gatherer societies to more sedentary societies. American Indians had to adapt to different environmental and geographic conditions to survive. Lack of a written language or common spoken language helped produce societies that created an individual identity for themselves while sharing some aspects of other cultures.

7.

Answer	Learning Objectives	Historical Thinking Skills	Key Concepts in the Curriculum Framework
C	WXT-1.0	Analyzing Evidence: Content and Sourcing	2.1

Explanation: Spanish discoveries of huge stores of precious metals in Central and South America left the Spanish eager to explore North America. However, after fruitlessly following American Indian stories of cities of gold, the Spanish began to lose interest in North America and concentrated their efforts on developing resources in Central and South America.

Short-Answer Question

Learning Objectives	Historical Thinking Skills	Key Concepts in the Curriculum Framework
WXT-2.0	Causation Patterns of Continuity and Change over Time Analyzing Evidence: Content and Sourcing	1.2

What a good response might include

a)   Examples of the ways in which the French and Indians interacted economically with each other would include:

   ◆ Many French traders came to the New World in search of animal fur, especially beaver.
   ◆ Indians in what is now Canada sold pelts to French traders in return for manufactured goods ranging from kettles to guns.

b) Examples of ways in which the Spanish and Indians interacted economically with each other would include:

✦ After the Spanish conquered native peoples in the Western Hemisphere, they extracted huge quantities of gold and silver, which they sold abroad or sent back to Spain to enrich the national coffers.

✦ The Columbian Exchange introduced new crops to Europe such as maize, tomatoes, and potatoes. Native economies were altered by the introduction of cattle and horses. The Spanish introduced deadly diseases to the native population.

✦ The *encomienda* system gave Spanish conquerors control over the labor and the products of native communities.

✦ As the Spanish exerted economic and political authority in the Americas, Spanish missionaries arrived in the New World and converted Indians en masse to Christianity.

c) Examples of how economic interaction between the French or the Spanish shaped the relationships between the French or the Spanish and native groups, including one piece of evidence that clearly links the economic interaction to the way it shaped relationships between Europeans and Indians, include:

✦ As trade relationships developed between the French and tribes like the Ottawas and the Hurons, French Jesuit missionaries arrived. Many of these missionaries lived in Indian communities where they cemented the relationships between Indians and the French.

✦ Although Indians often became suspicious of French missionaries, the groups often developed respect for each other.

✦ Since the French settlers did not arrive with families and the intent of forming permanent settlements, French trappers and traders often married Indian women and raised children with them.

✦ After the Spanish conquest of parts of the Americas, native people found themselves living in lands controlled by a centralized Spanish government and administered by Spanish institutions including Spanish legal codes and municipal councils.

✦ The establishment of the Spanish *encomienda* system enabled conquistadores to lay claim to Indian labor and Indian goods.

✦ As the demand for labor in Spanish territories in the New World grew, the Spanish brought thousands of Africans to the Western Hemisphere, resulting in racial mixing and the emergence of a casta system.

✦ Native religions were suppressed, but elements of those beliefs and practices infused and changed Spanish Catholicism.

✦ Contact with the Spanish and native susceptibility to European diseases like smallpox and yellow fever decreased the native population by 90 percent.

PERIOD 2
1607–1754

Overview

Period 2 begins in 1607 when the English established the first permanent North American colony at Jamestown, Virginia. The period focuses on colonial development and European rivalries in North America up to the eve of the French and Indian War. Included are comparisons of European interactions with American Indians, as well as the imperialist powers' approaches to colonization.

European colonizers had different goals and methods as each sought to expand their hold on North American territory. The Spanish maintained tight control of the areas they conquered, relying on military garrisons and working to convert the native population to Catholicism. The French and the Dutch were much less disruptive, working to forge trade alliances that involved fewer Europeans and often intermarrying with American Indians as they sought to build networks to acquire furs and other goods for European markets. The English sought to establish permanent colonies, clearing large tracts of land for agriculture, which disrupted Indian hunting and resources, leading to hostile encounters.

Because English colonists often came as family groups, they rarely intermarried with the native population or with Africans who were brought over as slaves, thereby creating a society marked by strict social and racial lines. As English indentured servants became fewer and the demand for labor to produce goods for European markets grew, southern colonists in particular increasingly turned to slave labor. Slavery in the English colonies gradually became more widespread and rigid, with slaves and their offspring held in perpetuity. In spite of these difficult circumstances, Africans managed to maintain many of their cultural and traditional values, and they found numerous ways to resist their captors.

Differences in climate, geography, and available resources resulted in striking regional differences among the British colonies in North America. New England, settled mainly by Puritans, developed into a closely knit region with an economy built around shipping, commerce, and farming. The middle colonies were the most diverse, relying on trade as well as agriculture. The Chesapeake region depended on tobacco, relying first on the labor of indentured servants and then increasingly on slaves. Farther south and in the West Indies, colonists grew other staple crops, sugar in particular, and depended heavily on slave labor.

As the European empires expanded in North America, they competed for land and resources and came into conflict with each other and with American Indians. They often tried to make alliances with various Indian groups to further their own interests. When the emerging British Empire attempted to assert imperial control over its North American colonies, the colonists began to find themselves at odds with the mother country.

American Indians grew alarmed as the colonial holdings expanded. Threats to their traditional ways of life and the dangers of European diseases began to outweigh their desire for European trade goods. Although the Spanish made some accommodations to Indian culture after the Pueblo Revolt in 1680, English colonists refused to make concessions. Conflicts between American Indians and Europeans were made more destructive by the introduction of European weapons and alcohol.

Colonies in eighteenth-century North America were part of the commercial, political, and cultural network known as the Atlantic world. Goods traveled to and from the Americas and Europe, and Africa became a ready source of slave labor for the New World.

The British colonies exhibited many characteristics of life in England, including political institutions, religious denominations, commercial interests, and an admiration for the ideals of the Enlightenment. The growing reliance on slave labor and the reluctance to accept either slaves or American Indians as equals led to a colonial society with clearly drawn racial divisions, unlike those of the French or the Spanish.

The British government attempted to assert stricter control over their North American colonies as they grew more important to the economy and prestige of the empire. Periods of benign neglect had led the colonists to recognize their ability to be self-reliant and to lessen their sense of being distinct regions. They began to realize their similar interests and advantages, which often did not fit neatly with the demands of the British government. British mercantilist policies often went against colonial interests, and resistance to imperial control became more frequent.

This period of history ends with colonial resistance on the rise as the colonists became more experienced in self-government, more accepting of religious diversity, more dissatisfied with British imperialist economic control, and more interested in the ideals of the Enlightenment.

Key Terms

Be sure that you understand the meaning of these terms and their relevance in U.S. history.

Anglicization	Natural rights
Chattel slavery	Overt and covert resistance
Deism	Print culture
Enlightenment ideas	Protestant evangelism
Freeholder ideal	Royal and proprietary colonies
Indentured servitude	Salutary neglect
Mercantilism	Tribalization

Questions to Consider

As you study Period 2, keep the following thematic questions in mind.

American and National Identity

- ✦ To what extent did British American colonists develop a sense of identity separate from that of English men and women?
- ✦ What factors encouraged and what factors impeded the development of an "American" identity?
- ✦ What group and regional identities emerged in the thirteen British American colonies?
- ✦ Why and how did the English, the Spanish, and the French develop different views on race?

Work, Exchange, and Technology

- ✦ How did patterns of exchange shape the societies that emerged in North America between 1607 and 1754?

- How did British American colonists react to the implementation of the British economic policies of the late seventeenth and early eighteenth centuries?
- How did new technologies lead to increasingly destructive conflicts between European and American Indians?

Migration and Settlement

- What were the various models of colonization that the Spanish, French, Dutch, and English in North America adopted?
- What settlement patterns emerged in this period in North America, and how did these shape colonial society?
- What factors shaped the institution of slavery in the British North American colonies?

Politics and Power

- In what ways did British American colonists model their political institutions on England? How did these colonists adapt these institutions in a way that seemed uniquely "American"?
- What were the sources of conflict between native peoples and Europeans in the seventeenth century and the first half of the eighteenth century? How did the resolution of these conflicts change the lives of American Indians and those of European descent?
- In what ways did African Americans resist slavery?

America in the World

- What factors led to increasing opposition to both British and Spanish authority in North America?
- How did rivalries and competition between European nations affect the lives of colonists, Indians, and African Americans in North America?

Geography and the Environment

- How did the colonial environment shape the lives of the colonists in ways that contributed to their eventual separation from England?
- What was the role of the natural environment in shaping regional and group identities in colonial North America?

Culture and Society

- How did religion shape the development of colonial societies?
- What role did religious discord play in colonial communities?
- How did cultural differences shape the relationships among Europeans, Native Americans, and African Americans in colonial America?
- What regional differences in religion, family life, and community values emerged in the British American colonies? What accounted for these differences?

America's History Chapter Summaries

(required AP® content in bold)

Chapter 3
The British Atlantic World, 1660–1750

Chapter 3 examines the changes in politics and society in the British North American colonies in the century leading up to the American Revolution. The British government sought to tighten control over colonial commerce with the imposition of numerous Navigation Acts, which only increased the colonists' desire to regulate their own trade. King James II further angered the northern colonies when he abolished their own assemblies and created his own Dominion of New England, an organization that fell apart during England's Glorious Revolution in 1688. The years that followed saw sporadic periods of salutary neglect when colonists were able to regulate their own affairs, though the British periodically reasserted control, which led to even more colonial resentment. These years also saw the enormous expansion of the slave trade and slave system, particularly in the southern colonies and the West Indies, a system of labor that had an impact of workers throughout the colonies.

In the 1660s, King Charles II of England reinvigorated colonial expansion with the creation of the Carolina colony, the establishment of the colony of Pennsylvania, and the acquisition of New York and New Jersey. He sought to give Britain a **mercantilist advantage and to maximize British profits** by restricting colonial trade with a series of Navigation Acts. After his death, his brother, James II, continued these policies, adding another layer to colonial control with the imposition of his Dominion of New England, which gave the king and his representative authority in decisions about local government, trade, and charters. These restrictions were weakened by the Glorious Revolution, though the British reasserted their authority in various ways. The colonists began to see both the **advantages of self-government and their own abilities to be successful at managing their own affairs**.

The colonists were further disillusioned by their involvement in England's colonial wars with European rivals, as they found themselves fighting proxy battles. The **colonists were often dissatisfied with the territorial settlements that ended these wars**. The wars also led to increasing conflicts with American Indians, as the various tribes sought to make alliances with both Europeans and each other that they thought might benefit them. Few of these alliances had any long-term rewards for the Indians.

The growth of the Atlantic world economy and the North American slave trade brought tremendous wealth to England and its colonies, but at tremendous cost to the peoples of West and Central Africa. Millions of Africans were captured, transported across the Atlantic in unspeakable conditions, and sold into slavery in the New World. The **enormous number of Africans transported had a significant impact on life in Africa and in the colonies**. Those who survived the dreaded Middle Passage were destined for a life of hardship. West Indian-style slavery came to the Carolinas and Chesapeake to cultivate rice and tobacco. In spite of the harsh conditions under which they lived, the slave communities that emerged were marked with distinct signs of African cultural traditions and values. Major rebellions were few in the early days of slavery, but **many more subtle forms of resistance were common**. Southern colonies in particular developed a **rigid social hierarchy**, setting the landowners apart from the landless and all whites apart from the slaves.

As the southern colonies became increasingly dependent on slave labor, the northern colonies developed a thriving maritime economy and a more urban society. Wealthy merchants headed society, but a middle class of artisans and shopkeepers slowly developed. Propertyless workers made up the next tier of society, with a relatively small percentage of slaves at the bottom.

During the occasional periods of salutary neglect that the colonists enjoyed, interest grew in self-government. Colonial assemblies became increasingly powerful and outspoken, challenging the restrictions of the **British mercantilist system**. Periods of salutary neglect led colonists to long for more permanent control over their own affairs. The British responded with determination to reassert control over what they saw as **rebellious subjects who posed a threat to the imperialist system**. The stage was being set for a political showdown between the colonies and Great Britain.

Chapter 4
Growth, Diversity, and Conflict, 1720–1763

Chapter 4 examines the social changes that occurred in British North America in the mid-eighteenth century. It begins by tracing the changes in the New England colonies and then examines the diversity of the middle colonies. It also explores the tremendous cultural changes that were the result of advances in transportation and print technology, the ideas that emanated from the Enlightenment, and the major religious upheavals in both the northern and southern colonies. The final section focuses on the French and Indian War (also known as the Seven Years' War) and the continuing struggle over land and expansion.

The New England colonies experienced dramatic population growth in the eighteenth century, largely the result of natural increase. Closely knit Puritan **families and communities continued to rely on a mixed economy**. While colonists saw their communities as models of democracy, women remained second-class citizens, and a social hierarchy grew as some families were able to increase their wealth while many others remained relatively poor. The fast-growing population also strained the New England colonies as good farmland became scarce.

The **middle colonies were quite diverse**, with Dutch colonists in New York and the Hudson Valley, Quaker Englishmen and women in Pennsylvania, and Presbyterian Scots-Irish and German Protestants of various denominations throughout the region. The cities of Philadelphia and New York were centers of trade and destinations for new immigrants, giving the region a flourishing economy. Most groups retained characteristics of their different cultures.

A road network developed that supplemented the "Great Wagon Road" that ran through the Shenandoah Valley. These roads carried people, produce, and merchandise east and west, along with newspapers and pamphlets. The **print revolution that was occurring in Europe quickly spread to the British colonies, bringing with it new ideas that would reshape the colonial mind-set.**

Colonial culture was also influenced by the ideas of the European Enlightenment, the religious revival known as the Great Awakening, and the impact of British trade. The old idea that political authority was given by God to monarchs was replaced with the concept of natural rights, that is, the idea that people had the right to change governments if they felt their needs were not being met. Traditional religion was also challenged with some speculating that they might be better served by rational thought and scientific solutions to their problems rather than worrying about appeasing a vengeful Calvinist God. Some colonial intellectuals like Benjamin Franklin and Thomas Paine leaned toward deism, relying on **"natural reason" to help them define right and wrong**. Others sought to renew interest in religion through Pietism, the belief that worship should be more emotional and personal, a shift away from the academic approach of the earlier Puritan clergy. New England saw the rise of charismatic preachers like Jonathan Edwards and George Whitefield, leaders in what became known as the Great Awakening.

As these changes were sweeping the colonies, more challenges to traditional ways of life were brewing in Europe. Britain and France, along with their various Indian allies, fought each other in **several imperial wars**. The largest of these conflicts, the Seven Years' War (also known as the French and Indian War), resulted in the final **defeat of the French in North America**. At the same time, **British colonists were demanding the right to move farther west, regardless of the potential for conflicts with both European powers and the Indians.**

Thematic Timeline

THEME	REQUIRED CONTENT	SUPPORTING EXAMPLES
AMERICAN AND NATIONAL IDENTITY	• English colonies were characterized by a rigid racial hierarchy and were not tolerant of sexual relationships between European settlers and American Indians or Africans. • Africans in the British colonies developed both covert and overt methods to resist the dehumanizing aspects of slavery. • The British colonies became increasingly Anglicized as the colonists and those in Great Britain shared a common heritage, religion, and print culture. • Racial stereotyping increased in the British colonies, resulting in the development of strict racial categories. • The Spanish and French were more accepting of racial gradations. • The British colonies came to share a common pattern of culture, laws, institutions, and government.	**1607–1700** • Puritans identify themselves as God's chosen people (mid-seventeenth century). • Puritan women are viewed as subservient to men and face legal and cultural restrictions, but they maintain key roles in the church. • By the 1660s, Maryland and Virginia define chattel slavery and pass laws increasing restrictions on Africans. • Increased warfare and the ravages of disease lead to tribalization of Indian groups (late seventeenth century). • European immigrants to the middle colonies come from many different nations, and most cling to their old traditions and religions. • Slaves from different parts of Africa eventually lose much of their identities as members of specific families or clans and instead form a common identity as Africans. • Slaves maintain many elements of African cultures: music, hairstyles, religion. • Southern plantation owners identify themselves as members of British high society, though they are often viewed as inferior by the British gentry. • Especially following Bacon's Rebellion, the Virginia gentry encourage middle-class and poor whites to identify with them rather than empathizing with nonwhites. Lower classes of whites are given lower taxes, jobs, and expanded voting rights. **1700–1754** • Slaves in the British colonies demand rights such as Sundays off. • Slaves undermine masters by stealing and working slowly. • Stono Rebellion (1739).
WORK, EXCHANGE, TECHNOLOGY	• Relatively few French and Dutch came to the New World. These countries were primarily interested in acquiring products like furs for export to Europe. They made trade alliances with American Indians and accepted intermarriage between European men and Indian women.	**1607–1700** • A colony at Jamestown is founded to generate wealth for its settlers and investors in England (1607). • Tobacco becomes a valuable cash crop in the Chesapeake. • The headright system is used in Virginia to attract a larger labor force; by 1700 the majority of settlers are indentured servants. • Massachusetts Bay founded as a joint-stock company (1630).

THEME	REQUIRED CONTENT	SUPPORTING EXAMPLES
WORK, EXCHANGE, TECHNOLOGY (*continued*)	• The Atlantic slave trade flourished as the indentured labor force proved insufficient, there was difficulty in enslaving native peoples, and demand for colonial goods increased. • Slavery was most prevalent in the Chesapeake colonies and in the South. • European colonies focused on finding sources of labor and producing goods for European consumption, which further emphasized the competition between the parent countries in Europe. • As the economies on both sides of the Atlantic grew, so did the shared labor market and the exchange of goods.	• As the population of New England increases, families are unable to divide their land among all of their children. • By the 1640s, planters in the Caribbean and Brazil turn to sugar as a profitable cash crop. • The institution of slavery is increasingly molded to suit the needs of southern planters. • French settlers in North America establish the beaver trade. • British impose Navigation Acts on their colonists. • By the late seventeenth century, the British American colonies become an integrated economic sphere. **1700–1754** • In the eighteenth century, water and transportation networks expand in the Middle Atlantic and New England colonies. • Rice cultivation in South Carolina results in a greatly increased demand for slaves. • The South Atlantic System, centered in Brazil and the West Indies, depends on the sale of sugar produced by African slaves. • By the early eighteenth century, the economies of New England and the West Indies are linked by sugar. • When the British attempt to control colonial trade, colonists respond by smuggling and bribing officials. • Colonial assemblies establish public land banks but are restricted by the Currency Act (1751).
MIGRATION AND SETTLEMENT	• Because of their different goals, customs, and beliefs, the Spanish, French, British, and Dutch developed different forms of colonization. • The government in Spain tried to tightly control colonization from afar and intended to convert or exploit the native population.	**1607–1700** • Jamestown is established as first permanent English colony (1607). • Champlain founds Quebec (1608). • The French explore the Mississippi River Valley all the way to Louisiana, though far fewer French settlers than British come to the New World. • The first women and first Africans are brought to Jamestown (1619). • British settlers come to the Caribbean (1620s). • Dutch found New Netherlands (1621). • Pilgrims arrive at Plymouth (1620). • Puritans led by John Winthrop establish their "holy commonwealth" at Massachusetts Bay (1630). • Maryland is established as a haven for Catholics (1634).

THEME	REQUIRED CONTENT	SUPPORTING EXAMPLES
MIGRATION AND SETTLEMENT (*continued*)	• The English wanted to establish permanent colonies. Many English men and women immigrated to North America, and relations with the Indians often became hostile.	• New Netherland becomes New York as the English take control (1664). • The Carolinas are settled (1660s). • William Penn and Quakers found Pennsylvania, the last of the Restoration Colonies (1682). • Penn's Frame of Government promotes political equality. • By 1700 there are three distinct types of European colonies in the Western Hemisphere: tribute colonies (Mexico and Peru), plantation colonies (Brazil, Jamestown, Maryland, and the Caribbean), and neo-European colonies (New France, New England, Middle Colonies). **1700–1754** • Georgia, the last of the thirteen colonies, is founded (1732). • After the seventeenth century, the increase in the population of slaves is largely due to natural increase rather than importation. • By 1800 6.1 million African slaves have been brought to the Western Hemisphere by way of the Middle Passage. • Increased trade creates wealth and stimulates the growth of cities in the northern colonies. • Large numbers of German and Scots-Irish arrive in the colonies in the first half of the eighteenth century. In Pennsylvania, the growth of these numbers threatens Quaker domination. • German immigrants come to the New World for religious reasons (the Mennonites) and economic opportunity. • Throughout the eighteenth century, tensions increase between rich and poor in the British American colonies.
POLITICS AND POWER	• Political instability continued in North America as European conflicts spread across the Atlantic. • British, French, Dutch, and Spanish colonies armed and allied with American Indians. • Especially in the British American colonies, distrust increased between colonial settlers and their European governments.	• House of Burgesses meets in Jamestown (1619). • Increasing tensions like the Powhatan conflict between white settlers in Virginia and Indians. • Pattern for relations between European settlers and Indians: uneasy welcome, rising tension, war. • Virginia Indian War of 1622. • James I makes Virginia a royal colony (1624). • Mayflower Compact (1620). • Puritans establish the town meeting as the model for political participation in New England.

THEME	REQUIRED CONTENT	SUPPORTING EXAMPLES
POLITICS AND POWER (*continued*)	• Issues that divided settlers and European governments included territorial settlement and frontier defense. • Deadlier weapons and alcohol served to make warfare more destructive. • In the face of growing unrest in the colonies and international competition, the British government felt it necessary to strengthen its control over the colonies. • These efforts, which served only to increase colonial resistance, met with minimal success, and by the late seventeenth century, the British government maintained a pattern of relative indifference toward the colonies.	• War between English settlers and Pequots in New England (1637). • Metacom's War (King Philip's War), 1675–1676. • Bacon's Rebellion (1676). • First comprehensive slave legislation in Barbados (1661). • Parliament annuls Massachusetts Bay charter (1684). • Dominion of New England (1686). • Leisler's Rebellion. **1700–1754** • European wars affect American colonists, forcing them to arm and make alliances with Indian tribes. This also gives leverage to the Indians. • Under salutary neglect, colonial assemblies grow more powerful. • In the mid-eighteenth century, after a period of salutary neglect, the British attempt to reassert authority over their colonies.
AMERICA IN THE WORLD	• Interactions between people living in the New World, both Indians and Europeans, and European governments varied greatly, depending on the goals of colonization and the ability of European bureaucracies to regulate activities in the Western Hemisphere. • Conflicts in Europe spread to North America, leading to continued political instability.	**1607–1700** • English Civil War begins (1649). • Stuart Restoration (1660). For a period after this, the British tried to exert more control over the colonies. • Glorious Revolution (1688). • Increased British involvement in foreign wars (Second Hundred Years' War) leads to salutary neglect of the colonies beginning in the late seventeenth century. **1700–1754** • Treaty of Utrecht (1713). • War of Jenkins's Ear (1739–1741). • War of the Austrian Succession (1740–1748).

THEME	REQUIRED CONTENT	SUPPORTING EXAMPLES
GEOGRAPHY AND THE ENVIRONMENT	• The availability of land for farming increased the demand for slaves. • Climate, the availability of natural resources, and other environmental factors resulted in the emergence of regional differences in the British colonies. • The geography of New England encouraged the development of a mixed economy of farming and commerce. • Environmental and geographic factors encouraged an export economy in the middle colonies and the labor-intensive tobacco economy of the Chesapeake colonies and North Carolina. Farther south, the economy was based on staple crops and a slave labor force.	**1607–1700** • A harsh environment nearly causes the failure of the Jamestown colony (early seventeenth century). • Although there are many farms in New England, the harsh climate and rocky soil make many New Englanders turn to the sea for a living. • Iroquois Confederacy is strengthened by its strategic location between the French and Dutch colonies. • Environmental factors determine which crops can be grown in European colonies and what labor force can be used.
CULTURE AND SOCIETY	• The British believed in their own racial and cultural superiority. This belief buttressed their willingness to enslave black people in perpetuity and also helped account for the many violent confrontations between British colonists and native peoples. • Slavery altered relationships between African men and women, as well as kinship relationships. • Their focus on religion helped the Puritans form a closely knit and homogeneous society.	**1607–1700** • Toleration Act issued in Maryland (1649). • Jesuits arrive to convert Indians in New France. • Pilgrim separatists arrive to freely practice religion in Plymouth (1620). • Puritans establish Massachusetts Bay as a colony based on religious conformity in belief and practice (1630). • Roger Williams and then Anne Hutchinson banished from Massachusetts Bay for calling for freedom of conscience in matters of religion (1636 and 1637, respectively). • Late-seventeenth-century witchcraft trials in New England, especially Salem, attempt to control women. • Quakers in Pennsylvania assert gender equality.

THEME	REQUIRED CONTENT	SUPPORTING EXAMPLES
CULTURE AND SOCIETY (*continued*)	• As contact increased between American Indians and Europeans, there were significant cultural and demographic changes for both. • Especially after the Pueblo Revolt, the Spanish colonizers made some accommodations with Indian culture; however, contact and conflict with Indians only served to reinforce English beliefs on land and gender roles. • Enlightenment ideas spread through the British colonies. • Many British colonists came to hold beliefs that set them at odds with the British government. These included belief in self-government, liberty, the ideals of the Enlightenment, religious diversity and toleration, and opposition to imperial corruption.	• Glorious Revolution prompts Parliament to force the new monarchs to issue the Declaration of Rights, basing their claim to increased authority on the ideals of the Enlightenment, especially those of John Locke, author of *Essay on Human Understanding* (1690) and *Two Treatises on Government* (1690). **1700–1754** • Two intellectual movements, the Enlightenment and Pietism, are increasingly at odds. • Deism reflects Enlightenment beliefs. • Some religious figures, like Cotton Mather who supports smallpox inoculations, attempt to link religion and reason. • Jonathan Edwards ignites the Great Awakening (1730s). • George Whitefield arrives in the colonies (1739). • The Great Awakening splinters colonial churches and challenges spiritual authorities. "Ordinary" colonists feel a new sense of power (mid-eighteenth century). • New Light universities established. • Baptist, Methodists, and Presbyterian churches gain new adherents. • Anglican churches in the South are challenged by Presbyterians. • Ideas spread rapidly in the emerging print culture. • The Great Awakening message of equality reaches African Americans. • Benjamin Franklin emerges as the colonist most representative of Enlightenment ideas. • *Poor Richard's Almanac* first published (1732). • Franklin founds the American Philosophical Society (1743).

Period 2 Practice Questions

Multiple-Choice Questions

Questions 1–3 refer to the excerpt below.

"And it is further enacted by the authority aforesaid, that from and after the first day of April, which shall be in the year of our Lord one thousand six hundred sixty-one, no sugars, tobacco, cotton-wool, indigoes, ginger, fustic, or other dyeing wood, of the growth, production, or manufacture of any English plantations in America, Asia, or Africa, shall be shipped, carried, conveyed, or transported from any of the said English plantations to any land, island, territory, dominion, port, or place whatsoever, other than to such other English plantations as do belong to his Majesty, his heirs and successors, or to the kingdom of England or Ireland, or principality of Wales, or town of Berwick upon Tweed, there to be laid on shore . . ."

Excerpt from the Navigation Acts, 1660–1696

1. The above act was part of a British attempt to
   - (A) encourage the British North American colonies to increase trade with the Dutch.
   - (B) enforce an economic system that believed colonies existed for the good of the mother country.
   - (C) increase colonial production of manufactured goods.
   - (D) establish a high protective tariff on colonial goods entering Great Britain.

2. Acts such as the one above encouraged
   - (A) the growth of the shipbuilding industry in New England.
   - (B) the production of diversified food crops in the South.
   - (C) the dominance of manufacturing industries in the middle colonies.
   - (D) an increased demand for indentured servants by 1700.

3. Which of the following is NOT true of the series of English acts that regulated trade during the seventeenth century?
   - (A) They benefitted both the colonies and England in certain ways.
   - (B) They were largely ignored by the American colonies if they were not beneficial.
   - (C) They required that colonial goods be carried in English ships with English crews.
   - (D) They sparked frequent violent rebellions over British authority beginning with King Philip's (Metacom's) War.

Questions 4-6 refer to the excerpt below.

"[New Englanders] are at present a numerous and thriving people and in 20 years more are likely . . . to be mighty rich and powerful and not at all careful of their dependence upon old England. . . . I take the way of roughness and peremptory orders, with force to back them, to be utterly unadvisable. For they are already too strong to be compelled . . . and though I apprehend them yet not at that point to cast us off voluntarily and of choice; yet I believe if we use severity towards them in their government civil or religious, that they will (being made desperate) set up for themselves and reject us."

Earl of Sandwich, "Comments upon New England," 1671

GO ON TO THE NEXT PAGE.

4. Which of the following is best reflected by the above passage?

   (A) New England was threatening the world trade dominance of Great Britain in the late seventeenth century.
   (B) The majority of American colonists favored separation from Great Britain in 1671.
   (C) Britain's inability to provide the colonists with adequate defense from American Indians led the colonists to issue the Declaration of Independence.
   (D) Some colonists were beginning to feel a sense of identity separate from Great Britain by the late seventeenth century.

5. The above passage indicates that the New England colonies

   (A) were operating outside the British mercantilist system.
   (B) rejected the Anglican Church, leading to English repression.
   (C) dominated trade with American Indians, reducing British profits.
   (D) were dependent on Great Britain for raw materials.

6. Which of the following best represents a reason for the development of the New England colonies as expressed by the Earl of Sandwich?

   (A) The commitment of British troops to protect the New England colonists from American Indian allies of the French
   (B) The continued naval dominance of the Spanish fleet
   (C) British preoccupation with internal and European affairs
   (D) The failure of New England to provide England with useful raw materials

Questions 7–9 refer to the excerpt below.

"Now, know ye, that we, being willing to encourage the hopeful undertaking of our said loyal and loving subjects . . . that our royal will and pleasure is, that no person within the said colony, at any time hereafter shall be any wise molested, punished, disquieted, or called in question, for any differences in opinion in matters of religion, and do not actually disturb the civil peace of our said colony; but that all and every person and persons may, from time to time, and at all times hereafter, freely and fully have and enjoy his and their own judgments and consciences, in matters of religious concernments, throughout the tract of land hereafter mentioned."
Charter of Rhode Island and Providence Plantations, July 8, 1663

7. Founders of Rhode Island supported the above provision of the charter primarily because they

   (A) had experienced religious repression in the European countries from which they emigrated.
   (B) had experienced religious repression in the southern colonies.
   (C) were opposed to the institution of slavery.
   (D) had experienced intolerance of dissenting views in Massachusetts Bay.

8. Provisions such as those in the Rhode Island charter would ultimately encourage movement toward which of the following principles in colonial America?

   (A) Separation of church and state
   (B) Egalitarianism
   (C) Churches being ruled by congregations
   (D) Creation of a theocracy where the leaders of the church and state are the same

GO ON TO THE NEXT PAGE.

9. Which of the following colonies would be most similar to Rhode Island in granting religious freedom during the 1600s?
   - (A) Virginia
   - (B) Pennsylvania
   - (C) North Carolina
   - (D) Connecticut

Questions 10–12 are based on the excerpt below.

"That for all persons . . . which during the next seven years after Midsummer Day 1618 shall go into Virginia with intent there to inhabit, if they continue there three years or die after they are shipped there shall be a grant made of fifty acres for every person . . . which grants to be made respectively to such persons and their heirs at whose charges the said persons going to inhabit in Virginia shall be transported."

Virginia Company Instructions to Sir George Yeardley, November 18, 1618

10. The system described above was primarily initiated to
    - (A) protect colonists settling in Virginia from attacks by American Indians.
    - (B) encourage the growth of an elite class of plantation owners.
    - (C) provide an adequate labor force to make the land profitable.
    - (D) encourage the deportation of riffraff from England.

11. As a result of the system eluded to above,
    - (A) slavery replaced indentured servitude as the chief labor source in Virginia by 1618.
    - (B) a majority of English people emigrating to Virginia came as indentured servants prior to 1650.
    - (C) there was little dissension between the backcountry and the Tidewater prior to 1700.
    - (D) the Anglican Church was firmly established as the state church of Virginia by 1660.

12. Because no such system was established in New England,
    - (A) the average size of landholdings was smaller in New England than in the Chesapeake.
    - (B) New England was the last colonial region to become "overpopulated."
    - (C) African slaves became the chief labor source in New England.
    - (D) the Chesapeake colonies became more homogeneous than New England in both religion and ethnic background.

END OF MULTIPLE-CHOICE SECTION

Short-Answer Question

"SIR, Having notice that under color of a trade to Newfoundland for fish, great quantities of wine, brandy and other European goods, are imported from thence into his Majesty's plantations, particularly New England, on an allegation, that the said New Foundland is accounted as one of the said plantations. To which purpose, it is now become a Magazine of all sorts of goods brought thither directly from France, Holland, Scotland, Ireland and other places, which is not only contrary to law, but greatly to the prejudice of his Majesty's Customs, and to the trade and navigation of this Kingdom. To the end, therefore, that so destructive and growing an evil may be timely prevented, we desire you . . . to give public notice to all persons concerned . . . that they be very careful not to suffer any European goods, other than what are by the aforesaid law and Proclamation accepted, to be imported into New England."

Commercial Orders to Governor Andros (1686–1687)

Using the excerpt above, answer a, b, and c.

a) According to this document, how did colonists in New England avoid restrictive British commercial laws?

b) What name was given to the economic goals and policies that the British used in the seventeenth and eighteenth centuries to strengthen their empire? What area in British colonial North America might have been a better fit for this system than New England was?

c) Explain how either New England or the region discussed in part b reacted to more restrictive laws passed by Great Britain in the late seventeenth and early eighteenth centuries.

END OF SHORT-ANSWER SECTION

Document-Based Question

Directions: The following question in based on the accompanying documents. The documents have been edited for this exercise. Spend approximately 15 minutes planning and 45 minutes writing your answer.

Write an essay that does the following:

+ States an appropriate thesis that directly addresses all parts of the question.
+ Supports the thesis or argument with evidence from all or all but one of the documents AND your knowledge of U.S. history beyond the documents.
+ Analyzes all or all but one of the documents.
+ Places each document into at least one of the following categories: intended audience, purpose, historical context, and/or point of view.
+ Uses historical evidence beyond the documents to support your argument.
+ Places the argument in the context of broader regional, national, or global processes.
+ Incorporates all of the elements above into a convincing essay.

Question: Analyze the similarities and differences between the New England colonies and the Chesapeake colonies to 1750.

Document 1

Source: Letter from indentured servant in Virginia to His Parents in England, 1623

I am not half a quarter so strong as I was in England, and all is for want of victuals, for I do protest unto you, that I have eaten more in [a] day at home th[a]n I have allowed me here for a week.

Document 2

Source: John Winthrop, *A Modell of Christian Charity,* 1630

We shall be as a City upon a hill. The eyes of all people are upon us. So that if we shall deal falsely with our God in this work we have undertaken, and so cause him to withdraw his present help from us, we shall be made a story and a by-word throughout the world.

GO ON TO THE NEXT PAGE.

Document 3

Source: John Underhill, *Newes from America; Or, A New and Experimentall Discoverie of New England* (London, 1638).

May 1637 Massacre at Pequot Village

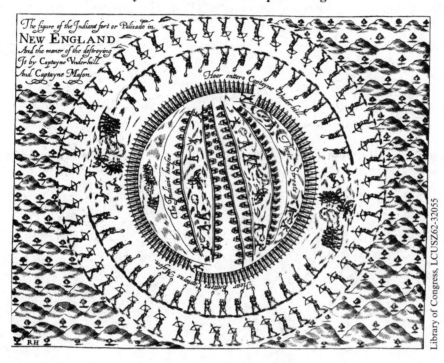

Library of Congress, LCUSZ62-32055

Document 4

Source: Nathaniel Bacon, *Declaration,* 1676

Another main article of our guilt is our open and manifest aversion of all, not only the foreign but the protected and darling Indians.

Document 5

Source: An act for preventing Negroes Insurrections, Statutes of Virginia, June 1680–ACT X

Be it enacted by the kings most excellent majesty by and with the consent of the general assembly, and it is hereby enacted by the authority aforesaid, that from and after the publication of this law, it shall not be lawful for any negro or other slave to carry or arm himself with any club, staff, gun, sword or any other weapon of defense or offense, nor to go or depart from of his masters ground without a certificate from his master, mistress or overseer and such permission not to be granted but upon particular and necessary occasions.

GO ON TO THE NEXT PAGE.

Document 6

Source: Benjamin Wadsworth, selection from a Puritan marriage manual, 1712

Though the husband is to rule his family and his wife, yet his government of his wife should not be with rigor, haughtiness, harshness, severity; but with the greatest love, gentleness, kindness, tenderness that may be. Though he governs her, he must not treat her as a servant, but as his own flesh.

Document 7

Source: U.S. Bureau of the Census

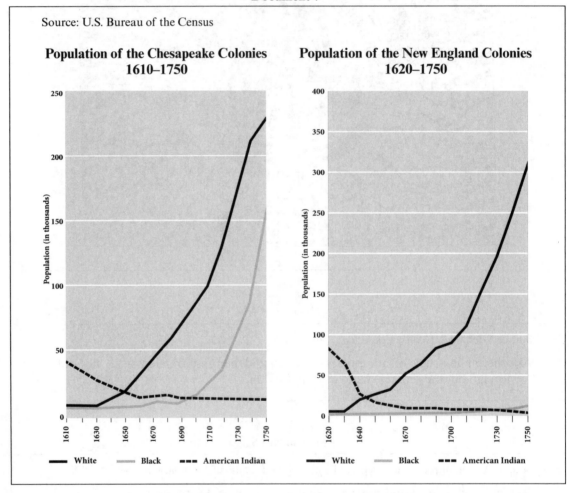

Population of the Chesapeake Colonies 1610–1750

Population of the New England Colonies 1620–1750

END OF DOCUMENT-BASED SECTION

Answer Key to Period 2 Practice Questions

Multiple-Choice Questions

1.
Answer	Learning Objectives	Historical Thinking Skills	Key Concepts in the Curriculum Framework
B	WXT-2.0	Causation Analyzing Evidence: Content and Sourcing	2.2

Explanation: The British mercantilist system saw colonies as existing for the good of the mother country. Colonies were to produce raw materials and consume manufactured goods. The Trade and Navigation Acts of the seventeenth century were designed to force that to happen. Certain goods mentioned in the document could be transported only to England. Colonists avoided that proscription by sending them first to Newfoundland and then to other foreign countries.

2.
Answer	Learning Objectives	Historical Thinking Skills	Key Concepts in the Curriculum Framework
A	WXT-2.0	Causation Analyzing Evidence: Content and Sourcing	2.2

Explanation: The Trade and Navigation Acts required that colonial goods be shipped in English ships with English crews. This encouraged the development of a colonial ship-building industry to meet the demand for increased tonnage. The South continued to be dominated by a one-crop economy because it fit well into the mercantilist economy. Colonial manufacturing was generally discouraged by the Trade and Navigation Acts.

3.
Answer	Learning Objectives	Historical Thinking Skills	Key Concepts in the Curriculum Framework
D	WOR-1.0	Contextualization	2.2

Explanation: King Philip's War (also known as Metacom's War) was a confrontation between colonists and American Indians and thus had nothing to do with the Trade and Navigation Act. The colonists benefited from a captive British market and the encouragement that trade be carried in English ships. They were hurt by having other potential foreign markets closed to their trade. They generally ignored acts injurious to their economies.

4.
Answer	Learning Objectives	Historical Thinking Skills	Key Concepts in the Curriculum Framework
D	NAT-1.0	Causation Analyzing Evidence: Content and Sourcing	2.2

Explanation: The passage indicates that some, but not the majority of, colonists were identifying themselves as separate and distinct from Great Britain. *Salutary neglect* meant that England had not monitored the colonies as closely as necessary to ensure that the colonies were behaving as mercantilist colonies should. As a result, colonists adhered to orders that benefitted them but ignored ones that injured them without serious repercussions.

5.

Answer	Learning Objectives	Historical Thinking Skills	Key Concepts in the Curriculum Framework
A	WXT-2.0	Analyzing Evidence: Content and Sourcing	2.2

Explanation: Under the mercantilist system, colonies existed for the good of the mother country. Indications that New England was "not at all carefull of their dependence on old England" is an indication that they were operating outside the mercantilist concept.

6.

Answer	Learning Objectives	Historical Thinking Skills	Key Concepts in the Curriculum Framework
C	WOR-1.0	Causation Analyzing Evidence: Content and Sourcing	2.2

Explanation: Salutary neglect, or preoccupation of Britain with internal and European affairs, meant that England could not monitor or regulate New England sufficiently. Colonists were largely on their own in terms of protection from American Indians until the French and Indian War. After the defeat of the Spanish Armada in 1588, England had naval dominance throughout the seventeenth century. New England did supply England with raw materials.

7.

Answer	Learning Objectives	Historical Thinking Skills	Key Concepts in the Curriculum Framework
D	CUL-1.0	Causation	2.2

Explanation: Rhode Island was founded by colonists who had been banished from Massachusetts Bay for their dissenting views on religion. Because they had varied beliefs concerning religion, the way to protect their own religious freedom was to protect the religious freedom of all residents. Despite the fact they may have emigrated from Europe to gain a degree of freedom, they felt that freedom threatened by the authorities of Massachusetts Bay.

8.

Answer	Learning Objectives	Historical Thinking Skills	Key Concepts in the Curriculum Framework
A	POL-1.0	Patterns of Continuity and Change over Time Analyzing Evidence: Content and Sourcing	2.2

Explanation: The idea of separation of church and state began to gather momentum during the early colonial period. As more diverse immigrants entered the colonies, pressure was placed on the colonial establishment to loosen religious restriction. Relatively low population densities made it more difficult to monitor the religious behavior of colonists.

9.

Answer	Learning Objectives	Historical Thinking Skills	Key Concepts in the Curriculum Framework
B	NAT-1.0	Patterns of Continuity and Change over Time	2.1

Explanation: Pennsylvania, founded by William Penn, was a haven for Quakers, who had endured significant religious intolerance. Penn's invitation to diverse ethnic and religious groups to settle in Pennsylvania could be attractive only if full religious freedom was granted. The homogenous makeup of Connecticut meant that the Puritan church would still dominate. Southern colonies generally adopted the Anglican Church as a state (tax-supported) religion.

10.

Answer	Learning Objectives	Historical Thinking Skills	Key Concepts in the Curriculum Framework
C	MIG-1.0	Patterns of Continuity and Change over Time Analyzing Evidence: Content and Sourcing	2.1

Explanation: The above passage describes the headright system instituted by the Virginia Company to populate the colony and make it more productive. Once tobacco became the chief cash crop of Virginia, an adequate supply of labor was needed to make the crop profitable. The headright system brought many indentured servants to America prior to the institutionalization of slavery later in the century.

11.

Answer	Learning Objectives	Historical Thinking Skills	Key Concepts in the Curriculum Framework
B	WXT-1.0	Patterns of Continuity and Change over Time	2.1

Explanation: Prior to the mid-seventeenth century, the vast majority of English people who came to Virginia came as indentured servants. Slavery did not become the dominant system of labor until well after midcentury. Bacon's Rebellion of 1676 clearly illustrates the tensions between the backcountry and the Tidewater prior to 1700. And although the Anglican Church was the state church in Virginia, it was not because of indentured servitude.

12.

Answer	Learning Objectives	Historical Thinking Skills	Key Concepts in the Curriculum Framework
A	MIG-1.0	Comparison	2.1

Explanation: The introduction of the headright system allowed Virginia landowners to amass large estates. By contrast, New England was settled according to the township system, which only allowed individuals to amass modest amounts of land. Townships were also relatively small, which further prevented individuals from amassing large acreage. A short growing season, limited supply of labor, and difficult terrain also served to limit landholdings in New England.

Short-Answer Question

Learning Objectives	Historical Thinking Skills	Key Concepts in the Curriculum Framework
WXT-2.0 WOR-1.0	Analyzing Evidence: Content and Sourcing Contextualization	2.2

What a good response might include

a) The New England merchants purchased forbidden foreign goods but not directly from the French, the Dutch, or other Europeans. Instead they attempted to circumvent the Navigation Acts by purchasing in New Foundland "all sorts of goods brought thither directly from France, Holland, Scotland, Ireland and other places." By buying these goods in a country that the New Englanders argued was also a British "plantation," they were not clearly in violation of the law.

b) The New Englanders opposed this system, called mercantilism, which they believed hurt two key components of their economic system: manufacturing and trade. The British wanted their colonies to produce raw materials to be sent to England and also to buy manufactured goods from the mother country. Since they were based on farming staple crops and had little manufacturing, colonies in what would be the American South may have been less opposed to the restrictions placed on them by British mercantilism.

c) Since England was so far away and unable to enforce all of its laws, New England merchants often simply ignored mercantilist laws. Planters throughout the colonies continued to trade with other European nations, and smuggling was common. In Maryland, a Chesapeake colony, Protestant farmers removed the Catholic governor from power.

Document-Based Question

Learning Objectives	Historical Thinking Skills	Key Concepts in the Curriculum Framework
MIG-1.0	Patterns of Continuity and Change over Time Comparison Contextualization Argumentation Synthesis	2.1

What a good response might include

This question clearly expects you to craft a thesis based on the historical thinking skill of comparison which, as defined by the *AP® United States History Course and Exam Description*, means that you should be able to "describe, compare, and evaluate multiple historical developments . . . between different societies." You might also include other skills, including **contextualization** and **patterns of continuity and change over time**. Your thesis must do more than simply repeat the prompt: it must state just what you are going to prove. You are being asked to analyze both the similarities and the differences between the New England colonies and the Chesapeake colonies to 1750. Note that you are to address both similarities AND differences.

In order to earn the maximum of 3 points for document use, in this case you must analyze *all* or *all but one* of the documents (meaning at least six in this DBQ) and address how these documents provide evidence of the causes of expansion. Do not forget the requirement to address one of these points for each document you use: audience, purpose, historical context, or point of view. If you are not certain how to do this, ask your teacher to show you some examples. You cannot merely name the intended audience or simply state the speaker's point of view. Instead, you must link this discussion to the directive at hand: to analyze the similarities and differences between the New England colonies and the Chesapeake colonies to 1750.

In the body of your essay, you are required to demonstrate understanding of the context in which English settlers came to North America, integrating into your essay both outside information and inferences from the documents. Never merely summarize a document. Weave the documents and other knowledge that you have into your essay; both documents and this outside information serve as evidence to buttress the argument you make in your thesis.

Think about some ways in which the colonies were similar. They were settled by men and women from England who risked much to come to North America in the seventeenth century in search of a better life. In both areas, settlers sometimes challenged established authority. As Document 4, Nathaniel Bacon's *Declaration*, indicates, some colonists in Virginia rebelled against the existing power structure. In New England, dissidents like Roger Williams and Anne Hutchinson differed with the beliefs and policies of Puritan leaders. And in both colonial regions, violent conflicts sometimes characterized relationships between white settlers and Indians. Document 3, the woodcut showing the massacre at Pequot Village, is one example of the evidence you can use to analyze these conflicts.

Even before you turn to the documents, it is helpful during your planning time to generate a list of outside information you might bring to your essay. For example, the documents do not mention John Smith, Roger Williams, and Anne Hutchinson, or Metacom's War. It is your job to integrate information like this into your discussion of the documents. Together, outside information and use of the documents serve as the evidence you need to write a strong essay.

Often a study of the documents will remind you of other things that you know. For example, Document 1 is a letter from an indentured servant. Use this opportunity to explain how and why indentured servitude in the South largely gave way to slavery. John Winthrop's *A Modell of Christian Charity* (Document 2) gives you a chance to talk about just why it was that the Puritans braved the passage to America and to demonstrate your understanding of the differences between the New England settlers, who arrived with their families and intended to establish permanent communities, and the men who arrived in Jamestown seeking their fortunes. Bacon's *Declaration* (Document 4) becomes truly meaningful only when you examine Bacon's grievances and the revolt that bears his name. If your class read any of Anne Bradstreet's poetry, refer to her work when analyzing Benjamin Wadsworth's advice on marriage (Document 6) and how it reflects the Puritans' emphasis on family and community.

Connect documents that work together to strengthen your argument. For example, both Documents 3 and 4 indicate tensions between white settlers and Indians and show that these tensions were present in New England and in the Chesapeake. The letter from the indentured servant (Document 1), the Virginia statute preventing slave insurrections (Document 5), and the charts giving data on population change (Document 7) can be used together in a discussion of slavery in the Chesapeake region. Your reference to a document should read like this: "Nathaniel Bacon, the leader of a rebellion against the colonial governor of Virginia, William Berkeley, and the power of wealthy planters, argued in his 1676 *Declaration* that the yeoman farmer was being exploited by the rich, who failed to provide settlers in the backcountry with sufficient protection against Indians." You must include specific references to the documents. For example, if you merely state that the Puritans stressed the importance of family, you have not really "used" Document 6, Benjamin Wadsworth's manual on Puritan marriage. Instead specifically discuss Wadsworth's advice to a Puritan husband on the "government" of his wife.

Keep in mind that a strong essay also demonstrates awareness of broader historical processes and issues. In your comparison of colonial New England and the Chesapeake colonies, you should refer to the ongoing colonization of the New World by England and many other European nations. Link that to the exploitation of native populations, the increasingly widespread slave trade, and the financial motivation that led so many European nations to engage in exploration and colonization.

Do not refer to the documents as "Document 1" or "Document 6." Instead, refer to the type of document (painting, address to Congress . . .), its context, and reference the author, the title of the work, and his purpose, audience, or point of view. Be certain to link the document to your thesis. One of the worst errors you can make is to do what is called "laundry listing" the documents.

When you finish writing, look over your essay. Be certain that you have included all of the required elements. If you do not already have a copy of a generic rubric, ask your teacher to give you one so you will be absolutely certain that you understand what the person who scores your essay is looking for. The rubric is a sort of map for your essay. Remember that if you go on a journey without a map, you might never know when you arrive at your destination. So commit that rubric to memory, and pay attention to your destination and what it takes to get there.

PERIOD 3
1754–1800

Overview

Period 3 traces the developments that led to the expulsion of the French as a factor in the imperial struggle for North America and the subsequent American Revolution. It then focuses on the efforts by the new United States to define its government, policies, identity, and place in the world.

Although the British were victorious over France in the Seven Years' War ending in 1763, they faced new problems with their North American colonies and the Indian tribes. British acquisition of lands west of the Appalachians and in the Ohio Valley meant dismantling of the French-Indian trade networks and new waves of colonial settlers. The opening of lands west of the Appalachians led to rapid settlement and renewed conflicts with both Indians and the British who remained in the Ohio Valley. Colonists in the backcountry developed an independent yeoman culture, increasing tensions as they sought to defend their new homes. Indians tried to form new alliances to ward off these threats, and the British sought to limit migration of settlers into western territories.

Colonists, frustrated at attempts to stop western settlement, were also angered when the British began to tighten control over trade and taxes in an effort to clear debts left from the Seven Years' War. Colonial resistance was fueled by the ideas of the Enlightenment as well as the determination to be treated fairly under British law. In spite of British military and financial advantages, the resulting revolution succeeded due to colonial resilience, ideological commitment, and timely foreign intervention.

The late eighteenth century was a time of international debate about religion, politics, and new forms of government, leading to new theories that challenged old imperial systems and beliefs. Americans embraced the ideals of the Enlightenment, hoping to create a model republican government that would guarantee natural rights and protect the people from both autocratic leaders and the rule of the mob. Thomas Paine's *Common Sense* made the case for a republic. The first attempt at government of the new country was the Articles of Confederation, which concentrated power in the hands of the legislature and had no chief executive. This document proved too limited and the central government it created was too weak to be effective. The Articles were replaced by the Constitution after long deliberations about the proper role of the federal government and a series of compromises about representation. Ratification almost failed when some states felt there were not strong enough guarantees of individual rights, but the addition of the Bill of Rights calmed those fears. Continuing debates in the new government over federal power, foreign policy, and economics eventually led to the formation of political parties.

The new United States also had to deal with foreign policy issues. Early leaders felt the best course to take with Europe was that of neutrality in order to protect the new nation's borders and secure favorable trade alliances. The French Revolution presented a special challenge because the French had aided the colonists in their own revolution. President Washington restated his belief in the importance of neutrality, though others in government continued to debate the wisdom of this approach.

Slavery remained a point of disagreement among the states in the new nation. Many felt the existence of slavery ran counter to the ideals of the American Revolution and the Declaration of Independence. To ensure passage of the Constitution, debates over slavery were postponed, though the issue continued to be at the forefront of political debate for decades.

In California, the Spanish continued to expand their mission settlements, which offered some social mobility to soldiers and settlers. The Northwest Ordinance created an orderly way for land to be sold and new states to be admitted, while also providing for public education and prohibiting slavery. Indian claims and rights remained unaddressed, however, and they continued to lose land to settlers. Increasing need for access to the Mississippi River led to new problems for the new country with both the Spanish and the British.

People in the United States still wrestled with the tension between regional identity and loyalty and their loyalties to the federal government. The South's determination to expand slavery into new territories conflicted with states in other parts of the country that were moving to end the institution. Women also confronted the disconnect between the ideals of equality promoted by the Enlightenment and the Revolution with their second-class status in the new country. White women had to be content with the ideal of "republican motherhood," seeing their role as that of forming good citizens as they raised their children at home rather than playing a role in public life.

Key Terms

Be sure that you understand the meaning of these terms and their relevance in U.S. history.

Atlantic world	Federalism
Artisans	Loyalists
Assimilation	Nullification
Backcountry cultures	Republican motherhood
Checks and balances	Tariffs
Ethnic tensions	Yeoman farmers

Questions to Consider

As you study Period 3, carefully consider each theme and the questions that relate to that theme.

American and National Identity

- ✦ What accounted for the emergence of an American identity in the years between the French and Indian War and the beginning of the American Revolution?
- ✦ What factors accounted for the formation of regional and group identities in the years between 1754 and 1800?

Work, Exchange, and Technology

- ✦ What economic factors influenced the decision of the American colonists to wage a war for independence from Britain?
- ✦ What beliefs guided the founders as they set about establishing the American economic system in the years following the American Revolution?

Migration and Settlement

+ How did the movement of English colonists to the west affect relations with the French and Indian nations in the mid-eighteenth century?

Politics and Power

+ What factors led to the outbreak of war between the French and British in both Europe and North America?
+ Why and how did both the French and the British forge alliances with Indians in the French and Indian War?
+ What goals did native groups hope to achieve by making alliances with the French and British before and during the French and Indian War?
+ What accounted for the colonial victory over the British?
+ What values were reflected in the political institutions that Americans established during and after the American Revolution?
+ What factors accounted for the continued tensions between white Americans and American Indians after the end of the Revolution?
+ What tensions emerged in the debate over the writing of the Constitution? Why did this occur, and how were these tensions resolved?
+ Why did political factions, and eventually political parties, emerge in the years after the American Revolution?

America in the World

+ How did events in Europe exacerbate the tensions between the British and the American colonists in the years between 1754 and 1776?
+ What factors determined the foreign policy of the new nation during the Washington and Adams presidencies?
+ How successful was the American government in asserting itself on the world stage during this period?

Geography and the Environment

+ What environmental factors influenced settlement patterns and the formation of regional identities in this period?

Culture and Society

+ What influence did Enlightenment thinkers have on the colonists' decision to go to war against Britain?
+ In what ways did Americans' beliefs about race and gender change in the years following independence from Britain?
+ Why did the Articles of Confederation prove ineffectual, and how did the framers of the Constitution attempt to remedy their shortcomings?
+ What are republican values, and how were they manifested in American political, religious, and cultural institutions in the last half of the eighteenth century?

America's History Chapter Summaries

(required AP® content in bold)

Chapter 5
The Problem of Empire, 1763–1776

Chapter 5 covers the period of time between the end of the French and Indian War (also known as the Seven Years' War) and the formal Declaration of Independence of the American colonists from Great Britain. It details Britain's attempts to affirm control over the North American colonies and colonial resistance to these efforts, culminating in the American Revolution. Poor British leadership, enormous imperial debt, and an aggressive Parliament ran headlong into colonial demands for more political and financial autonomy, along with their determination to expand settlement into territories they felt they had earned due to their participation in the war. The clash led to the emergence of a new nation.

The end of the Seven Years' War left the British with a huge debt, which they expected their American colonists to help pay. The colonists, however, had long been used to being able to manage their own affairs to a large degree. The British hoped to make up wartime expenses by stricter enforcement of taxation and tariff collection in the colonies. Additional **fears of French rebellions in Canada and Indian uprisings in the Ohio Valley led to decisions to increase military strength in North America as well**. The British were angered when the colonial merchants and assemblies resented what they saw as military occupation and extortion.

Prime Minister George Grenville was the first to propose a series of laws designed to boost the British treasury at the colonists' expense. The Stamp Act of 1765 led to the first open confrontation with colonists, who convened the Stamp Act Congress and demanded an end to taxes within the colonies they were not allowed to vote on themselves—what they called "internal taxes." They rejected the British claim that they had "virtual representation" and **claimed what they felt were their rights as British citizens**. Britain responded with sending even more troops under a new Quartering Act, requiring the colonists to provide food and shelter for troops. The Stamp Act Congress was followed by violence in the streets, with citizens' groups such as the Sons of Liberty destroying stamp warehouses and attacking the British stamp agents. The colonists based their actions on **both the traditions of British common law and the ideas of the Enlightenment. What they saw as imperial oppression did not fit with new ideas of natural rights and the obligations of the government to the governed**.

These popular resistance movements caught the attention of Parliament. Charles Townshend replaced Grenville as prime minister, and the Declaratory Act repealed the Stamp Act, while still maintaining that the British government had the right to tax the colonies. Townshend imposed a new round of taxes and duties that led to **renewal of colonial resistance**. Colonial women led the call for nonimportation of British products they could make themselves. Men followed their lead, and British commercial profits dropped. The British responded by increasing the number of troops stationed in the colonies.

New troubles were brewing in the Ohio Valley as **colonial settlers ignored the Proclamation Line of 1763, which prohibited any new settlements west of the mountains in what was then Indian country**. Thousands had already moved west, and they were not likely to be driven back. Lord North replaced Townshend in 1770, and he agreed to repeal most of the Townshend duties. As Parliament debated Lord North's proposals, trouble broke out in Boston in March 1770 when British soldiers fired on a group of colonists. Though the soldiers were later acquitted, the event became known as the Boston Massacre and further inflamed sentiment against imperial power.

While the repeal of the Townshend duties restored order for a while, colonial resentments were never far beneath the surface. Several colonial assemblies set up committees of correspondence to keep in touch without having to use British mails in the event of a crisis. Such a moment was not long in coming when **Parliament passed a new Tea Act in 1773 to bolster the fortunes of the imperial East India Company**. Colonists reacted to the proposed monopoly with new calls for boycott, and in Boston they dumped an entire shipment of tea into the harbor. The British responded with the Coercive Acts, hoping to make an example of Boston and the Massachusetts colony. The Quebec Act opening the Ohio Valley to Canadian settlers inflamed the colonists even more.

The First Continental Congress was called to meet in Philadelphia in September 1774. Some who attended wanted more boycotts, others favored a move to independence, and still others hoped for compromise. They agreed to demand repeal of the Coercive Acts and threatened complete boycott if the British refused. The colonies remained deeply divided as to how to respond to British policies. Some remained loyal to the crown while others simply wanted to be left alone. Growing tensions in the Ohio Valley and in New England pushed people on all sides into open conflict by spring 1775. The British occupying Boston heard claims of armed militia in the countryside and sent troops out to capture colonial leaders and supplies. The battles that ensued at Lexington and Concord became the opening round of the American Revolution.

The Second Continental Congress set up a temporary government and authorized raising a militia as the British prepared to launch another attack on Boston. King George III and the British Parliament ignored last-ditch efforts at compromise by the Congress, and skirmishes broke out in the South and West as well as New England. **Pamphleteer Thomas Paine sought to rally the undecided to the Patriots' cause with the publication of** *Common Sense* **in which he made the case to end the tyranny of monarchy and establish a republic**. In the summer of 1776, the Declaration of Independence was signed, **using the ideas of the European Enlightenment to make the case for independence and the rule of popular sovereignty**.

Chapter 6
Making War and Republican Governments, 1776–1789

Chapter 6 examines two related sets of events. The first is the American Revolution against the British Empire, which began in 1776 and ended in 1783. The **colonists won through a combination of outstanding leadership, the resilient Continental army and militia, and support from allies abroad**. The second focuses on the Patriots' attempts to build an effective form of republican government, culminating in the ratification of the Constitution of 1787, the national charter that endures today.

Colonial leaders **wrote and signed the Declaration of Independence in 1776**, just as the British began large-scale military assaults in New England. The British seemed to have more advantages in the conflict, as the colonists were economically and militarily weak. After a number of setbacks in the early years of the war, the Patriots' prospects improved dramatically in 1778 when they formed a formal alliance with France. The British tried to focus on the South, where they thought they would find greater Loyalist support. They also hoped to win slaves to the British cause by offering freedom to any who would rebel against their colonial masters. However, by October 1781, the British were forced to concede defeat at the seaport of Yorktown, Virginia, thus ending the American Revolution.

Shortly after the signing the Declaration of Independence, the Continental Congress adopted the **Articles of Confederation, a document that created a loose union of the states as an association of equals**. Although the Confederation held powers to make war and treaties, requisition funds from the states, and manage Indian affairs, there were major weaknesses as well. The Articles provided for no chief executive or federal judiciary, could not tax, and lacked the power to enforce its provisions. Even so, ratification came after a dispute involving land claims in the Ohio Valley was settled by the creation of a federally administered Northwest Territory. The Northwest Ordinance of 1784 and the Land Ordinance of 1785 later provided for the orderly settlement of the territory and included a ban on slavery. While a boon for settlers, **these policies effectively ended Indian claims to any of the lands in the Ohio Valley**.

Financial problems quickly emerged as the war ended and states began to deal with their war debts. Some states tried to clear these debts by raising taxes, which placed a heavy burden on already financially strapped small farmers. Revolt broke out in Massachusetts with Shays's Rebellion, led by former Patriot soldiers who now faced the possibility of losing the land they had fought for because they could not pay the new taxes. The **national government under the Articles of Confederation had no way to help solve such problems, and many began to support demands for the creation of a stronger central government**.

In May 1787, a national convention met in Philadelphia to consider changes in the Articles. The delegates quickly realized that revisions would be inadequate; the country needed a completely new framework. The **result of their deliberations and compromises was the creation of the U.S. Constitution**, a document that created a stronger federal government with a chief executive and a judiciary, yet one that would still share many powers with the individual states. The final Constitution created a two-house legislative branch. Smaller states got equal representation in the Senate, while larger states won representation based on population in the House of Representatives. The issue of slavery was too controversial to deal with definitively, so the new Constitution simply set a time for the end of the international slave trade but **left the question of slavery for another generation to solve**. Those who hoped the new government would move to end slavery altogether were disappointed. Southern delegates did get the right to count slaves proportionally in determining representation in the House of Representatives. Women who hoped the new Constitution would offer citizenship to them were disappointed as well. They were relegated to continuing **their roles as wives and mothers and contenting themselves with raising good future citizens**.

The ratification process proved to be more difficult than the framers had expected. Two camps quickly emerged: the Federalists, who felt a strong national government was a necessity, and the Antifederalists, who worried that the states were giving up too much power. Legislators in Massachusetts declared **they would vote against ratification if a more explicit Bill of Rights were not added to the document, spelling out certain individual rights they felt were left too vague in the Constitution itself**. With the promise of the addition of a Bill of Rights, states voted to ratify the Constitution and the new government was officially established. Nevertheless, **debates over the limits of federal and state power would continue for some time**.

Chapter 7
Hammering Out a Federal Republic, 1787–1820

Chapter 7 explores three interrelated themes: public policy (both domestic and foreign), party politics, and westward expansion. The chapter discusses the rise of mass democracy, the struggle to define the limits of state versus federal power, the first major extension of national boundaries beyond the Mississippi River, the growth of the first political parties, and the social pressures that accompanied this rapid expansion of political, economic, and technological change. It examines the breakup of the old Federalist order with the election of Thomas Jefferson and then moves to the development of the First Party System with the rise of the Virginia Dynasty presidents and the Democratic-Republicans. The addition of the Louisiana Territory meant changes for the nation in terms of rapid westward expansion, more complicated international diplomacy, new economic opportunities, and new social and cultural issues. The United States moved from its status as a small emerging nation to one with the beginnings of a world presence, even though many internal social and political issues still needed resolution

During the 1790s, the new nation debated its role in foreign conflicts, especially the war between Great Britain and France triggered **by the French Revolution, which was itself partially inspired by the American Revolution. The American Revolution also helped spark the Haitian Revolution** beginning in 1791, which established the first black republic in the Atlantic world.

Prior to 1800, during the first administration of President George Washington, the government ratified **the Bill of Rights**. Throughout the 1790s, the nation moved to **more participatory democracy** with the development of new political parties, with the **Democratic-Republicans** successfully challenging the Federalists in the election of 1800. The Supreme Court played a role in defining the **supremacy of federal power over state power and solidified the role of the judiciary in making determinations about the meaning of the Constitution** (ex: *Marbury v. Madison*; *McCulloch v. Maryland*).

The country also experienced **growing regional economic diversification**, which also led to political and social differences. **The expansion of slavery** became a central issue for the nation, especially **as slavery expanded west across the Lower South** with the **increasing demand for cotton for the newly emerging textile industry** The acquisition of lands from the **Louisiana Purchase** led to further debate about the expansion of slavery, an issue settled only temporarily by the **Missouri Compromise** in 1820.

Expansion also led to increased **conflicts with American Indians** who resisted expansion (ex: Tecumseh) yet often found themselves on the unfavorable side of increasingly restrictive treaties (ex: Treaty of Greenville). **Homesteaders and entrepreneurs sought to push farther west**, leading to a constant demand for more land.

While the United States was intent on expanding its national borders, the new nation also wished to stay out of European conflicts. Even so, foreign involvement was inevitable, as the government negotiated the **purchase of the Louisiana Territory** from France and later **sought to control the North American continent**, leading in part to further conflict with Great Britain. While the nation's leaders talked of isolation, **the country was slowly finding itself involved in world affairs**.

Thematic Timeline

THEME	REQUIRED CONTENT	SUPPORTING EXAMPLES
AMERICAN AND NATIONAL IDENTITY	• After the colonists' victory in the American Revolution, Indian tribes wanted to trade with the new Americans yet also tried to maintain their tribal identity and hold onto their land. • Despite the colonists' decision to fight for independence, many colonists remained loyal to Britain. • Concerned that the British were placing unwarranted constraints on their economic and political liberties, colonists united. • As economic, social, and political factors shaped regional identities after the Revolution, people formed political parties to articulate and implement policies that they supported.	**1754–1775** • After the French and Indian War, the British insistence that colonists had "virtual representation" serves to unite many colonists in opposition to the mother country. • From the mid-1760s to the outbreak of the Revolution (1775), many colonists develop a national identity without shedding their regional and group identities. • Patrick Henry attacks George III in the Virginia House of Burgesses (1765). • Stamp Act Congress (1765). • Sons of Liberty (1765). • Popular resistance leads to the nullification of the Stamp Act (1766). • Daughters of Liberty (1768). • By 1770, many Patriots, including Benjamin Franklin, Patrick Henry, and Samuel Adams, refuse to accept authority of Parliament. • Many colonists (15 to 20 percent of whites) remain loyal to Britain. They distrust some Patriot leaders and fear anarchy. Quaker pacifists refuse to support war. **1776–1800** • During the American Revolution, colonial political identities change as colonists felt the "abstract bonds of citizenship." Many, however, remain loyal to Britain. • During the American Revolution, the British recruit slaves by promising them freedom. • Many American Indians ally with the British. • Despite some attempts at assimilation of Indians after the American Revolution, Indians refuse to give up loyalty to their clan, the essence of tribal structure. • Many Indians incorporate elements of Christianity into their traditional religion. • Indians reject attempts to turn them into farmers. • Fear of slave revolts intensifies after Toussaint L'Ouverture leads Haitians against the French (1798).

Theme	Required Content	Supporting Examples
WORK, EXCHANGE, TECHNOLOGY	• After the French and Indian War, Indians wanted to maintain trade with Europeans but also resisted the English presence on Indian land. • Competition for resources between the British colonists and Indians continued after the French left North America. • One reason the British attempted to control the colonial economy after 1754 was the debt incurred during the French and Indian War. • The weaknesses of the Articles of Confederation, including the difficulty of raising revenue, led many to call for revisions to the Articles. • Debates over economic policy eventually led to the formation of two political parties.	**1754–1775** • Colonial demand for British goods increases in the mid-eighteenth century, resulting in a trade deficit with Britain. • The cost of maintaining British forces in North America greatly increases after 1754. • The expense of the French and Indian War plus British extension of credit to the colonists leads the British government to seek additional sources of revenue. • The per capita tax burden in Britain is 20 percent (1760s). • Many colonial merchants oppose British economic policies because they have made fortunes from smuggling in their effort to circumvent British laws. • George Grenville becomes prime minister and convinces Parliament to impose economic reforms, many of which the colonists oppose (1763). • Currency Act (1764). • Sugar Act (1764). • Stamp Act (1765). • Townshend Act imposes duties on colonial imports (1767). • Debate rages over internal versus external taxes. • Colonists organize boycotts of British goods (mid-eighteenth century). • Women are key to the efforts of the nonimportation movement (1768). • Tea Act (1773). • Boston Tea Party (1773). • British impose Coercive Acts (1774). **1776–1800** • Following the outbreak of the Revolution, the colonial economy is hurt by the British blockade. The Americans have no reliable source of funds until the 1778 treaty with France. • Publication of Adam Smith's *The Wealth of Nations* (1776). • After the Treaty of Paris (1783), some Loyalist property is seized, and merchants who supported independence prosper. • Shays's Rebellion demonstrates frustration with the economic policies of the Massachusetts government (1786–1787). • Economic issues are at the core of debate over the new American government: debts, tariffs, taxes.

THEME	REQUIRED CONTENT	SUPPORTING EXAMPLES
WORK, EXCHANGE, TECHNOLOGY (*continued*)		• The Constitution provides for honoring of national debt and the power to tax. • Along with the three-fifths compromise, framers of Constitution agree that slave trade cannot be banned until 1808. • Two competing economic visions vie for support in the early years of the new republic. • Washington appoints Alexander Hamilton as the first secretary of the treasury. Hamilton's economic plan is designed to increase the authority of the central government. • Bank of the United States established (1790). • Hamilton submits three economic reports: on public credit, on the national bank, and on manufactures (1790–1791). • Hamilton proposes a revenue-raising tariff (1791). • Hamilton's rival, Thomas Jefferson, envisions a society that rests on the labor of independent yeoman farmers. • Eli Whitney invents the cotton gin (1793). • Pennsylvania farmers wage the Whiskey Rebellion to protest an excise tax (1794).
MIGRATION AND SETTLEMENT	• After the defeat of the French and their withdrawal from the continent, new conflicts arose between white settlers and Indians along the western border of colonial America and then the United States. • Backcountry cultures and social and ethnic tensions emerged when settlers moved westward. • In the middle and late eighteenth century, the Spanish expanded their mission settlements in California, leading to a new cultural blending. • Those who joined the movement for independence from Britain included colonial elites, laborers, artisans, and women.	**1754–1775** • By 1754, the British and the French, as well as various Indian groups, lay claim to the Ohio Valley. • Colonists defy the Proclamation of 1763. As they move west, they engage in conflicts with Indian groups. • Pontiac's Rebellion (1763). • As British colonists move west, conflicts over economic issues and colonial Indian policies increase. • Paxton Boys in Pennsylvania (1763). • Regulator Movement in South Carolina (1763). • Regulator Movement in North Carolina (1766). **1776–1800** • After the 1783 Treaty of Paris, Indian tribes feel abandoned by the British. • 1784 Treaty of Fort Stanwix takes land from Iroquois. • Additional treaties result in Indians' ceding most land in what will become Ohio (1785). • Formation of the Western Confederacy. • Battle of Fallen Timbers (1794).

THEME	REQUIRED CONTENT	SUPPORTING EXAMPLES
MIGRATION AND SETTLEMENT (*continued*)	• As Americans moved westward, republican institutions moved with them, often intensifying conflicts between American Indians and white settlers. • With the expansion of slavery in the Lower South and in the West, and the gradual abolition of slavery elsewhere in the United States, regional attitudes developed toward slavery.	• Greenville Treaty sparks white migration into Ohio and Tennessee River valleys (1795). • White settlers move in large numbers to Kentucky (late eighteenth and early nineteenth centuries). • As cotton becomes a more profitable crop, many Americans move to the Deep South.
POLITICS AND POWER	• As the English expanded into the interior of North America, Indian tribes shifted alliances among European nations. • After the mid-eighteenth century, British colonists in North America blamed their economic and political grievances on the British crown, and a movement for independence gained momentum. • Thomas Paine's *Common Sense* and the Declaration of Independence clearly showed colonists' belief in natural rights and republican self-government. • Superior colonial leadership was a pivotal factor in ensuring colonial victory in the American Revolution.	**1754–1775** • Before and during the French and Indian War, the Iroquois forge alliances with the British; other tribes ally with the French. • Governor Dinwiddie sends George Washington to the confluence of the Allegheny and Monongahela rivers to reassert British claims (1754). • Albany Congress (1754). • Colonists begin to raise questions about British political and economic policies: taxation imposed from London and trial by vice admiralty courts (1760s). • British policy of salutary neglect ends. • Stamp Act (1765). • Quartering Act (1765). • Declaratory Act (following repeal of Stamp Act in 1766). • Tax on tea left in place after repeal of Townsend Acts (1770). • Boston Massacre (1770). • Committees of Correspondence form (early 1770s). • First Continental Congress meets (September 1774). • Battles of Lexington and Concord (April 1775). • Battles of Bunker Hill (May 1775). • Declaration of the Causes and Necessities of Taking Up Arms (1775).

THEME	REQUIRED CONTENT	SUPPORTING EXAMPLES
POLITICS AND POWER (*continued*)	• After the American Revolution, state constitutions and the Articles of Confederation confirmed Americans' suspicion of both too much centralized power and excessive popular influence, placing limits on each, with power in the legislature and restrictions on suffrage and citizenship. • Political compromise allowed for the creation of the Constitution, a document that strengthened the federal government but also placed limits on it. • Political parties were formed in the early years of the Republic, reflecting Americans' differences on the issues of federalism, economic policy, and foreign policy. • While many after the American Revolution called for greater democracy and the abolition of slavery, the framers delayed a solution to the issue of slavery and the slave trade, ensuring that these would be debated for many years. • The Northwest Ordinance provided for the admission of new states and supported public education, private property, and the restriction of slavery.	**1776–1800** • Patriot governments are weak at the start of the Revolution. • Battle of Saratoga is a turning point of the American Revolution (October 1777). • Valley Forge (winter of 1777–1778). • After French come to their aid, American forces are able to defeat the British at Yorktown (1781). • Treaty of Paris (1783) gives United States land south of the Great Lakes and east of the Mississippi River. American navigation on the Mississippi is guaranteed. • Articles of Confederation are adopted. Fear of a too-powerful executive results in a central government with no chief executive, no judiciary, and no power to tax (November 1777). • The Northwest Ordinances provide for five new states, where slavery is banned and funds for schools are mandated (1784–1787). However, claims by Indian tribes are essentially invalidated. • In the wake of Shays's Rebellion, a convention is called to revise the Articles (May 1787). • Virginia and New Jersey plans adopted as key part of the new Constitution, viewed as the Great Compromise (1787). • Ratification of the Constitution promoted by *The Federalist*, written by Hamilton, Jay, and Madison (1787–1788). • "Federalist No. 10" based on the ideas of Montesquieu. • Compromises during the writing of the Constitution ensure the debates over slavery will not be resolved soon. • In order to ensure ratification and provide guarantee of individual rights, Federalists pledge to include a Bill of Rights. • National court system created by the Judiciary Act of 1789. • Bill of Rights ratified (1791). • Supporters of Hamilton and Jefferson increasingly develop allegiance to political factions. By 1794, these factions are known, respectively, as Federalists and Democratic-Republicans (often called Republicans). • By 1796, the First Party System emerges in the context of conflict over Hamilton's economic program.

THEME	REQUIRED CONTENT	SUPPORTING EXAMPLES
POLITICS AND POWER (*continued*)	• In his Farewell Address, George Washington warned about the dangers of political parties and "entangling" foreign alliances, but increasing tensions with France and Britain led to bitter partisan debates about both political parties and foreign policy.	• Federalists pass the Alien and Sedition Acts to weaken support for the Republicans (1798). • Kentucky and Virginia resolutions (1798). • Americans debate the legacy of the French Revolution as Federalists side with the British and Republicans voice admiration for the French (after 1789).
AMERICA IN THE WORLD	• During the American Revolution, European nations provided considerable support for the colonists, helping them defeat the British. • European powers remained in North America after the end of the American Revolution. Their presence provided many challenges to the new American government as it attempted to promote trade and other economic interests and protect its borders. • Following the French Revolution, Americans debated both domestic policy and America's place in the world. • Many criticized the Articles of Confederation for hindering the implementation of a strong foreign policy; this led to calls for significant revision of the Articles and a stronger central government. • The American Revolution affected events in France, the Caribbean, and Latin America. • The United States used diplomacy to lessen tensions with Spain that rose over use of the Mississippi River and to deal with a continuing British presence in North America.	**1754–1775** • By the mid-eighteenth century, Britain is the world's commercial and industrial leader. • After the war between the French and British begins in North America, the conflict spreads to Europe and is known as the Seven Years' War (1756–1763). • Treaty of Paris (1763). **1776–1800** • After the Battle of Saratoga, Americans make a treaty with France. France provides money and troops (1778). • Spain joins the conflict on the side of the British (1779). • The French Revolution is inspired by republican ideas and the model of the American Revolution (1789). • After the American and French revolutions, many Americans were divided as to whether to support the British or the French and debated which nation shared American values and beliefs about government and foreign policy. • Proclamation of Neutrality (1793). • Jay's Treaty viewed as too conciliatory toward the British (1795). • XYZ Affair (1798).

THEME	REQUIRED CONTENT	SUPPORTING EXAMPLES
GEOGRAPHY AND THE ENVIRONMENT	• The geography of eastern North America contributed to rising tensions among colonists, Indians, and the British in the years leading up to the American Revolution. • Partly due to their familiarity with their environment, the colonists were able to defeat the British. • After the American Revolution, the Mississippi River and access to New Orleans became a focus of international rivalry.	**1754–1775** • As colonial settlements are built in the West, the British government must extend its authority and resources into a new and difficult environment. **1776–1800** • Following the end of the American Revolution, white settlers move in large numbers to new environments in the West and the South and confront new challenges. • Indian groups must adapt to new environments as they are pushed westward by white settlement.
CULTURE AND SOCIETY	• Those who supported the colonial fight for independence based their arguments on the ideals of the Enlightenment, the rights of Englishmen, and belief in individual liberty. The colonists' commitment to these ideals helped them achieve their goals. • In the eighteenth century, people around the Atlantic world debated new ideas about politics and religion and experimented with new political structures. • The Enlightenment emphasis on individual talent rather than hereditary privilege inspired American thinkers.	**1754–1775** • The intellectual roots of the Patriots' resistance come from many sources: English common law, used by James Otis to oppose writs of assistance in 1761, Enlightenment rationalism and belief in natural law as articulated by Locke and Montesquieu, (many in the colonies begin to see slavery as a violation of natural law), and Republican and Whig traditions in England, for example, the movement toward a constitutional monarchy. **1776–1800** • *Common Sense* by Thomas Paine (January 1776). • Declaration of Independence (July 1776). • Women assume a larger role while men are fighting for independence, so they come to expect expanded rights when the war is over. • Although women in New Jersey could vote until 1807, women's efforts to end restrictive laws are largely ignored after the Revolution. • There is some expansion of educational opportunities for women. • Women's role in the new nation is based on the idea of "republican motherhood," a notion further refined in the nineteenth century with the popular idea of the "cult of domesticity."

THEME	REQUIRED CONTENT	SUPPORTING EXAMPLES
CULTURE AND SOCIETY (*continued*)	• While fighting for independence from Britain and then establishing a new government, Americans continued debating the balance between liberty and order. • Belief in individual liberty was one reason that many successfully demanded that a Bill of Rights be added to the Constitution. • Enlightenment ideas and a need to establish a role for women in the political life of the new nation promoted the idea of "republican motherhood."	• By the turn of the century, republican principles form the basis of American political thought. These include: representative democratic government within prescribed limits and based on popular sovereignty, rule of law (a written constitution), a dynamic market economy, private ownership, government responsibility for enhancing the "common wealth," equality in family and social relationships (in the North), aristocratic republicanism (in the South), and opposition to an established church.

Period 3 Practice Questions

Multiple-Choice Questions

Questions 1–3 refer to the image below.

Paul Revere, Engraving of the Boston Massacre, 1770

1. The above engraving was used as propaganda to promote which of the following?
    (A) Grassroots mobilization to defend the rights of colonial British subjects
    (B) A memorial for British losses during the Revolutionary War
    (C) A condemnation of the threat to property created by riots in Boston
    (D) An increase in Bostonian support of British rule to preserve peace in the colonies

2. All of the following causes led up to the event portrayed in the engraving EXCEPT
    (A) imperial control over North American markets.
    (B) British implementation of what colonials believed to be unfair taxation.
    (C) the British navy's refusal to protect colonial interests from the Barbary pirates.
    (D) Great Britain's massive debt from the Seven Years' War.

3. The above engraving represents a general trend of colonial discontent occurring in which of the following time periods?
    (A) 1491–1607
    (B) 1607–1754
    (C) 1754–1800
    (D) 1800–1848

GO ON TO THE NEXT PAGE.

Questions 4–6 refer to the excerpt below.

"The next wish of this traveler will be to know whence came all these people? They are a mixture of English, Scotch, Irish, French, Dutch, Germans, and Swedes.

"What then is the American, this new man? He is either an European, or the descendant of an European, hence that strange mixture of blood, which you will find in no other country. I could point out to you a family whose grandfather was an Englishman, whose wife was Dutch, whose son married a French woman, and whose present four sons have now four wives of different nations. He is an American, who leaving behind him all his ancient prejudices and manners, receives new ones from the new mode of life he has embraced, the new government he obeys, and the new rank he holds. He becomes an American by being received in the broad lap of our great Alma Mater."

St. Jean de Crèvecoeur, "What Is an American?" *Letters from an American Farmer*, 1782

4. The above passage best indicates what fundamental difference between English colonies and Spanish and French colonies in North America?

    (A) The propensity of English colonies to grant religious freedom while the French and Spanish were much more restrictive

    (B) The adherence of Britain to a mercantilist economic system while the French and Spanish created free-market economies

    (C) Less restrictive policies than the French or Spanish introduced on who could or could not emigrate to the colonies

    (D) The willingness of the British to allow greater political freedom than either the French or Spanish

5. By the time of the American Revolution, the above passage indicates that

    (A) the majority of Americans favored independence.

    (B) many colonists felt a sense of American identity.

    (C) nativist sentiment was significantly on the rise.

    (D) religious freedom would be a casualty of any rebellion against England.

6. The above passage supports which of the following statements about the American Revolution?

    (A) Great Britain hired mercenaries to assist them in fighting the Patriots.

    (B) The Patriots had a reasonable expectation that European countries would provide military and financial aid.

    (C) American Indians tended to side with the British rather than the colonists.

    (D) The Revolution began because Great Britain prohibited people from other nations to emigrate to the colonies.

Questions 7–9 refer to the excerpt below.

"Art. II. Each State retains its Sovereignty, Freedom, and Independence, and every Power, Jurisdiction, and Right, which is not by this Confederation expressly delegated to the United States in Congress assembled.

"Art. V. In determining Questions in the United States, in Congress assembled, each State shall have one vote.

"Art. VIII. The Taxes for paying that Proportion shall be laid and levied by the Authority and Direction of the Legislatures of the several States, within the Time agreed upon by the United States in Congress assembled.

GO ON TO THE NEXT PAGE.

"Art. IX. All Controversies concerning the private Right of Soil claimed under different Grants of two or more States, whose Jurisdictions, as they may respect such Lands . . . shall, on the Petition of either Party to the Congress of the United States, be finally determined . . .

"Art. XIII. . . . And we do further solemnly plight and engage the Faith of our respective Constituents, that they shall abide by the Determinations of the United States in Congress assembled, on all Questions which by the said Confederation are submitted to them, and that the Articles thereof shall be inviolably observed by the States we respectively represent, and that the Union shall be perpetual."

Articles of Confederation, November 1777 (ratified 1781)

7. The primary reason the Articles of Confederation restricted the power of the federal government was fear
   (A) that the national government would create a monarchy.
   (B) that anarchy would sweep the nation following victory over Great Britain.
   (C) of tyranny that many colonists believed they had suffered under British rule.
   (D) that the French would attempt to recapture land they had lost in the French and Indian War.

8. Despite its weaknesses, the Articles of Confederation experienced their greatest success in
   (A) securing from Spain the right to peacefully navigate the entire length of the Mississippi River.
   (B) setting up a system of survey and disposal of western lands.
   (C) removal of the British from the Northwest forts.
   (D) agreement from the French to halt the impressments of American sailors.

9. Disagreement over determining state representation in the Articles of Confederation Congress led to the Constitutional Convention to incorporate which of the following into the Constitution?
   (A) The first ten amendments limiting the power of the federal government
   (B) A federal system that divided power between the national and state governments
   (C) A clause that allowed Congress to stretch its power as necessary
   (D) The division of Congress into two branches, the House of Representatives and the Senate

Questions 10–12 refer to the excerpt below.

" 'Why did I go?'
   'Yes,' I replied; 'My histories tell me that you men of the Revolution took up arms against intolerable oppression.'
   'What were they? Oppressions? I didn't feel them.'
   'What, were you not oppressed by the Stamp Act?'
   'I never saw one of those stamps. . . . I am certain I never paid a penny for one of them.'
   'Well, what then about the tea-tax?'
   'Tea-tax! I never drank a drop of that stuff; the boys threw it all overboard.'
   'Then I suppose you had been reading Harrington or Sidney and Locke about the eternal principles of liberty.'
   'Never heard of 'em. We read only the Bible, the Catechism, Watt's Psalms and Hymns, and the Almanac.'
   'Well, then, what was the matter? and what did you mean in going to the fight?'

GO ON TO THE NEXT PAGE.

'Young man, what we meant in going for those red-coats was this: we always had governed ourselves, and we always meant to. They didn't mean we should.'"

Interview of Ninety-Year-Old American Revolutionary War
veteran Captain Preston, 1842

10. The above account best reflects which of the following about the American Revolution?
    (A) It was fueled by specific acts of British oppression.
    (B) It was in part the result of serious propaganda campaigns by the colonial elite.
    (C) It was in part the result of a changing American identity.
    (D) It resulted in a serious divide between Loyalists and Patriots.

11. Which of the following would most likely lead a historian to question the accuracy of the passage cited above?
    (A) The reliability of a firsthand account collected long after the event
    (B) The reliability of a firsthand account from a poorly educated individual
    (C) The reliability of interviewers to accurately record firsthand accounts of events
    (D) The reliability of conflicting accounts from firsthand witnesses of the same event

12. The above excerpt best illustrates the fact that colonists
    (A) had developed a sense of self-government before the Declaration of Independence.
    (B) would call for a strong central government following the Revolution.
    (C) developed a lasting sense of egalitarianism following the Revolution.
    (D) supported the expansion of natural rights to disadvantaged classes before the Revolution.

END OF MULTIPLE-CHOICE SECTION

Short-Answer Questions

"And be it further enacted, That if any person shall write, print, utter or publish, or shall cause or procure to be written, printed, uttered or publishing, or shall knowingly and willingly assist or aid in writing, printing, uttering or publishing any false, scandalous and malicious writing or writings against the government of the United States, or either house of the Congress of the United States, or the President of the United States, . . . then such person, being thereof convicted before any court of the United States having jurisdiction thereof, shall be punished by a fine not exceeding two thousand dollars, and by imprisonment not exceeding two years."

The Alien and Sedition Acts, July 14, 1798

1. Using the quotation above, answer a, b, and c.

    a) Identify whom the act targeted and why.

    b) Identify the circumstances that led to the passage of the act.

    c) Cite one piece of additional evidence that explains the reaction to the act by the group it targeted.

GO ON TO THE NEXT PAGE.

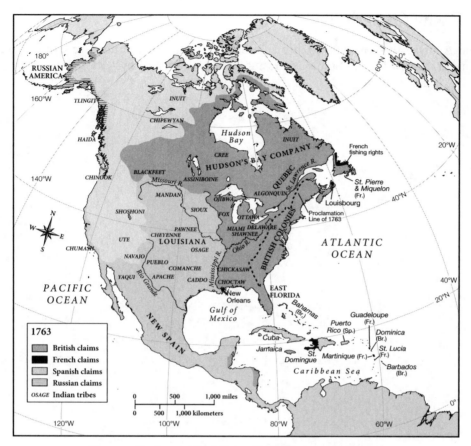

Europe Redraws the Map of North America, 1763

2. Using the map above, answer a, b, and c.

a) Briefly explain the international consequences of the French and Indian War.

b) Explain why Great Britain attempted to limit colonial expansion.

c) Explain why efforts to limit British colonial expansion failed.

END OF SHORT-ANSWER SECTION

Long Essay Question

Question: Analyze the continuities and significant changes in political, economic, and social conditions in the new United States as a result of the American Revolution.

END OF LONG ESSAY SECTION

Answer Key to Period 3 Practice Questions

Multiple-Choice Questions

1.

Answer	Learning Objectives	Historical Thinking Skills	Key Concepts in the Curriculum Framework
A	NAT-1.0	Causation Analyzing Evidence: Content and Sourcing	3.1

Explanation: The engraving of the Boston Massacre was designed to sway wavering colonists toward the cause of independence. While it caused a temporary withdrawal of activism against British control, in the long run it had significant appeal as a propaganda device.

2.

Answer	Learning Objectives	Historical Thinking Skills	Key Concepts in the Curriculum Framework
C	NAT-1.0	Causation	3.1

Explanation: British attempts to end salutary neglect and raise money to counter the debt incurred during the French and Indian War increased tension between the colonies and Great Britain. Acts such as the Stamp Act infuriated colonists, who began to form structured organizations like the Sons of Liberty to combat new restrictions. Attempts to more stringently regulate colonial trade (Townshend Act) and restrict colonial movement westward (Proclamation of 1763) also increased tensions.

3.

Answer	Learning Objectives	Historical Thinking Skills	Key Concepts in the Curriculum Framework
C	NAT-1.0	Periodization	3.1

Explanation: Gathering tension between the colonies and Great Britain was increasingly felt during and after the French and Indian War (1754–1763), reaching a climax with the Declaration of Independence and the Revolutionary War in the 1770s.

4.

Answer	Learning Objectives	Historical Thinking Skills	Key Concepts in the Curriculum Framework
C	MIG-1.0	Comparison	2.1
		Analyzing Evidence: Content and Sourcing	3.1

Explanation: Both France and Spain exercised greater administrative control over who could settle in their colonies, largely limiting it to their own nationality and religion. French and Spanish colonies tended to be extractive rather than settlement colonies. The British had to rely on agriculture and the harvesting of raw materials. The more people who settled in the British colonies, the more productive vast areas of agricultural lands could be.

5.

Answer	Learning Objectives	Historical Thinking Skills	Key Concepts in the Curriculum Framework
B	NAT-1.0	Contextualization Analyzing Evidence: Content and Sourcing	3.1

Explanation: The blending of different nationalities and religions created a new sense of American identity and weakened their ethnic and cultural ties to their former country. Independence was not favored by the majority of Americans, and nativism would be an outgrowth of dramatically expanded immigration in the 1840s.

6.

Answer	Learning Objectives	Historical Thinking Skills	Key Concepts in the Curriculum Framework
B	WOR-1.0	Causation Analyzing Evidence: Content and Sourcing	3.1

Explanation: The idea that the American colonies were creating a separate identity from Great Britain encouraged European powers to settle old grudges and weaken the dominant power in Europe. Multinational military leadership aided the colonial cause significantly. Once the colonies demonstrated a reasonable chance of success (at the Battle of Saratoga), European countries were more willing to assist.

7.

Answer	Learning Objectives	Historical Thinking Skills	Key Concepts in the Curriculum Framework
C	NAT-2.0	Causation Analyzing Evidence: Content and Sourcing	3.2

Explanation: Confrontation with Great Britain left the colonists leery of placing too much power in the hands of a central government. Colonies were reluctant to give up their autonomy to a national government because of the perception that the British government had become a tyranny by taking away the natural rights of man. In the subsequent Constitutional Convention and early republic, the fear of tyranny was a continued subject of debate.

8.

Answer	Learning Objectives	Historical Thinking Skills	Key Concepts in the Curriculum Framework
B	MIG-2.0	Causation	3.3

Explanation: The Land Ordinances of 1785 and 1787 set up the process by which Northwest Territory lands would be surveyed and sold. The Northwest Ordinance also established the process by which territories could become states. The Confederation Congress was unsuccessful in securing the right of deposit at New Orleans or at removing British troops from Northwest posts. Britain rather than France was responsible for impressing U.S. sailors.

9.

Answer	Learning Objectives	Historical Thinking Skills	Key Concepts in the Curriculum Framework
D	POL-3.0	Causation	3.2

Explanation: The Constitution divided Congress into two branches, with representation in the House of Representatives being based on population while representation in the Senate was equal for all states. The Great (or Connecticut) Compromise satisfied the concerns of Virginia Plan that favored large states and the New Jersey plan that favored small states.

10.

Answer	Learning Objectives	Historical Thinking Skills	Key Concepts in the Curriculum Framework
C	NAT-1.0	Analyzing Evidence: Content and Sourcing	3.1

Explanation: The American colonists developed a sense of identity around the perception that they had been self-governing for a significant period of time. That perception led them to feel that they were different from the British and that the government of Great Britain was threatening their rights as a self-governing people.

11.

Answer	Learning Objectives	Historical Thinking Skills	Key Concepts in the Curriculum Framework
A	NAT-1.0	Analyzing Evidence: Content and Sourcing	3.1

Explanation: In looking at the accuracy of historical evidence, historians must take into account potential bias as well the possibility that memory fades and stories change over time. Part of that is caused by subsequent events that distort the original memory.

12.

Answer	Learning Objectives	Historical Thinking Skills	Key Concepts in the Curriculum Framework
A	POL-2.0	Analyzing Evidence: Content and Sourcing	3.1

Explanation: The passage indicates that colonists believed they had governed themselves for a considerable period of time prior to the Declaration of Independence. British attempts to assert control in the years leading up the American Revolution left the colonists suspicious of centralized power. There is nothing in the account to suggest either egalitarianism or the fact that disadvantaged classes lacked natural rights.

Short-Answer Questions

1.

Learning Objectives	Historical Thinking Skills	Key Concepts in the Curriculum Framework
NAT-1.0 POL-1.0	Causation Analyzing Evidence: Content and Sourcing	3.2

What a good response might include

a) A good response will identify the key targets of the Alien and Sedition Acts. Some examples include:

   ✦ As illustrated by the excerpt, the Alien and Sedition Acts clearly targeted anyone who spoke out against the Federalist-controlled government in general, and the president and Congress in particular. This criticism could take many forms: making speeches, distributing newspapers critical of the government, writing an essay critical of the government.

   ✦ The Republicans and their leader, Thomas Jefferson, were specific targets of the Alien and Sedition Acts. Republicans had supported the French Revolutionaries, whom the Federalists vehemently opposed.

   ✦ Republicans also had set their sights on the White House and Congress and often criticized the Federalists who controlled both the presidency and Congress.

   ✦ Immigrants were also targeted by the Alien and Sedition Acts, as these laws made it easier to deport foreigners. Immigrants were more likely to support the Republicans than the Federalists.

   ✦ Politicians and newspaper editors were targets of the Alien and Sedition Acts. More than twenty politicians and editors were arrested, and many of them were convicted and jailed.

b) Several key issues and events led to the issuance of the Alien and Sedition Acts and the ensuing opposition to them. Some examples include the following:

   ✦ Despite the absence of any reference in the Constitution to political parties, two parties emerged in the early years of the republic: the Federalists and the Republicans. These parties differed in their view of the role of government and in their approach to banking and economic development. As political discourse became more heated, the dominant party of the late 1790s, the Federalists, feared that their popularity was on the wane, and they supported the Alien and Sedition Acts in order to quell dissent.

   ✦ Increasing tensions between the dominant nations in Europe, France and England, put pressure on the U.S. government to take sides in this conflict. Federalists Alexander Hamilton and John Adams leaned toward the British, while Republican Thomas Jefferson was more sympathetic toward the French. Foreign policy became one battleground between the two American political parties and led to the Adams administration's support of the Alien and Sedition Acts, hoping to limit criticism of the government's foreign policy. Additionally, immigrants to the United States tended to support the Republicans, giving rise to efforts to deport them.

   ✦ The presidential election of 1800 was approaching. During the administrations of the first two presidents, George Washington and John Adams, the Federalists controlled the presidency and Congress. As the Republicans increased their efforts to lead the government, John Adams and his Federalist administration proposed the Alien and Sedition Acts to quiet their critics and lessen the chances that Thomas Jefferson would become president.

   ✦ Newspaper readership was on the rise in the new nation. Newspapers and their editors played a key role in adding to the fervor of political discourse. As Republican newspapers became more outspoken in their opposition to the Federalists and their policies, Federalists determined that the Alien and Sedition Acts could be used to mitigate the influence of the press.

c)   A good response will explain one example that serves as evidence of the reaction Republicans and their followers had to the passage of the Alien and Sedition Acts. Some of these responses include the following:

   ✦ In 1798, Thomas Jefferson and James Madison authored the Virginia and Kentucky Resolutions, which supported the notion of states' rights and asserted the right of the states to determine whether federal law was legitimate. This idea, which came to be called "nullification," would later be used to support the rights of slave owners.

   ✦ Republicans also reacted by increasing their efforts to elect Thomas Jefferson to the presidency in 1800. His election, called the Revolution of 1800, effectively killed the Alien and Sedition Acts, as Congress refused to extend them. Jefferson and his congressional allies shrunk the size of the federal government and ousted many of the men Adams had appointed to the courts.

2.

Learning Objectives	Historical Thinking Skills	Key Concepts in the Curriculum Framework
WOR-1.0 NAT-1.0	Patterns of Continuity and Change over Time Contextualization	3.2

What a good response might include

a)   A good response might include the following:

   ✦ The defeat of the French and their Indian allies gave the British control over half of North America, including French Canada, all of the French territory east of the Mississippi River, and Spanish Florida.

   ✦ The war also resulted in a reshaping of British/colonial and British/Indian and colonial/Indian relations.

b)   A good response might include the following:

   ✦ The British attempted to limit colonial expansion west of the Appalachian Mountains because this area was both difficult and expensive to control.

   ✦ The British had made agreements with Indian leaders, most notably Pontiac, that gave Indian groups continued control of the trans-Appalachian West.

c)   A good response might include the following:

- ✦ British American colonists felt confined because their population was increasing rapidly and the amount of available land east of the Appalachian was dwindling just as rapidly.
- ✦ Would-be landowners moved west and sparked conflicts over Indian policy, in particular the restriction of settlement in the backcountry.
- ✦ Faced with poor land and mounting debt, many backcountry settlers formed vigilante groups known as Regulators, to challenge the rights of Indians to their lands. One such vigilante group was the Paxton Boys of Pennsylvania.
- ✦ The British, hampered by the debts incurred in the fighting of the French and Indian War, did not have the resources or manpower to stop western settlement.

Long Essay Question

Learning Objectives	Historical Thinking Skills	Key Concepts in the Curriculum Framework
CUL-1.0 CUL-2.0 CUL-3.0 NAT-1.0	Patterns of Continuity and Change over Time Argumentation Synthesis	3.2

What a good response might include

A solid essay demonstrates mastery of several historical thinking skills including **historical argumentation** and **synthesis**, but most important, this essay requires analysis of **patterns of continuity and change over time**, in this case from the beginning of the American Revolution to the end of the Federalist period in 1800. You must develop a thoughtful thesis that clearly states the argument you will craft. Your essay must synthesize a significant body of evidence and must support your thesis. Remember not to rush through your essays; rather, take the time to make sure that you are answering the question and not merely summarizing events and ideas but rather analyzing them. After you write your introductory paragraph, put down your pen and carefully read what you have just written. It is far easier to make changes in your essay at the beginning rather than trying to correct your mistakes as time expires. Also, occasionally stop writing as you work on the rest of your essay and examine your work to ensure that you are saying just what you want to say.

Look at the prompt carefully, and make sure you understand the meaning of every word in it. Take this opportunity to provide a more sophisticated analysis. For example, try to determine just how and to what extent the American Revolution fostered change. Clearly link the Revolution to the changes—or the continuities—you include in your essay. Be careful to address nuance in your response. In other words, try to avoid taking a position that commits you to defending the notion that everything changed as a result of the American Revolution or, on the other hand, arguing that nothing changed. A nuanced approach might argue that there was considerable change, but that some things did not change very much. Or you could argue that despite some significant changes, the political, social, and economic values, goals, and institutions developed after the Revolution remained largely the same as before. A nuanced essay might also argue that change was more apparent in some areas than in others; for instance, you might assert that there was more significant political change and less social transformation. Or you could claim that the economic system did not change as much as the social fabric of the new nation.

You are free to argue what you wish as long as you provide substantial evidence to support your argument. Of course, always keep in mind that your essay must present an argument, not simply a summary of events.

Here are some examples to consider in crafting your essay.

Political

- ✦ The Revolution ended royal authority in the colonies.
- ✦ When the Articles of Confederation proved inadequate, the founders wrote a national constitution that clearly delineated the powers and the limits of government and explicitly guaranteed individual liberties, certainly a major change.
- ✦ The colonists borrowed heavily on English traditions, in particular the constitution and Bill of Rights that came out of England's Glorious Revolution.
- ✦ Ideas about personal liberties, religious diversity, and the right of people to overthrow their governments were not new. English philosophers like John Locke and other thinkers of the Enlightenment like Mary Wollstonecraft, Voltaire, and Emmanuel Kant had advocated many of the changes that the new American nation adopted.
- ✦ By basing authority on popular sovereignty, the Constitution established a new form of government.
- ✦ Over 100,000 Loyalists left the new Republic, most of them to British-controlled Canada.
- ✦ By the 1790s, political parties had formed as Americans were guaranteed the right to debate and criticize.
- ✦ Even under the new government, many of the same political elites assumed important positions in government. It was not infrequent that leaders questioned the wisdom of allowing the masses to assume more power.
- ✦ Although in some states, property requirements for voting were lowered or eliminated (but only for white men), in most states these requirements remained in place.
- ✦ Women, blacks, and Native Americans were not granted the political rights held by white men.

Social

- ✦ Northern states began to abolish slavery; however, slavery became even more entrenched in the South.
- ✦ The Constitution did not abolish either slavery or the slave trade, but it did open the door to ending the slave trade after 1808.
- ✦ The Northwest Ordinance banned slavery in the territories that became the states of Ohio, Indiana, Illinois, Michigan, and Wisconsin.
- ✦ Even in Virginia, a southern state, legislation was passed in 1782 allowing manumission of slaves. However, that law was repealed in 1792.
- ✦ Middle-class white women were given a new role in the new republic, that of "republican mothers," but they remained disenfranchised and without many of the political, social, and economic opportunities that white men enjoyed.
- ✦ Educational opportunities for white women increased. There was also growing support for public education, but in some colonies, particularly in New England, public support for education had long been in place.

Economic

- ✦ Social and economic mobility for white men rose.
- ✦ The new government abolished primogeniture.
- ✦ Although many in the middle class enjoyed new economic opportunities, many merchants and southern plantation owners who thrived during the colonial period maintained their elite status in the new economy.

✦ As the manufacturing sector grew, economic opportunities for white men increased, but women, blacks, and Native Americans did not reap the same benefits.

✦ As the nation spread westward after the Revolution, Indians were forced to surrender even more of their land.

✦ States increased their commitment to building the nation's infrastructure.

✦ The federal government maintained much the same kind of control over business and trade as Parliament had; Secretary of the Treasury Alexander Hamilton's financial program included a national bank, a tariff, and excise taxes.

PERIOD 4
1800–1848

Overview

Period 4 focuses on the history of the United States between 1800 and 1848. This division highlights the new nation's move from an emerging postcolonial country to one that controlled most of a continent and had to redefine the meaning of both democracy and citizenship. This was an era of competing political, social, and economic "revolutions," as dramatic changes in voting rights, the economy, and society led to a mass democracy and a growing, if contested, sense of a national identity.

The end of the Federalist era and the emergence of the Democratic-Republicans marked the beginning of the process of broadening participatory democracy. The four decades that followed the turn of the nineteenth century saw the broadening of the franchise (the right to vote) from the privileged few to most white males. To be sure, many were still left without voting rights—women, American Indians, most African Americans (whether enslaved or not), and many newly arrived immigrants—but the move toward a more open definition of citizenship gained momentum.

The creation of modern political parties also began during this period as the United States moved from the Federalist decade of the 1790s to the formation of the Democratic-Republicans and later the Democratic and Whig parties. As the voter base broadened and the nation expanded, questions arose about the proper role of the federal and state governments in the growing republic and the expanding economy. Some of these issues were decided by the U.S. Supreme Court; for example, in *McCulloch v. Maryland*, Supreme Court decided that state laws could be ruled unconstitutional. Other issues surfaced in the context of new economic conditions that saw the emergence of factories in the North and the development of slavery as a uniquely southern institution. The diverging economic structures of the North and South led to a sharpening of distinct regional identities. All of these changes left many Americans struggling to match democratic ideals with the harsher realities surrounding them, touching off a series of reform efforts—the Second Great Awakening, the movement for women's rights, and abolition (the move to abolish slavery)—that ultimately served both to unite and divide the country.

During this period, the United States also embarked on unprecedented territorial and economic expansion. The boundaries of the United States doubled with the Louisiana Purchase in 1803, opening the prospect of landownership to millions and beginning the rapid westward movement that transformed the continent. Along with access to new lands came revolutionary changes in technology and economic specialization that brought both prosperity and increased focus on regional interests that had an impact on markets as well as politics. This rapid development resulted in significant changes in the lives of everyone regardless of gender, race, ethnicity, or socioeconomic group. Many people were able to take advantage of new opportunities, while others, such as American Indians like the Cherokee and the Iroquois nation, found themselves further marginalized in the name of "progress."

Rapidly changing technology fueled the expansion of American commerce into the global market as factories expanded in the North and cotton cultivation came to dominate the southern economy. Efforts to organize the national economy, including proposals such as the American System, which sought to use tariff revenues to fund internal improvements, strengthened economic ties between the North and the newly opening West but further isolated the slaveholding South. Efforts to modernize transportation fostered regional division, as canals and roads tended to connect the Northeast to the West, while the South continued to rely on rivers for transportation and trade. The lives of people in all parts of the country were affected by this economic growth as the nature of the workplace changed.

Entry into the global economy also complicated U.S. foreign policy. Territorial expansion and growing markets required involvement with the rest of the world. At the same time, the United States sought to remain isolated from European political conflicts. Territorial expansion also raised questions about the role of slavery in the newly acquired areas. The existence and expansion of slavery emerged during this period as issues of overarching national concern. The slavery question was settled temporarily by political expediency, such as the Missouri Compromise, which divided the Louisiana Territory into free and slave areas, but there was no final resolution to the debate over slavery in this era.

Key Terms

Be sure that you understand the meaning of these terms and their relevance in U.S. history.

Economic specialization	Primacy of the judiciary
Human perfectibility	Regional identity
Interchangeable parts	Republicanism
Internal improvements	Romantic beliefs
Market revolution and market economy	Social hierarchy
Mass democracy	Sovereignty
National culture	Transcendentalism
Nativism	

Questions to Consider

As you study Period 4, keep the following thematic questions in mind.

American and National Identity

+ What characteristics of national identity emerged in the first half of the nineteenth century?
+ What factors encouraged and which impeded the formation of a national identity?
+ Why during this period did Americans form both a national and a regional identity, and how did the two conflict with each other?
+ How did government policies shape the formation of regional identities in the North, South, and West?
+ How did both free and enslaved African Americans preserve their identity and their culture in the face of increased barriers that confronted them?

Work, Exchange, and Technology

+ How were Americans affected by innovations in markets, technology, and transportation in the first half of the nineteenth century?
+ How did changes in both agriculture and manufacturing change labor systems and affect the lives of American workers?
+ How did government policies affect the manufacture and distribution of goods in the United States?

Migration and Settlement

+ What caused the emergence of nativism in the mid-nineteenth century?
+ In what ways did immigration change the social, economic, and political fabric of America?
+ How did technological changes affect immigration patterns?

Politics and Power

+ Why did political parties emerge in the early years of the Republic?
+ In what ways, and why, did the positions taken by the Federalists and the Democratic-Republicans change over time?
+ How did the Supreme Court help shape the political and economic landscape of the United States in the first half of the nineteenth century?
+ Why and how did many Americans attempt to expand democratic ideals in the early and mid-nineteenth century?
+ What were the similarities and differences between the Jeffersonian Republicans and the Jacksonian Democrats? Account for these similarities and differences.

America in the World

+ What were some turning points in the development of American foreign policy?
+ Why were these turning points so important?
+ How did the U.S. government use foreign policy to advance its interests?

Geography and the Environment

+ How did environmental factors contribute to the western movement that occurred in the first half of the nineteenth century?
+ What was the impact of western migration on American Indians?

Culture and Society

+ How did the Second Great Awakening shape reform in education, women's rights, abolitionism, temperance, and the prison system?
+ What were the characteristics of the new national culture?
+ In what ways did literary and philosophical movements in the first half of the nineteenth century reflect changes in the economic and social order?

America's History Chapter Summaries

(required AP® content in bold)

Chapter 8
Creating a Republican Culture, 1790–1820

Chapter 8 explores the impact of the developing ideology of republicanism on the economy, society, and culture. It looks at the development of technology and transportation and the expansion of both manufacturing and agriculture in the early years of the nineteenth century. The chapter also explores new forms for private life and education, the growing debate over slaves, and the emergence of new religious sensibilities that culminated in the Second Great Awakening.

In the years following the American Revolution, the growth of the market economy led a number of states, as well as the federal government, to support private businesses that **expanded technology and transportation** and thus contributed to regional and national growth (ex: Lancaster Turnpike, canals). **These economic developments precipitated profound changes in business, manufacturing, and agriculture** and in the lives of many Americans. Rural families that previously relied on farming became the nation's first factory workers, while others **in rural areas began to produce goods for distant markets**, making them more prosperous but also more dependent on the market.

The new market economy led to changes in lifestyles in both urban and rural areas, which brought changes in social norms. The belief in legal equality resulted in greater social mobility for some, but women were constrained by traditional views of gender roles. Still, **women's experiences in the American Revolution and in the Enlightenment stressed the ideology of "republican motherhood" for white women.** The ideal gave women within the family a new role in promoting republican culture. The ideas of a unique American identity based on the idea of the United States as a unique experiment in democracy led to the **emergence of a new and independent national culture in the arts and literature.**

While the **Enlightenment had given hope to some that the institution of slavery would disappear**, by the early decades of the nineteenth century, **slavery had become increasingly associated with the South's regional identity.** As slavery expanded across the South, the **region became more distinct from other regions of the country** and fueled **debates over the extension of slavery, leading to the Missouri Compromise of 1820.**

American religious and secular beliefs both changed in the early nineteenth century. Beginning in the 1790s, a series of religious revivals led to **the Second Great Awakening, based on the belief in human perfectibility.** These new beliefs, grounded in romanticism, also sparked a wave of **voluntary organization dedicated to social reform.** Women in particular began to take up reform work in areas that fit with white women's traditional concerns: raising children, the home, and campaigns for moral reform. Women increasingly played a role in other reform movements as well, finding opportunities to work for better education for children, temperance, and abolition. The **Second Great Awakening** also led to changes in Protestantism, how many people viewed the role of religion in national life, and the increasing insistence that Christians had an obligation to bring about meaningful reform in society.

Chapter 9
Transforming the Economy, 1800–1860

Chapter 9 examines the causes of the economic transformation of the first half of the nineteenth century, as well as the consequences that resulted from these changes. The two driving forces of economic growth during this period were the Industrial Revolution and the development and expansion of the market economy. These developments brought with them social transformations as well: the rise of an urban society, growing ties between the Northeast and the Midwest along with the further isolation of the South, and increased tensions among different social groups throughout the country, including newly arriving immigrants from Ireland and Germany.

Industrialization unfolded in the United States between 1790 and 1860 and included the development and growth of the modern factory system, with a distinct division of labor and enormous increases in production. Textile factories in particular illustrated the favorable combination of new technologies, newly discovered power sources, identification of new labor pools, and the support of **government economic policies such as protective tariffs**. The creation of interchangeable parts further aided the growth of manufacturing.

Many of the early workers in textile factories were women, though their labor was soon supplemented **by low-skilled men**, who produced the goods that supplied both local and international markets. Many soon found themselves at odds with management over low pay and harsh working conditions, leading to early labor organization and disagreements about what the rights of working classes should be. Advances in manufacturing technology led to greatly increased production in many new industries, particularly **textiles** (ex: Lancaster model, Lowell model, Samuel Slater, the Boston Associates, Eli Whitney).

The national economy benefitted from advances in the construction of roads and canals, transportation networks that facilitated both commerce and **movement of settlers to the West**. Cities and towns grew along these trade routes, while Atlantic seaports remained centers of both foreign and domestic trade.

The rapidly expanding domestic and international market economy led to debates about both the government's role in that expansion and the **regional differences** that were developing. **State-sponsored roads and canals** facilitated that expansion and led to calls for more government involvement in such infrastructure improvements (ex: **American System**, the Erie Canal, the National Road).

The Market Revolution **widened the gap between the rich and poor**, creating a business elite in many towns and cities, as well as a growing middle class **that set themselves apart** from the working classes. Women who could stay at home saw themselves as the guardians of the futures of their children, continuing the **transformation of gender and family roles**. This transformation separated middle-class women from women who did not have the luxury of staying out of the workplace. For middle-class men, many came to see their success as a result of their willingness to work, giving rise to the image of the self-made man. This perception obscured the hard work done by those at the poorer end of the economic scale and led to further class divisions.

Chapter 10
A Democratic Revolution, 1800–1844

Chapter 10 examines the causes and consequences of the political changes that accompanied the economic transformation of the early nineteenth century. It follows the rise of popular politics and the decline of the dominance of the wealthy "notables"—northern landlords, southern planters, and seacoast merchants. The chapter also explores the rise and presidency of Andrew Jackson and the emergence of the Second Party System.

The **growth of mass democracy began** as the right to vote was extended to more white men, though many still remained unable to claim full citizenship. Concurrent with the expansion of democracy was the rise of political parties, often run by professional politicians such as lawyers or journalists. The election of 1824 pitted the older "notables"—John Quincy Adams and Henry Clay—against William Crawford, a protégé of Thomas Jefferson, and Andrew Jackson, the rising hero of the War of 1812. Jackson, backed by a group of supporters who called themselves "democrats" to emphasize their egalitarian policies, won the most electoral votes but did not win a majority, and the House of Representatives voted to elect John Quincy Adams as president. As president, John Quincy Adams faced fierce **opposition to his support of protective tariffs** and his support of Clay's proposed **American System**.

Andrew Jackson's run for the presidency in 1818 produced a huge voter turnout that signaled the real beginning of mass democracy in the United States. As president, Jackson enjoyed support for his policies of decentralization, but he also confronted some of his own supporters in South Carolina who tried to assert that **state's right to reject federal law** in the nullification crisis. Jackson also struck at both the American System and **supporters of centrally controlled economy**, which symbolized the Bank of the United States. Jackson also threw his full support behind the Indian Removal Act, which called for the **relocation of American Indians**. The Cherokees attempted to use the **Supreme Court's power** to fight the state of Georgia and removal. Although the Supreme Court sided with the Cherokees in *Worcester v. Georgia* (1832), Jackson's negotiators pushed through the fraudulent Treaty of New Echota to effect removal. By the time Jackson left office in 1837, the **Second Party System, consisting of the Democrats and the newly formed Whig Party**, had emerged. The economic chaos that resulted from the Panic of 1837 led to disillusionment with Jackson's successor, President Martin Van Buren, resulting in a Whig victory in the election of 1840.

Chapter 11
Religion and Reform, 1800–1860

Chapter 11 examines a number of reform movements in the first half of the nineteenth century. The transcendentalist movement led to unique American art and culture and emphasized individualism, especially among the middle class. The chapter also explores the rise of utopian movements and religion and looks at the rise of urban popular culture and a wave of European immigration. Finally, it focuses on the rise of abolitionism and the women's rights movement.

A number of communitarian movements emerged in the middle years of the nineteenth century, growing out of the **Second Great Awakening's support for the doctrine of perfectibility** and the search for utopia on earth (ex: Brook Farm, the Shakers, the Oneida Colony, the Fourier communities). The Mormons also emerged during this period. Out of Brook Farm, in particular, a number of American artists and writers helped create a distinctly **American national culture through literature and art** (ex: Ralph Waldo Emerson, Henry David Thoreau, Walt Whitman, Nathaniel Hawthorne, Herman Melville, Charles Willson Peale).

During these same years, a new urban popular culture arose as East Coast cities grew in size and population. Part of this expansion was **due to a wave of immigration from Europe**. While cities seemed to promise success and adventure, many found a much harsher reality there, living on subsistence wages in poor housing. Immigrants often confronted particularly virulent **xenophobia**.

This reform era also saw the expansion of abolitionist and women's rights movements. The abolitionist movement in particular found support among free African Americans (ex. David Walker) **and from enslaved African Americans** (ex. Nat Turner). Growing out of the abolitionist movement, the early women's rights movement drew on **middle-class women's experiences** as they stepped out of their culturally prescribed roles to advocate for property and voting rights (ex: Seneca Falls).

Chapter 12
The South Expands: Slavery and Society, 1800–1860

Chapter 12 traces the expansion of the South and the plantation culture from the Upper South to the Mississippi Valley and beyond during the first half of the nineteenth century. It focuses first on the domestic slave trade and then explores the culture of white southerners. It also examines the expansion of slavery and the rise of the Cotton South. Finally, it looks at the culture of southern African Americans, both enslaved and free.

The invention of the cotton gin led to the rapid spread of short-staple cotton cultivation in areas that had not been suitable for the long-staple cotton that had to be cleaned by hand. **Southern cotton furnished raw materials for manufacturing and fueled the internal slave trade**. Cotton was critical to the national economy, and slavery was a critical piece of cotton agriculture.

As plantation agriculture spread west in the first half of the nineteenth century, slavery spread with it. Slaves came into the newly opened regions through the international slave trade only until 1808, when the Constitution abolished the international slave trade. After the end of the international slave trade, slaves moved from the Upper South to the Mississippi Valley through the internal or domestic slave trade. This trade involved the breaking up of families and forced migration to new parts of the country. Slaves who were "sold South" rarely saw their loved ones again.

Most of the political leaders in the South had some stake in the slave system, and few emancipation initiatives ever got very far in southern legislatures. In fact, **many Americans in the South felt pride in the institution of slavery and insisted that the federal government should defend the institution**. John C. Calhoun, a U.S. senator from South Carolina who had served as Andrew Jackson's first vice president, called slavery a "positive good." While most southern whites did not personally own slaves, most were caught up in the society the slave system created.

The slave economy resulted in southern dependence on foreign and domestic trade for other necessities, particularly manufactured goods. Even the development of schools and municipal institutions languished because the slaveholding elite voted down taxes that would have paid for such advances.

The settlement and eventual annexation of Texas in the 1820s and 1830s became entangled with the slavery issue. Indeed, throughout the nineteenth century, the **American acquisition of new lands in the West led to heated debate over the extension of slavery**.

Within the context of slavery, **enslaved and free African Americans created communities** that were a synthesis of African- and European-derived cultures. Many African Americans relied heavily on the **evangelical Christianity of the Second Great Awakening**. The church became a core institution in the black community. Free blacks in both the North and the South worked in various ways to negotiate rights and further the cause of abolition. In the North, African Americans were **prominent in the abolitionist movement**.

Many state governments continued to restrict African Americans' citizenship. Freed blacks in the South and most in the North were treated as second-class citizens without the right to vote, attend public schools, or attend white churches. Only in Massachusetts could African Americans testify in court. The federal government did not allow blacks to work for the postal service, claim public lands, or hold a U.S. passport.

Thematic Timeline

THEME	REQUIRED CONTENT	SUPPORTING EXAMPLES
AMERICAN AND NATIONAL IDENTITY	• A distinct American identity emerged. • Regional identities solidified. • In the South, whites asserted their identity through an increased resolve to maintain slavery. • Identities emerged based on gender, race, and religion. • African Americans, both slave and free, created and maintained communities and family structure. • Tensions increased between national and regional identities, with regional loyalties often trumping national identity. • Issues such as slavery, tariffs, the national bank, and internal improvements shaped regional identities.	**1800–1820** • Republican motherhood, marriage, and family life. • Notion of "separate spheres" for men and women. • Northern states abolish slavery. • Gabriel Prosser plans unsuccessful slave revolt (1800). • African Methodist Episcopal Church founded (1816). • A distinct national culture emerges. **1821–1836** • The cult of domesticity defined for women. • Women's role in churches expands during the Second Great Awakening. • Southern defense of slavery expands based on both constitutional and religious arguments. • Nat Turner leads slave revolt in Virginia (1831). • Freed black David Walker writes *Appeal to the Colored Citizens of the World* (1829). • American Anti-Slavery Society founded. • Working Men's Party founded (1828). • Francis Trollope's *Domestic Manners of the Americans* published (1832). • Alexis de Tocqueville's *Democracy in America* published (1832). • Anti-Masonic Party organized. **1836–1848** • *Commonwealth v. Hunt* (1842) determines that labor unions are legal. • Seneca Falls Convention for women's rights (1848).
WORK, EXCHANGE, TECHNOLOGY	• Emergence of a national and international market economy resulted in a growing middle class but also in wider gaps between rich and poor. • The market economy promoted changes in gender and family roles. • Technological innovation significantly changed both industry and agriculture.	**1800–1820** • The Industrial Revolution expands. • The power loom and mechanical reaper affect industry and agriculture. • Interchangeable parts make American industry more efficient. • Construction of the National Road begins. • Robert Fulton invents the steamboat (1807). • Construction starts on Erie Canal (1817). • Second Bank of the United States (1816). • Tariff of 1816. • Panic of 1819.

THEME	REQUIRED CONTENT	SUPPORTING EXAMPLES
WORK, EXCHANGE, TECHNOLOGY (*continued*)	• Key innovations included the textile industry, steam power, interchangeable parts, transportation networks, and the telegraph. • Specialization, especially in southern cotton, shaped the economy. • The American System, which included a national bank, tariffs, and internal improvements, was designed to unify the national economy.	**1821–1836** • *Gibbons v. Ogden* rules that Congress has the right to regulate interstate commerce. • Lowell system established. • Middle class grows rapidly. • Rapid urbanization disrupts social order. • Tariff of Abominations (1828). **1837–1848** • Panic of 1837. • Railroad era begins. • Industrialization moves westward. • John Deere and McCormick manufacture farm equipment.
MIGRATION AND SETTLEMENT	• Increasing xenophobia was one response to increased immigration. • Settlement patterns reflected economic specialization. • Canals and roads made it easier for Americans to move westward.	**1800–1820** • Alien and Sedition Acts expire (1801). • Tecumseh and the Western Confederacy organized (1808). • American Colonization Society formed (1817). **1821–1836** • Samuel F. B Morse writes *Foreign Conspiracy against the Liberties of the United States*, one of many nativist responses to immigration (1834). • Andrew Jackson signs the Indian Removal Act (1830). **1837–1848** • Irish immigrate to the United States in large numbers. • Anti-Irish discrimination increases ("No Irish Need Apply"). • After unsuccessful resistance, Cherokee people removed on the so-called Trail of Tears (1838). • Anti-Catholic riots break out in Philadelphia.
POLITICS AND POWER	• A two-party political system formed, beginning with the Federalists and the Democratic-Republicans and, later, the Democrats and the Whigs.	**1800–1820** • Thomas Jefferson elected president in the Second American Revolution (1800). • John Adams appoints "midnight judges" before leaving office (1801). • John Marshall is appointed chief justice of the Supreme Court (1801).

THEME	REQUIRED CONTENT	SUPPORTING EXAMPLES
POLITICS AND POWER (*continued*)	• Americans debated the proper role of government in the emerging market economy. • The federal and state governments placed further restrictions on African Americans even though the slave trade was abolished and there were increasing numbers of free African Americans. • The Missouri Compromise, though short-lived, provided a truce on the issue of slavery. • The Supreme Court expanded its authority by asserting its right to interpret the Constitution and through decisions that increased federal power. • Government became more participatory. • Resistance to federal power came from many quarters • Territorial expansion of the nation resulted in more efforts to limit the liberties of American Indians.	• *Marbury v. Madison* (1803), *McCulloch v. Maryland* (1819). • Hartford Convention meets (1815). • Missouri Compromise (1820). **1821–1836** • "Corrupt bargain" is blamed for the election of John Quincy Adams (1824). • Andrew Jackson elected president (1828). • Jackson introduces the "spoils system." • Nullification crisis (1828). • Bank War (1828). • Jackson appoints Roger Taney as chief justice of the Supreme Court (1835). • Daniel Webster, John C. Calhoun, and Henry Clay lead the Whig Party. **1837–1848** • Jackson succeeded as president by Martin Van Buren. • William Henry Harrison elected first Whig president (1840).
AMERICA IN THE WORLD	• Beginning with the Louisiana Purchase, the United States sought to expand its borders and markets. • The United States sought to become the dominant power in North America.	**1800–1820** • Louisiana Purchase (1803). • Embargo Act (1807). • War Hawks urge war against the British. • War of 1812. • Treaty of Ghent ends the War of 1812 (1814). • Adams-Onís Treaty leads to U.S. acquisition of Florida from Spain (1819). **1821–1836** • Monroe Doctrine (1823). **1837–1848** • Texas admitted to Union (1845). • War with Mexico begins (1846).

Theme	Required Content	Supporting Examples
GEOGRAPHY AND THE ENVIRONMENT	• As arable land in the Southeast shrank, southerners moved to the Southwest, increasing sectional tensions.	**1800–1820** • Lewis and Clark explore the Louisiana Purchase and the Missouri River (1805).
CULTURE AND SOCIETY	• During the Romantic era, a new American culture emerged, combining elements of European culture with regional American culture. • The Second Great Awakening, along with a belief in perfectibility, led to a series of reform movements designed to promote abolition and women's rights.	**1800–1820** • The United States begins to achieve cultural independence from Europe. • Noah Webster promotes American English. • Washington Irving and James Fenimore Cooper pen American novels. • Emma Willard promotes education for women. **1821–1836** • Charles Grandison Finney becomes the best-known preacher of the Second Great Awakening. • William Lloyd Garrison begins publishing *The Liberator*, an abolitionist newspaper (1831). • The Grimké sisters, Lyman Beecher, and Sojourner Truth are leading abolitionists. • Shaker communities form. • Joseph Smith publishes the Book of Mormon (1830). • Transcendentalism emerges as a dominant American philosophy. • Hudson River School artists express the romantic vision in painting. **1837–1848** • Ralph Waldo Emerson delivers "The American Scholar" address (1837). • Dorothea Dix calls for reform of prisons and mental institutions (1841). • Brook Farm community is formed (1841). • Seneca Falls Convention is organized by Elizabeth Cady Stanton (1848). • Margaret Fuller, Henry David Thoreau, and Walt Whitman are prominent transcendentalists. • John Humphrey Noyes organizes the Oneida Community (1848).

Period 4 Practice Questions

Multiple-Choice Questions

Questions 1–3 refer to the excerpt below.

"We admit, as all must admit, that the powers of the Government are limited, and that its limits are not to be transcended. But we think the sound construction of the Constitution must allow to the national legislature that discretion with respect to the means by which the powers it confers are to be carried into execution which will enable that body to perform the high duties assigned to it in the manner most beneficial to the people. Let the end be legitimate, let it be within the scope of the Constitution, and all means which are appropriate, which are plainly adapted to that end, which are not prohibited, but consist with the letter and spirit of the Constitution, are Constitutional."

U.S. Supreme Court, *McCulloch v. Maryland*, 1819

1. The above quotation most focuses on which of the following debates that characterized the new republic?
   - (A) The extension of slavery into the territories
   - (B) The formation of a national currency
   - (C) Loose versus strict interpretation of the Constitution
   - (D) The application of the Bill of Rights to states

2. The above decision reflected which of the following tendencies of the early Supreme Court?
   - (A) To side with big business over labor
   - (B) To favor national over state power
   - (C) To uphold the sanctity of contract
   - (D) To look unfavorably on the institution of slavery

3. Which of the following groups would be most likely to support the above decision?
   - (A) Western farmers
   - (B) Jacksonian Democrats
   - (C) Know-Nothings
   - (D) Former Federalists

Questions 4–6 refer to the excerpt below.

"We might feel a pride in the reflection, that our young country . . . was the first to adopt with any efficacy, the penitentiary system of prison discipline, and the first to attempt to prevent the commission of crimes, by seeking out the youthful and unprotected, who were in the way of temptation, and by religious and moral instruction, by imparting to them useful knowledge, and by giving them industrious and orderly habits, rescuing them from vice, and rendering them valuable members of society. . . . To confine these youthful criminals . . . where no, or scarcely any, distinction can be made between the young and the old, or between the more or less vicious, where little can be learned but the ways of the wicked, and from whence they must be sent to encounter new wants, new temptation, and to commit new crimes, is to pursue a course, as little reconcilable with justice as humanity: yet, till the House of Refuge was established there was no alternative."

Society for the Reformation of Juvenile Delinquents in the City of New York, *Fourth Annual Report*, 1829

4. The above account best reflects what growing reform sentiment during the period 1820 to 1848?

   (A) Belief in the perfectibility of man
   (B) Commitment to egalitarianism
   (C) Acceptance of transcendental philosophy
   (D) Commitment to the philosophy of predestination

5. Reform movements concerned with all of the following emerged in the same time period EXCEPT

   (A) women's rights.
   (B) environmental preservation.
   (C) temperance.
   (D) public education.

6. During the period 1800 to 1848, reform movements were most successful in achieving their goals in which of the following?

   (A) The granting of women's suffrage through the Nineteenth Amendment
   (B) Prohibition established through the Eighteenth Amendment
   (C) State laws focusing on improved public education
   (D) Establishment of federal standard for minimum wage and maximum hours

Questions 7–9 refer to the excerpt below.

"This transformation of the condition of the country from gloom and distress to brightness and prosperity, has been mainly the work of American legislation, fostering American industry, instead of allowing it to be controlled by foreign legislation, cherishing foreign industry. The foes of the American System, in 1824, with great boldness and confidence, predicted, first, the ruin of the public revenue, and the creation of a necessity to resort to direct taxation; The gentleman from South Carolina (General Hayne), I believe, thought that the tariff of 1824 would operate a reduction of revenue to the large amount of eight millions of dollars; secondly, the destruction of our navigation; thirdly, the desolation of commercial cities; and fourthly, the augmentation of the price of objects of consumption, and further decline in that of the articles of our exports. Every prediction which they made has failed, utterly failed."

Henry Clay, *In Defense of the American System*, 1832

7. The system that Henry Clay describes above was designed to create

   (A) government ownership of the means of production.
   (B) a foreign trade system that favored Great Britain over France.
   (C) a national market economy.
   (D) dominance of state government over the national government.

GO ON TO THE NEXT PAGE.

8. The following were components of the American System that Henry Clay envisioned EXCEPT

    (A) federally funded internal improvements.
    (B) government ownership of railroads.
    (C) a second Bank of the United States.
    (D) tariffs to protect infant industries.

9. By 1848, which component of the American System was still used to benefit business?

    (A) A third Bank of the United States
    (B) Providing business with free raw materials from government-owned land
    (C) A protective tariff
    (D) The elimination of corporate income taxes

Questions 10–12 refer to the excerpt below.

"In 1831 Lowell was little more than a factory village. Several corporations were started, and the cotton-mills belonging to them were building. Help was in great demand; and stories were told all over the country of the new factory town, and the high wages that were offered to all classes of work-people, — stories that reached the ears of mechanics' and farmers' songs, and gave new life to lonely and dependent women in distant towns and farmhouses. . . . Troops of young girls came by stages and baggage-wagons, men often being employed to go to other States and to Canada, to collect them at so much a head, and deliver them at the factories."

Harriet Hanson Robinson, *Loom and Spindle,* 1898

10. The above account best represents a departure from which of the following beliefs about the role of women in the early nineteenth century?

    (A) Prevalence of the concept of "republican motherhood"
    (B) Aspirations of women to become "career" women
    (C) Aspiration of women to become "visible saints"
    (D) Prevalence of the concept of "the cult of domesticity"

11. Early industry began in the Northeast for all of the following reasons EXCEPT

    (A) swift-flowing streams that provided a good source of power.
    (B) a relatively high population density to supply both labor and markets.
    (C) a highly skilled labor force as a result of the apprenticeship system.
    (D) an efficient mean of transportation provided by good natural harbors.

12. The original mill girls mentioned above were subsequently replaced by which of the following groups?

    (A) Immigrant women
    (B) Native-born children
    (C) Retired farmers
    (D) Immigrant children

END OF MULTIPLE-CHOICE SECTION

Short-Answer Questions

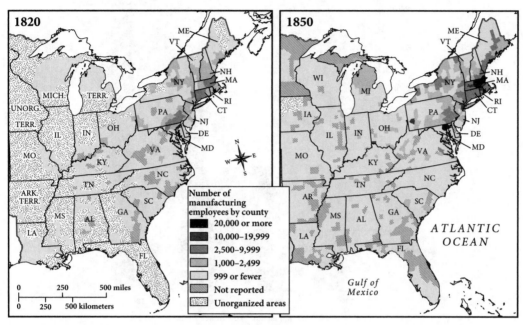

U.S. Manufacturing, 1820 and 1850

1. Using the two maps above, answer a, b, and c.

   a) Identify the major continuity reflected in the maps.

   b) Identify the major change over time reflected in the maps.

   c) Identify one major factor that accounts for this change over time.

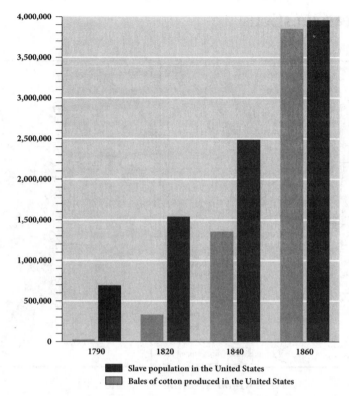

Growth of Cotton Production and the Slave Population, 1790–1860

2. Using the figure above, answer a, b, and c.

    a) Account for the rapid increase in slave population given the fact that Congress banned the international slave trade in 1808.

    b) Identify a major factor that led to increased cotton production between 1790 and 1840 and explain how this led to increased production.

    c) What conclusions can be drawn from the above figure concerning the efficiency of cotton production over time?

END OF SHORT-ANSWER SECTION

Document-Based Question

Directions: The following question is based on the accompanying documents. The documents have been edited for this exercise. Spend approximately 15 minutes planning and 45 minutes writing your answer.

Write an essay that does the following:

+ States an appropriate thesis that directly addresses all parts of the question.
+ Supports the thesis or argument with evidence from all or all but one of the documents AND your knowledge of U.S. history beyond the documents.
+ Analyzes all or all but one of the documents.
+ Places each document into at least one of the following categories: intended audience, purpose, historical context, and/or point of view.
+ Uses historical evidence beyond the documents to support your argument.
+ Places the argument in the context of broader regional, national, or global processes.
+ Incorporates all of the elements above into a convincing essay.

Question: Analyze the political, economic, and social factors that encouraged Americans to move west between 1800 and 1848.

GO ON TO THE NEXT PAGE.

Document 1

Source: The USCen Web Census Project, www.US-Census.org

1800 U.S. Census

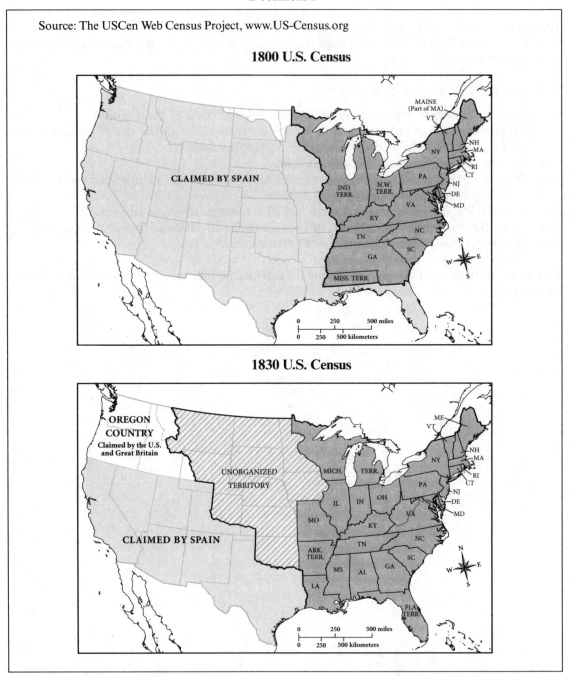

1830 U.S. Census

Document 2

Source: American Explorer Zebulon Pike, 1806

From these immense prairies may arise one great advantage to the United States, viz: The restriction of our population to some certain limits, and thereby a continuation of the Union. Our citizens being so prone to rambling and extending themselves on the frontier will through necessity be constrained to limit their extent to the west to the borders of the Missouri and Mississippi, while they leave the prairies incapable of cultivation to the wandering and uncivilized aborigines of the country.

Document 3

Source: Land Act of 1820

That from and after the first day of July next [1820], all the public lands of the United States, the sale of which is, or may be authorized by law, shall when offered at public sale, to the highest bidder, be offered in half quarter sections [80 acres]; and when offered at private sale, may be purchased, at the option of the purchaser, either in entire sections [640 acres], half sections [320 acres], quarter sections [160 acres], or half quarter sections [80 acres].

Document 4

Source: John William Hill, *View of the Erie Canal*, 1829

Art Resource, NY

GO ON TO THE NEXT PAGE.

Document 5

Source: President Andrew Jackson's Case for the Removal Act, First Annual Message to Congress, December 8, 1829

It gives me pleasure to announce to Congress that the benevolent policy of the Government, steadily pursued for nearly thirty years, in relation to the removal of the Indians beyond the white settlements is approaching to a happy consummation. Two important tribes have accepted the provision made for their removal at the last session of Congress, and it is believed that their example will induce the remaining tribes also to seek the same obvious advantages. . . .

Toward the aborigines of the country no one can indulge a more friendly feeling than myself, or would go further in attempting to reclaim them from their wandering habits and make them a happy, prosperous people. I have endeavored to impress upon them my own solemn convictions of the duties and powers of the General Government in relation to the State authorities. For the justice of the laws passed by the States within the scope of their reserved powers they are not responsible to this Government. As individuals we may entertain and express our opinions of their acts, but as a Government we have as little right to control them as we have to prescribe laws for other nations.

Document 6

Source: John O'Sullivan on America's "Manifest Destiny," 1839

America is destined for better deeds. It is our unparalleled glory that we have no reminiscences of battle fields, but in defense of humanity, of the oppressed of all nations, of the rights of conscience, the rights of personal enfranchisement. Our annals describe no scenes of horrid carnage, where men were led on by hundreds of thousands to slay one another, dupes and victims to emperors, kings, nobles, demons in the human form called heroes. We have had patriots to defend our homes, our liberties, but no aspirants to crowns or thrones; nor have the American people ever suffered themselves to be led on by wicked ambition to depopulate the land, to spread desolation far and wide, that a human being might be placed on a seat of supremacy. . . .

The far-reaching, the boundless future will be the era of American greatness. In its magnificent domain of space and time, the nation of many nations is destined to manifest to mankind the excellence of divine principles; to establish on earth the noblest temple ever dedicated to the worship of the Most High—the Sacred and the True. Its floor shall be a hemisphere—its roof the firmament of the star-studded heavens, and its congregation an Union of many Republics, comprising hundreds of happy millions, calling, owning no man master, but governed by God's natural and moral law of equality, the law of brotherhood—of "peace and good will amongst men."

GO ON TO THE NEXT PAGE.

Document 7

Source: Adapted from Table 40 in Lewis Cecil Gray, *History of Agriculture in the Southern United States to 1860*, vol. 2 (Gloucester, MA: Peter Smith, 1958), 1026.

American Production of Raw Cotton, 1790–1860 (bales)

Year	Production	Year	Production	Year	Production
1790	3,135	1815	208,986	1840	1,346,232
1795	16,719	1820	334,378	1845	1,804,223
1800	73,145	1825	532,915	1850	2,133,851
1805	146,290	1830	731,452	1855	3,217,417
1810	177,638	1835	1,060,711	1860	3,837,402

END OF DOCUMENT-BASED SECTION

Answer Key to Period 4 Practice Questions

Multiple-Choice Questions

1.

Answer	Learning Objectives	Historical Thinking Skills	Key Concepts in the Curriculum Framework
C	POL-1.0	Analyzing Evidence: Content and Sourcing	4.1

Explanation: Arguments over the expansion of federal power in the necessary and proper clause of the Constitution provided an ongoing dispute during both the First and Second American Party Systems. The extension of slavery into the territories became an issue later in the time period, while the application of the Bill of Rights to the states would ultimately be an issue decided by the Supreme Court.

2.

Answer	Learning Objectives	Historical Thinking Skills	Key Concepts in the Curriculum Framework
B	NAT-2.0	Periodization Analyzing Evidence: Content and Sourcing	4.1

Explanation: The early Supreme Court, with Federalist John Marshall as chief justice, consistently favored the growth of federal power over the states. John Marshall, a Hamiltonian Federalist who sat on the Court until 1836, had tremendous influence over the justices on the Supreme Court. Additional early decisions such as *Fletcher v. Peck* and *Cohen v. Virginia* also increased the power of the federal government.

3.

Answer	Learning Objectives	Historical Thinking Skills	Key Concepts in the Curriculum Framework
D	NAT-2.0	Analyzing Evidence: Content and Sourcing	4.1

Explanation: Federalists, under the leadership of Alexander Hamilton, favored a loose interpretation of the Constitution that would increase federal power. Eventually the Federalists would morph into the Whig Party that also favored increasing the power of the national government by supporting initiatives such as the Bank of the United States, federally funded internal improvements, and protective tariffs to promote American industry.

4.

Answer	Learning Objectives	Historical Thinking Skills	Key Concepts in the Curriculum Framework
A	CUL-4.0	Patterns of Continuity and Change over Time Analyzing Evidence: Content and Sourcing	4.1

Explanation: The Second Great Awakening's belief in the perfectibility of man stimulated the growth of reform movement in the early nineteenth century. That belief led to the formation of multiple reform groups such as those advocating women's rights, abolitionism, temperance, and reforms in public education.

5.

Answer	Learning Objectives	Historical Thinking Skills	Key Concepts in the Curriculum Framework
B	CUL-4.0	Causation	4.1

Explanation: Environmental preservation did not become relevant for most Americans until late in the nineteenth century. Through most of the century, Americans tended to view natural resources as inexhaustible because of the vast area of free or cheap land available. The Census Bureau did not declare the frontier closed until 1890.

6.

Answer	Learning Objectives	Historical Thinking Skills	Key Concepts in the Curriculum Framework
C	CUL-2.0	Periodization	4.1

Explanation: States began to regulate public education largely as a result of the work of Horace Mann. Those reforms included increased state funding for education, the establishment of normal schools for teacher training, and a lengthened school year. The Eighteenth and Nineteenth Amendments were products of the Progressive movement of the early twentieth century, while wage and hour legislation was not enacted until the New Deal of the 1930s.

7.

Answer	Learning Objectives	Historical Thinking Skills	Key Concepts in the Curriculum Framework
C	WXT-2.0	Interpretation Analyzing Evidence: Content and Sourcing	4.2

Explanation: Henry Clay wished to create a national market economy linking all sections of the country economically. The American System was designed to accomplish that through creation of the Second Bank of the United States, protective tariffs, and federally funded internal improvements.

8.

Answer	Learning Objectives	Historical Thinking Skills	Key Concepts in the Curriculum Framework
B	WXT-2.0	Analyzing Evidence: Content and Sourcing	4.2

Explanation: Henry Clay's American System did not envision government ownership of railroads. Populists of the late nineteenth century would advocate public ownership of utilities in the Omaha Platform. Clay was successful in the creation of the Second Bank and in the institution of a protective tariff, but was largely unsuccessful in securing federally funded internal improvements.

9.

Answer	Learning Objectives	Historical Thinking Skills	Key Concepts in the Curriculum Framework
C	POL-3.0	Patterns of Continuity and Change over Time	4.2

Explanation: The government continued to support a relatively high protective tariff throughout the nineteenth century. The Bank War during the Jackson presidency effectively killed the Second Bank of the United States, and federally funded internal improvements never became prominent. Corporate income taxes were not in place until the twentieth century.

10.

Answer	Learning Objectives	Historical Thinking Skills	Key Concepts in the Curriculum Framework
D	CUL-3.0	Patterns of Continuity and Change over Time Analyzing Evidence: Content and Sourcing	4.2

Explanation: Employment of "Lowell Girls" challenged the concept of the cult of domesticity, which advocated separate spheres for women that included creating a nurturing home environment rather than work outside the home. Republican Motherhood was an outgrowth of the American Revolution, which emphasized the training of children to be responsible citizens.

11.

Answer	Learning Objectives	Historical Thinking Skills	Key Concepts in the Curriculum Framework
C	WXT-3.0	Causation	4.2

Explanation: As the first Industrial Revolution began, unskilled workers took the place of skilled artisans, lessening the need for highly skilled workers. Swift-flowing streams in New England allowed industrialization through the harnessing of water power, while the township system of settlement in the Northeast provided a relatively high population density, and a multitude of good natural harbors provided for access to international markets.

12.

Answer	Learning Objectives	Historical Thinking Skills	Key Concepts in the Curriculum Framework
A	WXT-1.0	Patterns of Continuity and Change over Time	4.2

Explanation: By 1840, immigrant women who viewed factory work as permanent began to replace native-born women who viewed such work as temporary. Increased immigration from Ireland and Germany during the 1840s and 1850s continued to provide low-cost labor for employers with the added benefit that they viewed industrial work as permanent and employers were not responsible for monitoring their behavior after the workday.

Short-Answer Questions

1.

Learning Objectives	Historical Thinking Skills	Key Concepts in the Curriculum Framework
WXT-1.0 WXT-2.0	Analyzing Evidence: Content and Sourcing Patterns of Continuity and Change over Time	4.1 4.2

What a good response might include

a) A good response will describe one way in which the two maps reflect a similar phenomenon. Some examples are:

   ✦ Manufacturing in both 1820 and 1850 was most concentrated in the Northeast, from Pennsylvania to Maine.
   ✦ More people were employed in manufacturing in the Northeast than in other sections of the nation.
   ✦ Manufacturing centers in both years tended to be in areas with access to water so that products could be more easily transported.

b) A good response will describe one change illustrated by the two maps that occurred in manufacturing between 1820 and 1850 and may include one of these:

   ✦ The nation was more industrialized in 1850 than in 1820.
   ✦ By 1850, manufacturing centers were emerging near the Great Lakes and in the South.
   ✦ There was more manufacturing in the West and the South in 1850 than there had been in 1820.
   ✦ In 1850, there were fewer areas that did not report manufacturing statistics or were unorganized than there had been in 1820.

c) A good response will explain one reason for the change described in b. Examples may include the following:

   ✦ After 1820, the textile industry grew significantly, especially in Massachusetts and Rhode Island, as water power was harnessed and a surplus labor force was available to work in textile mills.
   ✦ Women from rural areas in New England moved into towns and cities to take jobs in the growing textile industry.
   ✦ Increased immigration from Europe, especially from Ireland, increased the labor pool, especially in the North.
   ✦ Discovery of coal and iron led to increased manufacturing in the Ohio Valley and near the Great Lakes.
   ✦ The invention of the cotton gin made the production of cotton much easier, contributing to the growth of the textile industry.
   ✦ Passage of protective tariffs limited the importation of foreign goods, especially from Great Britain.
   ✦ Manufacturing increased when the modern factory system with its division of labor and use of interchangeable parts was introduced into the manufacturing process.

♦ The transportation revolution of the early and mid-nineteenth century, characterized by the building of canals, the use of steamboats, and the beginning of the railroad industry, spurred a "market revolution" that included the spread of manufacturing to the Midwest and in a more limited way to some areas of the South.

2.

Learning Objectives	Historical Thinking Skills	Key Concepts in the Curriculum Framework
WXT-2.0 CUL-4.0	Comparison Contextualization Analyzing Evidence: Content and Sourcing Patterns of Continuity and Change over Time	4.2

What a good response might include

a) A good response will explain why the slave population increased between 1790 and 1860. Examples may include the following:

♦ Although the U.S. government ended the Atlantic slave trade in 1808, over 100,000 Africans had been imported in the previous thirty years. This significant increase, coupled with the natural birth rate among slaves, resulted in a substantial increase in the number of slaves in the United States.

♦ The demand for slaves grew as a result of the invention of the cotton gin. As cotton became cheaper to produce, the demand for slaves increased.

♦ As the United States expanded westward to places like Texas, the slave frontier also expanded to the West.

♦ Between 1800 and 1850, several new states were admitted to the Union. This included Missouri, Louisiana, Alabama, Mississippi, and Texas, all states that allowed slavery. The number of states permitting slavery grew from eight to fifteen between 1800 and 1850, contributing to the overall increase in the slave population.

♦ With the advent of the Industrial Revolution, the demand for textiles, especially cotton, markedly increased. In order to supply cotton to factories in the North, a larger supply of cheap labor was needed, and southern planters saw slavery as a way to increase the production of cotton.

♦ Sugar production in the Deep South also increased the demand for slaves.

♦ With the growth of the cotton industry, southerners became more strident in their defense of slavery, moving from a defense of slavery as a "necessary evil" to supporting slavery as a "positive good." Any hope that southern states would pass manumission laws was dashed as the demand for slaves grew.

b) Some examples of good responses include the following:

♦ Eli Whitney's invention of the cotton gin in 1793 made it much easier to take the seeds out of the cotton boll, thereby keeping the price of cotton down and increasing the demand for it.

♦ Eli Whitney and others also developed and improved on the idea of using interchangeable parts in textiles and in other industries. This also served to increase the demand for and production of cotton.

♦ Other inventions such as new lathes, planers, and boring machines made cotton production cheaper and more efficient, increasing the demand for cotton.

✦ Transportation was revolutionized when, in 1807, Robert Fulton built the first steamboat, making it easier to ship cotton.

c) A good response must demonstrate whether the increase in the number of slaves was accompanied by a substantial increase in the number of bales of cotton produced. Some examples of good responses include the following:

✦ Technological improvements such as the cotton gin resulted in more efficient production of cotton.

✦ As time passed, fewer slaves were needed to produce each bale of cotton.

✦ One must consider that the 1790 figures may be misleading, as the majority of slaves were probably working in tobacco fields in the Upper South, not cotton fields in the Deep South.

Document-Based Question

Learning Objectives	Historical Thinking Skills	Key Concepts in the Curriculum Framework
MIG-2.0	Causation	4.2
WOR-2.0	Periodization	4.3
	Contextualization	
	Argumentation	
	Analyzing Evidence: Content and Sourcing	
	Synthesis	

What a good response might include

This is a straightforward prompt. But you must determine what is meant here by the word *analyze*. You should not merely list some of the causes of westward expansion. Instead, try to clearly link each cause to an effect. Analysis here also requires that you put the various factors that encouraged westward expansion into one of three categories: political, economic, or social. Students are sometimes confused about what "social" means. When you are required to address "social" causes, first think about issues of race, ethnicity, gender, and religion. In this DBQ, consider the references the documents make to Indians and how the relations between white Americans and American Indians affected westward migration. Also address slavery and the role it played in the march west. Remember that "social" is not restricted to the four categories listed here, but they are a good place to start.

In order to earn the maximum of 3 points for document use, in this case you must analyze *all* or *all but one* of the documents (meaning, at least six in this DBQ) and address how these documents provide evidence of the causes of expansion. Do not forget the requirement to address one of these points for each document you use: audience, purpose, historical context, or point of view. If you are not certain how to do this, ask your teacher to show you some examples. You cannot merely name the intended audience or simply state the speaker's point of view. Instead, you must link this discussion to the directive at hand: to analyze the political, economic, and social factors that led Americans to expand westward.

Before you even begin writing—and remember to make good use of the 15-minute planning period that you are given—make a list of relevant information that you know about this period. For example, the time period covered in this DBQ, allows you to write about the early use and spread of railroads. You can mention the years after the end of the War of 1812 as the Era of Good Feeling, when there was a period of relative peace and prosperity and a lull in the political battles that characterized the dissent between Federalists and Republicans. An American identity was cemented and reflected in art and literature. Sectionalism had not yet proven to be the decisive force it would soon be as the nation moved toward civil war. Pay attention to the time frame dictated by the question. It is significant here that the Mexican War ended in 1848. That had a huge impact on movement west, even after the period covered by the DBQ. When you turn to the documents, use each one to expand your list of outside knowledge; this will strengthen your essay and improve your score.

Each document included in a DBQ is there for a reason; if used correctly, every document can help you respond to the prompt. Try to determine what the changes shown in the maps in Document 1 were and WHY they influenced immigration. Consider boundary changes due to treaties, purchases, and wars; improvements in transportation; the desire to spread slavery; and the demand for access to cheap land. Zebulon Pike (Document 2) brings up a social issue—the need to separate whites from Indians—which, he argues, mandates constraining white migration to the natural boundaries formed by the Mississippi and Missouri rivers. The Land Act of 1820 (Document 3) focuses on the sale of public lands, certainly an economic stimulus to westward migration. You might want to also consider the role that speculators caused in furthering a land boom.

Remember as you proceed that documents should be grouped and not just used in the order of their placement in the DBQ. And for each, your analysis must include specific discussion of audience, purpose, context, or point of view. This discussion must be directly connected to the question of the factors that led Americans to move to the West. (And remember that "West" need not refer to those areas that we consider to be in the West today.)

The painting of the Erie Canal (Document 4) reflects in many ways the romantic impulse portrayed in the art and literature of the early nineteenth century. The yeoman farmer, Thomas Jefferson's model of the ideal American, lives in partnership with the land. But this painting also shows the impact of the transportation revolution characteristic of the Era of Good Feeling and the decades that followed. Note that this mention of the context in which this painting was done can help you earn the contextualization point. Andrew Jackson's message on the Removal Act (Document 5) reinforces the social tensions that existed in the mid-nineteenth century and indicates the political power of the federal government. Note in your analysis of this document Jackson's use of terms like *happy consummation*, *friendly feeling*, and *happy, prosperous people* to justify his forced removal of Indian tribes from the southeastern part of the country.

John O'Sullivan (Document 6), who was famous for coining the term *Manifest Destiny*, addresses his white audience and tries to justify the expansion of the nation from the Atlantic to the Pacific, making it seem almost like a religious crusade, one certainly reflective of "God's natural and moral law." Be sure to address his point of view here in the context of the first half of the nineteenth century. Note that you can expand your use of outside information by carefully considering details like Manifest Destiny that may not be specifically referenced in the excerpt but should come to your mind when you read O'Sullivan's words. O'Sullivan's name might even make you think of the tens of thousands of Irish who came to America at this time. Although the Irish largely remained in northeastern cities, the Germans who arrived around the same time often took their families to America's heartland. To address the synthesis point, you might connect the Manifest Destiny impulse of the first half of the nineteenth century to the imperialism at the end of the nineteenth century, for many of the same arguments made to isolate Indians and take their land in the 1830s were also used to take the Philippines near the end of the century. Another way to earn the synthesis point is to examine contradictory evidence. If you can think of any factors that impeded immigration, address them and try to explain the reason that this contradictory evidence appears.

The final document, the chart indicating the rapid increase in cotton production, addresses the economic imperative that drove many farmers from the Upper South to the Deep South and also mandates analysis of the spread of slavery that accompanied the expansion of "King Cotton." Try to link different documents together; the chart on the expansion of cotton production ties in very well with the two maps showing the expansion of the United States between 1800 and 1830.

Do not refer to the documents as "Document 1" or "Document 6." Instead, refer to the type of document (painting, address to Congress . . .) and its context, and reference the author, the title of the work, and his purpose, audience, or point of view. Be certain to link the document to your thesis. One of the worst errors you can make is to do what is called "laundry listing" the documents.

When you finish writing, look over your essay. Be certain that you have included all of the required elements. If you do not already have a copy of a generic rubric, ask your teacher to give you one so you will be absolutely certain that you understand what the person who scores your essay is looking for. The rubric is a sort of map for your essay. Remember that if you go on a journey without a map, you might never know when you arrive at your destination. So commit that rubric to memory, and pay attention to your destination and what it takes to get there.

PERIOD 5
1844–1877

Overview

The years of Period 5 see the nation expand across the continent, though that growth comes with confrontations over slavery and different views of the place of the United States in the world. Many believed in the concept of Manifest Destiny—that the United States was ordained by God to rule the continent through a combination of racial and cultural superiority. As the country grew, however, the controversy over the extension of slavery followed. Another minority, American Indians, faced increasing pressure as more of their lands were forcibly taken from them. U.S. economic, diplomatic, and cultural interests even began to look beyond the West Coast to the possible extension of American influence into Asia.

As immigrants continued to pour into the United States, tensions grew between the new arrivals and established communities. Immigrants were often met with violent nativist movements, particularly aimed at Catholics. Many sought refuge in the West in the years after the Civil War. The need for labor to promote economic development often trumped nativist sentiment. As the settlement of the West progressed, Hispanics and American Indians came under particular hardship as many refused to accept their assimilation into American society.

Tensions between the North and the South over issues involving slavery came to a head in the 1840s and 1850s. The North relied increasingly on free labor, while the South grew more dependent on slave-based agriculture. Abolitionist groups became more outspoken and activist, leading to a growing paranoia among slaveholders. Southerners responded with states' rights claims, nullification bills, and increased reliance of racial stereotyping to bolster they case for maintaining slavery.

The 1850s saw repeated attempts to defuse the conflict, resulting in the Compromise of 1850, the Kansas-Nebraska Act, and the *Dred Scott* decision by the Supreme Court. Nothing seemed to slow down the growing sectionalism. Issues of slavery and nativism led to the realignment of political parties, with the Republican Party emerging in the Midwest and North, while Democrats still tried to hold the northern and southern factions of their party together. The election of Lincoln in 1860 on a platform calling for the end of the extension of slavery into new territories proved to be the tipping point that led to the breakup of the Union and the Civil War.

The Union victory in the war ended the constitutional issues of slavery and secession but left unresolved many disputes over what should be the limits of federal power. The North triumphed over the South in the war through a combination of industrial power, leadership, and the moral high ground of calling for an end to slavery. Lincoln's decision to issue the Emancipation Proclamation gained the Union cause support in Europe and mobilized many African Americans to fight for the northern cause. Northern strength eventually overcame southern resistance, as the war destroyed both the South's environment and its infrastructure.

While the Union victory settled the question of slavery once and for all, Reconstruction left unresolved many questions about federal versus state power, as well as many prewar social and economic patterns. The Thirteenth Amendment ended slavery, but many former slaves fell into the almost equally oppressive sharecropping system during Reconstruction and beyond. Some temporary progress was made in terms of African American voting rights and political participation, but these gains were short-lived when the rest of the country began to lose interest in Reconstruction programs as the country put the Civil War behind it. The Fourteenth and Fifteenth amendments promised full citizenship and voting rights to African American men, but as interest in Reconstruction faded, so did a commitment to the enforcement of these promises. Women felt particularly betrayed when the Fifteenth Amendment specified male voting rights but left women out altogether. In spite of these shortcomings, these two amendments became the basis for effective civil rights legislation in the twentieth century.

Key Terms

Be sure that you understand the meaning of these terms and their relevance in U.S. history.

Abolitionism	Manifest Destiny
Carpetbaggers	Nativism
Free-soil movement	Nullification
Ideal of domesticity	Personal liberty laws
Ideological debate	Popular sovereignty
Impeachment	"Redemption"
Imperialism	Sectional parties
Jingoism	Sectional tensions
Laissez-faire	

Questions to Consider

As you study Period 5, keep the following thematic questions in mind.

American and National Identity

+ How did westward expansion and the quest for "manifest destiny" both reflect and shape Americans' views on progress and identity?
+ What effect did the debate over slavery have on shaping regional identities in the period 1844–1877?
+ How did the Civil War and its aftermath change people's views about what it means to be American?

Work, Exchange, and Technology

+ How did the differing economies of the North and South contribute to both the outbreak of the Civil War and its outcome?
+ In what ways did events during the Civil War years, 1861–1865, shape the postwar economy?

Migration and Settlement

+ How did the influx of immigrants in the mid-nineteenth century change America?
+ Why did Americans and immigrants move west, and how did the federal government promote westward expansion?

Politics and Power

- How and why did political alignments change as a result of events in the period from 1844 to 1877?
- How did reformers and writers shape the arguments about slavery in the years before the Civil War?
- How successful was political compromise at resolving the issues facing the nation in the antebellum period? Account for the successes and failures of compromise.
- How did various groups use the Constitution to buttress their beliefs about slavery and post–Civil War reconstruction?
- What issues were left unresolved as the Civil War ended, and how were these addressed between 1865 and 1877?
- How did the Civil War and Reconstruction affect the balance of power between branches of the federal government and between the federal government and the states?
- How successful was Reconstruction in achieving its goals? Account for the successes and shortcomings of the effort to rebuild the nation and to guarantee the slaves rights and opportunities that others had.

America in the World

- In what ways did American efforts to increase the power and prestige of the United States bring the country into conflict with other nations?
- Why was the Mexican War, which ended in 1848, such an important factor in leading the U.S. into a civil war thirteen years later?
- How did foreign involvement help determine the outcome of the Civil War?

Geography and the Environment

- What effect did geography have on Americans' quest for economic progress in the antebellum era?
- To what extent did geography have an impact on the events leading up to and during the Civil War?
- How was the western environment transformed as more and more settlers moved west in the mid-nineteenth century?

Culture and Society

- What were the unifying factors that linked the abolitionist movement to the efforts to achieve an expanded role for women in the mid-nineteenth century?
- How did Americans' views about race and ethnicity shape their views on expansion and the treatment of immigrants?
- How did the power of the pen shape Americans' views on slavery and the conflict between North and South?
- In what ways was expansion of republican ideals at the heart of debates over Manifest Destiny, slavery, and Reconstruction?

America's History Chapter Summaries

(required AP® content in bold)

Chapter 13
Expansion, War, and Sectional Crisis, 1844–1860

Chapter 13 examines four related themes: the idea of Manifest Destiny and the westward expansion beginning in the 1840s, the impact of traders and settlers on the Great Plains and in California, the impact of the Mexican War (1846–1848), and the disintegration of the two-party system as debates over the extension of slavery grew more acrimonious. Every addition of new territory to the Union brought with it the debate over whether that territory would be slave or free. The question was settled temporarily with the Compromise of 1850, but arguments over the Fugitive Slave Act and southerners' determination to open new lands to slavery made any future compromises difficult. The Whig Party disintegrated and was replaced by the Republican Party, dedicated to limiting slavery to the states and territories where it already existed. The Democratic Party splintered as well into a northern faction that looked for a way to limit slavery and a southern one devoted to protecting the institution. The 1850s was a decade that saw less and less room for compromise.

The decade of the 1840s saw Americans embrace the concept of Manifest Destiny—the belief that they had a God-given right to extend the blessings of **republican government across the continent to the Pacific**. This "right" carried with it the assumption of Anglo-American superiority. Oregon was the first target, followed soon by California, with little attention paid to the Spanish, Mexicans, and American Indians who were in those territories already. The Plains Indian culture had been made possible by the introduction of European horses and weapons. **The descendants of those same people now threatened the Indians' way of life**.

The presidential election of 1844 brought in an administration that revered expansionism, particularly into Texas and Oregon. The desire to annex Texas soon helped spark war with Mexico, a war that was fought on many different fronts in the Southwest. American victories in both California and Mexico itself led to the surrender by the Mexican government and a treaty that added vast new territories to the United States. Even before the treaty was ratified, **the issue of whether to allow the extension of slavery into these new territories began to split Congress along regional lines**.

This issue of whether any new states would be slave or free reached a crisis point quickly when gold was discovered in California and the population of the West Coast grew rapidly. **Rights of Mexicans and Indians were pushed aside as gold miners crowded in and began to stake claims. California had the added attraction of being a port of call toward Asia, a possibility many American merchants already appreciated.** Constitutional crisis followed California's application for statehood. Southern threats to leave the Union were temporarily put off with the passage of the Compromise of 1850, though many of the provisions of this bill led to more controversy. A free California was balanced by opening the rest of the territory gained from Mexico through popular sovereignty, and the South got a new, **more stringent Fugitive Slave Law**. The old **Two Party System crumbled as more aggressive antislavery advocates took the political stage. The Democrats splintered along regional lines while the new Republican Party replaced the divided Whigs**.

Northern abolitionists were quick to try and undermine the new Fugitive Slave Law, and antislave literature gained widespread popularity. Southerners responded with defense of the system, citing what they felt was the "positive good" of the institution. The economies of both North and South continued to move apart, with the North relying more and more on free labor while the South became ever more dependent on slaves.

Expansion continued as Congress sought to put the **Kansas and Nebraska territories** on the statehood track. The decision to handle the issue of slavery through popular sovereignty stirred up even more controversy, as the bill cancelled out the earlier Missouri Compromise and threw **these two territories open for renewed fighting over whether they would be slave or free.** The new Republican Party began to take the lead in the fight to contain slavery where it already was but to allow no new slave territories for states to be created. Fighting broke out in Kansas almost immediately, but Congress was able to do nothing to resolve the conflict. The next challenge to the Compromise of 1850 came in the form of a court case brought by a slave, Dred Scott, who asked that he be declared free because he was taken into free territory. The Supreme Court, dominated by southerners, not only denied his petition but went on to add that no one could be prevented from taking their "property" wherever they chose, **a position that undercut all political attempts to limit the spread of slavery.**

This was the political atmosphere in which **Abraham Lincoln won the office of the presidency in 1860, a Republican elected on a platform of protecting slavery where it already existed but preventing its spread into any new territories.** Many in the South viewed Lincoln's victory as the end of their chances to live a prosperous life in the United States. Secessionist sentiments ruled the day.

Chapter 14
Two Societies at War, 1861–1865

Chapter 15 chapter surveys the dramatic events of the Civil War. The political fire-eaters pushed the South toward secession and the Confederacy's attack on Fort Sumter. Although the South enjoyed early successes, the lack of industry, disrupted agriculture, and the weight of the slave system eventually combined to make the southern cause a lost one. The North began the war with weak military leadership but with industrial advantages, financial resources, and enormous manpower that eventually gave it the upper hand. Congress worked to create a more efficient banking system to finance the war effort. Lincoln changed the nature of the war with his Emancipation Proclamation, pushing the end of slavery to the forefront of Union war aims. His choice of better military leadership led the Union to victory. The war was hard on civilians on both sides. They faced high taxes, food shortages, inflation, and the constant fear of conscription and the deaths of loved ones. Although the North won, personal losses were heavy on both sides of the war.

South Carolina was the site of the first fighting in the Civil War with the attack on Fort Sumter in 1861, following the election of Abraham Lincoln. The other southern states soon rallied to the cause in the months before Lincoln's inauguration. All attempts at compromise failed, and Lincoln took office with a divided Union. **Both sides faced disagreements among their people, but the final division fell along the lines of slave or free states.** The South had a slight advantage in the first year of the war, as Lincoln sought a reliable general to lead the northern troops. A surprise victory at Antietam led **Lincoln to change the focus of the war by announcing the Emancipation Proclamation, making the end of slavery a northern war aim.** The Union strategies of blockade and the fight to control the Mississippi River soon left the South without supply lines, and the course of the war began to change. **Lincoln's choice of Ulysses S. Grant gave him the military leadership he needed to bring total war to the South.**

The war touched all parts of society in both the North and the South. **Conscription, wartime deprivations, and the constant fear of losing loved ones in battle haunted people throughout the Union and the Confederacy. Lincoln occasionally ignored constitutional safeguards in order to maintain control of border states like Maryland.** Women were called to do the work of men on the home front and on the battlefield, serving as farm and factory workers as well as nurses. **Many women hoped their contributions would lead to greater rights as citizens when the war ended.**

The North flourished during the war, with a streamlined banking system, busy factories, and a Republican Congress. The South was reduced to poverty and persistent inflation, particularly after the war moved deep into southern territory.

Lincoln's Emancipation Proclamation was extended in 1865 with the Thirteenth Amendment, which abolished slavery throughout the country. **Former slaves began to flock to Union lines, offering their services to the war effort.** By 1864, General Grant had driven the war into the heart of the Confederacy, with his generals taking Atlanta and his own troops surrounding Lee and the Army of Northern Virginia. Lincoln's reelection was secured as the news from the battlefields grew more optimistic, though he faced a party of **Radical Republicans in Congress who wanted harsher punishments for the defeated South than Lincoln's proposal to reestablish the Union as quickly and painlessly as possible.** The Confederacy finally collapsed in April 1865, leaving the Union preserved but hundreds of thousands dead and half the country in ruins. Slavery was gone, but it remained to be seen what real change would come to the nation as the states struggled to regain some semblance of normality.

Chapter 15
Reconstruction, 1865–1877

Chapter 15 focuses on the period following the Civil War, as Republicans tried to restore the defeated southern states to the Union and define the status of newly emancipated African Americans. Andrew Johnson assumed the presidency after Lincoln's assassination and determined to promote a lenient model for Reconstruction. The Radical Republicans in Congress disagreed, and when southern states began to enact oppressive laws like the Black Codes, they moved to push Johnson aside and take control of Reconstruction policies. They impeached Johnson, and though they failed to remove him from office, the Republicans took over the reins of government and imposed military rule on the South. Gradually, however, the Radical Republicans' control diminished, leaving many aspects of southern politics and culture similar to that before the war.

The end of the Civil War brought immediate questions about the status of the newly freed slaves in the reunited nation. President Johnson's goal was to bring the South back into the Union quickly. The southern states, however, moved to reestablish white supremacy, passing Black Codes that restricted black rights and attempting to force freedmen into agricultural labor, often on their former plantations. Radical Republicans responded with legislation creating the Freedmen's Bureau and passing the Fourteenth Amendment to the Constitution. The amendment granted citizenship to all born in the United States, regardless of previous status as slaves. Johnson's attempts to veto the legislation passed by the Radical Republicans, who won a majority in Congress in the 1866 elections, were quickly overturned. The Reconstruction Act of 1867 placed Congress in charge of all aspects of Reconstruction. That same year, Congress passed the Tenure of Office over Johnson's veto and used his violation of the act to draw up charges of impeachment against him. Though the Senate failed to get the necessary votes to remove Johnson from office, he was rendered powerless for the remainder of his term. **Radical Reconstruction moved forward, with southern states put under military control.**

The presidential election of 1868 brought General Ulysses S. Grant into office, and the Radical Republicans continued to hold a solid majority in Congress. One of their first acts was passage of the **Fifteenth Amendment to the Constitution, which granted voting rights to all American-born men.** Many women were disappointed with this amendment, as they felt they had earned the vote as well. African American women had a hard choice to make. **While some women felt they too should have the vote, they wanted to support any legislation that would ensure that their men had that right.**

As freedmen began to realize the limitations of their new status, they found themselves in conflict with northerners who wanted to revive southern cotton cultivation for international markets. Many ended up working the same land they had tilled as slaves, only this time they held the status of sharecroppers, a role in many ways even more economically precarious than the plight of slaves. Sharecroppers and tenant farmers nearly always fell into debt, and often they found themselves as bound to the land by that debt as closely as they had been by the bonds of slavery. As long as congressional Reconstruction lasted, the freedmen's community had some measure of protection, but that quickly disintegrated as the white southern power elite began to regain control of state governments in the mid-1870s.

In spite of these difficulties, black communities were able to flourish in many parts of the Deep South. Local churches became community focal points, quickly followed by small schools, civic organizations, and newspapers. While many hoped for general desegregation of all public facilities and institutions, neither Congress, the courts, nor the local power structure allowed that. **Despite the Civil Rights Act of 1875 requiring full and equal access to public accommodations, no real support would come for desegregation until the 1960s.**

Radical Republican control of Congress began to unravel in the mid-1870s. A financial panic in 1873 took the country's attention away from the plight of the freedmen and focused it on their own bank accounts. The scandals of the Grant administration further discredited the congressional majority. Many began to wish for a return to stability, and white Democrat leaders in the South promised just that. **As military troops were withdrawn from southern states, "Redeemer" governments assumed power, including many leaders from the former Confederacy.** Freedmen immediately began to find their rights constrained by local laws and the illicit activities of groups like the Ku Klux Klan. **Supreme Court cases further undermined the hopes of freedmen for support from the federal court, and they found themselves locked into a political world controlled by many of their former masters.**

What followed was the long, slow decline of Radical Republican policies and power. Though the Redeemers regained power in the South, slavery was indeed gone and black communities managed to thrive in spite of long odds against them. **The Fourteenth and Fifteenth amendments were part of the Constitution, though it would take another one hundred years for these two pieces of legislation to have the impact that was intended.** The South continued to lag behind the rest of the nation in both economic development and social progress, though the seeds were planted for the civil rights revolution that came in the twentieth century.

Thematic Timeline

THEME	REQUIRED CONTENT	SUPPORTING EXAMPLES
AMERICAN AND NATIONAL IDENTITY	• Racial and cultural superiority formed the basis for the idea of Manifest Destiny. • As the boundaries of the United States expanded and migrants moved to the West, there was increased interaction and conflicts between the U.S. government and Hispanics and American Indians. • The lives of Hispanics and Indians were altered by contact with white Americans and the U.S. government. • Debates occurred over the rights and status of Hispanics and Indians. • White southerners became more entrenched in their support of slavery, using states' rights, nullification, and racist stereotyping to define slavery as a positive good. • Regional identities strengthened in both the North and South, and Americans joined political parties that were regional rather than national. • The relationship between blacks and whites in the South was temporarily altered during Reconstruction. • Advocates for women's rights were both encouraged and divided by the adoption of the Fourteenth and Fifteenth amendments.	**1844–1860** • John L. O'Sullivan coins the phrase *Manifest Destiny* (1845). • American settlers in California proclaim the Bear Flag Republic (1846). • The American Party (the Know-Nothings) forms in opposition to immigration in general and Catholics in particular (1851). • South Carolina secedes from the Union as regional identity trumps national identity (December 1860). **1861–1865** • Other states in the Deep South follow South Carolina's lead. The northernmost tier of southern states except the border states secedes (1861). • West Virginia separates from Virginia and joins the Union (1863). • Women play an active role in the Civil War, joining the wage-earning labor force and serving as nurses, spies, and scouts. • As the Civil War proceeds, many slaves seize their own freedom by deserting plantations. **1865–1877** • Women's groups are frustrated by the failure of Reconstruction amendments to grant women voting rights. • The women's movement divides into two factions: the American Woman Suffrage Association and Elizabeth Cady Stanton's National Woman Suffrage Association. • Wyoming Territory grants voting rights to women (1869). • In *Minor v. Happersett*, the Supreme Court rules that the rights of citizenship do not include suffrage (1875). • African Americans accept the northern ideal of domesticity. • Through family ties, schools, churches, social organizations, and newspapers, African Americans build strong communities.

THEME	REQUIRED CONTENT	SUPPORTING EXAMPLES
WORK, EXCHANGE, TECHNOLOGY	• Americans moved to the West to take advantage of the availability of natural resources, opening up new economic ventures for many. • In the years before the Civil War, the contrast increased between the free-labor manufacturing system of the North and the slave-based agricultural economy of the South. • The North's economic advantages over the South contributed to its victory in the Civil War. • Following the abolition of slavery, white southerners exploited former slaves through the sharecropping system.	**1844–1860** • While California is still under the control of Mexico, merchants in New England provide a market for California leather and tallow and send agents there. • Gold discovered at Sutter's mill in California (1849). • The gold rush begins as 80,000 forty-niners arrive in California (1849). • The Gadsden Purchase (1853) opens the way for a transcontinental railroad. **1861–1865** • The North had many advantages entering the Civil War, including more people and more economic resources. • The southern economy during the Civil War continues to depend on revenues from the sale of cotton. • The Union government moves to increase industrial and agricultural production, strengthen the banking system, and impose tariffs. • The National Banking Acts of 1863 and 1864 give the federal government control over the banking system. • The North finances 65 percent of its war costs through the sale of bonds and 15 percent by printing paper money. • Railroad companies are granted subsidies to build a transcontinental railway. • Northern industrial production increases to meet the needs of the war effort. • Despite opposition by states' rights advocates, the Confederacy assumes more control over the southern economy. • The Confederacy pays 60 percent of its war expenses by printing paper money, creating significant inflation. **1865–1877** • Reconstruction fails to redistribute land in the South to American Americans; instead, sharecropping becomes the dominant postwar labor system in the South. • Sharecropping and the continued southern dependence on cotton depress the southern economy. • By the mid-1870s, Republicans concerned about the expansion of federal power advocate laissez-faire economic policies. • Economic scandals weaken the Grant administration.

THEME	REQUIRED CONTENT	SUPPORTING EXAMPLES
MIGRATION AND SETTLEMENT	• In the mid-nineteenth century, many people immigrated to the United States, forming ethnic communities and often maintaining their religion, language, and culture. • As white settlers moved westward, they took land from American Indians. • Those who moved to the West, including Asians, African Americans, and white people, sought both economic opportunity and religious freedom.	**1844–1860** • In the 1840s, Americans view Oregon as a place for economic opportunity, leading to "Oregon fever." • By 1860, 250,000 Americans had traveled the Oregon Trail. • Americans moving to the Great Plains confront Comanches, Kiowas, Sioux, and other Plains tribes that had adopted a horse culture and acquired firearms. • Annexation of Texas (1845). • Indians in Oregon lose title to much of their land. • Many Chinese arrive on the West Coast and are often employed in gold mines (1850). • Many Mexican families in California are denied claims to their land grants. **1861–1865** • The decimation of the buffalo herds and the loss of land to white settlers have catastrophic effects on the Plains Indians. • Due to disease and extermination campaigns, the California Indian population drops to 30,000 by 1860, down from 150,000 in 1848. • Homestead Act (1862).
POLITICS AND POWER	• In the mid-nineteenth century, debates about Manifest Destiny were central to American political life. • During and after the Civil War, the American government passed legislation that promoted economic development and westward migration. • In the years before the Civil War, many attempts were made to arrive at compromise. Among these were the Compromise of 1850, the Kansas-Nebraska Act, and the *Dred Scott* decision. These compromises failed to reduce sectional conflict.	**1844–1860** • James Polk elected president largely due to his support of expansion (1844). • Expansionists argue for the annexation of Texas and sovereignty over Oregon. • The Wilmot Proviso proposes to ban slavery in any land acquired from Mexico; however, it fails to pass in Congress (1846). • The free-soil movement forms in opposition to extension of slavery into U.S. territories. • The Free-Soil Party forms (1848). • Zachary Taylor, defender of slavery but not its extension to the territories, elected president (1848). • California's application for statehood inflames passions over the extension of slavery (1849). • Stephen Douglas champions "popular sovereignty" as a solution to the debate over the expansion of slavery. • The Compromise of 1850 provides a temporary remedy to the issue of the expansion of slavery.

THEME	REQUIRED CONTENT	SUPPORTING EXAMPLES
POLITICS AND POWER (*continued*)	• The Second Party System (Whigs and Democrats) ended as issues like nativism and slavery drove Americans to hold fast to regional identities. • In the wake of the demise of the Second Party System, sectional parties emerged, most importantly the Republican Party in the North and Midwest. • Lincoln ran for president on a free-soil platform, and his victory in 1860 led many southern leaders to support secession. • The North's superior political and military leadership and Lincoln's decision to issue the Emancipation Proclamation were crucial to northern victory in the Civil War. • Southern military leaders were often effective early in the Civil War but were overcome by the North's advantages. • There were some on both sides who opposed the policies of their governments. • The Thirteenth Amendment abolished slavery, but obstacles to racial equality remained. • Radical and moderate Republicans in Congress worked to reconstruct the South and altered the balance of power between Congress and the president. • For a short time after the Civil War, former slaves gained some political opportunities.	• The Fugitive Slave Act proves to be the most controversial part of the Compromise of 1850. • Some northern states pass personal liberty laws. • A new political party structure emerges as the Whig Party disintegrates (early 1850s). • The Kansas-Nebraska Act repeals the Missouri Compromise and propels the nation toward civil war (1854). • A new Republican Party formed by Whigs, Free-Soilers, and abolitionists, all united in opposition to slavery (1854). • Violence erupts in Kansas (Bleeding Kansas) over the issue of slavery and the ratification of a new territorial constitution (1856). • John Brown kills proslavery settlers in Kansas (1856). • James Buchanan, a prosouthern northerner, elected president (1856). • In his decision in *Dred Scott v. Sandford*, Chief Justice Roger Taney declares that blacks, both free and enslaved, are not U.S. citizens and that no territory has the right to prohibit slavery (1857). • Lincoln-Douglas debates and Douglas's Freeport Doctrine (1858). • Lincoln's House Divided speech (1858). • Southern Democrats divide into moderates and "fire-eaters" in the late 1850s. • John Brown's raid at Harper's Ferry, Virginia (1859). • Lincoln is elected president (1860). • The Crittenden Compromise fails (1861). **1861–1865** • Secessionists form the Confederate States of America with Jefferson Davis as its president (January 1861). • Shots fired at Fort Sumter begin the Civil War (April 1861). • Border states decide to remain in the Union, but Virginia, Arkansas, North Carolina, and Tennessee secede (1861). • Confederate victories at Battles of Bull Run and Richmond (1861). • Union victory at the Battle of Shiloh (1862). • Radical Republicans pass Confiscation Acts and legislation aimed at ending slavery in the District of Columbia. • The Confederacy implements first draft in American history (1862).

THEME	REQUIRED CONTENT	SUPPORTING EXAMPLES
POLITICS AND POWER (*continued*)	• Radical Republicans tried to change southern attitudes and establish the Republican Party in the South, but they eventually failed due to southern resistance and northern war weariness. • The Fourteenth and Fifteenth amendments granted citizenship, equal protection, and voting rights to African Americans but blacks lost many of these through segregation, violence, Supreme Court decisions, and local political tactics. • Implementation of the rights guaranteed in the Civil War Amendments was slowed for many years but later became the basis for court decisions that upheld civil rights.	• Lincoln issues the Emancipation Proclamation (January 1863). • After the Emancipation Proclamation is issued, nearly 200,000 African Americans join the Union army. • The Union draft begins in 1863. Anticonscription riots follow in New York City. • Union victories at Vicksburg and Gettysburg (1863). • Lincoln appoints Ulysses Grant to command Union forces (1864). • Lincoln runs for reelection with Andrew Johnson as his running mate (1864). • Sherman implements the tactic of "hard war" as he marches through Georgia (1864). • The Thirteenth Amendment ends slavery (1865). • Robert E. Lee surrenders at Appomattox Court House, ending the Civil War (April 1865). • Lincoln's Ten Percent Plan is not implemented, and Lincoln pocket-vetoes the ensuing Wade-Davis Bill (1864). **1865–1877** • The southern states enact Black Codes (1865). • Freedmen's Bureau established and Civil Rights Act of 1866 passes; Johnson vetoes both, but Congress overrides both vetoes. • The Reconstruction Act of 1867 establishes military districts in the South. • President Johnson impeached (1867). • Congress passes the Fourteenth Amendment (1868). • Fifteenth Amendment ratified (1870). • Reconstruction government undertakes impressive reforms in education, social services, transportation, law, and commerce. • Many African Americans elected to public office. • Civil Rights Act of 1875. • By the mid-1870s, Republican resolve to continue Reconstruction wanes in the face of economic crisis, allowing former Confederates to increase their efforts to regain control, an effort they call "Redemption." • The Ku Klux Klan spreads through the South.

THEME	REQUIRED CONTENT	SUPPORTING EXAMPLES
POLITICS AND POWER (*continued*)		• In response to Klan violence, Congress passes Enforcement Laws. • In the *Slaughterhouse Cases*, *U.S. v. Cruickshank*, and the *Civil Rights Cases* of the 1870s, the Supreme Court undercuts the Reconstruction Amendments and the Civil Rights Act of 1875. • A deal made to resolve the controversial 1876 presidential election effectively ends Reconstruction.
AMERICA IN THE WORLD	• In the aftermath of the Mexican War (called the Mexican-American War in the framework) Americans differed on whether slavery should be allowed in land won from Mexico. • In order to expand trade, the United States looked across the Pacific to Asia, and economic, diplomatic, and cultural initiatives ensued. • After Lincoln issued the Emancipation Proclamation, foreign governments decided not to support the Confederacy.	**1844–1860** • Slidell mission to Mexico fails, providing Polk with an excuse to go to war (1846). • Polk agrees to divide the Oregon Country at the forty-ninth parallel (1846). • The Mexican War (1846–1848) divides the nation and becomes a focus of the debate over the expansion of slavery. • The Treaty of Guadalupe Hidalgo ends the war with Mexico (1848). • Supporters of slavery urge expansion into the Caribbean, especially Cuba, and try to get presidential approval of the Ostend Manifesto. **1861–1865** • The Battle of Antietam convinces Britain not to support the Confederacy (1862).
GEOGRAPHY AND THE ENVIRONMENT	• As settlers moved westward, they transformed the environment that they encountered. • Greater resources and the North's wartime destruction of the South's environment and infrastructure contributed to the northern victory in the Civil War.	• Fertile grassland in the Great Plains attracts American farmers and ranchers, increasing tensions between white Americans and the Plains Indians. **1861–1865** • Although the South had the advantage of fighting on familiar ground, the Confederacy could not overcome the North's superior industrial base and transportation network.

THEME	REQUIRED CONTENT	SUPPORTING EXAMPLES
CULTURE AND SOCIETY	• In the mid-nineteenth century, a nativist movement emerged in response to increased immigration. This movement was anti-Catholic, determined to limit the power and influence of immigrants, and often turned violent. • In the period before the Civil War, abolitionists, though in the minority in the North, increasingly mounted attacks against slavery. Their tactics included arguing against slavery, helping slaves escape, and sometimes a willingness to use violence. • Southerners and their state governments used nullification and states' rights to defend slavery.	**1844–1860** • By 1840, many Americans support the ideology of expansion. • Conscience Whigs lead the opposition to the Mexican War. • Free-soilers view slavery as a threat to republican values and to Jefferson's celebration of the independent yeoman farmer. • In 1852, *Uncle Tom's Cabin* is published, further igniting passions over slavery. • Hinton Helper, a southerner, criticizes slavery in his book *The Impending Crisis of the South* (1857). **1865–1877** • The debate over how to reconstruct the nation after the Civil War largely hinges on the question of whether the southern states had legally left the nation.

Period 5 Practice Questions

Multiple-Choice Questions

Questions 1–3 refer to the excerpt below.

"We are glad at last to get a clear case, one on which no shadow of doubt can hang. This is not meddling with other people's affairs—this is other people meddling with us. This is not going crusading after slaves who it is alleged are very happy & comfortable where they are: all that amiable argument falls to the ground, but defending a human being who has taken the risks of being shot or burned alive, or cast into the sea, or starved to death or suffocated in a wooden box—taken all this risk to get away from his driver and recover the rights of man. And this man the Statute says, you men of Massachusetts shall kidnap & send back again a thousand miles across the sea to the dog-hutch he fled from. And this filthy enactment was made in the 19th century, by people who could read & write. I will not obey it, by God."

Ralph Waldo Emerson, 1851

1. In the above passage, Emerson is critical of which act as being "this filthy enactment"?
    - (A) The designation of an arbitrary dividing line between slave and free states
    - (B) An act allowing Congress to upset the balance of power in the Senate in favor of slave states
    - (C) Federal law requiring states to assist in the capture and return of slaves
    - (D) A Supreme Court decision that prevented Congress from banning slavery in the territories

2. The above passage could be construed as encouraging northern states to
    - (A) emancipate slaves.
    - (B) violate federal law.
    - (C) oppose the restrictions on the discussion of slavery in the U.S. House of Representatives.
    - (D) violate personal liberty laws.

3. The act referenced above was part of a compromise to
    - (A) allow Missouri to enter the Union as a slave state.
    - (B) allow a southern route for a transcontinental railroad.
    - (C) allow California to enter the Union as a free state.
    - (D) end the threat of southern states nullifying the protective tariff.

Questions 4–6 refer to the excerpt below.

"Hon. Horace Greeley:

"Dear Sir. . . . I would save the Union. I would save it the shortest way under the Constitution. The sooner the national authority can be restored the nearer the Union will be 'the Union as it was.' If there be those who would not save the Union unless they could at the same time save Slavery, I do not agree with them. If there be those who would not save the Union unless they

GO ON TO THE NEXT PAGE.

could at the same time destroy Slavery, I do not agree with them. My paramount object in this struggle is to save the Union, and is not either to save or destroy Slavery. If I could save the Union without freeing any slave, I would do it, and if I could save it by freeing all the slaves, I would do it, and if I could save it by freeing some and leaving others alone, I would also do that. What I do about Slavery and the colored race, I do because I believe it helps to save this Union, and what I forbear, I forbear because I do not believe it would help to save the Union. I shall do less whenever I shall believe what I am doing hurts the cause, and I shall do more whenever I shall believe doing more will help the cause. I shall try to correct errors when shown to be errors; and I shall adopt new views so fast as they shall appear to be true views. . . . Yours, A. Lincoln."

Abraham Lincoln to Horace Greeley, August 22, 1862

4. The above letter helps to best explain which of the following?

   (A) The Emancipation Proclamation
   (B) The ratification of the Thirteenth Amendment
   (C) The establishment of the Freedmen's Bureau
   (D) Congressional Reconstruction

5. The Emancipation Proclamation was most designed to

   (A) free all slaves.
   (B) prevent a British alliance with the Confederacy.
   (C) spur on enlistments in the Union army.
   (D) end slavery in the border states.

6. Which of the following was NOT a result of the Civil War?

   (A) The theory of perpetual union was validated.
   (B) The South became the industrial center of the nation by 1877.
   (C) Wartime legislation encouraged westward expansion.
   (D) The Republican Party dominated the presidency until 1884.

Questions 7–9 refer to the map below.

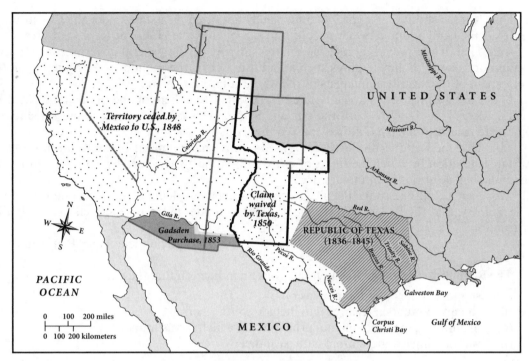

The Mexican Cession, 1848

7. The Mexican-American War resulted in

(A) Texas being annexed by the United States.
(B) the elimination of slavery west of the Mississippi.
(C) the breaking of U.S. diplomatic relations with Spain.
(D) renewed debate over the expansion of slavery.

8. The territory that the United States gained as a result of the Mexican-American War

(A) led to the division of Kansas and Nebraska into separate territories.
(B) entered the Union slave free as a result of the Wilmot Proviso.
(C) was largely unsuited to slavery.
(D) put to rest the idea that popular sovereignty was a workable means of governing the extension of slavery into the territories.

9. The Mexican-American War and its aftermath led most directly to which of the following?

(A) A northern majority in the legislative branch
(B) Completion of the transcontinental railroad
(C) An easing of sectional tension
(D) Secession of South Carolina from the Union

GO ON TO THE NEXT PAGE.

Questions 10–12 refer to the excerpt below.

"11. That Kansas should, of right, be immediately admitted as a state under the Constitution recently formed and adopted by her people, and accepted by the House of Representatives.

"12. That, while providing revenue for the support of the general government by duties upon imports, sound policy requires such an adjustment of these imposts as to encourage the development of the industrial interests of the whole country. . . .

"13. That we protest against any sale or alienation to others of the public lands held by actual settlers . . . and we demand the passage by congress of the complete and satisfactory Homestead measure which has already passed the House.

"14. That the Republican Party is opposed to any change in our Naturalization Laws, or any State legislation by which the rights of citizenship hitherto accorded by emigrants from foreign lands shall be abridged or impaired. . . .

"16. That a Railroad to the Pacific Ocean is imperatively demanded by the interests of the whole country; that the Federal Government ought to render immediate and efficient aid in its construction."

Republican Party Platform, 1860

10. The Republican Party platform of 1860 was an indication that the party
    (A) supported the abolition of slavery.
    (B) sought to broaden its appeal to include southerners.
    (C) maintained the fundamental principles on which it was founded.
    (D) was moving toward a more nativist stance.

11. The Republican Party platform of 1860 attempted to broaden its appeal to include
    (A) northern manufacturing interests.
    (B) a southern route for a transcontinental railroad.
    (C) support for filibustering expeditions into Latin America.
    (D) Know-Nothing supporters who had cost them the election of 1856.

12. The most immediate result of Lincoln's election in 1860 was that
    (A) attempts at compromise were abandoned.
    (B) the Civil War began.
    (C) South Carolina seceded from the Union.
    (D) the Emancipation Proclamation was made public.

END OF MULTIPLE-CHOICE SECTION

Short-Answer Questions

"The North may have won the war, but the white South won the peace. It preserved the essence:—a pool of cheap subservient labor—but escaped the capital outlays and social obligations that slavery imposed on its masters. . . .

"After all that can be said in their favor, the congressionally reconstructed governments were a disgrace, and in the end neither freedmen nor the Republican profited."

Samuel Eliot Morison, *Oxford History of the American People,* 1965

"In fact, Reconstruction governments were ambitious. They were hated in part, because they undertook impressive reforms in public education, family law, social services, commerce, and transportation. Like their northern allies, southern Republicans admired the economic and social transformations that had occurred in the North before the Civil War and worked energetically to import them."

James Henretta et al., *America's History,* Eighth Edition, 2014

1. Using the excerpts about Reconstruction above, answer a, b, and c.

    a) Provide one piece of evidence that supports Morison's position, and explain how and why it supports his position.

    b) Provide one piece of evidence that supports Henretta et al.'s position and explain how and why it supports that position.

    c) Provide an additional piece of evidence that supports either Morison's position or Henretta et al.'s position and explain why that evidence supports one or the other's point of view.

GO ON TO THE NEXT PAGE.

"But I take higher ground. I hold that, in the present state of civilization, where two races of different origin, and distinguished by color, and other physical differences, as well as intellectual, are brought together, the relation now existing in the slaveholding states between the two, is, instead of an evil, a good—a positive good. . . . I turn to the political; and here I fearlessly assert, that the existing relation between the two races in the South, against which these blind fanatics are waging war, forms the most solid and durable foundation on which to rear free and stable political institutions. . . . The condition of society in the South exempts us from the disorders and dangers resulting from this conflict; and which explains why it is that the political condition of the slaveholding states has been so much more stable and quiet than those of the North."

John C. Calhoun, Speech in the U.S. Senate, 1837

2. Using the excerpt above, answer a, b, and c.

a) How does the above account differ from southern perceptions of slavery prior to 1793?

b) Identify a specific event that might have led Calhoun to take this position.

c) Cite one specific example of something that fueled strong emotion over slavery in the middle decades of the nineteenth century, and explain how it increased sectional tension.

END OF SHORT-ANSWER SECTION

Long Essay Question

Question: To what degree and in what ways did the Civil War and Reconstruction alter the political, economic, and social fabric of American society?

END OF LONG ESSAY SECTION

Answer Key to Period 5 Practice Questions

Multiple-Choice Questions

1.

Answer	Learning Objectives	Historical Thinking Skills	Key Concepts in the Curriculum Framework
C	NAT-2.0	Patterns of Continuity and Change over Time Analyzing Evidence: Content and Sourcing	5.2

Explanation: The Fugitive Slave Law, passed as part of the Compromise of 1850, angered northerners, who saw slavery as a moral wrong. It drove many moderate abolitionists to a more extreme position. When coupled with other events from the 1850s such as *Uncle Tom's Cabin*, Bleeding Kansas, and the *Dred Scott* decision, it heightened the debate over slavery and made compromise less likely.

2.

Answer	Learning Objectives	Historical Thinking Skills	Key Concepts in the Curriculum Framework
B	POL-1.0	Patterns of Continuity and Change over Time Analyzing Evidence: Content and Sourcing	5.2

Explanation: The Constitution and federal law requiring states to return fugitive slaves were upheld by the Supreme Court in 1842 in the case of *Prigg v. Pennsylvania*. A number of states passed personal liberty laws that impeded the task of slave catchers by banning the use of state funds to assist in the capture and return. By the 1850s, abolitionist sentiment had grown to the point where mobs flouted federal law and actively sought to block the return of fugitive slaves.

3.

Answer	Learning Objectives	Historical Thinking Skills	Key Concepts in the Curriculum Framework
C	NAT-2.0	Causation Analyzing Evidence: Content and Sourcing	5.2

Explanation: The Compromise of 1850 was an attempt to overcome southern objections to the admission of California as a free state. This admission upset the balance of power in the Senate, giving the North control of the legislative branch of government. The compromise included a tougher Fugitive Slave Law to appease the South.

4.

Answer	Learning Objectives	Historical Thinking Skills	Key Concepts in the Curriculum Framework
A	NAT-1.0	Causation Analyzing Evidence: Content and Sourcing	5.3

Explanation: At the outset of the Civil War, Lincoln's primary objective was the preservation of the Union. Lincoln and the Republican Party believed in the free-soil principle that the federal government could control slavery in the territories but lacked the constitutional authority to do away with it in existing states. The Emancipation Proclamation was designed to keep slaveholding border states in the Union while broadening the motive of the war to ending slavery.

5.

Answer	Learning Objectives	Historical Thinking Skills	Key Concepts in the Curriculum Framework
B	WOR-2.0	Analyzing Evidence: Content and Sourcing	5.3

Explanation: The most important reason for the announcement of the Emancipation Proclamation was to prevent a possible European alliance with the Confederacy. European countries had done away with slavery, and popular opinion in Europe would not support an alliance predicated on the continued existence of slavery. Lincoln waited until the Battle of Antietam to issue the Emancipation Proclamation so that it wouldn't seem like a desperate move on the part of the Union.

6.

Answer	Learning Objectives	Historical Thinking Skills	Key Concepts in the Curriculum Framework
B	WXT-1.0	Patterns of Continuity and Change over Time	5.3

Explanation: Despite talk of the rise of the "New South," the South large remained a one-crop, cash-crop economy. The Civil War propelled the northern industrial machine to significant expansion that led to the second Industrial Revolution. By 1900 the North dominated the industrial productivity in the United States and had expanded to capture world markets.

7.

Answer	Learning Objectives	Historical Thinking Skills	Key Concepts in the Curriculum Framework
D	NAT-2.0	Patterns of Continuity and Change over Time	5.2

Explanation: Southern fire-eaters threatened secession if California, part of the Mexican Cession, was allowed to enter the Union as a free state. This threat prompted the major figures of Clay, Calhoun, and Webster to renew the debate over the extension of slavery and to hammer out the Compromise of 1850. President Zachary Taylor staunchly opposed any compromise, but his death and the ascension of Millard Fillmore to the presidency secured the compromise.

8.

Answer	Learning Objectives	Historical Thinking Skills	Key Concepts in the Curriculum Framework
C	GEO-1.0	Patterns of Continuity and Change over Time Analyzing Evidence: Content and Sourcing	5.1

Explanation: Some historians have used the phrase that "geography determined the issue of slavery in the Mexican cession." Arid conditions made the production of large-scale agricultural commodities impractical in the American Southwest. While California offered some opportunity for the extension of slavery, its admission to the Union as a free state meant that slavery would not gain a foothold there.

9.

Answer	Learning Objectives	Historical Thinking Skills	Key Concepts in the Curriculum Framework
A	NAT-2.0	Patterns of Continuity and Change over Time	5.2

Explanation: As a result of the Mexican-American War, the Compromise of 1850 admitted California as a free state, which upset the balance of power between slave and free states in the Congress. This allowed the North to dominate this branch of government. Southern sympathizers continued to dominate the presidency and Supreme Court until 1860.

10.

Answer	Learning Objectives	Historical Thinking Skills	Key Concepts in the Curriculum Framework
C	POL-1.0	Patterns of Continuity and Change over Time Analyzing Evidence: Content and Sourcing	5.2

Explanation: The Republican Party was formed as a free-soil party opposed to the extension of slavery into the territories. The 1860 Republican platform did not call for the abolition of slavery but for the prohibition of its spread. The eleventh plank of the platform calls for the admission of Kansas as a free state, thus remaining true to its founding principles that opposed slavery's extension.

11.

Answer	Learning Objectives	Historical Thinking Skills	Key Concepts in the Curriculum Framework
A	POL-1.0	Interpretation	5.2

Explanation: By the election of 1860, the Republican Party had become a purely sectional party appealing only to northerners. As a result, its platform attempted to broaden support by offering specific northern interests what they were interested in. In plank 12, the Republican Party shows support for a protective tariff beneficial to northern manufacturing interests. The party would not support either a southern route for a transcontinental railroad or filibustering expeditions because those ran contrary to northern interests. To sway immigrants, the platform included plank 14, which ran directly contrary to Know-Nothing's nativist thinking.

12.

Answer	Learning Objectives	Historical Thinking Skills	Key Concepts in the Curriculum Framework
C	NAT-2.0	Causation	5.2

Explanation: As an immediate result of Lincoln's election, South Carolina seceded from the Union in December 1860. Attempts at compromise (ex: the Crittenden Proposal, the Committee of 33) continued well into 1861. The Civil War did not begin immediately but required southerners to form the Confederate States of America. Lincoln did not issue the Emancipation Proclamation until 1863.

Short-Answer Questions

1.

Learning Objectives	Historical Thinking Skills	Key Concepts in the Curriculum Framework
NAT-2.0	Interpretation Analyzing Evidence: Content and Sourcing Contextualization	5.3

What a good response might include

a) A good response might include the following:
   + The South got what it really wanted out of Reconstruction as the southern black population was relegated to the status of second-class citizens, positions they were saddled with for almost another century through Jim Crow laws and the segregation system.
   + The system established at the end of Reconstruction kept black workers in powerless positions, and white employers had only to pay minimum wages rather than undertake the support that slavery entailed.
   + Toward the end of Reconstruction, Ku Klux Klan activities intensified, blacks were denied voting rights, and no mechanisms were left in place to ensure that black citizens would enjoy even minimal civil rights.

b) A good response might include the following:
   + While they were in power, Reconstruction governments energetically put people who were not associated with the pre–Civil War regimes in positions of authority.
   + During Reconstruction, a number of reforms worked to help newly freed slaves, including voter registration, the founding of Freedmen's Bureau schools, and the elevation of southern blacks to positions of leadership.
   + Reconstruction governments in the South ratified the Thirteenth, Fourteenth, and Fifteenth amendments to the Constitution.

c) A good response might include the following:
   + An additional piece of evidence that supports Morison's point of view that Reconstruction was a victory for southern goals was that as the "Bourbon" governments regained power, sharecropping and the crop lien system became the dominant form of agriculture. The majority of black farmworkers became trapped in this system and were never able to own their own land because they faced constant debt.

✦ A major success of Reconstruction was the establishment of strong black communities, bolstered by church, which were social centers and meeting centers. Although share-cropping was a system that kept blacks in debt and tied to the land, it was not slavery. Blacks could marry, receive an education, and establish businesses. The most enduring successes of Reconstruction were the passage and implementation of the so-called Reconstruction Amendments (the Thirteenth, Fourteenth, and Fifteenth), which became the cornerstone for the civil rights struggle in the twentieth century.

2.

Learning Objectives	Historical Thinking Skills	Key Concepts in the Curriculum Framework
WXT-1.0	Interpretation Analyzing Evidence: Content and Sourcing	5.2

What a good response might include

a) A good response might include the following:

  ✦ Many southerners referred to slavery in the late eighteenth and early nineteenth centuries as a "necessary evil," a practice that they often had difficulty reconciling with both democratic ideals and religious beliefs. The argument was made that the demands of southern staple crop agriculture made slave labor a necessity if the South was going to be economically viable.

  ✦ By the second decade of the nineteenth century, many slaveholders had switched to a defense of slavery as a "positive good," something that offered work and order to otherwise uncivilized Africans, as well as exposing them to a "higher culture" and the benefits of the Christian religion. Christianity was well suited to this defense, as those who suffered gladly in this life were guaranteed salvation in the next.

b) A good response might include the following:

  ✦ Southerners were under pressure to justify the slave system as the abolitionist movement began to gain strength in the North, particularly with the work of men like William Lloyd Garrison and groups such as the American Anti-Slavery Society. Talk of uncompensated emancipation meant the end of the southern economy as they knew it. They also began to look for moral as well as economic rationales for maintaining the slave system.

  ✦ Other events, like the slave uprising led by Nat Turner in South Hampton, Virginia, frightened many slave owners as well as white southerners who did not own slaves. The fear was that an end to the control of slavery could result in uprisings throughout the South that would destroy lives and property.

c) The 1850s saw the coming of many events that kept slavery at the front of national debate.

  ✦ The controversy over the Fugitive Slave Law that was a part of the Compromise of 1850
  ✦ Southern anger over northern and midwestern states and territories allowing personal-liberty laws that hindered the recapture of runaway slaves
  ✦ The 1852 publication of Harriet Beecher Stowe's novel, *Uncle Tom's Cabin*
  ✦ The events leading up to "Bleeding Kansas" in 1856
  ✦ The 1857 U.S. Supreme Court decision in *Dred Scott v. Sandford*
  ✦ The rise of the Republican Party, which sought to end the expansion of slavery into any new states or territories

Long Essay Question

Learning Objectives	Historical Thinking Skills	Key Concepts in the Curriculum Framework
WXT-1.0	Comparison	5.2
POL-1.0	Patterns of Continuity and Change over Time	5.3
CUL-2.0		

What a good response might include

This question begins with a sentence describing a historical **interpretation** about **patterns of continuity and change over time**, asking the writer to "support, modify, or refute" the interpretation. The essay should begin with the development of a relevant thesis. A good response to this question will support, modify, or refute the interpretation that the period of the Civil War and Reconstruction significantly altered the political, economic, and social fabric of American society. An essay supporting this interpretation would craft an argument using specific evidence that shows that the Civil War and Reconstruction did significantly change American society politically, economically and socially. A good response might also point out that the situation was nuanced. The essay might say, for the most part, that the historical evidence supports the claim of significant change in all three areas, while still pointing out that some evidence to the contrary exists as well.

Here are some examples to consider in crafting your essay.

Political
+ The nation set to rest the claim that secession was legal.
+ With the passage of the Thirteenth Amendment abolishing slavery, the question of the expansion of slavery into western territories was settled.
+ During the era of Radical Reconstruction, the South was divided into military districts and occupied by federal troops.
+ The Republican Party dominated national politics until well into the twentieth century.
+ After regaining control of their own state governments, the southern Redeemer governments move to regain control of local politics.
+ Redeemer legislatures in the South passed a number of laws designed to disenfranchise and marginalize African Americans.
+ Ordinary men still had little real power in Congress and other parts of government.
+ Despite the Fourteenth and Fifteenth amendments (ratified in 1868 and 1870, respectively), equal citizenship and voting rights were not realities for many blacks. However, these amendments laid the groundwork for the ongoing civil rights movement into the twentieth century.
+ Despite the agitation of the American Woman's Suffrage Association and other groups, women did not gain the right to vote during this era.

Economic
+ At the end of the war, northern business interests controlled the nation's economy.
+ Lackluster men were elected to the White House, leaving control of the nation's economy to the leaders of big business.
+ Legislation favored business interests.
+ The building of the transcontinental railroad concentrated enormous power in the hands of railroad and shipping interests.

- The American South was encouraged to remain agricultural but without the benefit of modern farming techniques.
- Workers often found themselves in jobs that offered little personal satisfaction or were sweatshop conditions. Farmers produced tremendous crops but they often made little money and remained at the mercy of banks and mortgage holders.
- Many southern laborers, both black and white, became tied to the sharecropping and crop lien systems that left many continually poor and in debt.

Social

- In the aftermath of the war, black men and women married and reunited with families when they could.
- Many African American families accepted and adapted the ideal of domesticity for their families.
- Jim Crow laws relegated African Americans to second-class citizenship.
- U.S. expansion into the western territories profoundly affected the lives and livelihoods of American Indians and Hispanic Americans already living there.
- A number of African Americans left the South for the West, most notably the group known as the "Exodusters," who settled in Kansas in the late 1870s.
- Despite being unable to vote in most states, women began to make slow gains in employment and educational opportunities. Women in the West were particularly valued, and, in 1869, women received the right to vote in the Wyoming Territory.

PERIOD 6
1865–1898

Overview

Between 1865 and 1898, the United States was transformed from a primarily agricultural society to one dominated by urbanization and industry. This shift brought with it many environmental, cultural, political, and economic changes. The rise of major industries led to increased migration to cities, resulting in changes in all areas of life for those living in urban areas. The federal government aided the growth of big business, as changes in technology and international communication linked American producers and consumers with the rest of the world.

In the years following the Civil War, the U.S. government subsidized industries that were viewed as essential to national expansion and aided the growth of new technologies and business models. The creation of monopolies allowed a small number of businessmen to expand their companies to dominate entire segments of the economy. These companies also expected that the government would help them control overseas resources. The prevalent belief in Social Darwinism, the idea that the more talented groups and individuals would and should rise to the top, helped justify the growing divide between the few very rich and the increasing numbers of poor. This discrepancy was particularly evident in urban areas, where the lifestyles of the rich were in sharp contrast to the more numerous poorer neighborhoods.

Various groups did offer challenges to the dominance of big business leaders. Labor movements gradually gained influence, hoping for better pay, better working conditions, and limits to child labor. The South continued to be primarily agricultural rather than industrial, with sharecropping and tenant farming replacing the old plantation system in what was called the "New South."

Westward migration continued to lead to conflicts about the management of natural resources. Some progress was made during this era in the establishment of the first national parks, though conservationists had an uphill battle. More efficient farming technology meant greater demands for land and more reliance on railroads to get farm goods to regional and national markets. Government favoritism toward business, coupled with unpredictable farming conditions, led to the creation of the People's (Populist) Party to represent the political and economic interests of farmers and other workers.

Immigrants, minorities, and women faced both progress and challenges during these years. America's cities became destinations for growing numbers of immigrants from Southern and Eastern Europe, as well as African Americans who sought better situations than they could find in the Deep South. They did find economic opportunities, but they also were relegated to poorer neighborhoods, often divided by race and class. Urban areas were often dominated by political machines that preyed on the needs of poorer classes, though some private efforts, such as the settlement house movement, sought to provide some relief to the working poor. Women's clubs worked to offer opportunities for middle-class women to become involved in civic and political issues.

The completion of the transcontinental railroad and the resulting flood of new settlers to the Great Plains and the West hastened the demise of independent Indian tribes. Those who survived military action were decimated by the loss of the buffalo on which their culture de-

143

pended. Reservations replaced tribal homelands in a misguided effort to force assimilation. Additional conflicts arose in the Southwest between settlers and Mexican Americans.

The rapid growth of big business during the Gilded Age was characterized by widespread corruption in both industry and government. Soon reformers were calling for changes, but they met stiff resistance from the powers in Congress, the Supreme Court, and the monopolists. Racism and nativism were reinforced with Supreme Court rulings like *Plessy v. Ferguson*. Even so, not all industrial leaders were Social Darwinists. A few suggested that the wealthy and successful did have an obligation to help the poor. Many reformers took up the goals of reform under the banner of the Social Gospel. Others directed their efforts at specific groups, especially African Americans and women.

Key Terms

Be sure that you understand the meaning of these terms and their relevance in U.S. history.

Capitalism	Naturalism
Commercial domesticity	Political machines
Consumer culture	Popular culture
Corporate ethic	Public sphere
Fact worship	Social Darwinism
Gilded Age	Spoils system
Literary realism	Suffrage
Management revolution	Vaudeville
Maternalism	

Questions to Consider

As you study Period 6, keep the following questions in mind.

American and National Identity

+ How did ethnic and regional identities help shape Americans' views of progress during the late nineteenth century?
+ In what ways did westward expansion transform Americans' national identity?
+ Why and in what ways did white Americans attempt to influence Indians to adopt white customs and behaviors?
+ What accounts for the emergence of the American labor movement in the Gilded Age?
+ How were immigrants able to become Americanized and at the same time maintain many elements of their traditional identities?
+ How did women's roles change during the Gilded Age, and what part did women play in bringing about change, especially in American cities?
+ What did Elizabeth Cady Stanton mean by the "solitude of the self," and what did women and women's groups do to facilitate this "solitude"?
+ What obstacles faced African Americans in the years after the Civil War, and how did they confront those obstacles?
+ What economic, political, and regional obstacles did farmers face in the late nineteenth century as they attempted to counter the power of big business?

Work, Exchange, and Technology

✦ What role did technological advances play in propelling American migration all the way to the Pacific Ocean?

✦ What were the forces that transformed the American economic system in the last half of the nineteenth century?

✦ How were a few industrialists able to consolidate so much production and profit in industries like steel, oil, and railroads?

✦ Why were tariffs such a source of passionate debate in the late 1800s?

✦ How did technological advances transform the lives the American farmers?

✦ What were the most significant obstacles faced by labor unions, and how did unions attempt to improve the lives of workers prior to 1900?

✦ What is a consumer culture, and how did the late-nineteenth-century consumer culture transform American life?

Migration and Settlement

✦ What tensions accompanied the arrival of white settlers in the trans-Mississippi West, and how did both Indians and white Americans react?

✦ What obstacles confronted immigrants who arrived in the United States between 1865 and 1900, and what steps did immigrants take in order to adapt to their new home?

✦ How did industrialization and immigration help to transform the American city in the late nineteenth century?

Politics and Power

✦ How did local governments and officials in Washington address the problems that accompanied the influx of Europeans into America during the Gilded Age?

✦ What role did the government play in restricting the opportunities and the liberties of racial and ethnic groups?

✦ What was the federal government's role in supporting the economic transformation that occurred during the Gilded Age?

✦ To what extent did "New South" emerge in the years following the Civil War?

✦ How were white southerners able to "redeem" the South in the aftermath of Reconstruction?

✦ Why, despite their shortcomings, were political machines able to become such a powerful force in America's cities?

✦ How successful were farmers in reaching their goals? What factors accounted for their successes and failures?

✦ Why, by the end of the nineteenth century, did the public increasingly demand political, social, and economic reform?

America in the World

✦ How and why did the role of the United States in the world change in the decades following the Civil War?

✦ How did economic changes at home affect U.S. policies abroad?

Geography and the Environment

+ Why, and in what ways, did the federal government implement new policies on land management in the late nineteenth century?
+ How did Indians forced from their homelands adapt to their changing environment?
+ Why did Americans in the late nineteenth century develop a love of the outdoors, and what resulted from this?

Culture and Society

+ How did nativism help shape government policy in the late nineteenth century?
+ What were some of the arguments that justified the rapid accumulation of wealth in the hands of a few in the late nineteenth century?
+ How did late-nineteenth-century literature reflect the problems confronting urban workers and farmers in this period?
+ In what ways did critics challenged the dominant "corporate ethic" of the American elites?
+ What were some characteristics of the new popular culture, including music, theater, and sports, that emerged in American cities in the last half of the nineteenth century?

America's History Chapter Summaries

(required AP® content in bold)

Chapter 16
Conquering a Continent, 1854–1890

Chapter 16 examines the expansion of the United States from 1854 through 1890. During these years, the United States expanded to the Pacific Coast and linked the East and West Coasts with a transcontinental railroad. The national economy grew at an unprecedented rate with the markets created by the war, the demands from new consumers, and the help of a business-friendly Republican government. Greenbacks competed with gold as the new currency as others sought to add silver coins as well. U.S. foreign policy became more expansive through the acquisition of Alaska and **increased international trade with the Pacific, Asia, and Latin America**. Those settling on the Great Plains became integrated into the national economy at the expense of the American Indians and the great herds of buffalo. Homesteaders transformed the **western environment to the point that the federal government began to set land aside for natural preserves**, another blow to the culture of the Indians who depended on these hunting grounds. After the end of the Civil War, President Grant sought treaties aimed at **assimilating Indians who would cooperate and exterminating those who would not**. By the late 1880s, most tribes had faced defeat and moved to reservations, though they persisted in their efforts to maintain their tribal identity. The United States was poised to become a major player on the world stage.

The completion of the first transcontinental railroad was a political as well as a technological triumph. Republicans had exercised nearly complete domination of Congress since the southern states left the Union in 1860 and 1861, and among their goals was the railroad, a stronger protective tariff, and the growth of the nation's industrial sector through various forms of public-private partnerships. The possibilities of new riches through overseas trade had been on the Republican agenda since the 1850s when trade with Japan began. Chinese labor had already proved valuable to American industry, and these workers played a major role in the building of the transcontinental railroad. The **new railroad companies transformed American capitalism with the creation of corporations**, all under the benevolent eye of the U.S. Congress. High tariffs protected American industry well after the end of the Civil War and the return of some southern Democrats to the government. Conservative appointments to the Supreme Court ensured favorable rulings for businesses as well. The nation also prospered from the discovery of **vast mineral wealth, particularly gold and silver**. These discoveries strengthened U.S. currency in the international markets and attracted European investment.

Congress moved to open the West on a grand scale with the Homestead Act of 1862. Farmers competed with miners and cattle ranchers in their race to the riches the West offered. Women played a significant role in this settlement as well, often finding greater political power in the territories than what was offered to them back east. Many homesteaders struggled with extreme environmental conditions, inadequate homestead allotments, and backbreaking labor as they worked to carve out a living from grasslands that often defied easy settlement. Among them were **African Americans who migrated out of the South** in search of independence and land in the newly opened frontier. Range wars were common between cattlemen and the newly arriving farmers, who fought over access to grazing land and water. Miners added another layer of competition, as the mining frontier began to move from west to east, encroaching on lands claimed by both farmers and cattlemen.

Often overlooked or underestimated in this scramble for western lands were the **numerous Indian tribes that also called the Great Plains home**. The systematic destruction of the vast buffalo herds on which Plains Indians depended for survival **led to Indian wars** and attempts by

Congress at mediation that rarely favored Indian interests. **Wars between the army and the Indians on the Great Plains began before the Civil War ended and intensified during Reconstruction.** Reservations set aside for Indians by the federal government proved to be woefully inadequate, with marginal land, poor supplies, and corrupt government officials who were charged with administering them, not to mention the loss of traditional ways of life for the Indian nations.

Lulls in the conflicts were always brief, and by the 1870s, the federal government was working to **force most Plains tribes onto reservations with false promises and increasing violence**. Assimilation meant boarding schools for children, life in near poverty on reservations, and efforts by well-meaning missionaries to substitute Christianity for native religions. The Dawes Act of 1887 sought to break up tribal lands into individual homesteads, **another step along the road to assimilation**. The Ghost Dance movement in the1890s was a last-ditch effort by Plains tribes to make a united stand against the U.S. military, but it was ended once and for all by the slaughter of more than one hundred Sioux at Wounded Knee, South Dakota. The world of the Plains Indians became the basis for entertainments like Buffalo Bill's Wild West Show, with rugged pioneers taking center stage and Indians and buffalo being relegated to background scenery.

Chapter 17
Industrial America: Corporations and Conflicts, 1877–1911

Chapter 17 explores the rise of the industrial United States between 1877 and 1911. Steel magnate Andrew Carnegie seemed to be a classic example of a poor immigrant who became a rags-to-riches success story through hard work and good timing. Although he knew firsthand the struggles of the laboring classes, workers at his mills felt they were not treated fairly and launched what became the Homestead Strike, an ill-fated union attempt to force concessions from management that resulted in loss of jobs and even of lives. **This era saw many such movements, most without resulting in many gains for the workers.**

Businesses boomed due to a **combination of new technology, more efficient management models, and access to seemingly unlimited resources**. The transcontinental railroad led to the rise of large industrial processing centers like Chicago and Cincinnati. Major industries were soon dominated by a **small handful of leaders who created trusts, monopolies that allowed them to control the production and sale of nearly all major commodities**. John D. Rockefeller's Standard Oil led the way in horizontal integration, which drove competitors out of business and allowed the creation of a complete monopoly in the oil industry. Other industries soon followed, and by 1900, America's largest one hundred companies controlled a third of the nation's productive capacity.

The work of these robber barons transformed the nation's economy. A **consumer culture arose**, and along with it, department stores developed. Montgomery Ward and Sears built mail-order empires, bringing merchandise to rural areas. A class of managers and salesmen arose, and women began to find jobs in corporate offices, though rarely in the areas of management. Skilled workers still had some autonomy in this new economy, but as industrialism advanced, the need for craft work began to decline. Mass production and scientific management theories valued speed and efficiency over craftsman skills. Many workers found the new factories to be dangerous and polluted places, which often operated with no concern for the surrounding environment. Child labor became common, particularly in coal mines and textile mills, and African Americans often found themselves at the bottom of most job opportunities and wage scales.

Immigrants, often willing to take jobs for **the lowest pay offered**, provided a boost to the labor force. Many native-born Americans resented them, feeling they drove down wages for everyone. **Many of those coming to America during these years were from Southern and Eastern**

Europe. Many Jewish immigrants came to escape the pogroms of Russia. Chinese immigrants had been arriving on the West Coast since the 1840s, and they faced some of the harshest treatment of all. Nativist pressure forced Congress to limit Chinese immigration with the Chinese Exclusion Act of 1882, the first such act of its kind, which created the legal foundation for future exclusionary policies.

Industrial workers began to look for ways to improve their situation and turned to labor unions. The Great Railroad Strike of 1877 was the first labor action to gain real public attention, a strike that quickly turned into riots and led state governments to call out troops to restore order. Writers began to take up the cause of workers, offering both practical and utopian suggestions about how society might address the workers' complaints. Farmers also felt themselves at the mercy of corporations, particularly the banks that held their mortgages and the railroads that charged whatever rates they wanted regardless of the hardship it caused their rural customers. An early political group, the Grangers, sought relief for farmers, soon merging their efforts into the Greenback-Labor Party. Despite some early successes in regulating railroad rates, the party found it lacked real power. Even the short-lived **Populist Party** would prove to be generally ineffective.

The first major labor union, the Knights of Labor, founded in 1869, hoped to represent all workers regardless of skill level. The Knights grew rapidly and enjoyed some early successes, although the organization was sprawling and decentralized. Their downfall came in May 1886 with an attempt to hold another nationwide railroad strike that was to begin with a gigantic rally in Haymarket Square in Chicago. A bomb blast turned the rally into a riot, and police fired into the crowd. Though no one ever knew for certain who was responsible, eight alleged anarchists were convicted of murder, and the reputation of the Knights of Labor suffered as well through guilt by association. The group never recovered its former strength and soon passed from the scene.

Farmers were attempting to organize through a series of **regional farmers' alliances**. Many had hoped to forge networks with labor groups in order to gain more national leverage. The federal government, feeling the mounting pressure of these different groups, did make some concessions in the 1880s. The Interstate Commerce Act created the Interstate Commerce Commission to investigate charges of unfair shipping rates. Though the commission looked promising on paper, there was no enforcement power built into its mandate and a **probusiness Congress and Supreme Court continued to give industrialists most of what they wanted at the expense of farmers and workers**.

The American Federation of Labor (AFL) moved in to fill the vacuum left by the end of the Knights of Labor. This group worked to serve skilled labor only, organizing individual craft unions under its umbrella of the AFL. Samuel Gompers led this organization for many years. He justified a more exclusive union on the grounds that this gave the group better bargaining power. Unskilled workers, women, tenant farmers, domestic workers, and other minorities were not allowed to become members. Although the AFL would enjoy little real success in the late nineteenth century, it was poised for better luck when new leadership came to the White House and Congress in the coming decades.

Chapter 18
The Victorians Make the Modern, 1880–1917

During these years explored in Chapter 18, the United States began to develop distinct working classes and a growing middle class. Global trade and mass production made consumer goods affordable, though large department stores allowed the working classes in only as clerks and cashiers. Those who could afford new electric lights and telephones installed them. The Pullman Palace Car company offered luxurious travel for those who could pay, with second-class and smoking cars for those who could not and for all minorities regardless of income. A dispute over segregated railroad cars led the **Supreme Court to affirm states' rights to impose Jim Crow laws with its decision in *Plessy v. Ferguson* in 1896**, a ruling that would stand until the 1950s.

Cities saw the growth of organizations like the Young Men's Christian Association and the popularity of sports competitions, particularly baseball. Here segregation also played a part, forcing the organization of Negro Leagues. Football began on elite college campuses and quickly gained popularity with the general public. Bicycling and camping gained devotees, with women taking part as well. Magazines began to praise the "New Woman," exemplified by the Gibson Girl, more educated, athletic, and independent than her mother or grandmother. **The establishment of national parks gained support through the work of conservationists** like John Muir, who founded the Sierra Club in 1892.

Women began to push again for political and economic rights, particularly as they began to take part in the urban reform movements that characterized this period. Families were smaller by this era, as women began to have greater access to rudimentary birth control. High school education was more readily available to boys and girls, and many schools were coeducational. Colleges moved from the traditional emphasis on Latin, Greek, and rhetoric to what was called a "liberal arts" curriculum, with many offering specific technical training in response to the needs of the job market. Booker T. Washington founded Tuskegee Institute in 1881, a school for African American youth that focused on industrial education as well as literacy and mathematics. Washington gained national fame when he spoke at the Cotton States Exposition in Atlanta in 1895, where he urged the races to work together so all could achieve economic success. **He hoped education and hard work on the part of African Americans would overcome racial prejudice**.

In spite of education and economic gains, women still found political equality elusive. **Various women's groups formed around the country**, making the argument that women should serve the community as well as the home and that such service was worthy of equal treatment under the law. Many women became involved in the temperance movement, working through organizations like the Women's Christian Temperance Union. They also organized the Daughters of the American Revolution, with southern women following up with the United Daughters of the Confederacy. Denied admission into these groups, **African American women formed the National Association of Colored Women, focusing on social initiatives as well as hoping to make a dent in racism**. Ida B. Wells-Barnett was a leader in this movement, taking up the campaign to try to get a national antilynching law. **Political rights for women were addressed by a number of groups**, including the National American Woman Suffrage Committee, though Congress still refused to entertain a constitutional amendment giving women the right to vote.

Rapid developments in science began to shake traditional religious foundations during these years. The 1893 World's Columbian Exhibition showcased scientific marvels of industry, transportation, and communication, showing the world rapidly becoming a very different place. The work of Charles Darwin challenged the Old Testament view of the world, though some felt his **theories of natural selection justified the Social Darwinist attitudes of many of the rich toward those who were worse off**. Some went even further and posed the theory of eugenics, suggesting that humans could be bred for certain traits. Such attitudes fed the nativism that plagued many new immigrants to this country.

The world of the arts responded to a more urban America with schools of realism in art and naturalism in literature. Many writers took a fairly bleak view of the direction in which the country was headed, feeling that men had lost a measure of control over their fates. Some, like Mark Twain, thought the United States was working for progress for its own sake rather than for the sake of those whose lives would be affected by it. Religions became more diverse with the huge numbers of immigrants arriving in the last decades of the nineteenth century. Catholics, Jews, and Eastern Orthodox vied with mainline Protestants in many large cities. This was a time of a great deal of missionary work overseas by Protestant denominations, and much of this fed into a growing determination that America was to serve as the example to the less fortunate of the world. Good intentions quickly took on an air of chauvinism, and the work of Christian missionaries sometimes became a justification for imperialism.

Racist groups like the American Protective Association vied with advocates of the Social Gospel about whether immigrants should be kept out or whether those who were better off should extend a helping hand. Groups like the Salvation Army worked to offer assistance to the urban poor, though America entered the twentieth century with many of these debates unresolved.

Chapter 19
"Civilization's Inferno": The Rise and Reform of Industrial Cities, 1880–1917

The rise of the industrial city brought many changes to traditional views of urban life, from sky-scrapers to subways to public parks and museums. There were neighborhoods of great wealth close to areas of grinding poverty, and these conditions led to questions about corruption, reform, and the obligations of the community to the individual.

Industrial cities combined traditional urban elements—neighborhoods, public meeting spaces, schools and churches—with centers of manufacturing, finance, and trade. Large populations and the need to get move about efficiently led to the development of mass transit, cable cars, and elevated trains. Steel girders, plate glass, and elevators made skyscrapers possible. Louis Sullivan became the leader in such architecture, and he put Chicago on the map as an innovative city in urban design. Electricity made nightlife possible, opening up all sorts of evening entertainment for city dwellers.

Immigrants flocked to America's cities, often settling in ethnic neighborhoods. They organized mutual aid societies to help ease the transition from overseas to their new lives. A small number of African Americans began to move north looking for better jobs and an escape from Jim Crow, though most could find work only in the service sector. **Race riots broke out periodically in northern cities, proving that racial prejudice was not only a southern problem**.

City planners responded to the **floods of immigrants by building low-cost five- and six-story tenement apartment buildings with cramped, airless apartments that were at least affordable**. These tenement neighborhoods quickly became overcrowded and rife with disease and infant mortality. Urban reformers took on these neighborhoods as they sought to find solutions to overcrowding and sanitation issues.

Despite these drawbacks, cities proved to be exciting places to live for many. Theaters and amusement parks showcased ethnic talent and drew large appreciative audiences. Social restrictions were lax in the city, and many young people found there was less supervision from parents and older relatives. Young women often lived in boardinghouses, and many of the older generation lamented their vulnerability to prostitution. Many cities had a more or less open gay subculture, something that would have been unheard of in earlier generations. Many cities also offered excellent art museums, often funded by wealthy patrons. Libraries and opera, theater, and literary guilds abounded. The popularity of libraries was testament to the gains made in general literacy in the decades after the Civil War. The daily press flourished in cities like New York and Chicago, though there were often no requirements for verification of the truth of stories that lured in readers. This was the era of "yellow journalism," when sensationalism was valued over close attention to the truth. **Some journalists took on the social ills of the time and called for reform**. These "muckrakers" often prodded politicians to address social problems they might otherwise have ignored.

Many major cities were ruled by unscrupulous political bosses and machines. Some, like Boss Tweed and G. W. Plunkitt, became notorious for their corruption. Newly arriving immigrants were their base of support. They gained votes in exchange for help finding housing and jobs and needed public services. The problems came when political greed took over and the machines benefitted more than their constituents did. By the financial depression of the 1890s, city political machines were unable to handle the crisis of unemployment, hunger, and mobs of the homeless. Voters began to demand more efficient and transparent government, and reform-minded politicians began to win elections. The era of Progressive reform was about to debut.

Progressivism was an urban movement first, an attempt to address the plight of those living in substandard housing, facing dangerous work for low wages, and dealing with hunger, poor sanitation, and infant mortality at home. Journalists used the newly available art of photography to graphically illustrate the poverty they sought to end. Public health moved to the forefront of reform when a number of epidemics broke out in northern cities. The "City Beautiful" movement sought to develop more urban park space for the relief of those living in overcrowded tenements. Social reformers sought to close down prostitution districts, though often no one bothered to look into the conditions that led many of these women to such a life.

The settlement house movement created community welfare centers in major cities, modeled on the first, Hull House, founded by Jane Addams in a working-class section of Chicago. **Settlement work led to other projects—health issues, calls for better schools, easier access to health services for women.** Margaret Sanger led the call for more open access to birth control. Reform did not come quickly or easily, but many middle-class women found fulfillment in this work. Women headed the National Consumers' League and the Women's Trade Union League. The call for safer working conditions became national news with the Triangle Shirtwaist Company fire in 1911. Over one hundred women died because there was no access to fire escapes in their New York building.

Progressive reform was just beginning at the dawn of the twentieth century. Over the next two decades, the crusade to improve the lives of those living in the nation's major cities would become a significant part of the national agenda.

Thematic Timeline

THEME	REQUIRED CONTENT	SUPPORTING EXAMPLES
AMERICAN AND NATIONAL IDENTITY	• Farmers, in order to protect their interests, organized and sought reform through the Populist Party. • Immigrants, facing many prejudices in American cities, attempted to "Americanize" and at the same time maintain their cultural identities. • Women frequently took the lead in urban reform, forming clubs and self-help groups to further intellectual pursuits. • Women and African American activists challenged the existing order, offering an alternate vision of equality. • American Indians' culture and identity were threatened as white Americans moved to the West. • U.S. military actions, the destruction of the buffalo, the reservation system, and assimilation policies reduced the Indian population and threatened Indian culture and identity.	• Booker T. Washington founds the Tuskegee Institute (1891). • Washington delivers his Atlanta Compromise address (1895). • Ida Wells begins her campaign against lynching (1890s). • As baseball becomes more popular, African Americans form Negro leagues. • General Federation of Women's Clubs formed (1890). • The National Association of Colored Women organizes (1896). • Mormon women in Utah pressure the territorial government to grant them suffrage, and after Utah becomes a state in 1896, several women are elected to the state legislature. • The Gibson Girl becomes the symbol of the "New Woman." • Elizabeth Cady Stanton speaks about the "solitude of self" (1890s). • Educational opportunities for women expand with the founding of colleges like Vassar and Smith. • The Daughters of the American Revolution founded (1890). • United Daughters of the Confederacy founded (1894). • "Reservation wars" fought in the late nineteenth century are followed by efforts to destroy Indians' traditional ways of life. • Sand Creek massacre (1864). • Fetterman massacre (1866). • Custer defeated at Little Big Horn (1876). • The Nez Perce are removed from their land and, under Chief Joseph, unsuccessfully attempt to flee to Canada (1877). • Dawes Severalty Act (1877). • Establishment of Indian boarding schools. • Supreme Court rules that Indians are not citizens (1903). • The National Grange of the Patrons of Husbandry founded (1867). • The Greenback-Labor Party forms (1870s). • Farmers' Alliance movement begins (1870s). • People's Party (the Populist Party) organizes and issues its Omaha Platform (1892).

Theme	Required Content	Supporting Examples
AMERICAN AND NATIONAL IDENTITY (*continued*)		• Populists call for monetary reform, public ownership of transportation and communication systems, and reform of the electoral and taxation systems. • Immigrants form mutual aid societies to help facilitate the transition to urban life in America. • Recent immigrants tend to cluster with others from their homeland in the workplace, urban neighborhoods, and their places of worship.
WORK, EXCHANGE, TECHNOLOGY	• The Gilded Age was characterized by technological innovation, large-scale production, and government support for industry. • Government provided subsidies for innovation and production in transportation and communication. • Monopolies became powerful by exploiting natural resources and a growing industrial labor force. • National economic issues—tariffs, currency, corporate expansion, and laissez-faire economic policies—were central to Gilded Age politics and led to calls for reform. • Government corruption and the excesses of big business caused the public to demand more popular control and reform of government at all levels. Some called for major changes in the capitalist system. • The industrial culture of post–Civil War America provided both opportunities and challenges, especially for women, African Americans, and immigrants.	**Technological innovation and its impact** • First transcontinental railroad completed (1869). • The federal government provides substantial financial support to private railroad companies, leading to the transformation of the American economy. • The Pullman Company makes railroad cars for the elite. • Led by the railroad industry, American companies increasingly form corporations and then trusts. • Alexander Graham Bell invents the telephone (1876). • The World's Columbian Exposition, held in Chicago, celebrates science and invention (1893). • Electricity, new ways of producing steel, and other modern technologies make it easier to live in the city. • Private enterprise takes the lead in modernizing the urban environment through building trolley lines and providing water, gas, and electricity. • Louis Sullivan pioneers the design and construction of skyscrapers. **The American economy** • In the Gilded Age, protective tariffs provide the bulk of funds to run the federal government. Fierce debates wage over tariffs. • First post–Civil War Economic depression begins (1873). • America goes on the gold standard (the "Crime of 1873"), although in 1878, the Bland-Allison Act mandates limited coinage of silver. The gold standard sharply limits the nation's money supply. • In *Munn v. Illinois*, the Supreme Court allows states to regulate key businesses (1877). This ruling is later struck down by *Wabash v. Illinois* (1886). • Another major depression begins in 1893.

THEME	REQUIRED CONTENT	SUPPORTING EXAMPLES
WORK, EXCHANGE, TECHNOLOGY (*continued*)	• A new consumer culture emerged as wealthy Americans could purchase new products, even though many others lived in poverty. • Farmers had to adapt to the realities of mechanized agriculture and the power of the railroads, so they formed organizations to resist the big corporations.	**The growth of industrial America** • Corporate leaders such as Andrew Carnegie and John D. Rockefeller use vertical and horizontal integration to form powerful monopolies. • The late-nineteenth-century "management revolution" enables corporations to operate more efficiently but often creates more distance and tension between workers and their bosses. • Transportation networks expand the national market. • A new model for organizing a business, the trust, is formed for the first time when John D. Rockefeller creates Standard Oil of Ohio (1882). **American workers respond to a changing workplace** • Immigrants from Southern and Eastern Europe fill the need for unskilled industrial labor. • Women enter the workforce in large numbers in secretarial and office work and as telephone operators. • Skilled workers lose much of their independence as goods are mass-produced and scientific management techniques spread. • The Knights of Labor forms (1869). • Mother Jones speaks out for American workers. • The Great Railroad Strike (1877). • Beginning in the1880s, the American Federation of Labor, under the leadership of Samuel Gompers, organizes workers. • The Haymarket incident hastens the demise of the Knights of Labor (1886). • Workers protest conditions at Carnegie's Homestead mill (1892). • Coxey's Army marches to Washington seeking help for the unemployed (1894). **The South and the West** • The Long Drive transforms the cattle industry. • Farmers seek ways to counter the power of large corporations. • In the South, attempts to unify white and black farmers fail. • Child labor is common, especially in the South. • African American workers suffer widespread job discrimination.

THEME	REQUIRED CONTENT	SUPPORTING EXAMPLES
WORK, EXCHANGE, TECHNOLOGY (*continued*)		**A consumer culture emerges** • John Wanamaker opens the first American department store (1875). • Montgomery Ward and Sears make it possible for people living far from large cities to buy a variety of products. • Advertising encourages and expands the consumer culture. • Mass readership of magazines and newspapers spreads through the introduction of cheap subscriptions.
MIGRATION AND SETTLEMENT	• Migration from overseas combined with large numbers of Americans moving from rural areas into cities changed the face of urban America and led to problems like low wages and an increase in child labor. • Immigrants from Asia and Southern and Eastern Europe, as well as African Americans leaving the rural South, moved into cities and to the West. • Cities provided challenges and opportunities as a mixture of classes, races, ethnic groups, and cultures coexisted in urban areas. • Settlement houses helped immigrants to adapt to their new life.	**In the Northeast** • In the late nineteenth century and continuing into the twentieth century, million of immigrants, especially from Southern and Eastern Europe, move into American cities. • Ellis Island receives its first immigrants in 1892. • Rather than the earlier model of the city as a center for finance and commerce, by the late nineteenth century, the "industrial" city is the norm. • Jane Addams and Ellen Starr found Hull House, one of the first settlement houses (1889). The settlement house movement propels women into other forms of social and political activism in education, workplace safety, and government reform. **In the West** • In the wake of the passage of the Homestead Act in 1862 and the end of the Civil War, westward expansion moves at a rapid pace. • Immigrants from Scandinavia and Germany, in a wave of "American fever," move to the American West. • Black "Exodusters" move west in the years after 1879. • The courts invalidate most land claims held by Mexican Americans (late nineteenth century). • Increasing racism against Chinese laborers in the United States results in the Chinese Exclusion Act (1882).

THEME	REQUIRED CONTENT	SUPPORTING EXAMPLES
POLITICS AND POWER	• Political machines formed in cities, filling the need for social services that governments were unable to provide. In return, the machines expected political support from urban dwellers, especially immigrants. • Workers formed unions in an attempt to combat the combined power of big business and government. • Some in the South called for a "New South," but sharecropping and tenant farming remained the norm. • Americans argued over the values of the American system as they debated the role of different groups in the political process.	**Regulation of big business** • The federal government partners with big business in support of industrial development. • The courts use the Fourteenth Amendment to protect corporations from excessive regulation. • Due in part to pressure from the Greenback-Labor Party, state Granger laws are passed, creating commissions to supervise railroad rates and policies, as well as insurance and utility companies. • The Supreme Court strikes down *Wabash v. Illinois* (1887). • The Interstate Commerce Act, despite its lack of enforcement powers, is an important step in government regulation of business (1887). • The Sherman Antitrust Act of 1890 is the first federal law to forbid corporations from acting "in restraint of trade." **Electoral politics** • "Waving the bloody shirt" rallies supporters of both parties after the Civil War. • Election turnout is higher from 1876 to 1892 than at any other time in U.S. history, although Gilded Age politics is characterized by corruption and stagnation. • From the inauguration of Ulysses Grant in 1869 to Wilson's inauguration in 1913, all presidents except for Grover Cleveland are Republicans. • Democrats sometimes hold one or both houses of Congress. • By the end of the century, white Democrats are fully in control in the "Solid South." Southern Democrats maintain a strong base in Congress. • In an attempt to rein in the spoils system, the Pendleton Act is passed (1883). • Mugwumps help elect Grover Cleveland, the first postwar Democratic president (1884). • Populist William Jennings Bryan runs for president in 1896. He is a candidate of both the Populist and Democratic parties, but Republicans win the election. • William McKinley elected president in 1896, showing the weaknesses of the Populist Party.

THEME	REQUIRED CONTENT	SUPPORTING EXAMPLES
POLITICS AND POWER (*continued*)		**Urban politics** • After the Civil War, Tammany Hall and other political machines become the driving force behind urban and state governments. • By the end of the nineteenth century, Americans become more aware of the limitations of machine politics, and calls for reform become louder. **Race, gender, and politics** • *Plessy v. Ferguson* allows Jim Crow laws to stand, establishing "separate but equal" as the law of the land (1896). • Supreme Court decisions in cases like the *Slaughterhouse Cases*, *U.S. v. Cruickshank*, and the *Civil Rights Cases* reverse much of the progress made during Reconstruction. • In *Williams v. Mississippi*, the Supreme Court rules that poll taxes and literacy tests are constitutional (1898). • The Comstock Act passes in 1873. • Women become active in the Prohibition Party and the People's Party (1880s and 1890s). • The National American Women's Suffrage Association merges two rival suffrage organizations in an attempt to invigorate the movement for women's suffrage.
AMERICA IN THE WORLD	• American businesses looked overseas, primarily to Asia, the Pacific, and Latin America, for resources and new markets.	• Following Mathew Perry's 1854 voyage to Japan, American businesses look to Asia for markets and resources. • Secretary of State William Seward supports American economic expansion in Asia. • The Burlingame Treaty guarantees the rights of U.S. missionaries in China (1868). • Seward negotiates a treaty with Russia for the purchase of Alaska (1869).
GEOGRAPHY AND THE ENVIRONMENT	• Conservationists and business interests locked horns, as those who wanted more protection of the environment called for the establishment of national parks. • The government, urged on by conservationist organizations, extended public control over land and other resources.	• The discovery of gold and silver in the West, along with the passage of the General Mining Act of 1872, leads to the growth of the mining industry and boom towns, along with a demand for western timber and produce. • Buffalo hunting and ranching transform the environment of the American West. • Homesteaders in the West confront environmental challenges such as finding water and battling insects. • Industrial dependence on fossil fuels transforms the natural environment.

THEME	REQUIRED CONTENT	SUPPORTING EXAMPLES
GEOGRAPHY AND THE ENVIRONMENT (*continued*)	• Competition for land in the West led to increased conflict between whites, Indians, and Mexican Americans.	• In the late 1800s, middle-class and wealthy Americans take to the outdoors. • Yellowstone is established as the first national park (1872). • John Muir founds the Sierra Club (1876). • John Wesley Powell publishes *Report on the Arid Region of the United States* (1879). • Frederick Jackson Turner writes "The Significance of the Frontier in American History" (1893).
CULTURE AND SOCIETY	• Many businessmen used Social Darwinism to justify their accumulation of wealth, though other Americans argued that the wealthy had the obligation to help the poor. • Racism and nativism were used to justify violence, discrimination, and segregation, as exemplified by *Plessy v. Ferguson*. • Utopianism and the Social Gospel were offered as alternate visions of society. • Science, morality, and philosophy were used both to support and challenge the existing social and economic order.	**Ideas on the economy and social issues** • Henry George, in his book *Progress and Poverty*, urges a single tax on land (1879). • Andrew Carnegie writes *The Gospel of Wealth* (1889). • William Graham Sumner champions Social Darwinism (late nineteenth century). • The Social Gospel calls for Christians to work for justice and social welfare (late nineteenth century). • Salvation Army founded (1879). • The YMCA serves as an example of "Muscular Christianity" (late nineteenth century). • Immigrants confront a religious dilemma: modernize or cling to traditional beliefs. • Militant Protestants form the nativist American Protective Association (1887). • Americans' opinions about prohibition often correlate with ethnic, religious, and class divisions. • Many couples attempt to limit family size in an effort to promote upward mobility, especially in cities. **Literature and the arts** • More young people attend college, and educators like Charles Eliot pioneer the liberal arts. • Andrew Carnegie donates millions of dollars to establish libraries throughout the United States. • Literary realism becomes a popular genre in the late nineteenth century. • Theodore Dreiser's *Sister Carrie* (1900), Stephen Crane's *Maggie: A Girl of the Streets* (1893), and works by Hamlin Garland are popular examples of realism. • Naturalist authors such as Frank Norris, Theodore Dreiser, Stephen Crane, and Jack London are widely read.

THEME	REQUIRED CONTENT	SUPPORTING EXAMPLES
CULTURE AND SOCIETY (*continued*)		• Mark Twain's *The Adventures of Huckleberry Finn* takes a bleak view of American society (1884). • New York City's Metropolitan Museum of Art and the Metropolitan Opera become icons of American high culture (1880s). • Booker T. Washington publishes *Up from Slavery* (1901). **Popular culture** • A popular culture emerges that seems to be more democratic, yet leads to debates over race, gender, inequality, and privilege. • P. T. Barnum promotes "commercial domesticity." • An urban culture evolves in the late nineteenth century: vaudeville, amusement parks, ragtime music, and dance halls. • The music of ragtime performers like Scott Joplin is popular with both white and black Americans. **A consumer culture** • The department store becomes an "Adamless Eden." • Team sports, especially baseball and football, become a fundamental part of American life. American men assume a consumer identity as sports fans. **The role of women** • Maternalism, the middle ground between domesticity and equality for women, leads many women to become more active in the life of their communities. • The Women's Christian Temperance Union is founded in (1874). This organization is a springboard for women to work for reform in many arenas. It stresses "womanliness" as a virtue and a goal. **In the West** • The Ghost Dance movement is followed by massacre at Wounded Knee (1890). • Buffalo Bill Cody's Wild West show attempts to create the western myth.

Period 6 Practice Questions

Multiple-Choice Questions

Questions 1–3 refer to the image below.

Killing the Bison, 1870s

1. The expansion of railroads to the West Coast led to the
   (A) destruction of American Indian habitats.
   (B) first American Industrial Revolution in the Northeast.
   (C) realization that private funding alone should build America's railroads.
   (D) admission of California as a free state.

2. How did railroad companies encourage immigration?
   (A) They offered free homesteads to those who would settle along rail lines.
   (B) They paid high wages to workers who would emigrate from their home countries.
   (C) They ran advertising campaigns in Europe for cheap railroad lands in the United States.
   (D) They lobbied the federal government to overturn the Chinese Exclusion Act.

3. The completion of the transcontinental railroad led to
   (A) increased sectional tension.
   (B) assimilation of Mexican Americans into society as equals.
   (C) hostility between the government and big business.
   (D) economic growth and the expansion of Asian markets.

GO ON TO THE NEXT PAGE.

Questions 4–6 refer to the excerpt below.

"We consider the underlying fallacy of the plaintiff's argument to consist in the assumption that the enforced separation of the two races stamps the colored race with a badge of inferiority. If this be so, it is not by reason of anything found in the act, but solely because the colored race chooses to put that construction upon it. . . . The argument also assumes that social prejudice may be overcome by legislation, and that equal rights cannot be secured except by an enforced commingling of the two races. . . . If the civil and political rights of both races be equal, one cannot be inferior to the other civilly or politically. If one race be inferior to the other socially, the Constitution of the United States cannot put them upon the same plane."

U.S. Supreme Court, majority opinion, *Plessy v. Ferguson*, 1896

4. *Plessy v. Ferguson* resulted in which of the following?
    (A) Integration of public schools
    (B) Violent riots that swept through major northern cities in the 1890s
    (C) Ratification of the Fifteenth Amendment by southern states that had been holding out
    (D) Second-class citizenship for African Americans

5. Prior to 1900, most African Americans in the post–Reconstruction South
    (A) migrated north and took jobs in industrial cities.
    (B) became sharecroppers or tenant farmers.
    (C) migrated west to take advantage of free homesteads.
    (D) left the United States and emigrated to Africa.

6. While mainstream African American leaders of the late Gilded Age differed in how they sought to end segregated society, many followed a moderate course that called for
    (A) violent protests.
    (B) nonviolent civil disobedience.
    (C) a "back-to-Africa" movement.
    (D) gradual accommodation.

Questions 7–9 refer to the excerpt below.

"The eighth wonder of the world is this: two pounds of iron stone purchased on the shores of Lake Superior and transported to Pittsburgh, two pounds of coal mined in Connellsville and manufactured into one and one-fourth pounds of coke and brought to Pittsburgh, one-half pound of limestone mined east of the Alleghenies and brought to Pittsburgh, a little manganese ore, mined in Virginia and brought to Pittsburgh, and these four and one-half pounds of material manufactured into one pound of solid steel and sold for 1 cent. That's all that need be said about the steel business."

Andrew Carnegie, *Ode to Steelmaking*, c. 1900

7. Andrew Carnegie reflects which of the following business models of the Gilded Age in the above quote?
    (A) Conspicuous consumption
    (B) Social Darwinism
    (C) Laissez-faire economics
    (D) Vertical integration

8. The rise of big business was fostered by all of the following during the Gilded Age EXCEPT

(A) improved transportation systems that opened new resources and market.
(B) the strict laissez-faire policy of the federal government.
(C) plentiful natural resources.
(D) a growing immigrant labor force.

9. The general business climate of the Gilded Age

(A) welcomed competition as a motivator to improve the quality of products.
(B) rejected overseas markets as unfeasible due to high transportation costs.
(C) endorsed the corporate model of the trust.
(D) rejected the notion of conspicuous consumption.

Questions 10–12 are based on the map below.

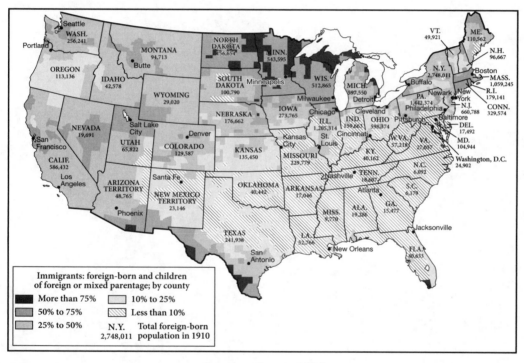

Immigration to 1910

10. Immigrants tended to settle

(A) in coastal cities in the South.
(B) in rural areas of the North.
(C) on the West Coast.
(D) in industrial cities.

11. The rapid increase in population in Gilded Age industrial cities led to

(A) neighborhoods composed of mixed classes where the rich mingled with the poor.
(B) the rich tending to move to the center city.
(C) immigrants moving to the city periphery because of easy access to streetcars.
(D) ethnic ghettos that tended to be settled by people of the same nationality.

12. The rapid increase in the pace and character of immigration after 1890 led to
   (A) increased nativist sentiment.
   (B) the resurrection of the Know-Nothings as a major third party in presidential elections.
   (C) massive deportations of Catholics and Jews.
   (D) the voluntary return of a majority of immigrants to their country of origin.

END OF MULTIPLE-CHOICE SECTION

Short-Answer Questions

"You come to us and tell us that the great cities are in favor of the gold standard. I tell you that the great cities rest upon these broad and fertile prairies. Burn down your cities and leave our farms, and your cities will spring up again as if by magic. But destroy our farms and the grass will grow in the streets of every city in this country. . . .

"Having behind us the commercial interests and the laboring interests and all the toiling masses, we shall answer their demands for a gold standard by saying to them, you shall not press down upon the brow of labor this crown of thorns. You shall not crucify mankind upon a cross of gold."

William Jennings Bryan, Cross of Gold Speech, July 8, 1896

1. Using the excerpt above, answer a, b, and c.

    a) Identify and explain why a specific group of people would have supported the ideas of William Jennings Bryan.

    b) Identify and explain why a specific group of people would have opposed the ideas of William Jennings Bryan.

    c) Explain why William Jennings Bryan received support from Populists when he was a Democratic candidate for president in 1896.

GO ON TO THE NEXT PAGE.

Puck Magazine, December 1882

2. Using the political cartoon above, answer a, b, and c.

a) Explain what prompted the Civil Service Reform Bill.

b) Explain the system that the civil service system was designed to replace.

c) Cite and explain one specific example of corruption in the Gilded Age at the national level.

END OF SHORT-ANSWER SECTION

Document-Based Question

Directions: The following question is based on the accompanying documents. The documents have been edited for this exercise. Spend approximately 15 minutes planning and 45 minutes writing your answer.

Write an essay that does the following:

+ States an appropriate thesis that directly addresses all parts of the question.
+ Supports the thesis or argument with evidence from all or all but one of the documents AND your knowledge of U.S. history beyond the documents.
+ Analyzes all or all but one of the documents.
+ Places each document into at least one of the following categories: intended audience, purpose, historical context, and/or point of view.
+ Uses historical evidence beyond the documents to support your argument.
+ Places the argument in the context of broader regional, national, or global processes.
+ Incorporates all of the elements above into a convincing essay.

Question: Analyze the ways in which laboring-class Americans in the Gilded Age (1865–1900) attempted to better their lives in the face of the power of big business and the federal government. Evaluate the degree of success their efforts attained.

Document 1

Source: Gift for the Grangers, 1873

Library of Congress, LC-DIG-pga-04170

GO ON TO THE NEXT PAGE.

Document 2

Source: I. G. Blanchard, "The Eight Hour Day," *Boston Daily Voice,* 1886

We mean to make things over,
We're tired of toil for naught,
With bare enough to live upon,
And never an hour for thought;
We want to feel the sunshine,
And we want to smell the flowers,
We're sure that God has willed it,
And we mean to have Eight Hours.
We're summoning our forces
From shipyard, shop, and mill;
Eight hours for work, eight hours for rest,
Eight hours for what we will!

Document 3

Source: The Haymarket Riot, *Harper's Weekly,* May 15, 1886

Library of Congress, LCUSZ62-796

GO ON TO THE NEXT PAGE.

Document 4

Source: National People's Party Platform, 1892

1. We demand free and unlimited coinage of silver and gold at the present legal ratio of 16 to 1.
2. We demand that the amount of circulating medium be speedily increased to not less than $50 per capita.
3. We demand a graduated income tax.
4. We believe that the money of the country should be kept as much as possible in the hands of the people, and hence we demand that all State and national revenues shall be limited to the necessary expenses . . .

TRANSPORTATION. — Transportation being a means of exchange and a public necessity, the government should own and operate the railroads in the interest of the people. The telegraph, telephone, like the post-office system, being a necessity for the transmission of news, should be owned and operated by the government in the interest of the people.

LAND. — The land, including all the natural sources of wealth, is the heritage of the people, and should not be monopolized for speculative purposes, and alien ownership of land should be prohibited. All land now held by railroads and other corporations in excess of their actual needs, and all lands now owned by aliens should be reclaimed by the government and held for actual settlers only.

Document 5

Source: Jacob Coxey, 1894

Up these steps the lobbyists of trusts and corporations have passed unchallenged on their way to committee rooms, access to which we, the representatives of the toiling wealth-producers, have been denied. We stand here to-day in behalf of millions of toilers whose petitions have been buried in committee rooms, whose prayers have been unresponded to, and whose opportunities for honest, remunerative, productive labor have been taken from them by unjust legislation, which protects idlers, speculators, and gamblers: we come to remind the Congress here assembled of the declaration of a United States Senator, "that for a quarter of a century the rich have been growing richer, the poor poorer, and that by the close of the present century the middle class will have disappeared as the struggle for existence becomes fierce and and relentless."

We have come to the only source which is competent to aid the people in their day of dire distress. We are here to tell our Representatives, who hold their seats by grace of our ballots, that the struggle for existence has become too fierce and relentless. We come and throw up our defenseless hands, and say, help, or we and our loved ones must perish. We are engaged in a bitter and cruel war with the enemies of all mankind — a war with hunger, wretchedness, and despair, and we ask Congress to heed our petitions and issue for the nation's good a sufficient volume of the same kind of money which carried the country through one awful war and saved the life of the nation.

GO ON TO THE NEXT PAGE.

Document 6

Source: Royal Melendy, "The Saloon in Chicago," 1900

In many of these discussions, to which I have listened and in which I have joined, there has been revealed a deeper insight into the real cause of present evils than is often manifested from lecture platforms, but their remedies are wide of the mark, each bringing forward a theory which is the panacea for all social ills. The names of Karl Marx and leaders of political and social thought are often heard here. This is the workingman's school. He is both scholar and teacher. . . . Many as patriotic men as our country produces learn here their lessons in patriotism and brotherhood. Here the masses receive their lessons in civil government, learning less of our ideals, but more of the practical workings than the public schools teach. It is the most cosmopolitan institution in the most cosmopolitan of cities. One saloon advertises its cosmopolitanism by this title, "Everybody's Exchange." Men of all nationalities meet and mingle, and by the interchange of views and opinions their own are modified. Nothing short of travel could exert so broadening an influence upon these men. It does much to assimilate the heterogeneous crowds that are constantly pouring into our city from foreign shores. But here, too, they learn their lessons in corruption and vice. It is their school for good and evil.

Document 7

Source: Jane Addams, *Twenty Years at Hull House,* 1912

Halsted Street is thirty-two miles long, and one of the great thoroughfares of Chicago. . . . Between Halsted Street and the river live about ten thousand Italians—Neapolitans, Sicilians, and Calabrians, with an occasional Lombard or Venetian. To the south on Twelfth Street are many Germans, and side streets are given over almost entirely to Polish and Russian Jews. Still farther south, these Jewish colonies merge into a huge Bohemian colony, so vast that Chicago ranks as the third Bohemian city in the world. To the northwest are many Canadian-French, clannish in spite of their long residence in America, and to the north are Irish and first-generation Americans. . . .

The policy of the public authorities of never taking an initiative, and always waiting to be urged to do their duty, is obviously fatal in a neighborhood where there is little initiative among the citizens. The idea underlying our self-government breaks down in such a ward. The streets are inexpressibly dirty, the number of schools inadequate, sanitary legislation unenforced, the street lighting bad, the paving miserable and altogether lacking in the alleys and smaller streets, and the stables foul beyond description. Hundreds of houses are unconnected with the street sewer.

END OF DOCUMENT-BASED SECTION

Answer Key to Period 6 Practice Questions

Multiple-Choice Questions

1.

Answer	Learning Objectives	Historical Thinking Skills	Key Concepts in the Curriculum Framework
A	MIG-2.0	Causation Analyzing Evidence: Content and Sourcing	6.2

Explanation: Expansion of railroads westward led to increased settlement and encroachment on American Indian lands. Beyond that, the railroads brought adventurers who decimated the buffalo herds that many tribes depended on for survival. As settlement extended westward, government policy sought to confine American Indians to small, scattered reservations.

2.

Answer	Learning Objectives	Historical Thinking Skills	Key Concepts in the Curriculum Framework
C	MIG-2.0	Causation Analyzing Evidence: Content and Sourcing	6.2

Explanation: Land grants to railroads by the federal, state, and local governments left railroads with a great asset. To maximize its potential, railroad companies advertised heavily in Europe to bring land-hungry immigrants to the United States. The vastness of the land grants meant that they could offer the land at affordable prices. Advertisements frequently misrepresented the climate and fertility of the land.

3.

Answer	Learning Objectives	Historical Thinking Skills	Key Concepts in the Curriculum Framework
D	WXT-3.0	Causation	6.1

Explanation: Prior to the completion of the Panama Canal in 1914, U.S. trade between the industrial Northeast and the Far East required passage around Cape Horn, the southern tip of South America. The completion of the transcontinental railroad allowed businesses to be competitive in the Far East market by significantly reducing travel time.

4.

Answer	Learning Objectives	Historical Thinking Skills	Key Concepts in the Curriculum Framework
D	NAT-2.0	Causation Analyzing Evidence: Content and Sourcing	6.3

Explanation: *Plessy v. Ferguson* ruled that separate but equal facilities were constitutional and did not violate the equal protection clause of the Fourteenth Amendment. This allowed state and local governments to enact Jim Crow laws that created a segregated society and left African Americans as second-class citizens. The formation of the National Association for the Advancement of Colored People in the early twentieth century initiated a long series of legal challenges to the system.

5.

Answer	Learning Objectives	Historical Thinking Skills	Key Concepts in the Curriculum Framework
B	WXT-1.0	Periodization	6.1

Explanation: Prior to 1900, although many African Americans hoped to leave the South to take advantage of homesteads or for jobs in industrial cities, it was beyond the means of most African Americans to do so. Thus, the majority of southern African Americans found themselves as sharecroppers or tenant farmers. Very few emigrated to Africa.

6.

Answer	Learning Objectives	Historical Thinking Skills	Key Concepts in the Curriculum Framework
D	POL-2.0	Periodization	6.3

Explanation: Booker T. Washington outlined his proposal for gradual accommodation of African Americans into American society as equals in his Atlanta Compromise speech. Washington advocated vocational instruction so that African Americans could gain social mobility through the accumulation of wealth, eventually resulting in full rights as equal citizens.

7.

Answer	Learning Objectives	Historical Thinking Skills	Key Concepts in the Curriculum Framework
D	WXT-2.0	Analyzing Evidence: Content and Sourcing	6.1

Explanation: Carnegie believed in vertical integration—owning all of the materials needed to make a finished product. In this way, middleman profit margins could be reduced, allowing Carnegie to sell steel at very low prices and capture a larger market share. Horizontal integration—owning all of the outlets of a finished product—was more associated with Rockefeller.

8.

Answer	Learning Objectives	Historical Thinking Skills	Key Concepts in the Curriculum Framework
B	WXT-2.0	Causation Analyzing Evidence: Content and Sourcing	6.1

Explanation: Transportation improvements, plentiful natural resources made more accessible by railroad, and an increased immigrant labor force willing to work for low wages all aided in the growth of big business. Despite professing to act in a laissez-faire manner, the federal government took a clearly probusiness attitude through land grants and subsidies, a high protective tariff, and a willingness to intervene in labor disputes on the side of big business.

9.

Answer	Learning Objectives	Historical Thinking Skills	Key Concepts in the Curriculum Framework
C	WXT-2.0	Contextualization Analyzing Evidence: Content and Sourcing	6.1

Explanation: The trust became the business model because it provided the possibility of raising greater capital and limiting liability. Competition was viewed, particularly by John D. Rockefeller, as a deterrent to efficiency because it directed focus away from improving quality and lowering prices. Particularly after the Panic of 1893, business leaders sought an increased overseas presence to protect themselves from domestic saturation.

10.

Answer	Learning Objectives	Historical Thinking Skills	Key Concepts in the Curriculum Framework
D	MIG-2.0	Periodization Analyzing Evidence: Content and Sourcing	6.2

Explanation: A majority of European immigrants entered the United States through ports in the Northeast. Generally they came with limited means, which meant they needed to seek employment quickly. Those opportunities were most plentiful in the major industrial cities of the Northeast and Midwest.

11.

Answer	Learning Objectives	Historical Thinking Skills	Key Concepts in the Curriculum Framework
D	NAT-4.0	Contextualization	6.2

Explanation: The advent of the electric streetcar allowed wealthier individuals to separate themselves from the downtown bustle and move to the periphery. Immigrants tended to cluster near the center city in ethnic enclaves. Because Southern and Eastern European immigrants faced major cultural and social barriers to assimilation, ghettos provided a safe haven. By the same token, living in these enclaves tended to delay their assimilation into American society.

12.

Answer	Learning Objectives	Historical Thinking Skills	Key Concepts in the Curriculum Framework
A	NAT-4.0	Causation	6.2

Explanation: Increased nativist sentiment came as result of an influx of immigrants after 1890. There were calls for literacy tests (adopted in 1917), and immigration restriction from groups like the American Protective Association and the Immigration Restriction League. Many in these group believed that unchecked immigration would result in the "mongrelization of the American race."

Short-Answer Questions

1.

Learning Objectives	Historical Thinking Skills	Key Concepts in the Curriculum Framework
POL-2.0 WXT-2.0	Contextualization	6.1 6.3

What a good response might include

a) A good answer would place the political support for William Jennings Bryan in the late nineteenth century. Examples of groups that might have supported Bryan include the following:
   ✦ Farmers, the laboring classes, and those who did not identify with big business or corporate leaders.
   ✦ Those in both the Democratic Party and the Populist Party who supported the concept of "free silver," silver coins minted at a ratio of 16-to-1 to gold coins.

b) A good answer would place political opposition to Bryan in the late nineteenth century. Examples of groups that might have opposed Bryan include the following:
   ✦ Republicans, who drew much support from industrialists and businessmen. Included in this group was Republic presidential candidate William McKinley, who won the 1896 presidential election over Bryan.
   ✦ Business leaders and others who opposed the idea of "free silver" and thought it would lead to inflation and a weaker economy.
   ✦ Those who called themselves "gold bugs" and wore tiny golden insects on their lapels as a demonstration of their conviction that gold currency was the only way for the currency to be structured.

c) A good answer might include the following:
   ✦ The Populists were among the first groups to call for silver currency, making it part of their platform in 1892. Populists had also called for the 16-to-1 ratio of silver coins mints in relationship to gold coins.
   ✦ Whatever the position of the Democrats that the Populists opposed, they were more in line with the views of the Democrats in 1896 than with the Republicans who supported—and were supported by—big corporations and business leaders.

2.

Learning Objectives	Historical Thinking Skills	Key Concepts in the Curriculum Framework
NAT-2.0	Analyzing Evidence: Content and Sourcing Contextualization	6.3

What a good response might include

a)   A good answer will explain the context in which the Civil Service Reform Bill was passed in 1883. Examples could include the following:

- ✦ The Civil Service Reform Bill, also known as the Pendleton Act, was signed into law in 1883 shortly after the assassination of President James Garfield by a man who felt he had been slighted in his quest for a federal job because of the old spoils system, which rewarded political supporters with federal jobs with the change of each new administration.
- ✦ Even before the assassination of President Garfield, reform groups had emerged that sought to stem the tide of political corruption as exemplified in the spoils system. The act created a list of government jobs to be filled on the basis of examinations administered by the new Civil Service Commission. While the original list covered only about 10 percent of all federal jobs, it was the first step in the direction of a more professional cadre of government workers.

b)   A good answer would include the following:

- ✦ The Civil Service Reform Bill was designed to replace the old patronage system, or spoils system, which left the appointment of people to fill vacant government positions primarily up to the president and those who advised him.
- ✦ Many jobs went to those who were owed political favors rather than people who were actually qualified to do the work required. The hope was that many government abuses of power would be eliminated by having qualified people in those positions rather than simply those who had supported a particular candidate.

c)   There are numerous examples of corruption in the Gilded Age that could be used as examples of misdeeds that civil service reform might have prevented. Some examples include the following:

- ✦ The Whiskey Ring scandal involved President Ulysses Grant's personal secretary, who defrauded the government of millions of dollars of excise tax on whiskey.
- ✦ Crédit Mobilier was a sham railroad corporation set up by Union Pacific Railroad to secure huge government grants and then protect the scam by paying off members of Congress.
- ✦ The Star Route Frauds involved the collection of payments for delivering federal mail to routes that had been long abandoned.

Document-Based Question

Learning Objectives	Historical Thinking Skills	Key Concepts in the Curriculum Framework
WXT-1.0 POL-2.0	Patterns of Continuity and Change over Time Comparison Contextualization Argumentation Synthesis	6.1 6.2 6.3

What a good response might include

Before you begin, determine exactly what the question is asking you to do. First, you must determine what is meant here by the word *analyze*. You should not merely list some of the ways in which laboring-class (or working-class) Americans attempted to better their lives. Instead, try to clearly link each cause to an effect. Analysis here also requires that you put the various ways in which working Americans tried to better their lives in the context of the power of big business and the federal government. That is, you must establish exactly what forces laboring Americans were up against.

The thesis must not simply restate the question. It should emphasize the historical thinking skills of **patterns of continuity and change over time** and **contextualization**. The thesis would emphasize the actions taken by specific groups of Americans and evaluate if and how their situations changed as a result of their actions. Their actions should be placed within the context of the Gilded Age and should emphasize the positions and policies of both big business and government.

In order to earn the maximum of 3 points for document use, in this case you must analyze *all* or *all but one* of the documents (that is, at least six in this DBQ) and address how these documents provide evidence of the causes of expansion. Do not forget the requirement to address one of these points for each document you use: audience, purpose, historical context, or point of view. If you are not certain how to do this, ask your teacher to show you some examples. You cannot merely name the intended audience or simply state the speaker's point of view. Instead, you must link this discussion to the directive at hand: to analyze the ways in which laboring-class Americans in the Gilded Age (1865–1900) attempted to better their lives in the face of the power of big business and the federal government and to evaluate how successful they were in their efforts.

Before you even begin writing—and remember to make good use of the 15-minute planning period that you are given—make a list of relevant information that you know about this period, for example, the time period covered in this DBQ. You are required to demonstrate understanding of the context in which laboring Americans lived and worked and explain why they felt the need to change their circumstances. Never merely summarize a document. Weave the documents and other knowledge that you have into your essay; both documents and this outside information serve as evidence to buttress the argument you make in your thesis.

Strong essays will link similar documents together to make a convincing argument. Documents 1 and 4, for example, address the concerns of farms and agricultural workers. Documents 2, 3, and 5 all address the situation of urban working people. A strong essay might also identify Document 7 as being in a separate category, as it deals with the efforts of urban middle- and upper-class women to bring about needed reforms in their own communities and through their influence with legislators. A strong essay might also use Document 6, a description of saloon culture in immigrant neighborhoods, as an example of an informal solution found by workers from diverse backgrounds for a social center of their own, a place where they were free to mingle and discuss their political and social concerns. While most of these groups achieved only limited success in the short run, their efforts set the stage for continuing reforms efforts during the Progressive Era.

As you study the documents, think about your outside knowledge and how it relates to each document. The image "Gift for the Grangers" (Document 1) celebrates the Granger movement, a farmers' group that led to the farmers' alliances that were briefly successful in challenging the railroad monopolies over high shipping rates and unfair pricing. The image represents the positive American ideal, the independent pioneer farmer.

"The Eight Hour Day" (Document 2) appearing in the *Boston Daily Voice*, a workingman's journal in the 1880s, was a rallying cry for workers demanding the eight-hour workday. The point of view reflects the sentiments of organized labor. The 1880s saw brief success for the Knights of Labor; the American Federation of Labor, which represented only skilled trades, had more than 2 million members by 1904.

The Haymarket incident depicted in Document 3 was the result of anarchist activism in Chicago in May 1886. Although the Knights of Labor, led by Terence Powderly, was not directly involved in the incident, the public perception was that they were. The labor movement, in particular the Knights of Labor, suffered a devastating setback because of the incident.

The Populist movement, whose platform is excerpted in Document 4, was a largely rural movement that sought to wrest control of the railroads from the hands of big business. The movement flourished for a time in the 1890s, and activists during the Progressive era advanced many of its ideas.

Jacob Coxey (Document 5) led a march on Washington, D.C., of unemployed men, many of them military veterans, hoping to get some financial relief from the federal government. He argued that ordinary people had no access to government and were affected by unfair laws. Coxey's point of view is one of sympathy with those who are out of work as he was facing the same circumstances. He was unsuccessful because most in government did not feel that relief programs were federal responsibility.

Reverend Royal Melendy's essay on saloon culture in Chicago (Document 6) describes a neighborhood saloon as an example of immigrants creating their own social centers, "a poor man's social club," a place to discuss political and social problems, a refuge from impoverished homes; he sees the saloon as a community institution rather than simply a bar, an essential part of the working-class social structure. His point of view, that these poorer classes can make their own institutions in spite of their difficulties, is somewhat optimistic and admiring.

Jane Addams, writing about her experiences during twenty years of work with Hull House (Document 7), speaks of Chicago as a city of immigrants who found themselves in rundown neighborhoods with few city services and no political voice when she organized the settlement house in 1889. She writes with sympathy for the people she served and a sense of obligation on the part of the better-off to help the poor. She speaks positively about urban reform. She had the benefit of financial backing and a position of influence in society to help her cause.

As you think about constructing this essay, think about how the documents link to each other. For example, Documents 1 and 4 express a point of view emanating from rural America, while Documents 2, 3, 6, and 7 come from an urban perspective. Document 5 bridges the two, in that while Coxey led a group of mostly urban men, his "army" gained a large rural following as well. There are other ways that documents might "speak" to each other and oppose each other. For example, by the 1890s, there was a growing movement against the use of alcohol and against saloon culture. Thus, while Melendy's perspective in Document 6 is mostly positive about saloon culture, many Americans, especially rural Americans, would not have agreed.

Do not refer to the documents as "Document 1" or "Document 6." Instead, refer to the type of document (painting, address to Congress . . .), its context, and reference the author, the title of the work, and his purpose audience, or point of view. Be certain to link the document to your thesis. One of the worst errors you can make is to do what is called "laundry listing" the documents.

When you finish writing, look over your essay. Be certain that you have included all of the required elements. If you do not already have a copy of a generic rubric, ask your teacher to give you one so you will be absolutely certain that you understand what the person who scores your essay is looking for. The rubric is a sort of map for your essay. Remember that if you go on a journey without a map, you might never know when you arrive at your destination. So commit that rubric to memory and pay attention to your destination and what it takes to get there.

PERIOD 7
1890–1945

Overview

Between 1890 and 1945, the United States became an international power, while at home issues surrounding industrialization, urbanization, and the demands of an increasingly diverse society came to the fore. As the U.S. economy became more dependent on large corporations and the production of consumer goods, people increasingly moved from rural areas to urban centers where jobs were available. Although these new jobs offered opportunities to many who had been underemployed, cycles of boom and bust created periodic instability. The Great Depression was the most dramatic of these economic downturns, leading to calls for more regulation of the national economy.

Progressive reformers began to call for government intervention in the economy to relieve the suffering of the urban working classes, who faced the greatest hardships. These reformers, often urban middle-class women, targeted reform of both social and political institutions. Another groups worked in the area of conservation of natural resources. National, state, and local leaders responded to this call for reform, particularly after the trauma of the Great Depression, and the result was the transformation of the government into a limited welfare state.

Franklin Roosevelt's New Deal built on many of the ideas of earlier Progressive reformers and created government programs to aid the poor and reshape the American economy. Roosevelt faced conservative opposition in Congress and from the Supreme Court, yet he was able to introduce reforms that made many feel more secure. His programs were identified with the Democratic Party and led a number of racial and ethnic groups to switch loyalties from the Republicans.

The years from 1890 to 1945 saw the introduction of many new forms of technology and communication. Although these advances helped many improve their standard of living, others felt their traditional ways of life were being threatened. These years were a time of traumatic change for many, with economic instability, world wars, and the stresses associated with migration. Conflicts emerged on a number of fronts: social, political, economic, and religious.

The xenophobia caused by World War I led the United States to enact a series of restrictive immigration laws in the 1920s. Fears of the spread of socialism and communism also inspired Congress to pass laws restricting citizens' civil liberties, all in the name of national security. A rash of labor strikes fed the fear of a "Red Scare," (called this because red was associated with the new Soviet Union), leading to even stricter overseas immigration controls. The nation opened borders within the Western Hemisphere, however, to allow in a steady supply of cheap labor. Although Mexicans were welcomed in the 1920s, they faced uncertain futures as migrant workers in the 1930s and 1940s.

African Americans also began to move out of the South in significant numbers to urban centers in the North, Midwest, and West Coast, seeking jobs and an escape from Jim Crow. This "Great Migration" had an impact throughout the country, particularly in New York City in the form of the Harlem Renaissance, a rich contribution to the national culture.

At the beginning of this time period, the United States took its first steps into the international arena. There was much disagreement within the United States as to whether such a move was in keeping with America's traditional position as a defender of the colonized. The War of 1898, or the Spanish-American War, left the country with island territories as well as military and economic interests to defend in the Caribbean and the Pacific. Debates over whether the United States should rightly be an imperialist power would continue for the rest of this century and beyond, although clearly the country was now an international presence.

World War I effectively ended the United States's long-term position as a neutral and isolated power, though debates over the U.S. role in international affairs continued in the 1920s and 1930s. The American Expeditionary Force entered in the last years of the war, which allowed Woodrow Wilson to play a role at the postwar negotiations at Versailles. The resulting Treaty of Versailles and Wilson's League of Nations proved unpopular in the United States, and the country spent the next two decades trying to follow a unilateral foreign policy and retreat back into isolationism, an ultimately unsuccessful effort.

The attack on Pearl Harbor in 1941 ended U.S. isolationism overnight and launched the country into World War II and a position of international political and military prominence that would not change with the end of the war. The mass mobilization required for the war effort effectively ended what was left of the Great Depression. Women and minorities benefitted from these jobs as well. American values came under scrutiny during the course of the war with the Japanese internment, the ongoing civil rights struggle, and the moral and ethical questions surrounding the decision to use atomic weapons on Japan. The United States and the Allies defeated the Axis powers through their combined military, economic, and technological strength. The United States emerged from World War II as the most powerful nation on earth.

Key Terms

Be sure that you understand the meaning of these terms and their relevance in U.S. history.

American exceptionalism
Appeasement
Belligerents
Chauvinism
Feminism
Fundamentalism
Cronyism
Culture wars
Dollar diplomacy
Economic collectivism
Fascism
General strike
Imperial presidency
Industrial unionism
Internal migration
Internationalism
Isolationism
Keynesian economics

Laissez-faire
Liberalism
Classical liberalism
Regulatory liberalism
Social welfare liberalism
Muckrakers
Pan-Africanism
Popular culture and high culture
Populism
Progressivism
Red Scare
Self-determination
Social settlements
Victorian morality
Welfare state
Welfare capitalism
Yellow journalism
Xenophobia

Questions to Consider

As you study Period 7, keep the following thematic questions in mind.

American and National Identity

1890–1917

+ What accounted for increased ethnic and racial tensions in American cities in the early years of the twentieth century?
+ What arguments were voiced by both black and white leaders about the rights and the roles of African Americans in the years leading to World War I?
+ Why and how did the relationships between men and women change between 1890 and 1920?
+ Why were women often in the forefront of Progressive reforms?
+ Why did gay subcultures emerge in American cities in the early twentieth century?

1917–1929

+ How was the United States able to mobilize for war so quickly?
+ What contributions did African Americans, Native Americans, and women make to the war effort?
+ How did World War I influence the debates over the role of women in the decade after this war?
+ Shortly after World War I ended, a journalist said, "The World War has accentuated all our differences." In what ways was this true in postwar America?

1929–1945

+ How did the depression exacerbate the struggles that Mexican Americans and Native Americans confronted?
+ Despite the fact that women and minorities gained relatively little from New Deal programs, many women and African Americans became part of the Roosevelt coalition. Why did this happen?
+ Wartime work for women "combined new opportunities with old constraints." What new opportunities did the war bring for women, and in what ways were they still constrained?
+ How did World War II influence debates about race and ethnicity during and after the war?

Work, Exchange, and Technology

1890–1917

+ Why was the coinage issue so controversial in the years leading to the twentieth century and even beyond, into the 1930s?
+ How were class differences reflected in the use of new technologies in the years prior to World War I?
+ What were the milestones in the struggle between American corporations and American workers in the years before World War I?
+ What role did Progressive presidents play in reforming the American economic system?
+ Progressive reforms that protected workers often turned out to be a double-edged sword. Why?

✦ In what ways was the Triangle Shirtwaist Company fire a watershed event in American history?

✦ What were the successes and failures of the American labor movement in the years prior to World War I? Account for these.

1917–1929

✦ Why was the automobile such a significant technological development?

✦ What were the most important characteristics of the consumer culture that emerged in the 1920s? Account for the emergence of consumerism in the 1920s, and explain how it differed from the consumer culture of the late nineteenth century.

1929–1945

✦ How did urban workers and farmers respond to the challenges they faced after the collapse of the stock market in 1929?

✦ How did economic forces affect the American political landscape in the years between the two world wars?

✦ What steps did Franklin Roosevelt's administration take to improve the American economy and the lives of workers?

✦ How did the American workplace change when the United States went to war in 1941?

✦ What impact did the development of the atomic bomb by the United States have on the American economy and on American culture in the decades following World War II?

Migration and Settlement

✦ As cities grew in the late nineteenth and early twentieth centuries, what new forms of amusement appeared? What functions did these new activities serve?

✦ What efforts were made to help the poor as they became increasingly visible in American cities?

✦ What demographic changes occurred in the United States as a result of American entry into each of the world wars? How did these demographic shifts affect the economic, political, and social fabric of the nation?

Politics and Power

1890–1917

✦ What did the Populists demand of government, and how responsive was government to the needs of rural Americans?

✦ Why was it that the Populists garnered so much support in the 1890s only to fade from the national political landscape a decade later?

✦ In what ways did the Populist movement of the late nineteenth century pave the way for the Progressive Era of the early twentieth century?

✦ What new challenges did American cities face at the turn of the century, and how did government address these problems?

✦ Many scholars argue that progressivism was largely a middle-class movement. Do you agree with this assessment? Why or why not?

✦ Government intervention was not the only approach used to combat the problems facing urban America. How successful were private individuals and organizations in effecting change in American cities?

- ✦ Your text argues that a major shift in Republican policy occurred when Theodore Roosevelt was in the White House. To what degree were Roosevelt's policies a major departure from those of his nineteenth-century Gilded Age predecessors?
- ✦ In what ways were the policies and actions of Theodore Roosevelt and Woodrow Wilson similar? Which president better deserves to be called "progressive"?
- ✦ Despite restrictions on the voting rights of blacks and immigrants, government actions in the early twentieth century gave more power to some voters. What changes strengthened democracy in the years prior to World War I?

1917–1929

- ✦ What were the most persuasive arguments in support of and in opposition to women's suffrage?
- ✦ What arguments were made in support of limited government in the 1920s? What specific government actions supported limited government, and which increased the scope of government?
- ✦ In what ways were the presidencies of Harding, Coolidge, and Hoover different from those of Roosevelt, Taft, and Wilson? Account for the changes that occurred in the role of the presidency in the years from 1900 to 1929.
- ✦ How did the United States justify limitations placed on individual liberty during World War I?
- ✦ Why did so many Americans oppose President Wilson's plans for the postwar world?

1929–1945

- ✦ What does your textbook present as the two competing visions of government? Compare these visions, and analyze how the battle between them shaped American politics from the 1930s to the present.
- ✦ What personal beliefs were at the heart of Herbert Hoover's response to the Great Depression? Why was his response to the problems confronting the nation considered inadequate?
- ✦ In what ways did the depression and the New Deal alter the structure and power of the federal government?
- ✦ What groups joined the Roosevelt coalition, and why did they feel that their interests were served by the Roosevelt presidency?
- ✦ What new challenges to his leadership did Roosevelt face in his second administration? How did he confront these challenges?
- ✦ How effectively did Franklin Roosevelt and Congress address the crises brought about by the Great Depression?
- ✦ In what ways did the Great Depression and New Deal contribute to a realignment of American political parties?
- ✦ What were the characteristics of the American welfare state that was established during the 1930s, and why was this development so significant?

America in the World

1890–1917

- ✦ What caused Americans to embrace imperialism in the late nineteenth century, only to reject it in the early twentieth century and into the 1930s?
- ✦ Why did the United States go to war against Spain in 1898?

✦ How wise do you think it was for the United States to intervene in Cuba and the Philippines?
✦ How did Theodore Roosevelt's foreign policy reflect the assertion of masculinity that was so prevalent in American culture?
✦ We often think of American intervention in other nations to be primarily military in nature. In what other ways did the United States involve itself in the political and economic life of other countries, especially in the Western Hemisphere, in the years before World War I?

1917–1929

✦ How was President Wilson able to reconcile his idealism with his decision to take the United States into war in 1917?
✦ To what extent were Wilson's Fourteen Points both idealistic and a reflection of global political and economic realities?
✦ How was the United States able to quickly mobilize for war in the years just prior to 1917 and 1941?
✦ In what ways did World War I set the stage for the outbreak of war only two decades later, in 1939?

1929–1939

✦ Despite the growing threat of fascism, why were so many Americans opposed to intervention in Europe? How did President Roosevelt overcome that opposition?
✦ What wartime strategies were most effective in achieving victory for the United States and its allies?
✦ In what ways was World War II also fought on the home front?
✦ In what ways were both World War I and World War II turning points in American history?
✦ In what ways did World War II hasten "profound social change" and expand the scope and authority of the federal government?
✦ Despite having other options, why did Harry Truman opt to use the atomic bomb on Hiroshima and Nagasaki?
✦ How did actions taken during World War II lay the groundwork for the Cold War?

Geography and the Environment

✦ How did urban reforms change the landscape of American cities in the years prior to World War I?
✦ What milestones in the environmental movement were due to the actions of Progressives?
✦ What environmental and geographic features contributed to the demographic changes of the World War II years?

Culture and Society

1890–1917

✦ In the late nineteenth and early twentieth centuries, America was becoming "modern." What did it mean to become modern, and in what ways did science, religion, literature, art, consumerism, popular culture, and feminism embrace modernity?

✦ How were the tensions between science and faith manifested in this period, and how did Americans attempt to reconcile "fact worship" and traditional religious beliefs

✦ How did the realist and naturalist writers at the turn of the century portray life in America? What accounts for this change in focus from previous literary portrayals of America?

✦ How did the new music of the turn of the century, ragtime and blues, both reflect and shape American culture?

✦ What is the difference between popular culture and high culture, and how did urban life in the early twentieth century reflect these differences?

✦ How did the emergence of mass culture affect the delivery of the news to Americans in the late nineteenth and early twentieth centuries?

✦ How do you define *progressivism*, and why were Progressives such an important force in the early twentieth century?

1917–1929

✦ What were the battlefields of the "culture wars" of the 1920s? How were these conflicts fought, and to what extent were they resolved?

✦ The conflicts of the 1920s can also be viewed through the lens of the tension between tradition and change. What caused this tension, and what were some examples?

✦ What accounted for the burst of creativity we call the Harlem Renaissance?

✦ What are some examples of the ways that critics of modern society in the 1920s challenged the prevailing views of war, technology, corporate power, and conformity?

1929–1945

✦ In what ways did New Deal programs facilitate "art for the millions"?

✦ How did beliefs held by many Americans before and during World War II influence policies toward Jews in Europe and Japanese Americans in the United States?

America's History Chapter Summaries

(required AP® content in bold)

Chapter 20
Whose Government? Politics, Populists, and Progressives, 1880–1917

From the end of the Civil War to the beginning of World War I, reformers in the United States concentrated on four areas: cleaning up political corruption, limiting the power of big business, reducing poverty, and working for social justice. **These years were known as the Progressive Era, and there were many reformers and reform agendas.**

The decades immediately after Reconstruction, known as the **Gilded Age, were years of political corruption and enormous industrial profits, while underlying it all were rising poverty, environmental pollution, and little attention paid to workers' rights**. A few reforms managed to win congressional approval: the Pendleton Act, which established the Civil Service Commission; the Interstate Commerce Act, which created the Interstate Commerce Commission; and the Sherman Antitrust Act, which was designed to identify and restrict monopolies. All of these pieces of legislation looked good on the surface but in fact lacked any enforcement power.

Frustration with the government to initiate any real reform led to the creation of the Populist Party, an attempt by farmers to force monetary and political reform. Their Omaha Platform in 1892 spelled out an agenda for regulation of monopolies, rate setting for railroads, more popular participation in choosing members of Congress, and currency based on silver rather than gold. The economic depression of 1893 led to the formation of Coxey's Army, hundreds of unemployed men who marched on Washington demanding government action to create jobs and provide relief. Republicans managed to retain power in the upcoming elections, but the problems facing the nation were not solved. The South was a stronghold for the Democrats, although they did not support the Populists because southerners felt that party did not support segregation and Jim Crow. The "Solid South" would remain until well into the next century.

Nationally the Democrats tried to make some gains from the Populists' positions and chose William Jennings Bryan as their presidential candidate in 1896. His positions mirrored many of those held by the Populists, including a call for bimetalism, or the use of silver coins as well as gold. The Democrats were not able to muster the votes to deny William McKinley, a Republican, the presidency, and over the next few years, the Populists began to fade from the political scene.

The Supreme Court was also a bastion of conservatism and generally hostile to attempts at political reform. The Court rejected attempts to limit workers' hours, **approved "separate but equal" facilities and schools for blacks and whites**, and endorsed monopolies. President McKinley was no friend of reform either, but his life was cut short by an assassin's bullet in 1901. Teddy Roosevelt proved to be a very different kind of president. Roosevelt was a supporter of private enterprise and big business, but he made a distinction between those who operated with the public good in mind and those who did not. He decided cases on their merits rather than simply siding with management. His administration supported the first trust-busting cases in the courts, and he signed the Hepburn Act into law, putting teeth into the Interstate Commerce Commission. He was also a **supporter of conservation, working with John Muir and Gifford Pinchot to identify potential national forest and parkland and creating irrigation projects that changed the face of the American West**. His successor, William Howard Taft, had neither Roosevelt's energy nor his devotion to reform, so he spent his one term in office trying to balance Roosevelt's expectations with his own less determined approach to progressive reform.

Many of the Populist ideals finally became law during the Progressive Era: initiative, recall, and referendum are a few. Changes in the Supreme Court led to decisions favoring limits to working hours, though only for women. Men did benefit from workmen's compensation laws. Little progress was made in the area of child labor, however.

The roots of the modern civil rights movement lay in the Progressive Era. African Americans found themselves divided by the pragmatic, industrial education approach of Booker T. Washington and the call for immediate equality and access to higher education coming from W. E. B. Du Bois. Du Bois would be a member of the Niagara Movement, a gathering that led to the creation of the National Association for the Advancement of Colored People (NAACP), which called for a more activist approach to make the promises of the Fourteenth and Fifteenth amendments a reality for African Americans.

Labor movements were still dominated by the American Federation of Labor, though this group was challenged by the new Industrial Workers of the World, a Marxist group that urged more strikes and activism on the part of workers.

The presidential election of 1912 saw the Republicans self-destruct with wrangling between their nominee, Taft, and Teddy Roosevelt, who launched a third-party "Bull Moose" candidacy. There was yet another candidate, Eugene V. Debs, who ran as a Socialist from a prison cell in Atlanta, Georgia, and polled almost 1 million votes. The Republican squabbles paved the way for the Democratic candidate, Woodrow Wilson, to come into office advocating his own brand of progressivism that he called the "New Nationalism." Wilson had the support of labor and farmers, but he did not draw many votes from African Americans. It would be during his term of office that the Great Migration of African Americans out of the South for urban areas in the North, Midwest, and West Coast began in earnest. Progressive promises had failed to make life under Jim Crow much easier, and millions decided to look for better opportunities on their own.

Wilson did initiate a number of landmark economic reforms. The progressive income tax became part of the Constitution with the Federal Reserve Act. The Federal Reserve System was organized. Monopolies were further regulated by the Clayton Antitrust Act in 1914. Wilson did not offer much to the African American community, and even went so far as to offer praise for the movie *Birth of a Nation*, which had a heroic depiction of the Ku Klux Klan.

While progressivism did not accomplish everything its reformers hoped to, there were tremendous economic and administrative improvements. Monopolies were brought under some control, women began to have more of a presence in public life, environmental gains were made with the creation of national parks and forests, conservation efforts were successful, and the lives of millions in the country's growing cities were made more comfortable. All of these reforms would be expanded in the coming decades.

Chapter 21
An Emerging World Power, 1890–1918

Chapter 21 explores the emergence of the United States as a world power and as a participant in world imperialism. The United States had long claimed to be uninterested in overseas expansion, even as the country expanded across the continent with little regard for the American Indians and other inhabitants who were already there. Earlier presidential administrations had seen access to global markets as a key to power, and **now expansionists added the concept of "American exceptionalism" to the argument, the idea that the United States had an obligation to foster democracy and higher civilization around the world**. Social Darwinism further fueled this belief.

Victory in the War of 1898 left the United States with new overseas possessions in both the Caribbean and the Pacific, touching off arguments about how the country should deal with these territories. Some favored independence; **others hoped for annexation or at least military and economic control**. The reelection of President McKinley in 1900 suggested that most of the country was comfortable with overseas acquisitions, though **debates over expansion and annexation would continue in Congress and the Supreme Court for years to come**. The United States also began to play a larger role in international diplomacy, negotiating the Open Door Note concerning China in 1899. Negotiations with Japan over that country's war with Russia further centered the United States on the world stage.

President Theodore Roosevelt also turned his attention to American relations with Latin America, as he thought the time to negotiate a Central American canal had arrived. Through a combination of diplomacy and devious tactics, he was able to secure rights to a canal and set in motion many years of U.S. involvement in Latin American affairs.

When World War I broke out in Europe, the United States hoped to remain neutral, though American businesses hoped to benefit from trade with the warring nations. Unfortunately American shipping and passenger lines came under attack, particularly from German U-boats. The Germans made the claim that anyone who traded with a country involved in the war was, in fact, no longer neutral. **President Woodrow Wilson spent his first term keeping the country out of the war, but soon after his reelection in 1916, a combination of unwarranted attacks on U.S. ships and angry diplomatic communications led him to ask Congress for a declaration of war on Germany and the Central Powers**.

Many Americans eagerly went to war, hoping their efforts would "make the world safe for democracy." General John Pershing led the American Expeditionary Force, which arrived at the Western Front in Europe in early 1918. America sent a multinational force that reflected the country's population, though African Americans served in segregated units. American Indians served in integrated units, but they were often given extremely hazardous jobs as scouts and snipers. American troops missed the misery of that war's prolonged trench warfare, but they still suffered from the war's efficient mechanized slaughter, as well as the great flu pandemic of 1918. Most on the home front supported the war, answering the call to ration, economize, and sacrifice consumer goods for the war effort. Labor unions agreed to postpone strikes, and housewives collected scrap metal and followed government requests to give up certain foods on certain days in order to send more supplies to the troops at the front. The government sought to stifle any criticism of the war effort through the work of the Committee on Public Information, a propaganda agency whose charge was to stir up patriotism. Congress went further, passing the Sedition Act of 1918, which **prohibited anything that would discourage dedication to the government and the war**.

Many African Americans took advantage of wartime jobs opening up in northern and midwestern cities and began to leave the Deep South and its Jim Crow system of segregation. **This movement became known as the Great Migration**, and even though African Americans often encountered discrimination in other parts of the country, most felt they had made progress for themselves and their families. **Mexicans were also encouraged to take vacant jobs, particularly as farmworkers**. Though some found a better chance here, many still faced harsh discrimination.

Women found many wartime job opportunities, working in both the service and industrial sectors of the economy. Though most realized their jobs would evaporate when the war ended and the men returned, they were glad to have the chance to work outside the home, and many felt their contribution might aid the cause of women's suffrage. The National American Women's Suffrage Association (NAWSA) wholeheartedly supported the war effort, volunteering for relief organizations and encouraging women to take industrial jobs. The National Women's Party (NWP), led by Alice Paul, was more confrontational, picketing the White House and demanding that women's efforts for the war should be translated into political equality. Some were arrested and treated badly in prison when they staged hunger strikes. President Wilson, perhaps in response to the publicity these women were generating, announced in January 1918 that he would support women's suffrage as a "war measure." In fewer than two years, the Constitution included the Nineteenth Amendment, guaranteeing women the vote.

The end of the war in Europe brought President Wilson to the peace conference held at the palace of Versailles outside Paris. **He arrived with his idealistic blueprint of the postwar world, the Fourteen Points**, unaware that his partners in peace—Lloyd George of Great Britain, Clemenceau of France, and Orlando of Italy—already had plans for a more punitive treaty. He saw many of his proposals collapse, but he held out for the creation of a League of Nations, an organization he felt would maintain world peace in the future through collective security. The Allies' determination to punish the Germans for the war, and the haphazard way they carved up the Ottoman Empire to satisfy their own imperialist aims, set the stage for the next war that would come in two more decades. **Wilson, however, remained optimistic that his cherished League would provide a way to sort out future conflicts without bloodshed**.

Wilson was disillusioned to find strong congressional opposition to both the treaty and his League when he returned to the United States. Many worried that the United States would be drawn into wars that were not in the country's best interests if they accepted membership in the League of Nations. Others simply did not want to be involved with the rest of the world on any terms other than trade. Wilson rejected all attempts to amend the treaty, and ultimately Congress rejected both the treaty and the League. Wilson suffered a stroke during his tireless campaigns to win the American people over to his plans for the postwar world, and he never fully recovered. The country quickly forgot about European problems as the 1920s ushered in an era of apparent prosperity and exuberant consumerism.

Chapter 22
Cultural Conflict, Bubble, and Bust, 1919–1932

Chapter 22 explores the 1920s and the early years of the Great Depression. The 1920s saw both expanding prosperity and growing cultural divides, as the country juggled the security of traditionalism with the allure and demands of modernism. The so-called Roaring Twenties came to a screeching halt with the onset of the Great Depression in 1929. The work of the earlier Progressives seemed to have evaporated.

Americans emerged from World War I to find a very different world. African Americans were no longer content to live under the Jim Crow system. **Those who left the South during the Great Migration found jobs in other parts of the country** but not the acceptance as equal citizens that they wanted. Race riots occurred in many parts of the country, showing racial prejudice to be a national problem rather than one limited to the South. Labor unions were also criticized for striking for higher pay at the war's end, but they received little sympathy from either the government or the courts. A few companies, including Ford, General Electric, and U.S. Steel, did offer workers' benefits, a form of welfare capitalism, but most workers had no safety net.

Tensions were also increased by the coming of a national "Red Scare," a fear of immigrants who might bring ideas of anarchy or communism (because the Bolsheviks, the leaders of the Russian Revolution, were known as "Reds"). The government authorized the attorney general, A. Mitchell Palmer, to investigate and arrest anyone under suspicion of sedition. The infamous Palmer raids led to the arrest and detainment of many innocent people. Suspicion of foreigners played a role in many arrests, even for offenses that did not pose issues of national security.

Republicans regained control of the White House in the 1920s, in part by arguing that strong businesses would guarantee the nation could remain secure. Women played a greater role in politics beginning in this decade, as they now had the vote and more experience working outside the home. Republican president Warren Harding personified the emphasis on business skills that many felt the country needed. Unfortunately, his proved to be a corrupt and ineffective term of office, and he was replaced at his death by Vice President Calvin Coolidge. Coolidge believed the "the business of America is business," and he supported bills that gave industries a freer hand. Foreign policy also reflected business interests during these years, with "dollar diplomacy" being the slogan of the day. Government policies were expected to support U.S. access to foreign resources and markets, even if they meant occasional military deployments. This policy lost steam with the coming of the Great Depression, as the "dollars" began to dry up.

The 1920s was also a decade of intense culture wars. Prohibition of alcohol was put in place by the Eighteenth Amendment at the end of the war. Organized crime flourished through black market sales of alcohol, while state and federal governments lost tax revenue. Public schools argued over Darwin's theory of evolution, with some feeling that science was launching an attack on Christian beliefs. **The government moved to limit foreign immigration even more with a series of acts designed to reduce the number of immigrants allowed into this country to a tiny fraction of what it had been in the 1890s.** Such measures were supported by nativist groups like the Ku Klux Klan, which saw a resurgence in the 1920s, picking up members throughout the nation rather than just in the South.

New York's Harlem proved to be a magnet for African Americans escaping life in the segregated South. **The flowering of art, music, and literature there in the 1920s became known as the Harlem Renaissance**. The jazz musicians showcased there influenced the development of music throughout the country. Marcus Garvey introduced pan-Africanism to American culture, an idea that would continue to resonate in the mid-twentieth century.

Many American writers took issue with what they saw as the superficiality of life in the United States in the 1920s. Some left for Europe, gaining the name the "Lost Generation." **Others stayed and wrote about what they saw as the narrowness and hypocrisy of small town and rural life**. Still others criticized what they felt was a slavish devotion to pleasure and material wealth.

Although the American economy seemed to be wildly successful in the 1920s, ominous signs were already visible in the agriculture sector. American farmers flooded the world markets with agricultural products, causing prices to drop. Those living in towns and cities, oblivious to the plight of farmers, rushed to buy consumer goods on readily available credit. Automobiles, also available on credit, became common. Movies reinforced longing for the luxurious life, and Hollywood introduced the figure of the "flapper" to young women. The flapper represented sexual and social emancipation, something that worried the older generation.

The party came to an end in October 1929, when the stock market dropped, taking most segments of the American economy with it. Unemployment meant a drop in consumer spending, bank failures, slowing industrial production — in short, tighter times for all and devastation for many. The destitute had to depend on family members and local private charities for what help there was. Those who looked to the federal government for relief found nothing. President Hoover and the Republican government hoped the market would correct itself if given sufficient time, but the American people were not willing to wait, and in 1932 they voted in Franklin D. Roosevelt, a Democrat who seemed to offer hope for a recovery.

Chapter 23
Managing the Great Depression, Forging the New Deal, 1929–1939

Chapter 23 focuses on the attempts of the United States to bring the country out of the Great Depression. In his first inaugural address in March 1933, **President Franklin Roosevelt pledged to ask Congress for the power to make war on the Great Depression**. The New Deal, as it was called, was a program of federal activism unprecedented in American history. FDR's brand of liberalism saw government as the guarantor of economic security for its citizens, something conservatives decried as a dangerous role for "big government." The American depression was part of an economic downturn that affected the entire world. Herbert Hoover had hoped to let it run its course and self-correct. His approach was to urge belt tightening and stick to traditional ways of operating, including continuing to tie the nation's currency to gold even when some European countries chose otherwise. High tariffs hindered international trade, something that might have helped the economy recover. The depression's grip on the United States remained strong, and Hoover became increasingly unpopular. The "Bonus Army" of unemployed veterans marched on Washington in the summer of 1932, demanding some sort of government relief. Fearing an outbreak of disease in their sprawling camp on the National Mall, Hoover had the men evicted using troops and tear gas, actions that proved to be a public relations nightmare. Franklin Roosevelt defeated him easily in the 1932 presidential election.

Roosevelt brought personal charm, political savvy, and willingness to experiment to the White House, all assets Hoover was lacking. He gained the confidence of the nation by holding weekly radio addresses, "fireside chats," which made people feel they were a part of solving the nation's problems. He greatly expanded presidential power, something a Democratic Congress was willing to let him do. His first "Hundred Days" in office saw fifteen sweeping **bills designed to focus on banking failures, farm overproduction, failing businesses, and rampant unemployment**. If he took liberties with the powers of his office, people were willing to accept this in the hope that his programs might turn the economy around. Landmark programs reorganized the banks, placed quotas on farm production while offering government subsidies, regulated private businesses, and provided government jobs. Other programs addressed the needs for housing, the plight of the elderly, and the need for jobs for the nation's youth. Roosevelt also proposed a regulatory agency for the nation's stock market, something designed to rein in the speculation that helped lead to the 1929 crash.

Roosevelt's New Deal was not without its critics. **Some on the right accused him of being a socialist; others accused him of destroying capitalism. Most of the justice on the Supreme Court had been appointed by Republicans in the 1920s, and they overturned several of Roosevelt's landmark programs, ruling them unconstitutional.** He also had critics who thought he had not gone far enough—people who felt the country would be best served by an open redistribution of wealth.

Roosevelt took on all these critics in his run for reelection in 1936, which he won in a landslide, gaining clear majorities in both houses of Congress as well. He launched his "Second New Deal" in an effort to address the both his critics and those who hoped for even more. Labor was pleased with his support of collective bargaining. The elderly poor were guaranteed government assistance when they were no longer able to work. Roosevelt was the creator of what became known as "New Deal Liberalism," the belief that the government should play a role in preserving individual economic well-being through assistance if it was required. This belief differed from "classical liberalism," which looked for individual welfare to come as the result of free-market policies and a weak government. These two different views of the proper role of government are still at play in American politics almost a century later.

Roosevelt's second term saw more employment programs initiated. He also began to attract large numbers of **African American voters, who saw the New Deal programs as offering more to them than traditional Republican policies**. After a brief struggle to realign the Supreme Court, Roosevelt dropped that effort when he realized that time and momentum were on his side as elderly justices began to retire and he could make his own appointments. A brief return of recession in 1937–1938 led Roosevelt to authorize more government spending, a Keynesian approach to economics that seemed to have some effect.

Roosevelt's New Deal not only fundamentally changed the relationship between American citizens and the government; it also encouraged other reforms. A labor union for unskilled as well as skilled workers, the Congress of Industrial Organizations, gained great popularity and took dominance away from the more exclusive AFL. Women played a greater role in public life, inspired by the work of Eleanor Roosevelt. African Americans saw some improvement in their situation, though **segregation and Jim Crow still remained in force in many parts of the country**.

American Indians saw the return of tribal ownership of land when Roosevelt signed the Indian Reorganization Act in 1934, ending many of the restrictions of the hated Dawes Act of 1887. **For Mexican Americans the New Deal was a mix of positive and negative**. Many who came during World War I as agricultural workers were deported. Yet many others were able to find jobs with New Deal agencies. Immigrants from Asia did not fare as well, laboring under exclusionary legislation from earlier years.

Roosevelt also faced enormous environmental issues, primarily the development of the Dust Bowl in the Great Plains. The New Deal developed soil conservation measures, including the planting of millions of trees to act as a continental windbreak through the middle of the country. Most important was the passage of the Tennessee Valley Authority, which established a system of dams and reservoirs throughout the Tennessee River Valley. This program brought erosion control, flood protection, and inexpensive electricity to millions of people in the Southeast. Even writers and artists found work through the New Deal's Federal Writers' project.

Though Roosevelt's New Deal was criticized for doing both too much and too little, no one could deny that his programs fundamentally changed the relationship between citizens and the government.

Chapter 24
The World at War, 1937–1945

Chapter 24 explores the outbreak and course of World War II. This war was truly a world conflict in every sense, involving six continents, killing more than 50 million people, and wounding hundreds of millions more. Much of the world lay in ruins at the war's end, and all were threatened from that point on by the specter of nuclear war. **The war changed not only U.S. history but also global history and relationships**.

When the war began in Asia and Europe, the United States hoped to remain neutral, though it was clear that Roosevelt suspected the country might be drawn in despite a neutral stance. Americans watched the rise of fascism and authoritarianism in Germany, Italy, and Japan with alarm, while congressmen like Gerald Nye worked to remind Americans that Europe's troubles were not their concern. Congress responded with a series of Neutrality Acts in the mid-1930s aimed at putting the world on notice that the United States would not be drawn into their war as had happened in World War I. Other groups felt the United States needed to be involved, particularly during the Spanish Civil War in the late 1930s. Some went to fight against the fascists as volunteers, though the majority of the country was content to leave European disputes alone.

Roosevelt watched with concern as Britain and France failed to appease Hitler's demands for more and more of Europe, but neither Congress nor the American public was ready to become involved. Roosevelt used public speeches as opportunities to remind Americans of what freedom meant here and how those values were threatened by events abroad, but isolationism remained strong. When Britain and France became involved in war with Germany, Roosevelt looked for creative ways to aid the Allied cause, lending ships and supplies when money began to run short. Congress went along, hoping such measures would allow the United States to remain on the sidelines.

Isolationism came to an end with the Japanese attack on the American naval base and airfield at Pearl Harbor in Hawaii. Congress passed the War Powers Act in 1941 that gave Roosevelt unprecedented control over the war effort. The **U.S. economy immediately mobilized for war**, with all needed civilian production directed to supplying troops. Steel mills and shipyards turned to war production, as did many of the country's largest corporations. Tens of millions of Americans joined the armed forces or the war industries workforces, or they became part of the civilian support team. The army still operated on a segregated basis, leading some civil rights groups to call for a "Double V"—victory against the Nazis abroad and racism at home. Roosevelt was able to shape some federal legislation in ways that furthered civil rights, demanding that any company receiving a government contract had to demonstrate fairness in hiring. American Indians served as communications liaisons with troops in both Germany and the Pacific, operating radios while speaking American Indian languages that neither German nor Japanese code breakers were able to understand. **Women served in the military in the war. Though barred from combat, many served in front units as nurses, and some flew transport and re-supply planes. Labor leaders pledged to hold off strikes until the war was won**.

Roosevelt won unprecedented third and fourth terms of office in 1940 and 1944. Voters preferred political continuity while the nation was involved in this world conflict. Families endured rationing, planted "victory gardens," and collected scrap metal. Hollywood produced patriotic films, and people sang patriotic songs. Once again, wartime jobs led to internal migration as people relocated to places where work was available. Racial tensions increased, with attacks on African Americans in Detroit in 1943, and the "zoot suit" riots of Los Angeles aimed at Hispanic teenagers in Los Angeles that same year. Wartime migration gave an unexpected boost to gay and lesbian communities in a number of urban centers, though the military still tried to screen out homosexuals.

Japanese Americans came in for especially harsh treatment during the war. Though many had lived in the United States for generations, **entire communities were forced to relocate to detention centers for the duration of the war because of fears that they might harbor loyalties to Japan**. Many lost everything: they had to abandon their homes and businesses with mortgages and give up pets, belongings, and the treasures of a lifetime. At the end of the war, many found they had no homes to return to, and some tried to seek restitution from the courts. The case of *Korematsu v. United States* was not decided in their favor until 1988, but this restitution represented only a fraction of what was lost.

The alliance of the United States, Great Britain, Free France, and the Soviet Union gradually began to get the upper hand in both Europe and the Pacific. By 1944, the tide had turned in favor of the Allies on both fronts. With the invasion of northern France on D-Day, on June 6, 1944, the Germans began a steady retreat back toward their own borders. With the Russians closing in from the east, Hitler committed suicide in April 1945, and the war in Europe ended one week later. The liberation of Europe also uncovered the German efforts to exterminate Jews, Poles, Slavs, Gypsies, political dissidents, and other "undesirables."

The war in the Pacific took some months longer to win. Island hopping had brought the Allies back to the Philippines and islands close to the Japanese archipelago. Military plans called for an invasion of Japan, an action that might cost up to 1 million lives. President Truman, who became president on Roosevelt's death from a stroke in early January 1945, made the decision to try to force a Japanese surrender by **dropping the newly developed atomic bombs on two Japanese cities**. The bombs were the result of the supersecret Manhattan Project and had been completed only that summer. The first was dropped on Hiroshima in early August 1945 and the second on Nagasaki several days later, resulting in more than 160,000 deaths in the two cities. The Japanese offered surrender on August 10, and the formal papers were signed on September 2, 1945. World War II was at an end, and **the United States emerged as the most powerful nation on earth**.

Thematic Timeline

THEME	REQUIRED CONTENT	SUPPORTING EXAMPLES
AMERICAN AND NATIONAL IDENTITY	**1890–1917** • Migration to and within the United States influenced the formation of racial and ethnic identities and sometimes led to tensions between various groups. • Gender roles and class identity changed in the face of economic, social, and cultural change. • Identity-based political and social movements emerged and were linked to increased activism in pursuit of civil rights. **1917–1929** • The post–World War I "Red Scare" made it more acceptable to attack radicals and immigrants. • Industrialization and urbanization provided new opportunities for women, Americans who moved internally, and immigrants from other nations. **1929–1945** • During the New Deal, African Americans, many ethnic groups, and workers came to identify with the Democratic Party. • American involvement in World War II led to debates about American national identity.	**1890–1917** • National American Woman's Suffrage Association (1890). • National Association Opposed to Woman Suffrage (1911). • "Feminists" call for complete equality for women. • The American Protective Association reflects growing xenophobia. • Immigrant communities promote ethnic identity and cohesion and form mutual aid societies. • In cities, tensions grow between African Americans and whites. • Theodore Roosevelt invites Booker T. Washington to the White House. • W. E. B. Du Bois and other leaders issue the Niagara Principles calling for full rights for African Americans (1905). • National Association for the Advancement of Colored People (NAACP) formed (1909). • Urban League organized (1911). • Imperialism is in part based on the belief that Anglo-Saxons are superior to others. **1917–1929** • Alice Paul forms the National Woman's Party, which is more confrontational in its approach to woman's rights than the NAWSA (1916). • Paul urges Congress to pass an Equal Rights Amendment (1923). • Many American women become active in the international peace movement, creating the International League for Peace and Freedom in 1919. • Actress Clara Bow is the model of the American "flapper," a symbol of the modern woman. • African Americans serve in segregated units during World War I. • After World War I, lynchings of blacks in the South increase, as do tensions between white and blacks in northern and midwestern cities. • White mobs kill dozens and destroy property in Tulsa, Oklahoma (1921). • Marcus Garvey leads the Universal Negro Improvement Association and champions black separatism and pan-Africanism.

THEME	REQUIRED CONTENT	SUPPORTING EXAMPLES
AMERICAN AND NATIONAL IDENTITY (*continued*)		• In the 1920s, nativists view immigration as the cause of moral decline in the United States. • The 1920s witness the resurgence of the Ku Klux Klan. This Klan, urged on by the release of the movie *Birth of a Nation*, adds immigrants, Catholics, and Jews to their list of targets. • In 1924, Congress passes the National Origins Act, severely restricting immigration, especially from Southern and Eastern Europe. • The execution of Nicola Sacco and Bartolomeo Vanzetti illustrates the legacy of ethnic and political tensions left by World War I (1927). • Several western states pass laws restricting the rights of Asian immigrants. **1929–1945** • The coalition of those who identify as Democrats broadens to include organized labor, farmers, white ethnic groups, African Americans, and many in the middle class. • Eleanor Roosevelt works to expand opportunities for women and African Americans, becoming known as the "conscience of the New Deal." • An informal "black cabinet," including Mary McLeod Bethune, advises New Deal agencies, although blacks made limited gains during the 1930s. • The conviction of the Scottsboro Boys demonstrates bias in southern law (1931). • Many black farmers join the Southern Tenant Farmers Union (1934). • The Indian Reorganization Act reverses the Dawes Act and gives tribes more autonomy (1934). • Half a million people of Mexican descent, many of them U.S. citizens, are deported between 1929 and 1937. • Although the Chinese Exclusion Act is repealed in 1943, Asian immigrants continue to face discrimination. • African Americans in the military remain segregated from other groups throughout World War II.

THEME	REQUIRED CONTENT	SUPPORTING EXAMPLES
AMERICAN AND NATIONAL IDENTITY (*continued*)		• Philip Randolph, leader of the Brotherhood of Sleeping Car Porters, plans a march on Washington, D.C., calling for a requirement for defense contractors to hire more black workers. Roosevelt issues Executive Order 8802, prohibiting discrimination in defense industry hiring (1941). • The Congress of Racial Equality is founded by James Farmer (1945). • Navajo "code talkers" play a crucial role in World War II. • During World War II, Mexicans are brought to the United States under the Bracero Program and are exploited. Mexican American civil rights leaders such as Dolores Huerta and Cesar Chavez lead the fight against this labor system. • Racial conflicts increase during the war, including attacks on "zoot-suiters" in Los Angeles. • Executive Order 9066 orders the removal of Japanese Americans on the West Coast to relocation camps. This action is upheld by the Supreme Court.
WORK, EXCHANGE, TECHNOLOGY	**1890–1917** • Rapid industrialization altered existing labor systems and changed American society and the lives of workers. • Large corporations dominated the American economy. • Debates over capitalism, industrialization, and the role of government influenced economic policies. • Economic competition with Europe encouraged support for American overseas expansion. **1917–1929** • New technologies improved the standard of living, increased mobility, and enhanced communications.	**1890–1917** • The National Consumers' League, led by Florence Kelley, advocates protection for workers. • In 1894, Eugene V. Debs leads the American Railway Union in the Pullman strike and in 1901 forms the Socialist Party of America. • Women's Trade Union League founded (1903). • Big Bill Haywood helps to organize the Industrial Workers of the World (1905). • The Elkins Act prohibits discriminatory railroad rates (1903). • The Hepburn Act allows the Interstate Commerce Commission to set shipping rates (1906). • In *Lochner v. New York*, the Supreme Court uses the Fourteenth Amendment to rule that New York cannot limit the workday of bakers (1905). • In its 1908 *Muller v. Oregon* decision, the Supreme Court upholds an Oregon law limiting the workday for women. • The Supreme Court forces the breakup of the Standard Oil monopoly (1911).

THEME	REQUIRED CONTENT	SUPPORTING EXAMPLES
WORK, EXCHANGE, TECHNOLOGY (*continued*)	• These technologies produced consumer goods, spread "modern" ideas, and created a new mass culture. **1929–1945** • The role of the federal government in regulating the economy changed over this period in response to instability in the market, especially the Great Depression. • The New Deal helped to reform the economic system and transform the United States into a limited welfare state. • Mobilization for World War II, with its demand for troops and a wartime workforce, ended the Great Depression. • World War II provided minorities and women with economic and social opportunities. • Technological advances and industrial production played a crucial role in the Allied victory in World War II.	• The fire at the Triangle Shirtwaist Company kills 146 people, mostly young immigrant women, igniting the call for labor reform (1911). • Many states pass laws providing workers with insurance to cover on-the-job accidents. • The Sixteenth Amendment enacts a progressive federal income tax (1913). • The Federal Reserve Act strengthens the banking system (1913). • Clayton Antitrust Act (1914). • Federal Trade Commission formed (1914). **1917–1929** • New technologies such as the machine gun and poison gas make the devastation of World War I even more horrible. • Close economic ties between the United States, Britain, and France eventually pull the United States into World War I. • The War Industries Board, led by Bernard Baruch, puts the United States on a war footing by regulating production. • The War Labor Board works with labor to support the war effort, granting the right to organize. • Herbert Hoover heads the U.S. Food Administration. • Following a spike in inflation immediately after the war, the economy grows and per capita income rises. • Court decisions and antiunion campaigns weaken unions in the years after World War I. • Seattle general strike (1919). • Governor Calvin Coolidge fires striking police in Boston (1919). • Welfare capitalism, an effort by management, offers some benefits to workers and attempts to head off labor unrest in the 1920s. • Herbert Hoover leads the Commerce Department and collaborates with companies in nearly every major industry to create trade associations; he hopes to create an "associated state" through voluntary cooperation between government and business. • Secretary of Interior Albert Fall convicted for his participation in the Teapot Dome scandal (1923).

THEME	REQUIRED CONTENT	SUPPORTING EXAMPLES
WORK, EXCHANGE, TECHNOLOGY (*continued*)		• Consumer culture explodes as Americans buy newly invented household appliances, radios, and, especially, automobiles. • Americans stretch their incomes, buying with easily available consumer credit. • In 1929, Americans spend $2.58 billion on automobiles. • Significant weaknesses in the economy continue, especially in the farming sector. • The stock market plunges in October 1929, and the nation soon enters the Great Depression. **1929–1945** • Banks fail, consumer spending drops, and the depression worsens in the aftermath of the crash and Hoover's inadequate response to it. • Republicans enact the Smoot-Hawley Tariff (1930). • The Reconstruction Finance Corporation provides federal loans to businesses (1931). • Roosevelt takes action to shore up the nation's banking system. • Roosevelt works to improve the lives of farmers through the Agricultural Adjustment Act (AAA), the Tennessee Valley Authority (TVA), and the Rural Electrification Administration (REA). • Roosevelt supports policies to increase production such as the establishment of the National Recovery Administration (NRA). • Relief for the unemployed is implemented through the Federal Emergency Relief Administration (FERA), the Public Works Administration (PWA), and the Civilian Conservation Corps (CCC) (1933). • The Federal Housing Administration (FHA) is formed (1934). • The Securities and Exchange Commission (SEC) is established to regulate the stock market (1934). • The Wagner Act upholds labor rights, and the Social Security Act provides pensions and support for the unemployed and disabled (1935). • Industrial workers find a voice in the Congress of Industrial Organizations (CIO). • The "Roosevelt recession" of 1937–1938 halts recovery; Roosevelt then adopts Keynesian economics and increases federal spending.

THEME	REQUIRED CONTENT	SUPPORTING EXAMPLES
WORK, EXCHANGE, TECHNOLOGY (*continued*)		• Despite some New Deal successes, mobilization for World War II is what ends the Great Depression. • The government heavily subsidizes defense industries, strengthening the influence of giant corporations. • Henry Kaiser revolutionizes shipbuilding. • Women hold defense jobs during the war; these women, despite receiving lower wages than men and being subject to sexual harassment, have opportunities to fill untraditional roles. • Unions emerge more powerful by the end of the war. • Consumer goods are rationed during the war.
MIGRATION AND SETTLEMENT	**1890–1917** • Throughout this period, the United States continued its transition from a rural to an urban society. • Internal and international migration in the years before World War I had a significant impact on urban life, the workplace, American culture, and reform. • Shortly before World War I, many, though not most, African Americans began a "Great Migration" from the South to the North seeking economic opportunity. • Although Congress established restrictive immigration quotas in the 1920s, legislators continued to allow unrestricted immigration from the Western Hemisphere. • During the Great Depression, many Americans moved in search of work.	**1890–1917** • The Tenement House Law of 1901 attempts to improve urban life. • Cities undertake efforts to make life easier and safer, including providing cleaner water and better transportation. • The "City Beautiful" movement advocates parks and gardens. **1917–1929** • In the Great Migration, more than 400,000 African Americans move to northern cities to take advantage of economic opportunities brought about by World War I. Nevertheless, blacks encounter discrimination in the North in housing, jobs, and education. • Between 1917 and 1920, more than 100,000 Mexicans enter the United States. **1929–1945** • During the Great Depression, some poor communities are called "Hoovervilles." • During World War II, migration increases to California, where defense installations were located.

Theme	Required Content	Supporting Examples
MIGRATION AND SETTLEMENT (*continued*)	• In the 1930s and 1940s, the many Mexicans who moved to the United States faced discrimination and poor working conditions. • As World War II approached, wartime production needs encouraged workers to move to areas where factories were busy mobilizing for war.	
POLITICS AND POWER	**1890–1917** • Progressive reformers were concerned about political corruption, economic instability, and social inequality, and they sought change through increased government intervention. • Progressives were generally urban and middle class and often female. • Progressives worked to change existing institutions at all levels of government and formed organizations to address the social problems that were prevalent in urban society. • The American government was changed following debates over the substance and structure of the Constitution. **1917–1929** • The presidents of the 1920s supported limited government and pro-business policies.	**1890–1917** • In a number of cities, including Cleveland and Galveston, urban reformers change the way cities are managed. • Progressivism, a varied and overlapping set of movements, works to combat the ills facing urban society. • Progressives want to clean up politics, limit the power of big business, reduce poverty, and promote social justice. • Governor Robert La Follette makes Wisconsin "the laboratory of democracy" by his efforts to intervene in the economy and give citizens the right of recall and referendum (1901–1905). • Theodore Roosevelt speaks in praise of the "strenuous life" and calls for reform. • The Supreme Court dissolves the Northern Securities Company (1904). • Roosevelt sponsors the first White House Conference on Dependent Children (1909). • Roosevelt runs unsuccessfully for president as the "Bull Moose" candidate of the Progressive Party and calls for a "New Nationalism" (1908). • Under the banner of "New Freedom," Woodrow Wilson is elected president (1912). • Wilson goes on to take bold economic initiatives but does not take a stand for civil rights and resists European-style social welfare programs. • The Seventeenth Amendment mandates popular election of U.S. senators (1913). • By the outbreak of World War I, the Progressive movement has helped create a more modern nation. • Wilson is reelected in 1916 on a pledge to stay out of war.

THEME	REQUIRED CONTENT	SUPPORTING EXAMPLES
POLITICS AND POWER (*continued*)	**1929–1945** • Franklin Roosevelt sought to remedy the problems caused by the Great Depression. He increased the power of the government in order to help the poor, stimulate economic recovery, and reform the economy. • Although not always successful in addressing the problems facing the nation, the New Deal left a legacy of reform and a long-term political realignment. • Pressured by radicals and unions and under attack from conservatives and the Supreme Court, Roosevelt sought even more extensive reforms in his second term. • Debates over the meaning and application of democratic values at home and abroad resulted in ideological and military conflicts. • In response to concerns over civil rights and civil liberties, the American political system underwent many changes.	**1917–1929** • As World War I rages, President Wilson promises that the United States will stay neutral. • In April 1917, at Wilson's request, Congress declares war. • Congress orders a military draft (1917). • In order to enforce "100 percent loyalty," the federal government curbs dissent by passing the Espionage Act and Sedition Act (1917 and 1918). • George Creel's Committee on Public Information creates and disseminates pro-American and prowar propaganda. • The American Protective League, in collaboration with the Justice Department, spies on other Americans, leads raids against peace activists, and incites nativism. • In *Schenk v. United States* and *Abrams v. United States*, the Supreme Court rules that Americans do not have the right to incite someone to resist the draft and also establishes the "clear and present danger" standard (1919). • The Nineteenth Amendment guarantees women's right to vote (1920). • During the Red Scare, Attorney General A. Mitchell Palmer arrests and deports thousands viewed as radicals and also denies constitutional rights to American citizens (1919–1920). • In a backlash against progressivism, the three Republican administrations of the 1920s, led by Warren Harding, Calvin Coolidge, and Herbert Hoover, reject activist government and support business interests. • The Sheppard-Towner Federal Maternity and Infancy Act, the first federally funded health-care legislation, is passed in 1921, only to be ended by Congress in 1929. • Governor Al Smith of New York is the first Catholic presidential candidate; he loses the 1928 election to Herbert Hoover.

THEME	REQUIRED CONTENT	SUPPORTING EXAMPLES
POLITICS AND POWER (*continued*)		**1929–1945** • Hoover's approach to the problems of the Great Depression includes reliance on individual character and voluntary action, maintenance of the gold standard, and high tariffs. • Many criticize Hoover for his response to the Bonus Army (1932). • In 1932, Franklin Roosevelt is elected to the first of four terms as president. • Roosevelt's "fireside chats" soothe Americans' fears. • Roosevelt's New Deal aims at increasing government activism. In the "Hundred Days," fifteen major bills are passed, altering the role of the American government (1933). • Secretary of Labor Frances Perkins becomes the first woman to hold a cabinet post (1933). • Critics on the right, including the Liberty League and the National Association of Manufacturers, assail Roosevelt's economic policies. • Populists such as Francis Townsend and Huey Long criticize Roosevelt for not doing enough for the poor and unemployed. • During the Second New Deal, 1935–1939, Roosevelt shifts tactics, adopting parts of the programs of Townsend, Long, and Charles Coughlin, and moving to the left. • The Works Progress Administration (WPA) puts millions to work on infrastructure projects (1935–1943). • When the Supreme Court strikes down the NRA and the AAA (in *Schecter v. United States*), Roosevelt responds by attempting to "pack" the Court, an attempt that fails (1937). • By the end of the 1930s, the United States has moved toward a social welfare state, creating a safety net for the old, the disabled, and the unemployed. • During the New Deal, the government's bureaucracy increases by 80 percent. • The War Powers Act grants Roosevelt complete control over the war effort, marking the start of the imperial presidency (1941). • The GI Bill of Rights (the Servicemen's Readjustment Act) is passed (1944).

THEME	REQUIRED CONTENT	SUPPORTING EXAMPLES
AMERICA IN THE WORLD	**1890–1917** • Americans debated the legality and morality of the expansion of U.S. power overseas. • Americans had differing motives for supporting expansionism, whether through diplomacy, military action, or economic means. • Global conflicts often led to change at home. • For a variety of reasons, the United States fought the War of 1898 (the Spanish-American War). • The U.S. victory in the War of 1898 led to the acquisition of Cuba and Puerto Rico and an increased presence in the Caribbean and Latin America. • Following the War of 1898, the United States became more involved in Asia and had to confront an insurrection in the Philippines. • The War of 1898 and others over the next decades propelled the United States into a new and dominant military, political, and economic role in the world. **1917–1929** • The debate between advocates of interventionism and isolationism continued as war broke out in Europe in 1914, and this debate lasted into the 1940s when America entered World War II.	**1890–1917** • Empire builders base their arguments on the idea of "American exceptionalism." • In *The Influence of Sea Power upon History*, Alfred Mahan supports imperialism by arguing for the need to maintain a strong navy (1890). • The United States invokes the Monroe Doctrine to intervene in Venezuela (1895). • After publication of the de Lôme letter and the explosion on the *Maine*, President William McKinley asks for a declaration of war against Spain (1898). • Teller Amendment issued (1898). • Congress votes to annex Hawaii (1898). • After victories in Manila Bay and at San Juan Hill, the United States defeats Spain and annexes the Philippines (1898). • Anti-imperialists oppose annexation of the Philippines. • Philippine rebel leader Emilio Aguinaldo leads an insurgency against the United States. • In the *Insular Cases*, the Supreme Court determines that the Constitution does not follow the flag (1901). • The Platt Amendment sets the terms for U.S-Cuban relations (1902). • Secretary of State John Hay calls for an "open door" policy in China (1899). • The president issues his Roosevelt Corollary (1904). • Roosevelt wins the Nobel Peace Prize for mediating a settlement between Japan and Russia (1906). • Root-Takahira Agreement (1908). • Roosevelt's belief that the United States should "speak softly but carry a big stick" impels him to support an independence movement in Panama, after which he leases land to build the Panama Canal (1903). • Panama Canal opens (1914). • During Woodrow Wilson's first term, tensions erupt between the United States and Mexico (1911–1914). • Rival blocs emerge in Europe, setting the stage for World War I. • Europeans go to war following the assassination of Archduke Franz Ferdinand in Sarajevo (1914). • A German U-boat sinks the *Lusitania* (1915).

THEME	REQUIRED CONTENT	SUPPORTING EXAMPLES
AMERICA IN THE WORLD (*continued*)	• In 1917, Woodrow Wilson led the nation into World War I, arguing that humanitarian concerns and defense of democratic values demanded U.S. action. • The American Expeditionary Force played a limited role in fighting World War I, but President Wilson was a key player in the settlement at Versailles and in the establishment of the League of Nations. The League and the postwar settlement were very controversial in the United States. • American foreign policy in the 1920s, while still largely isolationist, focused on economic investment, peace treaties, and limited military intervention. **1929–1945** • Prior to the attack on Pearl Harbor, most Americans opposed American participation in World War II. • Allied political and military cooperation contributed to the Allied victor; the United States emerged from this conflict as the most powerful nation on earth.	**1917–1929** • Despite its Sussex pledge, Germany resumes unrestricted submarine warfare (1917). • The Zimmermann telegram further angers Americans. • General John Pershing leads the American Expeditionary Force "over there" and into World War I. • Following the Bolshevik Revolution in November 1917, Russian leader Vladimir Lenin signs a peace treaty with Germany. • Germany signs an armistice ending the war (November 11, 1918). • Wilson issues his Fourteen Points, which includes a call for a League of Nations. (1919). • The U.S. Senate rejects the Treaty of Versailles (1920). • After the war, Republican presidents use "dollar diplomacy" to advance American business interests abroad. • U.S. forces occupy Nicaragua, Haiti, and the Dominican Republic for much of the period 1912 and 1934. **1929–1945** • Fascism, which originated in Italy in the 1920s, spreads to Germany, Spain, and Japan. • Japan defies the League of Nation and occupies parts of China. • In 1936, Germany invades the Rhineland and in 1937 forms the Rome-Berlin Axis with Italy. • Due to the allegations made by the Nye Commission and continued widespread isolationist sentiment, the United States vows to remain neutral. • Congress passes the Neutrality Act of 1935 and approves "cash-and-carry" restrictions on the sale of nonmilitary goods to belligerents in 1937. • Some Americans support the Popular Front movement and urge the defeat of Francisco Franco in Spain. • At the Munich Conference, France and Britain allow German annexation of the Sudetenland (1938). • Adolf Hitler and Joseph Stalin sign a nonaggression pact (1939). • World War II begins with the 1939 German invasion of Poland.

THEME	REQUIRED CONTENT	SUPPORTING EXAMPLES
AMERICA IN THE WORLD (*continued*)		• Roosevelt shows his support for France and Britain by allowing the sale of arms to the Allies on a cash-and-carry basis (1939). • Isolationists form the America First Committee with supporters who included aviator Charles Lindbergh (1940). • The first peacetime draft in U.S. history begins in 1940. • Roosevelt uses his Four Freedoms speech to demonstrate support for the war (January 1941). • Congress passes the Lend-Lease Act (March 1941). • Roosevelt and Winston Churchill announce the "Atlantic Charter" (August 1941). • As Japanese aggression in Southeast Asia increases, the United States stops trade with Japan and then freezes Japanese assets in the United States (July 1941). • Japan attacks Pearl Harbor on December 7, 1941. The United States declares war on Japan and then on Germany and Italy. • After war breaks out, the Allies differ over the opening of a front in France. At a meeting in Tehran, Churchill and Roosevelt agree to open the French front (1943). • In 1944, British and American troops take Rome and then invade France on D-Day (June 6). • World War II ends in Europe in May 1945. • Victories in battles in the Coral Sea and on Midway Island allow American forces to move toward Japan. • The Big Three meet at Yalta in February 1945. • President Roosevelt dies in April 1945, and Harry Truman becomes president. • The world learns that Hitler was responsible for the deaths of 6 million European Jews in the Holocaust. • After considering other options, such as a demonstration of the atomic bomb's power or advance warning, Truman orders these bombs, the product of the Manhattan Project, to be dropped on Hiroshima and Nagasaki on August 6 and 9, 1945. • Japan surrenders on August 10.

THEME	REQUIRED CONTENT	SUPPORTING EXAMPLES
GEOGRAPHY AND THE ENVIRONMENT	• In the late nineteenth and early twentieth centuries, their belief that the American frontier was now closed led many Americans to justify expansion abroad. • Beginning in the late nineteenth century, new policies regarding the use of resources and the protection of the environment were implemented.	• Theodore Roosevelt establishes three new national parks and dozens of wildlife refuges (early 1900s). • Newlands Reclamation Act (1902). • The U.S. Forest Service is created (1905). • Disaster strikes farmers in the "dust bowl" of the Great Plains (1930–1941). • Government agencies implement plans to avoid future environmental catastrophes in the plains. • The Tennessee Valley Authority, one of the programs of the Hundred Days, oversees the construction of dams and power plants (1933). • The CCC and WPA projects provide recreational opportunities for people around the country. • The Grand Coulee Dam is completed in 1941.
CULTURE AND SOCIETY	**1890–1917** • Beliefs in white superiority and American cultural superiority were used to justify the conquest of nonwhite nations. • In response to industrialization, urbanization, and immigration, American literature and culture changed to more accurately reflect life in American cities. • Culture and the arts both reflected and shaped American life, often effecting social and political change. • Journalists at the turn of the century worked with Progressives to improve American society. **1917–1929** • "Modern" values and a popular culture that reflected them influenced politics and society.	**1890–1917** • Realist authors like Theodore Dreiser and Hamlin Garland reject the romantic style of the past. • Naturalist authors like Stephen Crane and Jack London argue that humans are controlled by forces beyond their control. • Samuel Clemens (Mark Twain), the best-known American writer and creator of Tom Sawyer and Huckleberry Finn, bitterly criticizes the popular idea of progress. • "Modernism" emerges as the first important literary movement of the twentieth century. • Ash Can painters depict the grit of the American city and the isolation felt by people who live there. • Realist painters stage the Armory Show (1913). • Realism and modernism assert the importance of masculinity. • American Catholics try to maintain their religious traditions, in part by establishing Catholic schools. • American Jews embrace Reform Judaism. • The Social Gospel is an attempt to renew religious faith through efforts to promote social justice. • The Salvation Army serves as a primary example of the Social Gospel. • Evangelists like Dwight Moody and Billy Sunday focus on attaining eternal life.

THEME	REQUIRED CONTENT	SUPPORTING EXAMPLES
CULTURE AND SOCIETY (*continued*)	• The dominant social and economic order was both defended and challenged by using moral, scientific, and philosophical arguments. • During and after World War I, patriotism and xenophobia contributed to restrictions on speech and immigration. • In the 1920s, technological innovation, modernization, and demographic change led to increased cultural conflict, as Americans debated sensitive issues: tradition versus change, fundamentalist religion versus science, management versus labor, American-born whites versus blacks and immigrants, and idealism versus pessimism. • Industrialization and urbanization encouraged a variety of cultural expression, especially the Harlem Renaissance. • A shared national culture emerged, especially in the arts, movies, and mass media.	• Conservative Christians begin to call themselves "fundamentalists." • Urban dwellers develop a popular culture including vaudeville and amusement parks. • Musical innovations include ragtime and the blues. • Scott Joplin introduces ragtime at the Chicago World's Fair (1892). • W. C. Handy popularizes the blues. • The first American youth culture emerges. • Dating and casual sex characterize gender relations. • A vibrant gay culture challenges Victorian ideals. • High culture such as opera and the fine arts are cultivated by the upper classes. • Publishers William Randolph Hearst and Joseph Pulitzer practice "yellow journalism" while "muckrakers" expose corruption. • Jacob Riis writes *How the Other Half Lives* (1890). • Lincoln Steffens writes *The Shame of the Cities* (1904). • Upton Sinclair's *The Jungle* (1906), which exposes corruption and working conditions in the meatpacking industry, increases pressure for government reform of industry. • Cities increase efforts to eliminate prostitution. • Margaret Sanger crusades for birth control. • The film *Birth of a Nation* is considered a state-of-the art production but glorifies the Ku Klux Klan (1915). • In *Our Country*, Josiah Strong supports imperialism as a means to spread Christianity (1885). • Yellow journalists such as Hearst and Pulitzer promote war against Spain. **1917–1929** • Tensions between traditionalists and proponents of change result in culture wars throughout the 1920s. • Prohibition supporters succeed in convincing Congress to pass the Nineteenth Amendment (1918). • The battle over evolution plays out in the Scopes trial in Dayton, Tennessee, as the American Civil Liberties Union defends John Scopes (1925).

THEME	REQUIRED CONTENT	SUPPORTING EXAMPLES
CULTURE AND SOCIETY (*continued*)	**1929–1945** • American values were called into question with the internment of Japanese Americans during World War II; debates over civil liberties, race, and segregation; and the dropping of the atomic bomb. • The American commitment to the advancement of democratic values contributed to victory over the Axis powers.	• Writer and social critic H. L. Mencken attacks long-held American traditions and what he views as hypocrisy and small-mindedness. • Intellectual fervor and ferment arise from the social upheavals caused by World War I as intellectuals question prevailing assumptions about progress and the superiority of Western cultures. • Gertrude Stein, Ernest Hemingway, and other writers become known as the Lost Generation. • Sinclair Lewis attacks conformity in *Babbitt* and other novels, becoming the first American to win the Nobel Prize for literature. • Writers of the Harlem Renaissance, including Langston Hughes and Zora Neale Hurston, describe the richness of black culture and the struggles that African Americans face. • Jazz spreads nationwide, popularized by the radio, introducing musicians like Duke Ellington to whites and blacks alike. • Cars change the ways in which Americans spend their leisure time. • Hollywood becomes the world's film capital. **1929–1945** • New Deal liberalism adopts the ideas of John Maynard Keynes and argues that government must guarantee the basic rights of citizens. • The WPA funds the Federal Arts Project, the Federal Writers' Project, and the Federal Theatre Project, which enable artists, writers, actors, and playwrights like Jackson Pollock, Willem de Kooning, Zora Neale Hurston, Ralph Ellison, Orson Welles, and Arthur Miller to contribute to American culture. • John Steinbeck's iconic novel, *The Grapes of Wrath*, tells the story of those who left the Dust Bowl in hopes of a better life in California (1939). • The songs of Woody Guthrie tell the stories of those who live and struggle during the Depression. • Popular culture, especially the motion picture industry, supports the war effort.

Period 7 Practice Questions

Multiple-Choice Questions

Questions 1–3 refer to the excerpt below.

"All that this country desires is to see the neighboring countries stable, orderly, and prosperous. Any country whose people conduct themselves well can count upon our hearty friendship. If a nation shows that it knows how to act with reasonable efficiency and decency in social and political matters, if it keeps order and pays its obligations, it need fear no interference from the United States. Chronic wrongdoing, or an impotence which results in a general loosening of the ties of civilized society, may in America, as elsewhere, ultimately require intervention by some civilized nation, and in the Western Hemisphere the adherence of the United States to the Monroe Doctrine may force the United States, however reluctantly, in flagrant cases of such wrongdoing or impotence, to the exercise of an international police power."

Theodore Roosevelt's, Roosevelt Corollary to the Monroe Doctrine, Annual Message to Congress, December 6, 1904

1. The above message from Theodore Roosevelt foreshadowed
    (A) U.S. involvement in the War of 1998.
    (B) an increasingly active U.S. role in Latin American affairs.
    (C) retreat to the isolationism of the Gilded Age.
    (D) significantly increased trade with China.

2. The War of 1898 had convinced Roosevelt of the necessity of
    (A) acquiring Cuba.
    (B) building a canal connecting the Atlantic and Pacific oceans.
    (C) constructing a two-ocean navy.
    (D) completing a transcontinental railroad to quickly move troops and supplies to the West Coast.

3. Roosevelt's foreign policy initiatives broke with traditional U.S. foreign policy by
    (A) involving the United States prominently in world affairs.
    (B) involving the United States in European wars.
    (C) establishing passive tactics that shattered the notion of U.S. invincibility.
    (D) establishing U.S. colonies in Africa.

Questions 4–6 refer to the excerpt below.

"Just as he was an Elk, a Booster, and a member of the Chamber of Commerce, just as the priests of the Presbyterian Church determined his every religious belief and the senators who controlled the Republican Party decided in little smoky rooms in Washington what he should think about disarmament, tariff, and Germany, so did the large national advertisers fix the surface of his life, fix what he believed to be his individuality. These standard advertised wares—toothpastes, socks, tires, cameras, instantaneous hot-water heaters—were his symbols and proofs of excellence; at first the signs, then the substitutes, for joy and passion and wisdom."

Sinclair Lewis, *Babbitt*, 1922

GO ON TO THE NEXT PAGE.

4. Which of the following most clearly represents what Sinclair Lewis is criticizing in the selection from *Babbitt*?

   (A) U.S. failure to join the League of Nations following World War I
   (B) The growth of big business during the 1920s
   (C) Control of the U.S government by the Protestant religious establishment
   (D) The shallow and superficial nature of American society

5. A highly charged Tennessee court case in the 1920s reflected religious conflict between

   (A) Catholics and Protestants.
   (B) creationists and "big bang" theorists.
   (C) fundamentalist Christianity and scientific modernism.
   (D) adherents of Social Darwinism and adherent of the Social Gospel.

6. The foreign policy of the 1920s reflected what change from the two preceding decades?

   (A) An expansive role in international bodies like the World Court and League of Nations
   (B) Movement toward a more isolationistic posture
   (C) A more aggressive and jingoistic policy toward Latin American
   (D) A massive military buildup so the "preparedness would never again be an issue

Questions 7–9 are based on the excerpt below.

"Until four-thirty this morning I had hoped against hope that some miracle would prevent a devastating war in Europe and bring to an end the invasion of Poland by Germany.

"For four long years a succession of actual wars and constant crises have shaken the entire world and have threatened in each case to bring on the gigantic conflict which is today unhappily a fact. . . .

"It is easy for you and for me to shrug our shoulders and to say that conflicts taking place thousands of miles from the continental United States . . . do not seriously affect the Americas-and that all the United States has to do is to ignore them and go about its own business. . . .

"This nation will remain a neutral nation, but I cannot ask that every American remain neutral in thought as well. Even a neutral has a right to take account of facts. Even a neutral cannot be asked to close his mind or his conscience. I have said not once, but many times, that I have seen war and that I hate war. I say that again and again."

Franklin Roosevelt, Fireside Chat, September 3, 1939

7. The tone of Roosevelt's fireside chat reflects his belief that

   (A) the United States should remain completely neutral in World War II.
   (B) World War II will have little impact on the United States.
   (C) moral necessity would force the United States into the war.
   (D) Japan posed the greatest threat to U.S. interests.

8. Roosevelt's foreign policy in the late 1930s reflected what change from the foreign policy of the 1920s?

   (A) A return to the isolationism of the Gilded Age
   (B) A call for increased military invention in Latin America
   (C) More aggressive confrontation with the Soviet Union
   (D) Greater involvement in world affairs

GO ON TO THE NEXT PAGE.

9. By the time of U.S. entry into World War II in December 1941, the United States had done all of the following EXCEPT

    (A) provide the Allies with much-needed supplies.
    (B) move Japanese Americans to internment camps.
    (C) institute the first peacetime draft in U.S. history.
    (D) meet with Allied leaders to agree on war aims.

Question 10–12 refer to the graph below.

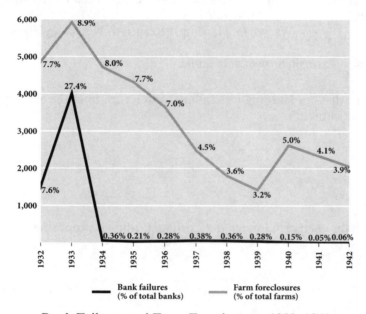

Bank Failures and Farm Foreclosures, 1932–1942

10. Which of the following statements is best supported by the graph above?

     (A) Farm foreclosures remained the same throughout the New Deal.
     (B) The rates at which banks failed and farms were foreclosed were about the same.
     (C) Banks recovered quickly in the early years of the New Deal.
     (D) Farm foreclosures went down steadily throughout the New Deal.

11. Which of the following represent(s) the greatest change in government policy ushered in by the New Deal?

     (A) The government was responsible for the economic well-being of the country.
     (B) The government should steadfastly retain a laissez-faire approach to economic recessions.
     (C) The government's primary role should be to defend the United States from foreign invasion.
     (D) Quack remedies would not put an end to the Great Depression.

12. The Great Depression was ended by

     (A) New Deal relief programs like the Federal Emergency Relief Administration.
     (B) work programs such as the Civilian Conservation Corps and Works Progress Administration.
     (C) industrial expansion fueled by acts like the Lend-Lease Act.
     (D) the Court-packing scheme, which upheld critical New Deal programs.

END OF MULTIPLE-CHOICE SECTION

Short-Answer Questions

"America's present need is not heroics, but healing; not nostrums, but normalcy; not revolution, but restoration; not agitation, but adjustment; not surgery, but serenity; not the dramatic, but the dispassionate; not experiment, but equipoise; not submergence in internationality, but sustainment in triumphant nationality. It is one thing to battle successfully against world domination by military autocracy, because the infinite God never intended such a program, but it is quite another thing to revise human nature and suspend the fundamental laws of life and all of life's acquirements."

Warren G. Harding, "Return to Normalcy," Boston, May 14, 1920

1. Using the above excerpt, answer a, b, and c.

   a) Explain what era Harding was calling for a return to in the above passage, and support your choice.

   b) Explain the change in foreign policy that Harding is proposing in the above passage.

   c) Explain Harding's position on Progressive reform.

GO ON TO THE NEXT PAGE.

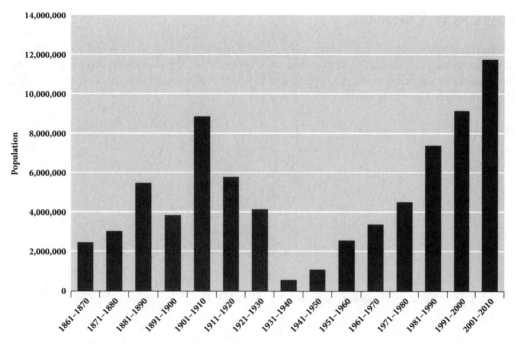

Immigration into the United States, 1861–2010

2. Based on the graph above, answer a, b, and c.

a) Explain the reasons for the decrease in immigration between 1911 and 1920.

b) Explain the reasons for the decrease in immigration between 1921 and 1930.

c) Explain the reasons for the decrease in immigration between 1931 and 1940.

END OF SHORT-ANSWER SECTION

Long Essay Question

Analyze the ways in which reformers during the Progressive Era attempted to improve life for average Americans through the regulation of big business, the democratization of the political process, and the institution of social welfare between 1900 and 1920, and assess the degree to which these efforts were successful.

END OF LONG ESSAY SECTION

Answer Key to Period 7 Practice Questions

Multiple-Choice Questions

1.

Answer	Learning Objectives	Historical Thinking Skills	Key Concepts in the Curriculum Framework
B	WOR-2.0	Analyzing Evidence: Content and Sourcing	7.3

Explanation: The Roosevelt Corollary to the Monroe Doctrine served notice that the United States would serve a more active role in policing the Western Hemisphere. In fact, Roosevelt sent in U.S. troops on several occasions, particularly when Latin American countries would not meet their debt obligations to European powers. Thus, the United States moved away from its traditional foreign policy of isolationism toward a more active role in world affairs.

2.

Answer	Learning Objectives	Historical Thinking Skills	Key Concepts in the Curriculum Framework
B	WOR-2.0	Causation	7.3

Explanation: The War of 1898 demonstrated the need for a canal through Central America to prevent the United States from having to build a two-ocean navy. The highly publicized trip of the U.S.S. *Oregon* from the West Coast, around Cape Horn, to Cuba demonstrated how time-consuming such a voyage was and worried Americans that battles might be lost because of the delay.

3.

Answer	Learning Objectives	Historical Thinking Skills	Key Concepts in the Curriculum Framework
A	WOR-2.0	Patterns of Continuity and Change over Time	7.3

Explanation: Roosevelt rejected the traditional isolationistic policy of the United States and was convinced that the country needed to be a major player on the world stage. His jingoistic "big stick" policy led to intervention in foreign countries that previous presidents would not have undertaken. His policies also set the stage for his successors to engage in "dollar diplomacy" under Taft and "moral diplomacy" under Wilson.

4.

Answer	Learning Objectives	Historical Thinking Skills	Key Concepts in the Curriculum Framework
D	CUL-2.0	Patterns of Continuity and Change over Time	7.2

Explanation: Like many "lost generation" writers of the 1920s, Sinclair Lewis was critical of the superficiality of American life. Disillusionment with the failure of World War I to attain the lofty goals of ending all wars and making the world safe for democracy led many intellectuals to abandon progressivism and self-sacrifice. As well, Progressives had watched much of their prewar accomplishment undone by the necessities of war.

5.

Answer	Learning Objectives	Historical Thinking Skills	Key Concepts in the Curriculum Framework
C	CUL-4.0	Comparison	7.2

Explanation: The Scopes trial, or monkey trial, provoked a media circus. The battle was one between fundamentalist Christianity, defended by William Jennings Bryan, and scientific modernism, espoused by defense attorney Clarence Darrow. Scientific modernism developed out of a need for many Christians to accommodate new scientific discovery with biblical accounts.

6.

Answer	Learning Objectives	Historical Thinking Skills	Key Concepts in the Curriculum Framework
B	NAT-3.0	Patterns of Continuity and Change over Time	7.3

Explanation: Between 1900 and 1920 the United States had become much more internationalist in foreign policy. To a degree, this represented a fundamental break with the traditional isolationist policy the United States had pursued during much of the nineteenth century. Disillusionment with the failure of World War I to meet idealistic expectations led the United States to withdraw to a more traditional posture of neoisolation. Evidence of this is the U.S. failure to join either the League of Nations or the World Court.

7.

Answer	Learning Objectives	Historical Thinking Skills	Key Concepts in the Curriculum Framework
C	WOR-2.0	Patterns of Continuity and Change over Time	7.3

Explanation: Roosevelt believed early on that Hitler was the greatest threat to the world and that the United States would ultimately be drawn into a European war. He inherited a political climate that favored isolationism as a result of the disillusionment with U.S. failure to meet its idealistic goals in World War I. He continued to push the United States toward active involvement in the face of such things as the Nye Committee Report and the America First Committee. His call to "quarantine" aggressor nations in 1937 aroused a storm of protest that forced Roosevelt to move more slowly toward his goal of involvement.

8.

Answer	Learning Objectives	Historical Thinking Skills	Key Concepts in the Curriculum Framework
D	NAT-3.0	Patterns of Continuity and Change over Time	7.3

Explanation: Though the United States had strong isolationist sentiments in the 1930s, Roosevelt cautiously moved the country away from Gilded Age policies and toward foreign involvement as the second world war began, battling and circumventing neutrality laws. At this time, Latin America and the Soviet Union were not a major concern of Roosevelt's.

9.

Answer	Learning Objectives	Historical Thinking Skills	Key Concepts in the Curriculum Framework
B	WOR-2.0	Contextualization	7.3

Explanation: Japanese internment did not occur until after the United States declared war. Allies had been supplied with necessary war materials through the "cash and carry" program and through the Lend-Lease Act prior to U.S. entry into the war. The Burke-Wadsworth Act, or Selective Service Act of 1940, instituted a peacetime draft that indicated foresight on the part of Roosevelt. Churchill and Roosevelt had discussed war aims in the Atlantic Charter in August 1941.

10.

Answer	Learning Objectives	Historical Thinking Skills	Key Concepts in the Curriculum Framework
C	POL-3.0	Analyzing Evidence: Content and Sourcing Patterns of Continuity and Change over Time	7.1

Explanation: The graph most clearly illustrates that banks recovered quickly in the early years of the New Deal. Farm foreclosures declined, for the most part, throughout the New Deal, although there was an upsurge in foreclosures in the late 1930s. The rate at which farms were foreclosed was clearly higher than the rate at which banks failed.

11.

Answer	Learning Objectives	Historical Thinking Skills	Key Concepts in the Curriculum Framework
A	POL-3.0	Patterns of Continuity and Change over Time	7.1

Explanation: The New Deal assumed government responsibility in helping to maintain a stable economy. This notion rejected the idea of rugged individualism and the Social Darwinist theory that economic depressions weeded out the unfit. Acceptance of the New Deal by the American public was extremely quick as it was codified into law in the Employment Act of 1946.

12.

Answer	Learning Objectives	Historical Thinking Skills	Key Concepts in the Curriculum Framework
C	NAT-3.0	Causation	7.3

Explanation: Roosevelt's belief that the United States would inevitably be drawn into European conflict led him to pursue a policy in which the United States would supply war material to "keep England fighting" while making the United States the "great arsenal of democracy." Programs like "cash and carry" and the Lend-Lease Act geared up U.S. industry toward wartime production, providing jobs and income that ultimately ended the Great Depression.

Short-Answer Questions

1.

Learning Objectives	Historical Thinking Skills	Key Concepts in the Curriculum Framework
NAT-3.0	Contextualization Periodization	7.3

What a good response might include

a) A good response will place Harding's comments in the context of his campaign to become the Republican Party's presidential nominee in 1920. His so-called return-to-normalcy speech was seen as a rallying cry not only against the international policies of outgoing President Woodrow Wilson but also in opposition to the activism of the Progressive Era. Some examples of what Harding was calling for might include the following:

+ The United States was weary of world commitments and somewhat disillusioned with the chaos in Europe that followed the end of World War I. Thus, Harding is calling for the United States to pull back and adopt a more isolationist foreign policy—what he calls "triumphant nationality."
+ After decades of reform activism that saw both the populists and progressives agitating for more government control of business and politics, he is calling for a return to the era before all this activism when the government maintained a hands-off position toward big business.

b) A good response will identify the changes Harding proposes as international isolationism even though it was a difficult position to maintain. Some examples might include the following:

+ The U.S. Senate, of which Harding was a Republican member, refused to ratify the Treaty of Versailles after World War I or participate in the League of Nations. This was a clear refutation of the goals set out by President Wilson.
+ While Harding does not discount the possibility of needing to battle "military autocracy" in World War I, he demurs from the idea that the United States should continue to be involved in trying to fix the world's problems.

c) A good response to Harding's position on Progressive reform as evidenced in this excerpt would include his determination to rein in many of the programs the progressives had introduced. Some examples might include the following:

+ Harding, and many of his Republican supporters, felt government-business cooperation was what the country needed, and they were happy to use federal policy and power to assist corporations.
+ As president, Harding appointed Herbert Hoover as secretary of commerce. Hoover established a policy of voluntary cooperation from business, which meant, in effect, giving corporate leaders greater policymaking power.
+ During Harding's tenure as president, labor unions saw membership drop.
+ The emphasis on social reform advocated by the progressives was deemphasized by the Harding administration.

2.

Learning Objectives	Historical Thinking Skills	Key Concepts in the Curriculum Framework
MIG-2.0	Causation	7.2

What a good response might include

a)   A good response might include one of the following:

  ✦ During this decade, much of the world, especially Europe, was engaged in World War I, so fewer people emigrated from there.

  ✦ In 1917, the United States began to institute various tests designed to prevent "undesirables" from immigrating. Many of those excluded were from Southern and Eastern Europe. Among these tests were those to determine literacy and health and demands that they sign statements promising that they were not anarchists and had not engaged in any "suspicious" political activities.

b)   A good response would include the following:

  ✦ Congress passed two laws the laws passed two laws—the Emergency Quota Act of 1921 and the National Origins Act of 1924—that set quotas for immigrants based on previous census data.

c)   A good response might include one of the following:

  ✦ The restrictions on immigration from the 1920s were still in effect.

  ✦ New laws restricted immigrants within the Western Hemisphere.

  ✦ The Great Depression, a global phenomenon, meant that fewer people could afford to emigrate out of their countries of origins.

Long Essay Question

Learning Objectives	Historical Thinking Skills	Key Concepts in the Curriculum Framework
POL-2.0	Analyzing Evidence: Content and Sourcing	7.1

What a good response might include

The long essay requires you to demonstrate your ability to use historical evidence in crafting a thoughtful historical argument. The question begins with a sentence describing a historical interpretation about continuity and change and then asks students to "support, modify, or refute" the interpretation. The essay should begin with the development of a relevant thesis. A solid thesis will take a stance that chooses one of these three options. In the rest of the essay, the student should answer the question in a way that demonstrates a sound knowledge of historical information relevant to the topic.

A good response to this question will support, modify, or refute the interpretation that the Progressive Era significantly improved the lives of average Americans through the regulation of big business, the democratization of the political process, and the enactment of social welfare legislation between 1900 and 1920. An essay supporting this interpretation would craft an argument using specific evidence that shows how the Progressive Era did significantly change the lives of average Americans during this time period. Although not required, a good response might also point out that the situation was nuanced. The essay might say, for the most part, that the historical evidence supports the claim of significant improvement in all three areas, while still pointing out that some evidence to the contrary exists as well.

A good response supporting the statement would cite historical facts from any number of sources as evidence of significant change in all three areas. The Progressive Era witnessed the passage of significant federal legislation aimed at regulating big business in an effort to protect consumers from unfair business practices. The Interstate Commerce Commission was strengthened by the Elkins Act of 1903, which specifically made secret rebates illegal and also held corporate leaders liable for such illegal activities. This act was a part of President Theodore Roosevelt's "Square Deal." The Hepburn Act in 1906 gave the Interstate Commerce Commission the power to set shipping rates and placed the burden of appeal on the shippers. The Clayton Anti-Trust Act of 1914 offered a clearer definition of what practices constituted an illegal trust and offered the government the power to set fair prices. This act also stipulated that labor unions were not the intended targets of laws like the 1890 Sherman Anti-Trust Act.

The Progressives also took on the issue of consumer protection with the passage of the Pure Food and Drug Act and the Meat Inspection Act in 1906. Trust-busting became a hallmark of the period, beginning with Roosevelt's mediation of the anthracite coal strike in 1902 and his efforts leading to the *Northern Securities* decision in 1904, the first time the Supreme Court ruled that a monopoly had to be disbanded. This case was the first of many brought to the Supreme Court during the Progressive Era, as monopolists finally faced a Supreme Court and a federal government that were willing to take them on. Further economic and political reform included the creation of the Federal Reserve System in 1912 to protect the nation from financial crises and monitor the currency supply.

The Progressive Era also saw the democratization of the political process with the ratification of the Seventeenth Amendment in 1913, which provided for the direct election of U.S. senators, and the ratification of the Nineteenth Amendment in 1919, which gave women the right to vote. The presidential election of 1920 was the first in which women were able to cast votes throughout the country.

There was also an effort during the Progressive Era to bring more openness and participation to local governments. Many cities moved to the city manager system in an effort to break the hold of big-city bosses who had historically made some urban areas their own political fiefdoms. While most black citizens continued to experience discrimination in many areas of their daily lives, efforts like the Niagara Movement, which organized the National Association for the Advancement of Colored People, began to look for ways to make equal rights a reality.

The Progressives also made sincere efforts to enact social welfare legislation. Many of the abuses that the Progressives addressed were brought to light through the efforts of journalists known as the muckrakers, who focused on a wide range of needed reforms in American society. Ida Tarbell, Jacob Riis, Lincoln Steffens, and Upton Sinclair, among other writers, worked to expose areas of American life that sorely needed reform. Many of their articles appeared in *McClure's* magazine, a publication that became a voice for reform in the Progressive Era. Ida B. Wells-Barnett worked to draw national attention to both women's rights and the plight of southern blacks, who were terrorized by lynching during these years. The National Child Labor Committee began to explore other ways to protect children in the workplace. There was an attempt to limit child labor with the Keating-Owens Act. The Children's Bureau was created within the U.S. Labor Department in 1912. The Adamson Eight-Hour Day Act in 1916 sought to provide working classes with more leisure time. Attempts to eliminate sex trafficking resulted in the Mann Act in 1910, a bill that provided penalties for interstate prostitution.

A good response might take the opposite approach and refute the assertion of the question, using persuasive evidence of ongoing problems that continued to resist the efforts of the Progressive reformers. While there was political reform during this period, many of the old problems persisted. Congress remained the domain of the wealthy and powerful, and monopolists continued to have enormous influence in both legislation proposed and bills passed. The

Progressive leaders were not consistent during the time period, with Roosevelt finding that Taft backed off on many of his initiatives, particularly in his dealings with Gifford Pinchot and some of the earlier environmental goals. Working classes, farmers, and minorities continued to be underrepresented in politics, and their needs were not consistently addressed. Despite the dedication to trust busting, many monopolies remained and regained strength during the 1920s.

While women got the vote at the end of the Progressive Era, they still faced obstacles in most areas of their lives, finding themselves unable in many states to establish bank accounts, hold professional jobs, or even obtain birth control information. Minorities, especially in the South, still struggled with the Jim Crow system and with white-dominated state and local governments that made political participation difficult if not impossible.

Even the Eighteenth Amendment could come under fire as a failed Progressive reform. Officially the production and sale of most alcohol was declared illegal, but many people chose to ignore the law. The demand for illegal alcohol eventually resulted in the rise of organized crime in the following decade.

Despite attempts to lessen dangers and stress in the industrial workplace, sweatshops persisted and factory owners often ignored regulations unless there was some publicity surrounding the poor conditions. The loss of life during the Triangle Shirtwaist Company fire in 1913 was a clear example of the many ways employers often ignored safety requirements as long as they could get away with it.

A good response might instead choose to modify the interpretation presented in the question. Such an answer would point out the many positive reforms and efforts that were part of the Progressive movement, while still including the fact that it was a work in progress and no reform movement could possibly correct all of the ills of society. There were many areas of success and, of course, others where efforts did not meet expectations. To make this argument, a good response would select facts supporting each of the two possibilities listed above, presenting proof that the final verdict on the successes of Progressive reform is ambiguous.

In all of the cases, a strong response would include proper chronology, a clear understanding of the issues, and the different approaches that Progressives chose to employ and would place progressivism within the context of the world of from 1900 to 1920.

PERIOD 8
1945–1980

Overview

The United States entered the post–World War II era as the most powerful country in the world. Among the challenges the country faced were the spread and containment of communism, leadership in the global economy, and maintenance of security both at home and abroad. The containment of communism during these years led to a number of "brushfire" engagements in other parts of the world, including Korea and Vietnam. The United States entered into a period of Cold War, with periodic crises followed by years of quiet coexistence.

The end of colonialism at the close of World War II opened the way for nationalist movements in Asia, Africa, and the Middle East, efforts complicated by the demands of the United States and the Soviet bloc that new countries choose sides in the Cold War. The United States also worked to ensure that friendly governments would emerge from newly created Latin American countries. Diplomatic relations with the Middle East were complicated by that region's vast oil supplies and the U.S. economy's dependence on that fuel source.

Fear of spreading communism played a significant role in domestic politics in the United States. While both political parties supported limiting communism's influence, there were disagreements about how this should be accomplished. The war in Korea resulted in some domestic protest; however, the war in Vietnam led to national, often violent, antiwar protests. Other issues were the proliferation of nuclear weapons, the influence of the military in domestic politics, and the proper role of presidential power in making foreign and military policy.

The 1950s and 1960s saw a rejuvenated civil rights movement challenging Jim Crow and segregation in the courts and in the streets. Landmark decisions resulted in the desegregation of the military, the end of separate but equal with the *Brown v. Board of Education of Topeka, Kansas* decision, and the sweeping Civil Rights Act of 1964. White segregationists continued to resist government attempts to end segregation, and civil rights activists themselves debated the best strategies to follow in the mid-1960s.

Calls for the end to segregation and Jim Crow led to calls for equal treatment from other minority groups, particularly women and gays and lesbians. Latinos, American Indians, and Asian Americans soon followed with demands of their own. Others spoke up for the poor, asking how a country known for its affluence could still have communities living in significant poverty.

President Lyndon Johnson's liberal domestic program, the Great Society, attempted to address many of these issues. His programs were supported by the Supreme Court, yet opponents of his approach began to gather strength as well. A new conservative movement began to question Johnson's vision of the scope of state and federal authority. Ironically his programs also came under fire from those on the far left who felt the government was not doing enough and who opposed America's foreign involvement in what they felt were local nationalist struggles.

The decades following World War II were a time of great economic growth and prosperity. Parents of baby boomers flocked to the suburbs in the 1950s and 1960s, demanding better schools, better infrastructure, and more opportunity for the growing middle class. Others saw the nation moving into conformity and spoke out against what they saw as a homogeneous mass culture. Conservatives worried that traditional values would be lost as urban and suburban areas grew further apart.

The United States continued to be the destination of choice for immigrants from around the world, especially after President Johnson liberalized immigration laws in 1965. Others focused on the growing awareness of the need to curb environmental pollution and begin to work more effectively at conserving natural resources.

As this time period drew to a close, new issues began to take over national debate. The traditional nuclear family was less in evidence as more women worked outside the home and divorce and single-parent households became more acceptable. The youth counterculture movement of the 1960s led to the rejection of the values of earlier generations, ushering in a sexual revolution and a much more informal culture.

Conservatives and liberals debated these social changes as well as issues about the proper role of the federal government and ways to offer greater protection of individual rights.

Key Terms

Be sure that you understand the meaning of these terms and their relevance in U.S. history.

Affirmative action
Black nationalism
Client regime
Cold War liberalism
Collective bargaining
Collective security
Consumer republic
Containment
Counterculture
Cultural conservatism
Decolonization
Deindustrialization
Détente
Domino theory
Economic feminism
Environmentalism
Evangelical Protestantism
Grassroots movements
Identity-based movements
Institutionalized racism

Labor feminists
Law-and-order issues
Left-wing and right-wing politics
Military-industrial complex
Moderate Republicanism
Mutual coexistence
New Left
Paternalism
Proxy wars
Restrictive covenants
Reverse discrimination
Right-to work laws
Rights liberalism
Rust Belt
Service economy
Silent majority
Stagflation
Third World
Traditional values

Questions to Consider

As you study Period 8, keep the following thematic questions in mind.

American and National Identity

✦ What did the American middle class want in the years after World War II? Account for the expansion of the middle class in postwar America.

✦ What caused the social tensions that the nation faced after World War II, and how were these tensions manifested?

✦ Why was it that the 1950s produced the phenomenon of the American teen culture ?

✦ Despite significant changes in gender roles, marriage, and the family, why did paternalism remain an important force?

✦ How did middle-class assumptions reflect the tensions between the traditional role of women and the forces promoting change?

✦ Why did some women reject feminism, and to what extent were conservative groups successful in thwarting the goals of the feminist movement?

✦ Besides women, what other groups challenged traditional authority? How effective were these groups in achieving their goals?

✦ What forces led to a significant change in Americans' views on racial equality in the two decades after World War II?

✦ Why were the Fourteenth and Fifteenth amendments, ratified one hundred years earlier, so central to African Americans' efforts to achieve civil rights in the 1950s and 1960s?

✦ What were some of the goals and strategies that black civil rights organizations used? To what extent were these different strategies successful?

✦ How and in what ways did student involvement help change the direction of the civil rights movement?

✦ What rifts threatened the black civil rights movement in the 1960s, and to what degree were differences in goals, methods, and leadership resolved?

✦ What challenges did Mexican Americans and Japanese Americans face during and after World War II, and how did they confront these challenges?

✦ How did the goals, issues, leadership, and methods of Chicano and Native American groups compare to those of African Americans?

✦ In what ways did "the new generation of Americans" that President Kennedy referred to in his inaugural address alter the political and social landscape of the 1960s and 1970s?

✦ What were the many constituencies of the antiwar movement of the 1960s and 1970s? How were the concerns of these disparate groups crystallized by the war in Southeast Asia?

✦ What did affirmative action programs attempt to do, and why were they so controversial?

✦ Despite the nation's move to the right in the 1970s, how were women, gays, and other groups able to sustain their efforts to expand civil rights?

Work, Exchange, and Technology

✦ In what ways were the rights of workers affected by the Cold War?

✦ Despite many achievements, labor unions remained vulnerable. What progress did unions make, and what storm clouds were on the horizon for American workers?

✦ In what ways did the divide between the rich and the poor increase in the 1970s? Why did this occur?

✦ In what ways did television play an important role in American politics and government?

✦ Why was Eisenhower so concerned about the "military-industrial complex"?

✦ What was the impact of the space race on science, education, and foreign policy?

✦ How did television transform American life?

✦ Why were the media able to have such an important role in shaping American opposition to the war in Vietnam?

✦ What factors accounted for limited economic growth in the 1970s?

✦ What effect did the gas crisis of the 1970s have on American assumptions and attitudes?

✦ What accounted for the transition from an industrial to a service economy?

Migration and Settlement

- ✦ Why did the United States become a suburban nation? What were the characteristics of this demographic change, and how did government policy, technology, and economic forces contribute to it?
- ✦ What groups made up the "other America" that Michael Harrington described? What efforts were made to address his concerns?
- ✦ In what ways was segregation in the North similar to southern segregation? How was it different?
- ✦ In what ways did the report of the Kerner Commission send a wakeup call to urban America and to those who governed American cities?
- ✦ What problems were specific to American cities in the 1970s, and how successfully did government address these problems?
- ✦ What were the effects of the changes made to U.S. immigration law in 1965?

Politics and Power

- ✦ What was "Cold War liberalism"?
- ✦ In what ways did President Truman alter FDR's vision of America?
- ✦ In what ways did American domestic policies reflect the tensions of the Cold War?
- ✦ To what extent do you feel that actions directed against communists in the United States were justified? Defend your argument.
- ✦ In what ways did American politics and policies reflect ideological differences in the Republican Party?
- ✦ How effective were President Eisenhower's policies in both combatting communism and solving problems at home?
- ✦ How successfully did President Kennedy confront the Cold War crises he faced?
- ✦ How did party politics reflect racial tensions in the decades following World War II?
- ✦ In what ways did opponents of the black civil rights movement attempt to link their opposition to the Cold War?
- ✦ What role did the courts play in formulating and enforcing policies that expanded civil rights?
- ✦ Account for the crumbling of the New Deal coalition in the 1970s and 1980s. How did the elections of Richard Nixon and Ronald Reagan reflect that realignment?
- ✦ What led to the decline of liberalism in the 1970s?
- ✦ Why did liberals and conservatives view government so differently?
- ✦ What were the contradictions that were characteristic of John Kennedy's life and presidency?
- ✦ What were Lyndon Johnson's goals as he assumed the presidency in 1963? How did his successes and failures reflect these goals?
- ✦ To what extent were the reforms of the New Deal and Johnson's Great Society similar?
- ✦ In what ways was the Great Society a manifestation of the centuries-old debate over the proper role of government?
- ✦ Richard Nixon is often considered a transitional figure. Why?
- ✦ Why did some Americans believe that the courts went too far in furthering the interests of the left?
- ✦ Why did the Nixon White House engage in such widespread abuse of power, and how did Nixon's actions change the nation?
- ✦ Is there a constitutional guarantee of privacy? If so, where in the Constitution is it found? Why has the right to privacy mattered so much in the years since World War II?

America in the World

- ✦ In what ways did World War II set the stage for the Cold War?
- ✦ Why did opposition to communism become such a key component of American foreign policy after World War II?
- ✦ What specific actions did the U.S. government take to combat communism?
- ✦ In what ways did actions taken by both the United States and the Soviet Union exacerbate the tensions between the two powers?
- ✦ As the Cold War escalated, the United States turned to two former enemies — Japan and West Germany — for support. Why?
- ✦ To what extent was containment an effective tool of U.S. foreign policy?
- ✦ The textbook notes that by 1955, "the two superpowers had institutionalized" the Cold War. What does this mean, and why did it happen?
- ✦ In what ways was NSC-68 a turning point in the Cold War?
- ✦ How did the memory of Munich inform American foreign policy after World War II?
- ✦ In what important ways had the world changed by 1964, and how did these changes force a change in U.S. foreign policy?
- ✦ What was more important in shaping American foreign policy in this period: the preservation and expansion of democracy or the search for stability?
- ✦ The textbook asserts that with regard to Vietnam, "the elemental paradox remained unchanged." What was this paradox, and what events supported this argument?
- ✦ Why did events in Vietnam escalate into a protracted and costly conflict?
- ✦ What factors led to American involvement in the Caribbean, the Middle East, and Africa?
- ✦ The Eisenhower Doctrine became yet another extension of Monroe's famous 1823 assertion of American foreign policy. What are the similarities and differences among these statements of American foreign policy: the Monroe Doctrine, the Roosevelt Corollary, the Truman Doctrine, the Eisenhower Doctrine, and the Nixon Doctrine?
- ✦ Many reform movements sprang from what the textbook calls "the progressive spirit" of the 1960s. How did these movements compare in their goals, methods, and leadership?
- ✦ What was the impact of the Vietnam War on U.S. politics, economy, and social movements?
- ✦ In what ways did world events in the 1970s change the lives of everyday Americans?

Geography and the Environment

- ✦ What were the historical precedents for the environmental activism of the 1970s?
- ✦ How did Richard Nixon's policies on environmental issues contribute to his reputation as a transitional president?

Culture and Society

- ✦ Changes in language often reflect and shape social change. In what ways was this true in the decades after World War II?
- ✦ The textbook argues that the Cold War "compromised, as much as supported, stated American principles." What evidence supports this statement?
- ✦ In what ways were the 1920s and the 1950s alike? How did they differ?
- ✦ What aspects of postwar culture were most targeted by intellectuals, writers, and other critics? Why did these critics believe that American society was in crisis?
- ✦ To what extent was the hippie culture of the 1960s similar to the culture of the Beats of the 1950s and the Lost Generation of the 1920s?

✦ Though many critics were pessimistic about America's future, many did not share their concerns. What gave Americans reason to be optimistic?

✦ How did music define the youth culture and reflect tensions in American society?

✦ Account for the rise of cultural conservatism. What factors supported the status quo, and which encouraged change in the decades after World War II?

✦ In the years since World War II, what forces have promoted change in the nature and function of the American family? In what ways has the American family changed?

✦ How has postwar popular culture reflected tensions in the family and in the workplace?

✦ What accounted for the sexual revolution of the 1960s and 1970s, and what was its impact?

✦ How was the sexual revolution portrayed in popular culture, and in what ways did popular culture serve to promote changes in sexual mores and behavior?

✦ What were the characteristics of the Fourth Great Awakening of the late twentieth century, and how did this religious movement compare to those that preceded it?

✦ In what ways did evangelical Christianity and its adherents craft and spread a message that appealed to many Americans?

America's History Chapter Summaries

(required AP® content in bold)

Chapter 25
Cold War America, 1945–1963

Chapter 25 examines the tensions that led to and maintained the era of the Cold War up to 1963. The end of World War II set the stage for the beginning of the Cold War, a time of tense relations and world competition of the United States and its Western allies with the Soviet Union and its client states. The Yalta agreements in the final months of the war, in addition to establishing the United Nations, allowed the Soviet Union to occupy and control most of Eastern Europe. At the Potsdam Conference in the summer of 1945, Stalin refused to compromise with Truman and refused to hold open elections in areas he controlled, thus maintaining Soviet power. Germany remained divided as it had been at the end of the war, with the West becoming a democracy and the East remaining under Soviet communist rule. Britain's Winston Churchill described Eastern Europe as trapped behind an "iron curtain" of Soviet rule, a term that became a watchword of the era.

The United States responded with a strategy that was dubbed **"containment," the determination to stop the spread of communist influence and control wherever it threatened to surface in the world**. Turkey, Greece, and Yugoslavia became early centers of this struggle. George Kennan, an advisor to the president, believed the Soviet system was unstable and would eventually collapse. He urged the United States to adopt the policy. President Truman took this advice and provided U.S. aid to Greece when that country was threatened with a communist uprising in 1947. At the same time, he issued the Truman Doctrine, outlining the policy of containment.

In response to the need to bolster the shattered economies of Western Europe—and also as part of a plan to bolster up noncommunist nations, the United States developed the Marshall Plan, which provided financial aid to any country in Europe that could demonstrate that it had a freely elected government. Western Europe's recovery quickly outstripped that of the East, which remained under Soviet control. In 1948, Stalin made an attempt to at least push Western powers out of the old German capital of Berlin by blockading the city. Truman responded with the Berlin Airlift, an around-the-clock stream of supply planes that brought supplies into the city for more than a year. Stalin finally abandoned the blockade, but Germany remained divided. Western powers formed the North Atlantic Treaty Organization (NATO) to deal with similar situations in the future.

Since the use of the atomic bomb during the war, many in the U.S. government worried about the inevitable proliferation of nuclear weapons, and in 1949. the Soviets detonated a bomb of their own. Congress passed the National Security Act in 1947, which created the National Security Council. That body's report in 1950, known as **NSC68, called for a massive buildup of the American military, the development of a hydrogen bomb, and whatever else it took to surpass the military power of the Soviet Union**.

China proved to be another theater of the Cold War. Civil war had been raging between the Western-backed Nationalists of Jiang Jieshi (Chiang Kai-shek) and the Communists under Mao Zedong. Mao triumphed and established the People's Republic of China in 1949, as the Nationalists fled to the island of Taiwan. The United States refused to recognize Communist China as the legitimate China.

In 1950, **Communist-backed North Korea launched a surprise attack on South Korea, an ally of the United States**. The United Nations came to the defense of South Korea, relying heavily on American troops under the leadership of General Douglas MacArthur. MacArthur's determination to press the war into China led President Truman to relieve him of command, and the

Korean War settled into a stalemate that became an issue in the presidential election of 1952. Republican candidate Dwight Eisenhower was able to turn this stalemate to his advantage in the presidential campaign.

The Democratic Party also suffered from the loss of labor support by 1952. A backlash against unions resulted in Congress's passing the Taft-Hartley Act in 1947 that weakened collective bargaining and initiated right-to-work laws prohibiting union shops. Truman had managed to win reelection in 1948 by a narrow margin, though his version of Roosevelt's domestic program, his Fair Deal, struggled with a Congress that did not often support him.

Fear of the spread of communism engulfed the country in the late 1940s and early 1950s. Congressional committees like the House Un-American Activities Committee were already calling suspect organizations and individuals to task. This committee was led by a freshman congressman from California, Richard Nixon, who made a special project of tracking down and working to convict Alger Hiss, a member of Roosevelt's inner circle, as a communist sympathizer. Senator Joseph McCarthy organized a Senate committee to investigate suspicious activities that quickly turned into a national witch hunt. In 1954, he was undone by making baseless accusations against the army and by being exposed as a bully and a fraud on national television. He died in disgrace several years later, though not before he had ruined many lives with his accusations.

Eisenhower won the presidential election of 1952, chosen because many hoped he would be a conservative alternative to the legacy of Franklin Roosevelt. In fact, Eisenhower proved to be a largely middle-of-the-road Republican who supported some New Deal programs while reining in others. **He was clearly a Cold Warrior, but one dedicated to containment rather than confrontation. The arms race accelerated, and Eisenhower appointed as secretary of state John Foster Dulles, who threatened those who disturbed international peace with "massive retaliation."** The newly created Central Intelligence Agency (CIA) intervened in the domestic politics of Iran, Central America, and Vietnam. Eisenhower and Dulles were **determined to intervene in Vietnam when the French decided to end their efforts to prevent a communist government from taking over in their former colony.** The United States picked up the support of the South Vietnamese forces at the Geneva Conference in 1954 as the French were pulling out. The goal was to install a Western-friendly regime there that would be a counter to the communist government of Ho Chi Minh in North Vietnam.

More controversy awaited in the Middle East, with the continuing conflict between the Israelis and the Palestinians, and now with the addition of a crisis involving Egypt and the Suez Canal. Egyptian support of the Palestinians led to a British and French attack on the Suez Canal, resulting in a stalemate that the United Nations had to sort out. The United States issued the Eisenhower Doctrine, reemphasizing American "support for any nation facing the threat of International Communism."

The year 1960 saw the election of Democrat John F. Kennedy, a Cold Warrior yet one who had the advantage of youth and charisma. In his inaugural address, Kennedy promised America a "New Frontier," and he brought in a cadre of young, highly educated advisors to make up his cabinet and staff. His administration immediately faced crises in Cuba and Berlin. **The ill-fated Bay of Pigs invasion was a disaster for the young president**, and many felt Kennedy's indecision emboldened Khrushchev to authorize the building of the Berlin Wall in August 1961. Kennedy redeemed himself by standing up to Khrushchev during the **Cuban missile crisis in October 1962, forcing the Russians to dismantle missile bases in Cuba under the threat of nuclear retaliation**. Under President Kennedy, the United States became even more mired in Vietnam. Kennedy authorized the use of military advisors and Special Forces, "Green Berets," whose specialty was unconventional warfare. American officials in Vietnam were dismayed at local protests against the government the United States supported, particularly Buddhist monks who chose to publicly burn themselves alive rather than endorse the government supported by the United States. The South Vietnamese government sponsored by the United States collapsed in a coup in November 1963, resulting in the assassination of Ngo Dinh Diem, the South Vietnamese president. South Vietnam was left without a popularly supported leader, but American foreign policy insisted that the North's Ho Chi Minh could not be considered a legitimate replacement. Vietnam remained a foreign policy problem for the United States. President Kennedy was assassinated a few weeks after the Vietnamese coup, and the question of what to do in Vietnam passed on to President Lyndon Johnson.

Chapter 26
Triumph of the Middle Class, 1945–1963

Chapter 26 examines the expansion of the middle class in the post–World War II decades. **One of the greatest social phenomena of the postwar period was the growth of the American middle class**. America dominated the global economy and had the highest standard of living in the world. The growth of the suburbs did not come without a dark side, however. Urban areas declined and racial segregation was on the rise. **Many on the margins of society, such as immigrants, minorities, the elderly, and the working poor, were not included in this prosperity**.

With Germany and Japan in shambles at the end of the war, **the United States entered a postwar economic boom in both internal and international marketplaces that would last for three decades**. The United States played a preeminent position in the creation of the World Bank and the International Monetary Fund, making the American dollar a currency valued worldwide. The General Agreement on Tariffs and Trades (GATT) fit America's vision of an open-market global economy as well. The Defense Department continued to offer enormous government contracts to private industries in the name of national security. The Soviet launch of *Sputnik* in 1957 led to the investment of even more millions in these programs under the National Defense Education Act (NDEA), as the United States was determined to keep pace with and then surpass the Soviet Union. Science, industry, and the military became so intertwined that Eisenhower, on leaving office, warned of the **potential dangers of what he termed the "military industrial complex."**

Corporate power characterized American capitalism during these years, employing huge numbers of white-collar workers. Some felt the working world in these corporations often stifled creativity, valuing "organization men" rather than original thinkers. Automation increasingly replaced blue-collar workers with machines, something that would have long-term effects on the economy by the end of the century. **While many enjoyed unprecedented prosperity, tenacious poverty lurked among those at the bottom of the economic ladder in both urban and rural areas.**

Prosperity meant seemingly endless waves of consumer goods. Returning GIs were able to take advantage of government programs to attend college in record numbers and to buy homes with low-interest loans. Workers rejoined trade unions on returning to work, though unions met with resistance in Congress, which passed legislation curbing some union powers. Management hoped to loosen the grip of unions in the decades to come. Americans bought homes, cars, and household appliances in record numbers. Their children, the "baby boom" generation, grew up as the focus of both their parents' attention and that of the advertising world. As they grew older, the marketing focus changed from games and television to music and the other interests of teenagers. Television became an essential part of nearly every American home, reinforcing the images of a good life through consumption of the latest goods and services. Television shows glorified the perfect suburban family, something that often fell short of the reality. Theirs was a vision of white middle-class tastes and values with little effort to add any nuance to the picture.

The teen culture of the 1950s and 1960s was also a new phenomenon. Elvis Presley provided the cross-over music that linked African American rhythm and blues to a young white audience. Youth rebellion became big business, with music, poets, writers, and artists providing the **younger generation with a rich alternative to their parents' predictable suburban lifestyle**. Church membership soared during the 1950s, in part because many felt **religion was an antidote to the threat of atheistic communism. In the 1950s the phrase "one nation under God" was added to the Pledge of Allegiance and "In God we trust" was added to the nation's coins.**

The baby boom lasted until about 1964 when birthrates began to decline. The boomers have given their generation a significant impact on the past six decades of American history because there are so many of them. They have enjoyed the best health care in history, have been generally well educated, and in many cases were indulged by parents who remembered the Great Depression and wanted to "give them the best." Many of their mothers stayed home because it was expected of them. Women who did work were usually relegated to "pink-collar" jobs as secretaries, nurses, or waitresses, to name a few. Most women also received less pay than men did for the same work. Many women had no choice but to work so that their families could pay their bills. The domestic ideal of the nuclear family with the father as the breadwinner was already crumbling around the edges.

The 1960s saw the coming of the sexual revolution. People began to talk about and acknowledge such topics as sex outside marriage and gay and lesbian relationships, and they began to have frank and open discussions of sexual matters that were previously kept out of public discourse. The baby boomers would be the first generation in history to have access to reliable birth control, another factor that would revolutionize sexual mores.

The growth of the suburbs was accelerated by the development of Eisenhower's Interstate Highway Act, a network of roads that made access to suburbs even easier. The subdivisions built by men like William Levitt became the young family's opportunity for independence, although minorities were not allowed to buy into them. Fast food outlets and shopping malls made life in the suburbs even more attractive. National demographics began to change as well, as plentiful jobs and pleasant weather led thousands to flock to the Sunbelt states of the South and Southwest. By the end of the 1960s, the nation was almost evenly divided between the urban and the suburban, with cities increasingly characterized by racial segregation, higher crime, poverty, and unemployment. Those in the suburbs felt protected from these woes by distance and wealth. Attempts at urban renewal met with limited success during these years. Immigrants often made their way to urban areas in search of inexpensive housing and what jobs they could get. The contradictory visions of America held by those in the cities and those in the suburbs would become a major part of the protest movements that characterized the 1960s.

Chapter 27
Walking into Freedom Land: The Civil Rights Movement, 1941–1973

Chapter 27 explores the era of modern civil rights that began during World War II and continued throughout the 1950s and 1960s. The modern civil rights movement began to emerge during World War II and the early Cold War era, with both grassroots efforts by churches and organizations like the Congress of Racial Equality (CORE) and **work through the courts to enforce the equal rights guaranteed in the Constitution to all American citizens.** Jim Crow had been a reality for African Americans living in the South since the days of Reconstruction, limiting both social equality and political participation. The North was only marginally better, with de facto rather than de jure segregation—low-paying jobs and separate neighborhoods with poor city services. Segregation and racial discrimination were a national rather than a regional problem.

The National Association for the Advancement of Colored People (NAACP) had been challenging racial segregation in a series of court cases since the group was formed in 1909. Marcus Garvey's United Negro Improvement Association attracted some attention in the 1920s. It was not until the emergence of a strong black middle class in the 1940s that progress began to seem possible. Churches and college students would provide the vanguard for the 1950s and 1960s.

A. Philip Randolph, head of the Brotherhood of Sleeping Car Porters, urged President Franklin Roosevelt to make racial fairness part of his wartime effort. Roosevelt signed into law Executive Order 8802, prohibiting racial discrimination in defense industries. This was followed by the Fair Employment Practices Commission, a weak body but a precedent nevertheless. Randolph also launched the "Double V" campaign, calling for victory over the Axis powers and over racism at home as well.

After the war, Jackie Robinson broke the color line in Major League Baseball, and President Truman appointed the Presidential Committee on Civil Rights and announced the desegregation of the armed forces. Truman's actions earned him enemies among southern politicians. In 1948 he faced a challenge from the States' Rights Democratic Party, the short-lived Dixiecrats, an early warning of the divisions that would face the Democratic Party in the years to come.

Other minorities endured discrimination as well. Mexican Americans in the Southwest faced a caste system similar to that of Jim Crow, including job discrimination and segregation in schools. Japanese Americans struggled to regain property lost during their forced internment during the war years.

The NAACP continued to look for the landmark court case that would turn segregation on its head. **Thurgood Marshall led the legal team that brought the case of *Brown v. Board of Education of Topeka, Kansas*, to the Supreme Court in 1954**. The Court ruled that segregation violated the principle of equal protection under the law, a clear breach of the guarantees of the Fourteenth Amendment. The South struck back, with 101 **southern political leaders signing the "Southern Manifesto," declaring that they would defy the Court's decision**. Only after President Eisenhower sent federal troops into Little Rock, Arkansas, to enforce desegregation did southern states begin to move grudgingly in the direction of compliance. The murder of a young black teen, Emmett Till, by Klansmen in Mississippi, resulted in a not-guilty verdict by a local court. That miscarriage of justice galvanized a generation of young African Americans to join the protest movements.

Desegregation of public facilities beyond schools was the next step, and Rosa Parks's arrest for refusing to give up her seat to a white passenger on a Montgomery, Alabama, bus provided the cause. The resulting bus boycott brought Martin Luther King Jr., a young Montgomery minister, to national attention. His advocacy of nonviolence changed the face of the civil rights movement and won respect for the protesters all over the world. He founded the Southern Christian Leadership Conference (SCLC) to organize protests and demonstrations, always with nonviolence as the watchword. Sit-ins by students in Greensboro, North Carolina, led to the creation of the Student Non-Violent Coordinating Committee (SNCC) to work with the SCLC. They staged Freedom Rides in an effort to desegregate interstate bus services, a tactic that resulted in serious injuries when the buses they rode were attacked by Klansmen in Alabama and other southern states.

The city of Birmingham, Alabama, became the scene of shocking violence when the local sheriff authorized the use of police dogs and fire hoses to break up civil rights demonstrations. King was arrested there and wrote his famous "Letter from a Birmingham Jail" to those who criticized his involvement in protests that were sure to turn violent. King was determined to see the passage of a national civil rights law that was before Congress in fall 1963. To lobby national support for the bill, he helped organize a march on Washington, D.C., in August that year to show Congress how much public support of it there was. Hundreds of thousands of people, black and white, converged on the nation's capital and heard King's famous "I Have a Dream" speech. Even so, it was not enough to get the necessary votes in Congress, and the bill was defeated that fall. **Lyndon Johnson would get Civil Rights Act passed the following year in 1964**.

The summer of 1964 saw SNCC's voter registration project, "Freedom Summer," begin in Mississippi. The students who participated were often naive about what they were facing, and three young workers were killed. An attempt to challenge Mississippi's segregated delegation to the Democratic National Convention that summer also failed, and many of the young SNCC members began to feel disillusioned. Even so, they had made gains: Congress passed the Voting

Rights Act of 1965, and this bill, along with the Twenty-Fourth Amendment, which outlawed poll taxes, enabled thousands of blacks to vote for the first time since Reconstruction.

The mid-1960s saw the rise of more activist civil rights group. Stokely Carmichael and others who left SNCC began to look for more concrete ways to attack the problems they felt faced minority communities. He advocated what he called "Black Power," black self-reliance in attacking poverty and injustice. A new generation of black nationalists looked to the earlier example of Marcus Garvey for inspiration. The Nation of Islam, the Black Muslims, gained popularity among African Americans, mainly in northern cities. Malcolm X, a leader of the Nation of Islam, broke with that group in 1964 and sought to work for civil rights through a broader Muslim organization that did not focus so much on the racial exclusiveness of Black Muslims. A much more militant approach was advocated by the Black Panthers, a radical nationalist group founded in Oakland, California, by Huey Newton and Bobby Seale. They also opposed the Vietnam War as a white man's war. Following this lead, the Puerto Rican community saw the organization of the Young Lords, a group calling for self-determination for Puerto Ricans.

Many young black politicians began to work within the system and win elective offices in major cities around the country. They even organized the National Black Political Convention that met in Gary, Indiana, in 1972, hoping to produce an agenda that would have an impact on the national Democratic Party meeting later that year to choose a presidential candidate. They were not successful, but black politicians continued to win elective office in the decades that followed.

The year 1965 saw the beginnings of violence and rioting in inner cities throughout the country. The riots in the Watts neighborhood of Los Angeles that summer were the first of many "long hot summers" for people living in urban ghettos. It became clear that poverty and racism were national problems rather than just southern issues. King hoped to expand his work to include issues of poverty and opposition to the Vietnam War as well as racism, but he was assassinated in April 1968. His civil rights work became fragmented with the loss of his leadership, as the leaders who followed did not have the charisma to replace him. The battle for equal rights now became tied to the antiwar movement as the decade of the 1960s drew to a close.

The nation also saw an organized Chicano movement emerge, under the leadership of Cesar Chavez, a champion for the rights of migrant workers and leader of the United Farm Workers (UFW). Young Mexican Americans, wanting a more activist approach, formed the Brown Berets, a group modeled after the Black Panthers, and organized a political party, La Raza Unida (The United Race), to promote Chicano interests. **The American Indian Movement (AIM) formed to work for better conditions on Indian reservations.** A takeover of the federal facilities at Wounded Knee, South Dakota, drew national attention to their cause.

The experience of African American civil rights advocates served as a model for similar civil rights movements among other minorities in the United States. All of these groups worked to achieve inclusion in mainstream American society, but each found themselves also including more nationalist celebrations of their own ethnic heritages as their movements developed and matured.

Chapter 28
Uncivil Wars: Liberal Crisis and Conservative Rebirth, 1961–1972

Chapter 28 charts the progress of liberalism and the resurgence of conservatism in the 1960s and early 1970s. **The liberal movements of the 1960s soon came under assault from a number of directions, from young people frustrated with the slow process of change and from conservatives who felt that change was coming too fast and that the size of government was getting out of control.**

By the end of the decade, the political pendulum began to move away from the reform minded toward the more traditional.

When Lyndon Johnson came into office after the assassination of John Kennedy, he hoped to create a domestic agenda that would finish the job the New Deal began. He called his program the "Great Society," and he immediately began to push for civil rights legislation as well as a full slate of other programs designed to alleviate the condition of the poor and marginalized. He spoke of a "War on Poverty," with the federal government leading the way.

Johnson won a term on his own in 1964, defeating the conservative Barry Goldwater. He also carried both houses of Congress, giving him a clear path for his legislative agenda. Among his first bills were Medicare and Medicaid, guaranteeing health care to, respectively, the elderly and the poor. The programs that followed, including environmental protection, education reform, aid to cities for transportation and housing, and even the arts, touched almost every segment of society. **Johnson proposed a significant change in immigration, replacing old quotas with numeric limits that were less discriminatory.**

While poverty rates did drop, not everyone was pleased with the impact of the Great Society vision. **Conservatives felt the programs were too expensive and argued that improvements would have come anyway with a stronger economy. Others pointed out that many problems remained, among them entrenched poverty and racial segregation.**

A number of groups did see progress, however. **The women's movement was revitalized as more women moved into the workplace and demanded equal pay for equal work.** Betty Friedan, author of the *Feminine Mystique,* was one of the founders of the National Organization for Women, a group dedicated to lobbying for equal treatment of women in the job and as citizens.

Hovering over the Johnson administration, however, was the growing war in Vietnam. As Kennedy had inherited this war from Eisenhower, so Johnson inherited the conflict from Kennedy. He saw South Vietnam as a vital outpost in the war to contain communism, so he was determined to prevent Southeast Asia "from going the way China went." Johnson used an alleged incident involving a U.S. destroyer in the Gulf of Tonkin in the summer of 1964 to get authorization from Congress for widening the war. The Gulf of Tonkin Resolution gave Johnson a free hand and led to a massive **escalation of U.S. involvement in Vietnam**, both through increases in ground troops and bombing raids on North Vietnam. As the casualties mounted, Johnson found American public opinion shifting against the war. Nightly television coverage showed the carnage, and the public began to doubt the rosy predictions of easy victory that came in a steady stream from the White House. Fueled by college students, many of whom had been involved in the civil rights movement, **antiwar sentiment began to grow and become more organized**. The Selective Service System became an early target of the antiwar effort as young people resisted the draft or applied for conscientious objector status. Antiwar demonstrations grew in numbers and strength through the Johnson years, while **young supporters of the war countered with the creation of the conservative Young Americans for Freedom**. The new counterculture, a movement rebelling against middle-class values and authority in general, blended antiwar energy with rock music, recreational drugs, and an open attitude toward sex that startled the older generations.

The year 1968 proved to be a watershed year of sorts, with protests against the war escalating as the military faced the Tet Offensive, an offensive by the North Vietnamese (at the time of the Vietnamese holiday of Tet) that showed U.S. gains in the South to be more at risk than the public had been led to believe. Johnson was discredited in the public eye, and many were no longer willing to believe his positive pronouncements on the progress of the war. Political assassinations rocked the country. Martin Luther King Jr. was killed in April, and Robert Kennedy, front-runner for the Democratic presidential nomination, was assassinated in June. The summer found the Democratic Party in disarray, holding a chaotic political convention in Chicago and choosing Vice President Hubert Humphrey as a less-than-inspiring candidate for the fall election. The Republicans took advantage of the Democrats' problems and nominated Richard Nixon as their conservative alternative, a man who promised to restore law and order to the country. Many voters, tired of the antiwar movement, the counterculture, and urban rioting, began to drift away from the Democratic Party. A third-party candidate, segregationist George

Wallace of Alabama, offered an alternative to southern voters, another group that felt they no longer had a political home with the Democrats. Nixon lured southern voters himself by downplaying his commitment to aggressively enforcing civil rights laws. Nixon won a narrow victory, and the country began a slow turn to the political right.

The struggle for civil rights continued, though some groups also took up the antiwar cause. **The women's liberation movement broadened its goals to support equal treatment of women in all areas of society**, and more women were elected to public office. A riot at the Stonewall Inn in New York focused **national attention on the issue of gay rights, and the Gay National Task Force was formed to organize lobbying efforts for nondiscrimination laws.**

President Nixon continued to insist that most Americans agreed with his basically centrist policies; he called them the "silent majority," as distinct from those who took to the streets in protest. He hoped to ease the country out of the war through what he called a process of "Vietnamization," letting the South Vietnamese gradually take over the war effort as America withdrew.

Nixon was determined to find a way out that would provide "peace with honor." As he approached the presidential election of 1972, he announced progress in the long-stalled peace talks with the North Vietnamese that had met sporadically in Paris for several years. In early 1973, he announced that the North and South Vietnamese had agreed to a Paris Peace Accord that would slowly allow the United States to withdraw, turning the war over to the South Vietnamese. When the United States did bring the troops home, the South Vietnamese government was not able to hold out on its own. In April 1975, the North Vietnamese defeated the South Vietnamese, and the country of Vietnam was unified under a communist government much like it might have been had they been allowed self-determination in 1954 when the French withdrew.

President Nixon was also able to change the direction of the Supreme Court, a body that had been predictably liberal for several decades. After his landslide reelection victory in 1972, he had the opportunity to make several Court appointments that began to shift the Court in a more conservative direction.

Chapter 29
The Search for Order in an Era of Limits, 1973–1980

Chapter 29 examines the crises of the 1970s. The early 1970s saw a growing backlash in the United States to the social and political upheavals of the 1960s. In addition, an international oil embargo in 1973 caused the economy to experience runaway inflation and the deepest economic slump since the Great Depression. United States support for Israel in the 1973 Yom Kippur War led the Arab members of the Organization of Petroleum Exporting Countries (OPEC) to support raising the price of oil in retaliation. The nation put conservation measures into place, such as lower speed limits, but prices on just about everything began to rise at alarming rates.

President Nixon introduced a number of environmental measures during his presidency. He had been impressed with Rachel Carson's book *Silent Spring*, which documented the effects of the overuse of pesticides on the environment. He signed into law a number of bills designed to protect the environment, including one that created the Environmental Protection Agency. The leak of radioactive material at the Three Mile Island reactor in Pennsylvania also brought the dangers of nuclear power to the forefront of public debate, slowing the development of nuclear power sources for decades.

The U.S. economy suffered under high unemployment, stagnant consumer demand, and inflation in the 1970s, a combination known as "stagflation." There was little that any presidential administration or Congress could do to improve the situation as long as oil prices remained high. Many American industries saw overseas competition cut into profits, leading to downsizing, automation, and attempts to invest in new technologies. Parts of the Northeast and Midwest that had been industrial centers declined and became known as the "Rust Belt." Deindustrialization also hurt labor unions as cheap overseas labor drew away jobs. Labor union membership declined to the lowest levels since the 1920s.

The growth of the suburbs contributed to a corresponding decline of urban areas. Suburban residents resented paying taxes to support government services and schools that they felt did not benefit them. **California led the way in the movement known as the "tax revolt," refusing to approve new taxes to fund services that taxpayers felt they did not need**. The generous spirit of the New Deal was unraveling.

Nixon was distracted from many of these problems by difficulties of his own. The Watergate scandal was threatening to consume his presidency. For a while, he successfully dodged questions about his involvement in the efforts to cover up the break-in at the Democratic National Committee headquarters in a Washington hotel during the 1972 presidential campaign. The story was doggedly pursued by reporters from the *Washington Post*, who eventually uncovered information that pointed directly at White House involvement. Nixon ultimately had to resign to avoid impeachment on charges of obstruction of justice. While dealing with this scandal, the president also found his power in foreign policy limited by the War Powers Act, which required congressional approval to deploy U.S. troops in anything less than an emergency.

The Watergate scandals and President Gerald Ford's decision to pardon Richard Nixon left many veteran politicians viewed poorly by the electorate. The elections of 1974 and 1976 brought many new faces to Congress, though government did not become much more efficient. The old Democratic coalition continued to crumble, though new alignments would not be evident for a few more years. The election of Democrat Jimmy Carter in 1976 was seen as the triumph of an outsider who was not involved in Washington's "business as usual." Despite his good intentions, Carter was not able to bring about much improvement in the economy, as gas prices stayed high. He was hurt as well by his inability to do much to protect American interests in the Iranian Revolution, failing to gain the release of hostages taken at the American embassy in Tehran.

Civil rights continued to be a major issue on the political agenda throughout these years. **The affirmative action policies of the 1960s faced new challenges by whites who saw such practices as reverse discrimination**. The Supreme Court **moved away from solid support for affirmative action in 1978 with the *Bakke* decision**, which rejected the use of quotas to ensure diversity in college admissions. Women's rights efforts were also curtailed by the states' rejection of the Equal Rights Amendment (ERA) in 1982. **A number of conservative women's groups joined the fight to stop ERA, and they were ultimately successful. Women did win the right to legal abortion with the *Roe v. Wade* decision in 1973, though controversy over that ruling continues today. Gay rights activists continued their work as well, though not without controversy and push-back from the conservative community**.

Nixon appointed Warren Burger as chief justice of the Supreme Court, thus beginning a shift toward greater conservatism within that body. Viewed in retrospect, many of the Burger Court decisions seem more centrist than conservative, but they were still a significant change from the liberal years of Chief Justice Earl Warren.

Many Americans worried over how life in the late twentieth century was changing traditional values. Single-parent households were on the rise, more women were moving into the workplace, and union workers were not able to depend on collective bargaining to advance their causes. Some popular culture centered on the lives of blue-collar workers. Rap and hip-hop spoke of the lives of working-class blacks in the deindustrialized urban city. **Access to birth control pills gave women control over reproduction, changing in many ways the traditional relationships between men and women. Sexuality and social problems became the focus of Hollywood. Many feared that traditional middle-class marriage would become a thing of the past**.

Churches responded with what some have called another "Great Awakening." Evangelical Protestantism gained popularity, using the medium of television to reach immense audiences. They sought to translate their "Christian family values" into a political agenda that would have a tremendous impact in the last decades of the twentieth century.

Thematic Timeline

THEME	REQUIRED CONTENT	SUPPORTING EXAMPLES
AMERICAN AND NATIONAL IDENTITY	• In the 1960s, many Americans identified themselves as liberals. • Civil rights activists achieved some successes in ending segregation, but progress was slow. • After 1965, differences over tactics and philosophy increased tensions between civil rights activists. • Some whites resisted efforts at desegregation. • Activists called for social and economic equality for women and gays and lesbians. • Latinos, American Indians, and Asians demanded social and economic equality and redress of past injustices.	**Setting the stage** • The Congress of Racial Equality is formed (1942). • During World War II, blacks serve in large numbers in the military and then demand equality at home. • World War II stimulates the growth of a large black middle class and increased enrollment of African Americans in college on the GI Bill. • Segregation is most prevalent in the South, but exists in other areas of the nation too. • During and after World War II, Mexican Americans live subject to discrimination similar to that in the Jim Crow South. **The Truman years, 1945–1953** • Truman issues Executive Order 9835, creating the Loyalty-Security Program (1947). • Before the civil rights movement of the 1950s, segregation underlies the social, political, and economic environment. • Impetus for change in race relations is fostered in large part by the legacy of World War II. • Cesar Chavez and Dolores Huerta become leaders of the emerging Mexican American civil rights movement. • The Japanese American Citizens League files lawsuits to help Japanese Americans regain property taken during World War II. **The Eisenhower years, 1953–1961** • By the late 1950s, the vision of America portrayed on television is nearly always white, Protestant, and middle class. • Attorneys including Thurgood Marshall, who will become the first African American on the Supreme Court, file suits to end discrimination. • *Brown v. Board of Education* overturns "separate but equal" (1954). • The Southern Manifesto denounces the *Brown* decision. • Emmett Till is murdered in Mississippi (1955).

THEME	REQUIRED CONTENT	SUPPORTING EXAMPLES
AMERICAN AND NATIONAL IDENTITY (*continued*)		• Rosa Parks refuses to give up her seat to a white man and triggers the Montgomery Bus Boycott (1957). • Martin Luther King Jr., a leader in the bus boycott, forms the Southern Christian Leadership Conference (1957). • On orders from President Eisenhower, Central High School in Little Rock, Arkansas, is integrated (1957). • Black college students begin the Greensboro sit-ins (1960). • Ella Baker and others form the Student Nonviolent Coordinating Committee (1960). • Women become conflicted as they are pulled in opposite directions by the middle-class domestic ideal and the expanding job market. • Homosexual activists organize to counter prejudice and to change the laws to prevent antigay discrimination. Although this activism begins in the 1950s, the gay rights movement does not gain steam until the 1970s. • A vibrant youth culture emerges in the 1950s. **The Kennedy years, 1961–1963** • Freedom Riders are attacked in Alabama, forcing the federal government to intervene (1961). • Thousands of marchers protest the white leadership in Birmingham, Alabama, and are met by force and Bull Connor (1963). • King writes his famous "Letter from Birmingham Jail" (1963). • King leads the March on Washington and delivers the "I Have a Dream" speech (1963). • Four black girls in a Birmingham church are killed by a bomb (1963). • Betty Friedan's *The Feminine Mystique* helps launch the women's movement (1963). **The Johnson years, 1963–1969** • President Johnson signs the far-reaching Civil Rights Act of 1964 that establishes the Equal Employment Opportunity Commission. • Affirmative action policies are increasingly implemented to address discrimination. • Whites respond by accusing the government of reverse discrimination. • The Freedom Summer campaign in Mississippi works to protect voting rights (1964).

THEME	REQUIRED CONTENT	SUPPORTING EXAMPLES
AMERICAN AND NATIONAL IDENTITY (*continued*)		• The Mississippi Democratic Freedom Party fights for representation at the Democratic National Convention (1964). • Marchers are attacked on the Edmund Pettus Bridge in Selma, Alabama (1965). • The emergence of black nationalism and the actions of the Nation of Islam signal a split in the civil rights movement (mid-1960s). • Riots strike large cities, beginning in the "long hot summer" of 1964. Thirty-four people die in Watts in 1965. • Malcolm X is assassinated (1965). • Stokely Carmichael and others advocate "Black Power" (1966). • Huey Newton and Bobby Seale organize the Black Panthers and inspire young Puerto Ricans to form the Young Lords Organization (1966). • Voters in Gary and Cleveland elect the first blacks to serve as mayors of large cities (1967). • The Kerner Commission issues an eye-opening report on race relations (1968). • Martin Luther King Jr. is assassinated (April 1968). • The National Organization for Women is founded (1966). • Mexican Americans form a significant voting bloc by the mid-1960s. • Students, dismayed by the conflict in Vietnam and the failure of the American Dream to reach all Americans, begin to organize. • Leaders of the Students for a Democratic Society, formed in 1960, call on young people to "look uncomfortably to the world we inherit." • The influence of the New Left spreads. • Students organize in opposition to the Selective Service System (1967). • A conservative youth organization, Young Americans for Freedom, attempts to counter the New Left. **The Nixon years, 1969–1974** • African Americans link the movement for civil rights to opposition to the war in Vietnam. • As feminists organize, words like *sexism*, *male chauvinism*, and *Ms.* enter the vocabulary.

THEME	REQUIRED CONTENT	SUPPORTING EXAMPLES
AMERICAN AND NATIONAL IDENTITY (*continued*)		• Many women of color are conflicted, torn between the civil rights movement and feminism. • Women are admitted to formerly all-male universities, and women's studies programs are offered at many colleges. • Publication of *Our Bodies, Ourselves* fuels the women's health movement (1971). • Title IX prohibits discrimination in education and has a huge impact on women's sports (1972). • Congress passes the Equal Rights Amendment in 1972, but ratification is derailed by the efforts of anti-ERA activists like Phyllis Schlafly. • *Roe v. Wade* establishes a constitutional right to abortion by affirming a right to privacy and sets the stage for a decades-long battle over reproductive rights (1973). • Young Mexican Americans begin to use the term *Chicano* to identify themselves and organize La Raza Unida (1970). • Gay activists demand their rights, especially after the Stonewall raid (1969). • The American Indian Movement (AIM) organizes and draws attention to poverty in Indian communities. • AIM activists occupy Wounded Knee (1973). **The Ford and Carter years, 1974–1981** • The decision in *Bakke v. University of California* energizes the opponents of affirmative action (1978). • Dozens of U.S. cities pass pro–gay rights ordinances. • Anita Bryant's "Save Our Children" campaign leads to the repeal of a gay rights ordinance in Dade County, Florida (1977). • Gay activist Harvey Milk is assassinated in San Francisco (1978).

THEME	REQUIRED CONTENT	SUPPORTING EXAMPLES
WORK, EXCHANGE, AND TECHNOLOGY	• Americans debated whether to maintain a large nuclear arsenal, often called the military-industrial complex. • Activists attempted to address the issue of poverty as a national issue. • The private sector strengthened. • Technological developments helped spur economic growth.	**In the aftermath of World War II/the Cold War** • The Marshall Plan establishes an extensive aid program aimed at promoting European economic recovery (1947). • The United States restores the Japanese economy in an effort to limit the spread of communism in East Asia. • The American economy: progress, prosperity, and poverty. • The United States dominates the world economy in the postwar era. • Government spending for domestic and military programs boosts the economy. • The military-industrial complex spurs the growth of the Sunbelt. • Three decades of economic growth are fueled by policies of the World Bank and the International Monetary Fund (called the Bretton Woods system), the expansion of the military-industrial complex, corporate growth, and consumer demand. • President Johnson calls for a War on Poverty (1964). • The Economic Opportunity Act creates Head Start, the Jobs Corps, and VISTA (1964). • The economy suffers due to its dependence on foreign oil and the power of OPEC to determine supply and price. • Following the Yom Kippur War, some Arab states declare an oil embargo, and Congress lowers the speed limit to 55 miles per hour (1973). • In the 1970s, the American economy struggles with a growing federal deficit, spiraling inflation, and foreign competition. • Stagnation contradicts basic economic principles. • An industrial and manufacturing economy gives way to a service economy. • Nixon addresses the nation's economic woes by taking the nation off the gold standard and imposing wage and price controls (1971). • Despite his efforts to WIP (Whip Inflation Now), President Ford is unsuccessful in stemming the nation's economic woes. • American cities are hit particularly hard by the economic downturn; New York City is forced to borrow from the federal government to avoid default (1975).

THEME	REQUIRED CONTENT	SUPPORTING EXAMPLES
WORK, EXCHANGE, AND TECHNOLOGY (*continued*)		• The middle class flees from the cities to the suburbs. • Jimmy Carter's economic policies, especially after the Iranian Revolution limits the supply of oil, fail to promote economic growth. • California's Proposition 13 becomes the symbol of a national tax revolt (1978). • The income inequality gap widens. **The American worker** • Congress passes the Taft-Hartley Act over Truman's veto, severely weakening the power of unions (1947). • Despite the Taft-Hartley Act, collective bargaining helps workers join the middle class in the two decades after World War II. • In the 1950s, due to the GI Bill and increases in federal funding for education, the U.S. workforce becomes the best educated in the world. • The 1963 Equal Pay Act establishes the principle of equal pay for equal work for women. • Women join the workforce in significant numbers as families become dependent on two incomes. • As educational and professional barriers fall, more women become doctors, lawyers, scientists, and business professionals. • In the 1970s, workers in the steel industry see their jobs disappear as heavy industry struggles to combat foreign competition. • The Rust Belt of the Northeast and Midwest are especially hard hit by deindustrialization. • Cesar Chavez and Dolores Huerta organize the United Farm Workers union (1962). • In the 1970s, deindustrialization greatly weakens the labor movement. • Between 1973 and the early 1900s, real wages for the typical worker decline 10 percent. **Technology and its impact** • *Sputnik* is launched in 1957, beginning the space race. • NASA funding and expenditures on education are increased. • Beginning in 1947, William Levitt uses new building techniques to build houses quickly and cheaply. • Dr. Jonas Salk develops the polio vaccine (1954).

THEME	REQUIRED CONTENT	SUPPORTING EXAMPLES
WORK, EXCHANGE, AND TECHNOLOGY (*continued*)		• Television demonstrates to the nation the violence of white supremacy and the dangers of zealots like Joseph McCarthy. • Television plays an important role in the 1960 presidential election. • The birth control pill, first marketed in 1960, revolutionizes the lives of American women. **An age of consumerism** • Patterns of consumption are driven by houses, cars, and children. • The Federal Housing Administration and the Veterans Administration encourage home-building by offering low mortgage rates. • The revolution in television advertising creates consumer demand. • Religious leaders promote consumption, arguing that those who live a moral life deserve material blessings. • The Equal Credit Opportunity Act guarantees married women access to credit (1974). • Beginning with the oil crisis in the 1970s, many Americans buy more efficient cars.
MIGRATION AND SETTLEMENT	• The Sun Belt experienced growth, and Sun Belt states became an economic and political force. • The baby boom led to the expansion of the suburbs. • Migrants, both international and internal, sought greater access to prosperity. • In 1965, significant changes to U.S. immigration laws encouraged increased immigration.	**The baby boomers and suburban America** • After World War II, Americans move to the suburbs in huge numbers: by 1960, one-third of Americans live in the suburbs. • The National Interstate and Defense Highways Act of 1956 authorizes the spending of billions of dollars to build the national highway system, making suburbanization possible. These new roads also make evacuation easier in case of a national nuclear emergency. • The population of the new suburbs is very homogeneous, made up of young, middle-class, white families. • Despite a court decision outlawing restrictive covenants, racial discrimination in the housing market is rampant. • Postwar marriages generally prove to be stable. • The baby boom explodes in the 1950s. • Mothers turn to Benjamin Spock's *Common Sense Book of Baby and Child Care* (1946) to help raise their children. • By the early 1960s, the baby boom subsides, and the divorce rate begins to increase. • Shopping malls and fast food restaurants like McDonald's emerge as visible symbols of the suburban environment.

THEME	REQUIRED CONTENT	SUPPORTING EXAMPLES
MIGRATION AND SETTLEMENT (*continued*)		**Urban America** • Urban renewal projects attempt to revitalize American cities. • Federally funded housing projects, meant to expand housing for the urban poor, often result in their isolation. **Immigration** • The Displaced Persons Act (1948), the McCarran-Walter Act, the Bracero Program, and the repeal of the Chinese Exclusion Act stimulate increased immigration. • Puerto Rican immigration increases, especially to New York City. • Many Cubans immigrate to Florida after Fidel Castro seizes power in Cuba in 1959. • The Immigration Act of 1965 ends the quota system, and the number of Latin American and Asian immigrants increases. **Going West** • Many Americans move to the South and the Southwest, now known as the Sunbelt; California experiences the greatest growth. • Disneyland opens (mid-1950s). • Mexican immigrants move into cities in the West and Southwest in large numbers.
POLITICS AND POWER	• Both American political parties supported the containment of communism, but Americans continued to debate the policies and methods that were proposed to deal with communism. • Shortly after the end of World War II, the military was desegregated. • Unlike the Korean conflict, where there was little domestic opposition, the war in Vietnam led to many, sometimes violent, protests. • The balance between liberty and order was at the center of much debate over the proper role of government and the power of the president.	**The Truman years, 1945–1953** • Truman orders the desegregation of the military (1948). • Governor Strom Thurmond of South Carolina leaves the Democratic Party and runs for president as a Dixiecrat (1948). • Truman defeats Dewey in 1948, embraces "Cold War liberalism," and proposes his Fair Deal. • HUAC hearings begin (1947). • Alger Hiss goes to prison in 1950. • Senator Joseph McCarthy asserts that he can name 205 Communists in the State Department (1950). • Although opponents of civil rights call racial integration "communistic," others believe that Cold War imperatives demand a more democratic America. • Because Democrats and Republicans seem to agree on most issues in the early 1950s, some in the media declare "an end of ideology," a sort of new Era of Good Feeling. However, several controversial issues soon divide the nation. **The Eisenhower years, 1953–1961** • The Rosenbergs are convicted and executed (1953).

THEME	REQUIRED CONTENT	SUPPORTING EXAMPLES
POLITICS AND POWER (*continued*)	• Some political leaders worked successfully to end segregation. • Civil rights activists used strategies including legal challenges, direct action, and non-violent protests. • The president, Congress, and the courts all participated in efforts aimed at desegregation. • *Brown v. Board of Education* and the Civil Rights Act of 1964 were milestones in the civil rights movement. • Liberals supported Lyndon Johnson's Great Society and believed in using federal power to end racial discrimination and eliminate poverty while confronting communism abroad. • The Supreme Court expanded liberal ideals, supported Great Society social programs, and buttressed the expansion of federal power. • The conservative movement grew in response to the ascendancy of liberalism, defending traditional views of morality and calling for more limited government. • Some on the left criticized liberals for their support of American policies abroad and for failing to adequately address racial and economic discrimination.	• Congress censures McCarthy (1954). • National Defense Education Act provides millions of dollars for American universities (1958). **The Kennedy years, 1961–1963** • John Kennedy defeats Richard Nixon (1960). • Kennedy's promotes policies he calls the New Frontier. • Kennedy proposes a civil rights act but is slain before action can be taken on it. • Kennedy is assassinated in November 1963, leaving many of his initiatives unfinished and promises unfulfilled. **The Johnson years, 1963–1969** • Lyndon Johnson succeeds Kennedy and is elected in his own right in 1964. • A conservative revolt begins, targeting what conservatives view as excessive permissiveness in American society. • Johnson calls for a Great Society to end poverty and racial injustice. • Despite southern opposition, Congress passes the Civil Rights Act of 1964. • The Civil Rights Act recognizes women as a category protected against discrimination. • Medicare and Medicaid, as well as the Elementary and Secondary Education Act, are hallmarks of Johnson's Great Society legislation. • Congress passes the Voting Rights Act in 1965. • *Griswold v. Connecticut* affirms a constitutional right to privacy (1965). • The Warren Court issues decisions expanding the rights of the accused. • Liberal activism in the 1960s fragments the New Deal coalition, as southern conservatives object to liberal initiatives. • Crisis strikes in 1968: the Tet Offensive, the assassinations of Martin Luther King Jr. and Robert Kennedy, and disruptions at the Democratic National Convention in Chicago. **The Nixon years, 1969–1974** • In his campaign for the presidency, Richard Nixon appeals to northern working-class voters and southern whites, breaking up the New Deal Democratic coalition (1968). • Nixon initiates his "southern strategy." • Nixon supporters become known as the "silent majority."

THEME	REQUIRED CONTENT	SUPPORTING EXAMPLES
POLITICS AND POWER (*continued*)		• George Wallace runs as a third-party candidate, calling for "law and order." • Women raise awareness of sexual politics and crusade for reproductive rights. • Conservatives mount an attack on what they view as the excesses of a liberal Supreme Court: *Miller v. California*, *Roe v. Wade*, and limitations on religious ritual in public schools. • Nixon appoints Warren Burger chief justice of the Supreme Court; however, the Burger Court maintains a liberal-moderate stance. • *Furman v. Georgia* strikes down capital punishment (1972). • Conservatives oppose school busing to achieve racial integration. • Nixon is reelected in a landslide in his 1972 campaign against George McGovern. • Vice President Spiro Agnew resigns after being accused of accepting kickbacks as governor of Maryland (1973). • The Nixon presidency unravels after the 1972 break-in at the Watergate offices of the Democratic National Committee. • Congress weakens presidential powers by passing the War Powers Act and the Freedom of Information Act (1973–1974). • Threatened with impeachment, Nixon resigns in August 1974. **The Ford years, 1974–1977** • Nixon's successor, Gerald Ford, is criticized for pardoning Richard Nixon. • Democrats assume a huge majority in the 1974 congressional elections and work to bring greater transparency to the federal government. However, the power of lobbyists increases and the end of bipartisanship makes government less efficient. • Political power shifts to the West and the South, signaling a conservative resurgence. • *Gregg v. Georgia* reinstates capital punishment (1976). **The Carter years, 1977–1981** • Jimmy Carter, touting his outsider credentials, defeats Gerald Ford in the presidential election of 1976. • Carter fails to develop close ties with Congress. • Carter attributes much of the nation's woes to a "crisis of the spirit."

THEME	REQUIRED CONTENT	SUPPORTING EXAMPLES
AMERICA IN THE WORLD	• The United States asserted its leadership in an effort to stem the expansion of communist ideology and military power. • U.S. foreign policy was based on collective security and influence of its economic power. • The American policy of containment led to military conflict in Korea and Vietnam. • Sometimes the Cold War involved direct and indirect military involvement; at other times, there was a period of mutual coexistence (or détente.) • The post–World War II decolonization and the emergence of nationalist movements in Asia, Africa, and the Middle East forced both the United States and the Soviets to forge new relationships with new nations, some of which remained nonaligned. • The United States supported noncommunist regimes in Latin America. These nations supported democracy to different degrees. • The United States became involved in the Middle East, dealing with ideological, military, and economic issues.	**1945–1953** • Despite the World War II alliance of the United States and the Soviet Union, the two nations are deeply divided by 1945. • The Yalta Conference establishes many of the conditions that would influence Europe in the postwar era (February 1945). • The three leaders who meet at Yalta agree to establish the United Nations. • Yalta and the conference at Potsdam (July 1945) set the stage for communist domination of Eastern Europe. • Cold War rivalries raise questions about the balance of power in Europe and Asia and the nature of independence movements in Asia, the Middle East, and Africa. • The U.S. government tends to view Third World nations as pawns of the Soviet Union. • Postwar Germany is first divided into four, and then two, sectors. • One American goal is to strengthen West Germany as a bulwark against communist expansion. • Churchill accuses Stalin of erecting an "iron curtain" around Eastern Europe (1946). • George Kennan enunciates the policy of containment (1946). • Concerned about communist expansion in Greece and Turkey, President Truman announces the Truman Doctrine (1947). • The CIA is established (1947). • Stalin blockades Berlin (1948). • The United States recognizes the new state of Israel (1948). • Tensions increase in the Middle East. • NATO is established in 1949. • NSC-68 is a turning point in the Cold War (1949). • Under the leadership of Mao Zedong, the People's Republic of China is established (1949). • The United States goes to war in Korea (1950). **1953–1961** • Eisenhower supports the New Look defense policy. • To achieve stability, the United States supports Iran, South Vietnam, and Nicaragua, allies that nevertheless have repressive governments.

THEME	REQUIRED CONTENT	SUPPORTING EXAMPLES
AMERICA IN THE WORLD (*continued*)		• The United States helps depose the leader of Iran, replacing him with Mohammed Reza Pahlavi (1953). • The CIA engineers a coup in Guatemala (1954). • Creation of SEATO (1954). • Suez Canal crisis (1956). • The president announces his Eisenhower Doctrine, extending the reach of containment (1956). • The domino theory drives U.S. foreign policy in Southeast Asia. • The United States helps finance the French war in Vietnam (early 1950s). • Eisenhower rejects the Geneva Accords that call for elections in Vietnam and instead lends U.S. support to the Diem government (1954). **1961–1969** • The Soviets construct the Berlin Wall (1961). • The Bay of Pigs fiasco damages U.S.–Soviet relations (1961). • The United States and the Soviet Union face off in the Cuban Missile Crisis (1962). • The National Liberation Front (Vietcong) works to undermine the Diem regime (beginning in 1961). • Diem is assassinated (1963). • The 1964 Gulf of Tonkin Resolution escalates the conflict in Vietnam. • Johnson initiates Operation Rolling Thunder (1965). • Television begins to turn Americans against the war in Vietnam. • Journalists accuse Johnson of creating a "credibility gap." • The antiwar movement crystallizes. • Following the Tet Offensive, American support for the Vietnam War plummets (1968). **1969–1977** • Nixon uses "Vietnamization" to reduce troop levels in Vietnam. • In 1969, the public learns of the 1968 My Lai massacre. • The bombing campaign in Cambodia and killings at Kent State and Jackson State energize the antiwar movement (1970). • Nixon begins to pursue détente. • SALT I signed (1972). • Nixon visits China (1972).

THEME	REQUIRED CONTENT	SUPPORTING EXAMPLES
AMERICA IN THE WORLD (*continued*)		• Before the 1972 election, Nixon sends Henry Kissinger to the Paris peace talks and then announces "peace is at hand." • Paris Peace Accords are signed, ending the Vietnam War (1973). • In 1975, North Vietnamese troops defeat the South Vietnamese and unite Vietnam. **1977–1981** • President Carter's idealistic foreign policy emphasizes human rights. • Carter makes the controversial decision to return control of the Panama Canal to Panama (1977). • Carter mediates a peace agreement between Egypt and Israel (1978). • The Senate rejects SALT II (1979). • To protest Soviet actions in Afghanistan, Carter declares an American boycott of the 1980 Olympics. • Iranian students seize the U.S. embassy in Tehran, Iran, and hold Americans hostage for over a year (1979). • Carter's popularity sinks due in large part to criticism of his foreign policy.
GEOGRAPHY AND THE ENVIRONMENT	• Because of crises over oil in the Middle East, the United States attempts to create a national energy policy. • Americans became increasingly concerned about the preservation of natural resources, calling for conservation measures and actions to lessen pollution.	• Rachel Carson's *Silent Spring* alerts Americans to the dangers of DDT (1962). • The shortage of oil in the 1970s prompts concern for the environment. • Environmental activists renew efforts to protect the environment. • Congress establishes the Environmental Protection Agency (1969). • Additional environmental protection laws are implemented, including the Clean Air Act, the Occupational Health and Safety Act, and the Endangered Species Act (1970–1973). • The first Earth Day is held (April 1970). • Environmentalism becomes a divisive issue, pitting corporate interests and many workers against environmental activists. • The debate over the merits and the dangers of nuclear power escalates after the incident at Three Mile Island (1979).
CULTURE AND SOCIETY	• In the 1960s, liberals were anticommunist and believed that government, especially the federal government, could be used to achieve social goals.	**Culture and government** • The Hollywood Ten go to jail for contempt of Congress by refusing to testify at the HUAC hearings (1947).

THEME	REQUIRED CONTENT	SUPPORTING EXAMPLES
CULTURE AND SOCIETY (*continued*)	• Support for liberalism reached its highest point in the mid-1960s. • While mass culture became more homogeneous, artists, intellectuals, and youth challenged conformity. • Conservatives more aggressively defended their ideology, one based in part on fear of juvenile delinquency, urban unrest, and what they perceived as attacks on the traditional family. There were increasing clashes between conservatives and liberals over social issues, the power of the federal government, and the movement for individual rights. • Despite the prevailing image of the nuclear family, the American family structure underwent significant changes, especially as more women entered the workplace. • The counterculture, which included many young people, rejected many of the values of their parents, and promoted a sexual revolution and greater informality in American culture.	• Johnson signs legislation establishing the National Endowment for the Humanities and the National Endowment for the Arts. • Debates rage over the government's role in regulating the music and film industries and in determining limitations on pornography. **Critics and rebels** • David Riesman writes *The Lonely Crowd*, a critique of corporate America (1950). • Michael Harrington's *The Other America* warns Americans not to ignore the poor (1962). • The Beats embrace jazz and question middle-class materialism. • Allen Ginsburg's "Howl" (1956) and Jack Kerouac's novel *On the Road* (1957) glorify spontaneity, sexuality, and drugs. • The hippies of the counterculture reject authority and middle-class respectability. • The Summer of Love draws thousands to San Francisco in 1967. **Race and culture** • Jazz flourishes among both African Americans and whites. • Rock and roll crosses over racial boundaries. • Jackie Robinson becomes the first black player in Major League Baseball (1947). • There are very few roles on television for black or Latino actors until the 1970s and 1980s. **The youth culture** • Hollywood promotes the teenage culture of the postwar decades, introducing stars like Marlon Brando and James Dean. • Rock and roll, which had its origins in African American music, becomes mainstream, as defined by Elvis Presley and other white musicians drawing on African American music. • The popularity of rock and roll icons, especially the Beatles and the Rolling Stones, is another indication of the growing divide between young and old. • Folk music is the musical inspiration for the counterculture. • In the 1970s, musicians including Bruce Springsteen and John Cougar Mellencamp sing about the plight of the working class. • Young African Americans develop new cultural forms like break dancing and rap music.

THEME	REQUIRED CONTENT	SUPPORTING EXAMPLES
CULTURE AND SOCIETY (*continued*)		**The media** • Television contributes to the end of Joseph McCarthy and the end of the war in Vietnam. • Archie Bunker both upholds and ridicules conservative views in the 1970s. • Mass-market books, television shows, and movies with sexual themes flood the market in the 1970s. • Televangelists use television to spread their message, building media empires. • Evangelical authors and publishing houses burgeon. **Faith in a changing America** • Many Americans reaffirm their faith as they become increasingly troubled by the threat of communism and nuclear war. • Religion plays a major role in the civil rights movement and the protest against the war in Vietnam. • Billy Graham, Norman Vincent Peale, Robert Schuler, and others adeptly use the media to spread an evangelical message. • In response to concerns about divorce rates, social unrest, challenges to traditional beliefs, feminism, legalized abortion, the counterculture, and homosexuality, evangelicals spark a Fourth Great Awakening in the late 1960s and the 1970s. • A primary goal of evangelicals is to strengthen the family, especially by restoring traditional gender roles. **The sexual revolution** • In the aftermath of World War II, the media celebrate paternalism, the nuclear family, and female domesticity. • Alfred Kinsley researches sexuality and brings taboo topics into the public discussion (late 1940s and 1950s). • A sexual revolution begins in the 1950s and, especially after the birth control pill becomes available, transforms American society. • Hugh Hefner starts his Playboy enterprise in the 1950s. • Critics of the sexual revolution blame television and comic books for promoting sex and violence. • Marriages face the challenges of rising divorce rates, changing sexual values, and critiques of the nuclear family. In response to these challenges, the therapeutic industry expands.

Period 8 Practice Questions

Multiple-Choice Questions

Questions 1–3 refer to the excerpt below.

"The Great Society rests on abundance and liberty for all. It demands an end to poverty and racial injustice, to which we are totally committed in our time. But that is just the beginning.

"The Great Society is a place where every child can find knowledge to enrich his mind and to enlarge his talents. It is a place where leisure is a welcome chance to build and reflect, not a feared cause of boredom and restlessness. It is a place where the city of man serves not only the needs of the body and the demands of commerce but the desire for beauty and the hunger for community.

"It is a place where man can renew contact with nature. It is a place which honors creation for its own sake and for what it adds to the understanding of the race. It is a place where men are more concerned with the quality of their goals than the quantity of their goods.

"But most of all, the Great Society is not a safe harbor, a resting place, a final objective, a finished work. It is a challenge constantly renewed, beckoning us toward a destiny where the meaning of our lives matches the marvelous products of our labor."

Lyndon Johnson, *The Great Society*, May 22, 1964

1. The Great Society of Lyndon Johnson's presidency resulted in
    (A) divisions within the Democratic Party.
    (B) the elimination of poverty in Appalachia.
    (C) significant deregulation of industry.
    (D) the elimination of environmental regulations for defense industries.

2. The Great Society was largely derailed by
    (A) lobbyists who poured massive amounts of money into Great Society opposition candidates.
    (B) the laissez-faire approach to government prevalent in the 1960s.
    (C) escalating costs of the war in Vietnam.
    (D) the Arab oil embargo.

3. The election of 1968 demonstrated
    (A) significant movement to the left with the candidacy of George Wallace.
    (B) dissatisfaction with protest and civil unrest.
    (C) validation of Great Society programs to end poverty.
    (D) increased support for the war in Vietnam due to the Tet Offensive.

GO ON TO THE NEXT PAGE.

Questions 4–6 refer to the 1953 political cartoon below.

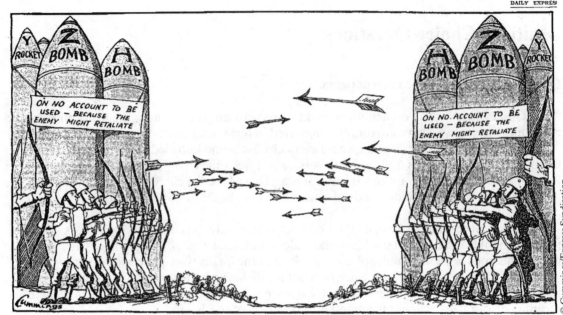

Back to where it all started . . .

British Daily Express, August 24, 1953

4. Which of the following BEST describes the primary focus of the above political cartoon?
   (A) The United States should launch a preemptive strike on the Soviet Union.
   (B) Defeating China would be a relatively easy task because of their use of primitive weapons.
   (C) The Soviet Union had gained a technological superiority over the United States in the 1950s.
   (D) Neither side would be successful in a nuclear war.

5. The above cartoon could be seen as encouraging the United States to
   (A) seek a diplomatic solution to U.S.-Soviet problems.
   (B) allow the building of missile bases in Cuba rather than risking a confrontation with the Soviet Union.
   (C) support the domino theory by sending troops to Southeast Asia.
   (D) allow the military-industrial complex to produce technologically superior weapons to give the United States a distinct advantage over the Soviet Union.

6. Which of the following best represents a partial realization of the spirit supported by the above political cartoon?
   (A) The U.S.-backed invasion of Cuba under President Kennedy
   (B) The shooting down of a U.S. spy plane over the Soviet Union
   (C) The policy of détente under President Richard Nixon
   (D) Escalation of the war in Vietnam under President Johnson

GO ON TO THE NEXT PAGE.

Questions 7–9 refer to the graph below.

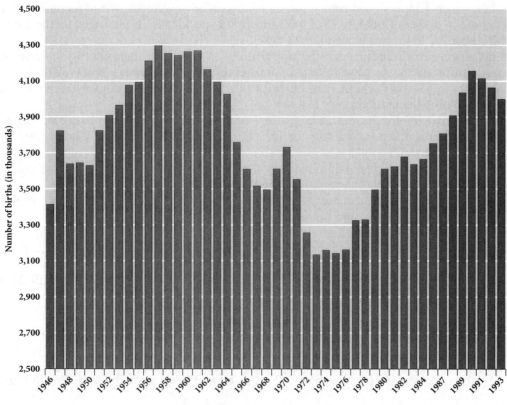

U.S. Birthrates, 1946–1993

7. The baby boom generation was sometimes referred to as a "pig in a python" because
   (A) society had to adjust to baby boomers as they passed through various life stages.
   (B) boomers were digested by society and had to assume traditional values.
   (C) the counterculture rejected cleanliness and lived a hedonist lifestyle.
   (D) of their increased concern over environmental pollution.

8. Which of the following best represents the most important impact the baby boom bulge in population had in the 1950s?
   (A) It caused the development of polio vaccine by Salk and Sabin.
   (B) It led to the first movement toward suburbs in American history.
   (C) It initiated a Red Scare with parents fearful their children would become communists.
   (D) It spurred consumerism as manufacturers produced age-specific products for "boomers."

9. As the baby boom generation reached late adolescence in the early 1960s, they tended to
   (A) challenge the traditional views and values of the older generation.
   (B) retreat in a shell of political noninvolvement.
   (C) attend college in lower numbers than any previous generation.
   (D) have children at an earlier and more rapid rate than their parents.

GO ON TO THE NEXT PAGE.

Questions 10–12 refer to the excerpt below.

"This bill, which I have signed today, substantially carries out most of the recommendations made by me in a speech on July 28, 1943, and more specifically in messages to the Congress dated October 27, 1943, and November 23, 1943:

"1. It gives servicemen and women the opportunity of resuming their education or technical training after discharge, or of taking a refresher or retrainer course, not only without tuition charge up to $500 per school year, but with the right to receive a monthly living allowance while pursuing their studies.

"2. It makes provision for the guarantee by the Federal Government of not to exceed 50 percent of certain loans made to veterans for the purchase or construction of homes, farms, and business properties.

"3. It provides for reasonable unemployment allowances payable each week up to a maximum period of one year, to those veterans who are unable to find a job.

"4. It establishes improved machinery for effective job counseling for veterans and for finding jobs for returning soldiers and sailors.

"5. It authorizes the construction of all necessary additional hospital facilities.

"6. It strengthens the authority of the Veterans Administration to enable it to discharge its existing and added responsibilities with promptness and efficiency."

President Franklin D. Roosevelt, Statement on Signing the GI Bill, June 22, 1944

10. The bill described above was primarily designed to

   (A) ease the adjustment of veterans into society and prevent a postwar depression.
   (B) demobilize the armed forces as quickly as possible.
   (C) prepare the United States to combat the Soviet Union on the world stage.
   (D) retain women's places in the workforce that had been necessitated by World War II.

11. A consequence of this bill in the 1950s was the movement toward

   (A) urban renewal designed to eliminate chronic slums.
   (B) the Sunbelt from the Rust Belt.
   (C) universal free college education.
   (D) the suburbs from the inner city.

12. In the 1950s, women's rights groups

   (A) introduced the Equal Rights Amendment.
   (B) gained strength as women's contributions to the war effort were highly publicized.
   (C) faced social pressure to return to a "cult of domesticity."
   (D) continued to lobby for the extension of voting rights and equal pay.

END OF MULTIPLE-CHOICE SECTION

Short-Answer Questions

"Let every nation know, whether it wishes us well or ill, that we shall pay any price, bear any burden, meet any hardship, support any friend, oppose any foe to assure the survival and the success of liberty. . . .

"But neither can two great and powerful groups of nations take comfort from our present course—both sides overburdened by the cost of modern weapons, both rightly alarmed by the steady spread of the deadly atom, yet both racing to alter that uncertain balance of terror that stays the hand of mankind's final war.

"So let us begin anew—remembering on both sides that civility is not a sign of weakness, and sincerity is always subject to proof. Let us never negotiate out of fear. But let us never fear to negotiate."

John F. Kennedy, Inaugural Address, 1961

1. Using the excerpt above, answer a, b, and c.

    a) Cite one example from the 1960s where negotiations with the Soviet Union were successful, and explain the consequences of that success.

    b) Cite one example of significant confrontation between the United States and the Soviet Union in the 1960s, and explain how the confrontation ended.

    c) Compare U.S.-Soviet relations at the end of the 1960s with U.S.-Soviet relations at the beginning of the decade.

GO ON TO THE NEXT PAGE.

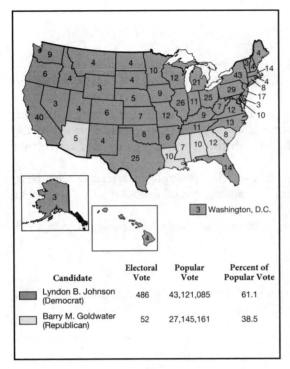

The Presidential Election of 1964

Candidate	Electoral Vote	Popular Vote	Percent of Popular Vote
Lyndon B. Johnson (Democrat)	486	43,121,085	61.1
Barry M. Goldwater (Republican)	52	27,145,161	38.5

The Presidential Election of 1968

Candidate	Electoral Vote	Popular Vote	Percent of Popular Vote
Richard M. Nixon (Republican)	301	31,770,237	43.4
Hubert H. Humphrey (Democrat)	191	31,270,533	42.7
George C. Wallace (American Independent)	46	9,906,141	13.5
Minor parties	—	239,908	—

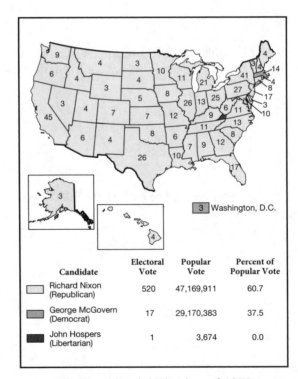

The Presidential Election of 1972

Candidate	Electoral Vote	Popular Vote	Percent of Popular Vote
Richard Nixon (Republican)	520	47,169,911	60.7
George McGovern (Democrat)	17	29,170,383	37.5
John Hospers (Libertarian)	1	3,674	0.0

GO ON TO THE NEXT PAGE.

2. Using the three maps on the facing page, answer a, b, and c.

    a) In the election of 1964, Lyndon Johnson won in a landslide. Identify one specific factor that helped lead to this landslide victory, and explain how it did so.

    b) In the election of 1972, Richard Nixon won in a landslide. Identify one specific factor that helped lead to this landslide victory, and explain how it did so.

    c) Explain why the election of 1968 was so tightly contested when sandwiched between landslide victories in 1964 and 1972.

END OF SHORT-ANSWER SECTION

Document-Based Question

Directions: The following question is based on the accompanying documents. The documents have been edited for this exercise. Spend approximately 15 minutes planning and 45 minutes writing your answer.

Write an essay that does the following:

+ States an appropriate thesis that directly addresses all parts of the question.
+ Supports the thesis or argument with evidence from all or all but one of the documents AND your knowledge of U.S. history beyond the documents.
+ Analyzes all or all but one of the documents.
+ Places each document into at least one of the following categories: intended audience, purpose, historical context, and/or point of view.
+ Uses historical evidence beyond the documents to support your argument.
+ Places the argument in the context of broader regional, national, or global processes.
+ Incorporates all of the elements above into a convincing essay.

Question: The 1970s have described by some as "the years of malaise," defined by dictionary.com as "a vague or unfocused feeling of mental uneasiness, lethargy, or discomfort." Analyze the foreign and domestic factors that led many Americans to feel this uneasiness with life in the 1970s.

Document 1

Source: David Falconer, U.S. National Archives, ca. 1973

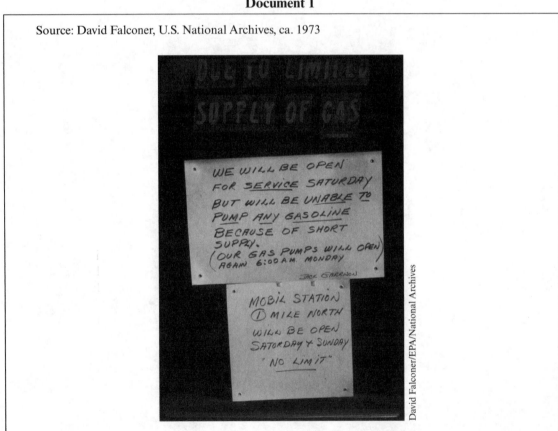

Document 2

Source: *New York Times*, August 9, 1974

Document 3

Source: President Gerald R. Ford, Address to Joint Session of the Congress on U.S. Foreign Policy, April 10, 1975

The North Vietnamese, from the moment they signed the Paris accords, systematically violated the cease-fire and other provisions of the agreement. Flagrantly disregarding the ban on the infiltration of troops, the North Vietnamese illegally introduced over 350,000 men into the south. In direct violation of the agreement, they sent in the most modern equipment in massive amounts. Meanwhile, they continued to receive large quantities of supplies and arms from their friends.

In the face of this situation, the United States—torn as it was by the emotions of a decade of war—was unable to respond. We deprived ourselves by law of the ability to enforce the agreement, thus giving North Vietnam assurance that it could violate that agreement with impunity. . . . Encouraged by these developments, the North Vietnamese, in recent months, began sending even their reserve divisions into South Vietnam. Some 20 divisions, virtually their entire army, are now in South Vietnam. The Government of South Vietnam, uncertain of further American assistance, hastily ordered a strategic withdrawal to more defensible positions.

GO ON TO THE NEXT PAGE.

Document 4

Source: John Jonik, cartoon about the Love Canal chemical disaster, 1978

Document 5

Source: *Report of the President's Commission on the Accident at Three Mile Island*, October 30, 1979

At 4:00 a.m. on March 28, 1979, a serious accident occurred at the Three Mile Island 2 nuclear power plant near Middletown, Pennsylvania. The accident was initiated by mechanical malfunctions in the plant and made much worse by a combination of human errors in responding to it. . . . During the next 4 days, the extent and gravity of the accident was unclear to the managers of the plant, to federal and state officials, and to the general public. What is quite clear is that its impact, nationally and internationally, has raised serious concerns about the safety of nuclear power.

GO ON TO THE NEXT PAGE.

Document 6

Source: Letter from U.S. President Jimmy Carter to Ayatollah Ruhollah Khomeini of Iran, November 6, 1979

In the name of the American people, I ask that you release unharmed all Americans presently detained in Iran and those held with them and allow them to leave your country safely and without delay. I ask you to recognize the compelling humanitarian reasons, firmly based in international law, for doing so.

Document 7

Source: U.S. inflation rate, 1960–2000.

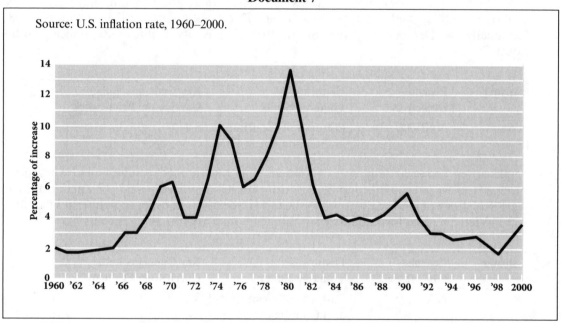

END OF DOCUMENT-BASED SECTION

Answer Key to Period 8 Practice Questions

Multiple-Choice Questions

1.

Answer	Learning Objectives	Historical Thinking Skills	Key Concepts in the Curriculum Framework
A	POL-3.0	Causation	8.2

Explanation: Southern Democrats were social conservatives who opposed many of the Great Society's social welfare programs. Ultimately this, along with disagreements over civil rights and law and order, led to a divided Democratic Party in the election of 1968. Eventually the Democratic "solid South" transformed itself into a Republican "solid South."

2.

Answer	Learning Objectives	Historical Thinking Skills	Key Concepts in the Curriculum Framework
C	NAT-3.0	Patterns of Continuity and Change over Time	8.1

Explanation: The escalating costs of Vietnam plus government spending on Great Society programs overheated the economy. Johnson himself reportedly said, "I knew from the start if I left a woman I really loved—the Great Society—in order to fight that bitch of a war in Vietnam, then I would lose everything at home. My hopes my dreams."

3.

Answer	Learning Objectives	Historical Thinking Skills	Key Concepts in the Curriculum Framework
B	NAT-2.0	Patterns of Continuity and Change over Time	8.2

Explanation: In the election of 1968, both Richard Nixon and third-party candidate George Wallace ran a "law and order" campaign against Vice President Hubert Humphrey. Both tapped into the opposition of the "silent majority" to antiwar and civil rights protests from the left. They also took issue with Supreme Court decisions that established new precedents for rights of the accused that conservatives believed hampered the ability of law enforcement to maintain a stable and orderly society.

4.

Answer	Learning Objectives	Historical Thinking Skills	Key Concepts in the Curriculum Framework
D	WOR-2.0	Interpretation	8.1

Explanation: The cartoon supports the idea of mutually assured destruction (MAD), the notion that neither side would come out the winner in a nuclear war scenario. The arms race during the 1950s left both sides leery of the cost of maintaining a policy of "massive retaliation" and the condition the world would find itself in following a nuclear war, prompting novels such as *On the Beach* and a fallout shelter building craze.

5.

Answer	Learning Objectives	Historical Thinking Skills	Key Concepts in the Curriculum Framework
A	WOR-2.0	Interpretation	8.1

Explanation: In the early 1960s the phrase *peaceful coexistence* became much more common. It held that although the United States and the Soviet Union had radically different political and economic systems, they could nevertheless exist without continual confrontation that brought the world to the brink of destruction. It evolved because of the fear that the consequences of a nuclear war to humanity would be too unimaginable to be rationally considered.

6.

Answer	Learning Objectives	Historical Thinking Skills	Key Concepts in the Curriculum Framework
C	WOR-2.0	Patterns of Continuity and Change over Time	8.1

Explanation: The political cartoon reflects the insanity of mutually assured destruction and strongly implies a more rational approach to peaceful coexistence. Richard Nixon's policy of détente was an attempt to defuse the Cold War. All of the other options reflect escalation of Cold War hostilities, which potentially could have led to atomic warfare.

7.

Answer	Learning Objectives	Historical Thinking Skills	Key Concepts in the Curriculum Framework
A	NAT-4.0	Contextualization	8.3

Explanation: The baby boom generation is referred to as "a pig in a python" because of the massive size of the cohort. As it moves through various life stages, society had to (and still is doing so) adjust to its mass. In the 1950s, for example, television shows and advertising became geared to children because they made up a significant market share. Elementary schools had to expand dramatically to meet the influx of school-age children.

8.

Answer	Learning Objectives	Historical Thinking Skills	Key Concepts in the Curriculum Framework
D	CUL-4.0	Patterns of Continuity and Change over Time	8.3

Explanation: Because the baby boomers made up such a significant portion of the population, manufacturers and advertisers catered to their needs (or desires). Fads such as "coonskin caps" and hula hoops were all the rage in the 1950s. As boomers continue to pass through life, manufacturers and advertisers are there to meet the needs of that life stage. Currently there is a proliferation of ads for medications that are associated with seniors as the baby boom generation enters that life stage.

9.

Answer	Learning Objectives	Historical Thinking Skills	Key Concepts in the Curriculum Framework
A	POL-2.0	Patterns of Continuity and Change over Time	8.2

Explanation: Many historians see the turbulent era of the 1960s as a reflection of baby boomers reaching the ages of eighteen to twenty-five. Many see this as the most volatile age of youth, in which their generation tends to challenge existing social norms. Seen in this light, the baby boom helps explains promotion of civil rights, antiwar protests, and the rise of the counterculture.

10.

Answer	Learning Objectives	Historical Thinking Skills	Key Concepts in the Curriculum Framework
A	WXT-3.0	Causation	8.3

Explanation: Roosevelt foresaw the possibility of a postwar depression if millions of servicemen and women reentered the job market following World War II. The Servicemen's Readjustment Act sought to delay an influx of workers until wartime industries had a chance to retool. As a result, the GI Bill provided educational benefits to veterans so that they could attend school, become more educated, and delay their entry into the job market.

11.

Answer	Learning Objectives	Historical Thinking Skills	Key Concepts in the Curriculum Framework
D	MIG-2.0	Patterns of Continuity and Change over Time	8.3

Explanation: The GI Bill granted low-interest home loans to veterans in hopes of inspiring a building boom to stimulate the economy. What transpired was a white flight from inner cities to suburbs where single-family houses were thought to provide a nurturing environment for children. This also had the impact of promoting automobile sales and the development of a modern highway system.

12.

Answer	Learning Objectives	Historical Thinking Skills	Key Concepts in the Curriculum Framework
C	CUL-3.0	Patterns of Continuity and Change over Time	8.3

Explanation: The 1950s witnessed a return to the "cult of domesticity" lifestyle that placed women in the home with their primary function to provide a nurturing environment for their children and husbands. Some have said that it was almost un-American to be married and not pregnant in the 1950s. As a result feminism reached a low point of the twentieth century and would face significant challenges in the 1960s.

Short-Answer Questions

1.

Learning Objectives	Historical Thinking Skills	Key Concepts in the Curriculum Framework
WOR-2.0	Contextualization Analyzing Evidence: Content and Sourcing	8.1

What a good response might include

a) A good response would choose one example from the 1960s in which negotiations with the Soviet Union were successful and explain the consequences of that success. Some examples might include the following:

- ✦ The United States and the Soviet Union were able to negotiate a peaceful resolution to the Cuban Missile Crisis in 1962, resulting in U.S. agreement not to invade Cuba while the Soviet Union agreed to dismantle missile bases on the island. This led to a slight thaw in U.S.-Soviet relations during the Cold War.
- ✦ An emphasis on "peaceful coexistence" between the United States and the Soviet Union also resulted in the establishment of a "hot line" between the two nations, which would make communication during times of crisis easier and more efficient.
- ✦ The United States and the Soviet Union signed the Limited Nuclear Test Ban Treaty in the summer of 1963, which placed limits on both the production and testing of nuclear weapons and testing. This was a major step toward limits in the arms race that had become a major factor in the Cold War.

b) A good response citing an example of a confrontation between the United States and Soviet Union might include the following:

- ✦ During the Cuban Missile Crisis in October 1962, the United States and the Soviet Union came perilously close to war. The crisis was resolved when the United States agreed to end a naval blockade of the island as the Soviet Union agreed to dismantle missile bases that were being built there.
- ✦ The United States and the Soviet Union also faced a crisis in August 1961 when a wall began to go up dividing the city of Berlin into a Soviet-controlled East and a NATO-allied West. The wall remained for decades and became a symbol of the Cold War tensions that existed between the United States and the Soviet Union.
- ✦ The Vietnam War was an ongoing confrontation with the Soviet Union, though indirectly. This war was one of many "proxy wars" that the United States and the Soviet Union engaged in during the 1960s. The Vietnam conflict did not end until 1975 and remained a difficult part of U.S. foreign policy throughout the 1960s.

c) In comparing U.S.-Soviet relations at the end of the 1960s with U.S.-Soviet relations at the beginning of the decade, a good answer might include the following:

- ✦ At the beginning of the decade, relations between the United States and the Soviet Union were quite tense and seemed destined to remain so. During the last year of President Dwight Eisenhower's presidency, the United States continued the policy of containment of communism begun under President Truman.
- ✦ Eisenhower was a strong advocate of the "domino theory"—the idea that when a country "fell" to communism, its noncommunist neighbors were likely to follow.

- ✦ Eisenhower's successor, John Kennedy, who became president in 1961, was also a committed Cold Warrior who worked to convince the American public that he could stand up to the Soviet Union.
- ✦ Kennedy inherited a disastrous plan drawn up by the Central Intelligence Agency (CIA) in the last months of the Eisenhower's administration to invade Cuba using former Cuban patriots trained in Central America. The so-called Bay of Pigs incident was disastrous for the U.S.-Soviet relationship and was a direct precursor of the Cuban Missile Crisis of 1962.
- ✦ By the end of the 1960s, President Richard Nixon had effected a decided change in U.S.-Soviet relations by formulating a new policy toward both the Soviet Union and China known as détente, or the gradual relaxation of tensions. He hoped to also bring about a quicker end to the Vietnam War by encouraging these two countries to end their aid to North Vietnam.
- ✦ Nixon also hoped to take advantage of the tensions that existed between China and the Soviet Union.
- ✦ Because of Nixon's policies, the more extreme polarization between the United States and the Soviet Union that characterized the Cold War in 1960 was reduced somewhat. Because Nixon had the reputation of being a strong anticommunist, his efforts to negotiate with the Soviet Union were more acceptable to the conservatives in his own political party.
- ✦ Negotiations on both the SALT I treaty, limiting nuclear weapons and the ICBM Treaty, limiting ballistic arms, were underway by the end of the 1960s, although they were not signed until the 1970s.

2.

Learning Objectives	Historical Thinking Skills	Key Concepts in the Curriculum Framework
POL-1.0	Patterns of Continuity and Change over Time Comparison	8.2

What a good response might include

a)   A good response would include one of several possible strong examples of why Lyndon Johnson won a landslide victory in the 1964 presidential election, which could include:
- ✦ Republican candidate Barry Goldwater was portrayed as a hardcore conservative whose "trigger-happy" talk of using nuclear weapons could possibly touch off a third world war.
- ✦ Johnson was seen as a steady, even-handed statesman who had handled the Gulf of Tonkin crisis that same year with what was seen at the time as skilled political maneuvering.
- ✦ Johnson benefitted from the promises of his Great Society program as well as the good feeling left from inheriting the Kennedy legacy.

b)   A good response as to why Nixon won in a landslide in the presidential election of 1972 could include one of the following:
- ✦ Nixon had managed through political negotiation and gradual withdrawal of troops to convince the country that the unpopular war in Vietnam was finally coming to a close.
- ✦ His Democratic opponent, George McGovern, was considered very liberal, and his campaign was plagued with difficulties, including the discovery that his original vice presidential running mate had undergone psychiatric treatment.

✦ Nixon had adopted a number of Democratic reforms during his first term, including the creation of the Environmental Protection Agency and the extension of Social Security, Medicaid, food stamps, and the Supplemental Security Income program.

✦ Nixon and the Republicans had secured the political support of the southern states through the use of what was known as the "southern strategy," a general downplaying of any big efforts to extend civil rights programs, the appointment of conservative justices to the courts, and lack of support for programs like busing to achieve racial balance in schools.

c) A good response as to why the presidential election of 1968 was so close, coming as it did between two landslide victories for different parties, could include one of the following:

✦ American society had become increasingly polarized during the Johnson administration over all sorts of issues, including the war in Vietnam as well as civil rights and social initiatives.

✦ The Republicans launched an appeal to Americans they referred to as the "silent majority," a group described as "unblack, unpoor, and unyoung."

✦ Many Americans had become alarmed as the civil rights movement began to splinter into rival groups, some of them favoring less nonviolence and more activism.

✦ The movement opposing the Vietnam War had grown dramatically, creating fault lines between many young people and an older generation that viewed the conflict through the lens of their experiences in World War II and Korea.

✦ The Democratic Party was divided after the assassination of Robert Kennedy, with many younger voters deciding to support the write-in candidacy of Eugene McCarthy rather than the Democratic candidate, Hubert Humphrey.

Document-Based Question

Learning Objectives	Historical Thinking Skills	Key Concepts in the Curriculum Framework
NAT-1.0 NAT-3.0	Patterns of Continuity and Change over Time Argumentation Analyzing Evidence: Content and Sourcing Synthesis Contextualization	8.1 8.2

What a good response might include

A good response must draw on *all* or *all but one* of the seven documents (that is, at least six) and must provide analysis of each element mentioned in the question. You are being asked to analyze both foreign and domestic factors that affected the mind-set of average Americans in the 1970s. You should be able to draw conclusions and make an argument about both U.S. foreign policy and domestic affairs.

You should craft a thesis based on the historical thinking skills of **patterns of continuity and change over time** and **contextualization**. You will use the documents to explore American attitudes over the course of the 1970s and offer insights into how and why these attitudes changed (or didn't) over the course of the decade. Your thesis must do more than simply repeat the prompt: it must state exactly what you are going to argue. The analysis of the documents must provide evidence to support the thesis AND explain how and why that evidence supports the thesis.

In the body of your essay, you are required to demonstrate understanding of the events of the 1970s, integrating both outside information and inferences from the documents into your essay. While evidence from at least six documents is required, you are expected to provide in-depth analysis from at least a majority of the documents (in this case, four documents) that focuses on at least one of the following: audience, purpose, context, or point of view. Never merely summarize a document. Weave the documents and other knowledge that you have into your essay; both documents and this outside information serve as evidence to buttress the argument you make in your thesis.

In constructing your essay, you are expected to bring in outside information that is not included in the documents. The notice about the service station being out of gasoline (Document 1) was the result of the 1973–1974 oil embargo by the Organization of Petroleum Exporting Countries (OPEC) against the United States and other countries that supported Israel in the 1973 Middle East War. The results of the nearly six-month embargo were gas rationing, limited gas supplies throughout the country, and skyrocketing prices for home heating oil and gasoline. The *New York Times*'s announcement of President Nixon's resignation in 1974 (Document 2) provides an opportunity to discuss the Watergate scandal, the Pentagon Papers, Nixon's "enemies list," and the national disillusionment with politics and politicians in general. You might draw a connection between Nixon's preoccupation with the Watergate hearings with his inability to make effective headway during the oil embargo. Gerald Ford's address to Congress in April 1975 (Document 3) explained the actions of the North Vietnamese that led ultimately to the fall of Saigon and the surrender of the South Vietnamese army, as well as an attempt to explain the failure of the U.S. military to prevail in Vietnam after two decades of engagement.

The image of "Love Canal cigarettes" (Document 4) including dioxin and pesticides offered with the ostensible approval of the U.S. regulatory agencies provides an opportunity to discuss high incidences of illnesses, birth defects, and dying landscapes caused by the chemical disposal site. Even if you are unfamiliar with the Love Canal incident, you should be able to draw some conclusions about its nature from the cartoon. The 1979 report on the Three Mile Island nuclear power plant leak (Document 5) reveals that news of the nuclear contamination was hidden from the public for a number of days after the leak occurred. Eventually over 100,000 people in the area around the power plant had to evacuate their homes. Both Love Canal and Three Mile Island raised environmental awareness and concerns about the safety of nuclear power and about the various governments (state, local, and federal) in managing these disasters.

President Jimmy Carter's appeal (Document 6) to the Ayatollah Khomeini to release Americans held hostage in Iran provides more evidence of U.S. weakness in international affairs. A later attempt to stage a military rescue the hostages failed in April 1980. The chart of the U.S. Inflation Rate, 1960–2000 (Document 7), shows a tremendous leap in inflation during the 1970s, the result of a number of factors.

Strong essays will link similar documents together to make a convincing argument. For example, a strong essay might link together Documents 1, 3, and 5 to illustrate examples of international events that had an impact on American attitudes about themselves and what some saw as the dwindling power of the United States in the international community. Documents 2, 4, and 6 represent domestic issues that left many Americans feeling disillusioned and powerless. Document 7 could be used to address both domestic problems and international pressures.

A strong essay will contain a conclusion that emphasizes the argument that you made in your opening thesis. You might argue, for example, that Americans' sense of malaise had more to do with domestic concerns than with foreign policy setbacks (or vice versa). You could also argue that, in fact, the characterization of the 1970s expressed in the question is wrong, though this would be quite tricky to do, since it would be difficult to use these documents to make that case. Whatever you have argued, your conclusion should summarize what you have written and explain how it supports your thesis.

1980–Present

Overview

The last decades of the twentieth century saw a resurgence of conservatism in the United States that stressed the importance of traditional values and rejected liberal views about society and the role of government. Conservatism was fueled by a loss of faith in the ability of the government to solve problems, a growth in religious fundamentalism, economic challenges, and disillusionment with elected officials. Evangelical Christian organizations became politically active and sought to limit the influence of liberal social and political trends of earlier decades.

Conservatives found that some of the government programs they wanted to end enjoyed wide popularity with the general public. They were more successful in their efforts to limit taxes and deregulate industries than they were with their moral and social initiatives. Many "big government" programs were too popular for Republicans to cut or eliminate.

The Reagan administration made anticommunism a centerpiece of its foreign policy, though the president's cordial relations with the Soviet leader, Mikhail Gorbachev, led to productive talks and arms reductions on both sides. With the end of the Cold War, the role of the United States changed dramatically from one of the two superpowers to a nation expected to be a global peacekeeper.

The attacks on the World Trade Center and Pentagon by Al Qaeda on September 11, 2001, however, placed the Middle East and the war on terrorism at the center of U.S. concerns. U.S. policy was refocused as the United States launched military attacks on both Afghanistan and Iraq, and efforts to achieve security and safety at home raised questions about the protection of civil liberties and the safeguarding of human rights.

As the twenty-first century dawned, the United States faced significant social, economic, and demographic changes. The country was now part of the global economy, and both information technology jobs and manufacturing jobs moved overseas. Union power declined, and real wages were stalled. Politicians were unable to agree on the right course concerning free trade agreements, tariffs, and government support for domestic industries. Continuing conflict in the Middle East threatened the oil supply, and local sources were not able to meet domestic demand. Computer technology and the Internet changed the way people did business, interacted socially, and were connected to the rest of the world.

The country's population continued to move to the South and West, in search of jobs and friendlier climates. These same regions saw an influx of immigrants from Latin America and Asia, who filled entry-level jobs in those parts of the country. Issues of citizenship and illegal immigration dominated political debates. These and other demographic changes led to further discussions over issues like gender roles, family makeup, and group identity.

Key Terms

Be sure that you understand the meaning of these terms and their relevance in U.S. history.

Axis of evil
Bipolar world
Culture wars
Debtor nation
Entitlement programs
Ethnic chauvinism
Ethnic cleansing
Faith-based agenda
Financial deregulation
Free markets
Globalization
Grassroots conservatives
Libertarian spirit

Majority-minority nation
Multiculturalism
Multinational corporation
Multipolar world
National debt
Neoconservatism
Pacific Rim
Reagan Democrats
Religious Right
Rockefeller Republicans
States' rights
Supply-side economics
Trickle-down economics

Questions to Consider

As you study Period 9, keep the following thematic questions in mind.

American and National Identity

✦ How has multiculturalism changed the American social, economic, and political landscape?
✦ Why has there been so much debate over immigration and multiculturalism in the past few decades?
✦ How does regional identity influence American politics in the twenty-first century?
✦ What issues have divided feminists from the Religious Right?

Work, Exchange, and Technology

✦ How was the Religious Right able to use the media so successfully to promote its message?
✦ What is supply-side economics, and why was this a central element of Ronald Reagan's economic policy?
✦ What were the most important achievements and the most notable shortcomings of Reagan's fiscal policies?
✦ What was the impact of deregulation on consumers, the federal bureaucracy, workers' rights, and the environment?
✦ What economic crises did Reagan face in his second term, and how did he confront them?
✦ How have computer technology and the omnipresence of the World Wide Web both illustrated the irony of free-market capitalism and served as a force for democratization?
✦ How do international organizations influence the operation of the American economy? Why are these organizations able to exert so much influence?

+ What were the key aspects of President George W. Bush's economic policies, and how effective were these policies in ensuring economic progress and stability?
+ What caused the Great Recession that began in 2007?
+ What economic policies were implemented by Presidents Bush and Obama to help the economy recover, and how successful were these policies?

Migration and Settlement

+ How and why have immigration patterns changed since 1965?
+ How have arguments over affirmative action been linked to the debate over immigration?
+ What demographic shifts have occurred since the 1980s, and what has been the impact of these changes?

Politics and Power

+ Why did conservatives oppose Great Society liberalism?
+ What were the three legs of the conservative movement, and how did conservatives attempt to implement their agenda?
+ Why did conservative religious groups become politically active?
+ In what ways did the Carter presidency make Ronald Reagan's path to the White House easier?
+ Why was Reagan able to build such a disparate coalition?
+ What were Reagan's domestic priorities, and to what extent did he achieve his goals?
+ What are the twin dilemmas that have defined the period from the end of the Cold War to the present, and how have they influenced the American political, economic, and social landscapes?
+ What was "the contradiction between New Right ideology and political reality"?
+ How successful was Reagan in using the courts to further conservatism?
+ During the Reagan years, why did government not shrink as much as Reagan would have liked?
+ In what ways was Reagan "a master of the politics of symbolism"?
+ Why was the Reagan administration slow to respond to the AIDS crisis?
+ What was Bill Clinton's "third way," and to what extent was he successful in changing the American political landscape?
+ Why was President Clinton impeached, and what were the consequences of his impeachment?
+ Why, despite opposition to wars in Iraq and Afghanistan and concern over rising deficits at home, was President Bush reelected in 2004?
+ What electoral shifts were seen in the presidential elections of 2008 and 2012?
+ Often in American history, we see that unexpected events shape a presidency. What examples do you see of this in the late twentieth and early twenty-first centuries?
+ What accounts for the extreme partisanship we see in American politics in the twenty-first century?
+ What issues and policies have caused decreased public trust in government?
+ What factors account for the emergence of the Tea Party as a force in American politics?

America in the World

+ How did President Reagan's approach to dealing with the Soviets differ from that of his predecessors?
+ What were the specifics of Reagan's Cold War policies?
+ Despite Reagan's commitment to the expansion of democracy, why did he sometimes support authoritarian dictatorships?
+ In what ways did the Iran-Contra affair threaten the Reagan presidency?
+ What factors were most significant in bringing about the fall of communism in the Soviet Union and Eastern Europe?
+ What was the impact of the September 11 attacks on American foreign and domestic policy?
+ What issues have contributed to the continued tensions between the United States and the people and governments of the Middle East?
+ What events best illustrate the difficulties the United States has had in the Middle East?
+ In what ways have globalization and the end of Cold War duality shaped regional, ethnic, and religious conflict in the twenty-first century?
+ What foreign policy challenges has President Obama faced, and how successfully has he addressed them?
+ Why, after achieving military victory in Iraq, was it so difficult to end the American military presence there?
+ What accounts for the continued destabilization of the Middle East?
+ What do you see as the promises and the dangers of globalization?
+ What twenty-first-century challenges do the expansion of the European Union and the emergence of China as an economic power present to the United States?

Geography and the Environment

+ What actions did Reagan take that alarmed many environmentalists?
+ Why has the topic of climate change stimulated so much conversation and controversy?

Culture and Society

+ In what ways did intellectuals contribute to the conservative resurgence?
+ What have been the most significant differences between liberalism and conservatism in the past thirty-five years?
+ How did Americans view "the culture of success"?
+ What have Americans continued to fight about what your textbook calls "the Battles of the 60s"?
+ What key battlegrounds have emerged in the clash over "family values"?
+ In what ways has the Supreme Court been a major player in the culture wars?

America's History Chapter Summaries

(required AP® content in bold)

Chapter 30
Conservative America in the Ascent, 1980–1991

Chapter 30 focuses on the ascendancy of conservatism in the 1980s. The 1970s witnessed a United States divided by the Vietnam War, worn out by social unrest, and panicked by economic uncertainty. **Many Americans developed a distrust of the liberalism of the Great Society, and the New Right took the lead in the Republican Party. Ronald Reagan was their champion, offering smaller government, deregulation of the economy, Christian morality, and a new determination to win the Cold War.**

Reagan built on the grassroots conservatism that had supported Barry Goldwater in his presidential bid in 1964. He also gained support from conservative women's organizations who did not feel comfortable with the women's liberation movements. The **new conservative movement rested on three principles: anticommunism, free-market economics, and religious moralism**. A number of journals and policy groups picked up this cause, among them William F. Buckley's *National Review* and the conservative Heritage Foundation. They were also supported by the new "Religious Right," **evangelical Protestants who opposed abortion, divorce, premarital sex, and feminism**. Their message was often spread by televangelists who sought to build a conservative coalition that would undo what they felt were the excesses of the Great Society.

This conservative coalition found a perfect target in President Jimmy Carter. Carter was elected in 1976 as a Washington outsider who had no taint attached to him of the Watergate scandal that had brought down President Richard Nixon. His outsider status proved to be his undoing, however, as many found him naive and idealistic when faced with international realities. His lasting legacy was the Camp David Accords, a "framework for peace" between the **Israelis and Palestinians in the Middle East**. Most of his other initiatives foundered: Strategic arms limitation (SALT II) was not approved by the Senate, a boycott of the 1980 Summer Olympics in Moscow was unpopular even though the Soviets had invaded Afghanistan, and the Iranian Revolution left more than fifty Americans held hostage in the Tehran Embassy for nearly a year.

In this climate of uncertainty and declining public trust, the Republicans seized their opportunity in 1980, nominating a confident and poised Ronald Reagan for the presidency. Reagan received over 50 percent of the popular vote in the election, and the New Right's bid for power was a success. Reagan had experience with the media from his years as a Hollywood actor, but he also had experience with industry and government, having worked with General Electric and served as governor of California. His core supporters were relatively affluent white Protestants who wanted balanced budgets, lower crime, and limits to social welfare. He also gained support from southern Democrats, who had been far too conservative to be comfortable with the Democratic agenda for some time. He spoke of supporting states' rights to a receptive audience. The Republicans also won the support of the Religious Right, as well as of blue-collar Catholics who shared many of their same concerns.

Reagan advocated increased defense spending to prosecute the Cold War. He advanced an economic policy that came to be known as "Reaganomics" or "supply-side economics." This approach advocated investment in production while at the same time lowering taxes on corporations and wealthy individuals, who would be expected to reinvest in the economy. Increasing supply would generate more demand, thereby energizing the economy for everyone. **Reagan supported tax cuts that benefitted primarily the wealthy, and he supported cuts in federal expenditures for a number of social programs**. Congress balked at these cuts, however. David Stockman, Reagan's budget director, began to voice some concerns about the soundness of supply-side economics, questioning the assumption that prosperity would "trickle down," as Reagan's program promised. In addition, **Reagan's increases in military spending increased the national debt, something the Republicans had promised to reduce**.

Attempts at the deregulation of federal agencies also led to unanticipated problems. Environmentalists, for example, were dismayed at attempts to undermine the Environmental Protection Agency, and eventually Reagan backed off somewhat. Reagan did have a lasting impact on the Supreme Court, appointing three Supreme Court justices with solid conservative credentials. Sandra Day O'Connor was the first woman appointed to the Supreme Court. In addition, Reagan appointed more than 350 federal court judges, most with conservative leanings. He chose William Rehnquist as chief justice of the Supreme Court, who led a Court that reversed a number of the more liberal decisions of the earlier Warren and Burger courts.

Reagan was president during the nation's first awareness of the HIV/AIDS epidemic, though it would take more than a decade for the country to see this virus as more than the "gay disease."

Reagan was easily reelected in 1984, emphasizing the economic recovery the country experienced during his first term, though some part of that was due to the OPEC decision to increase oil production and sales. **The nation's heavy industries continued to struggle with foreign competition, but service industries were growing, giving the country a sense of returning prosperity**.

The 1980s also saw the dawning computer age. The PC had arrived, thanks to the work of innovators like Bill Gates, Paul Allen, and Steve Jobs. **Computers would change the nature of both the work space and personal life in the next two decades**.

During Reagan's presidency, the Soviet Union collapsed as its leader, Mikhail Gorbachev, sought to reform Soviet society and foreign policy. **Reagan replaced a number of his hardline advisors and moved toward détente with the Soviet Union**. Soviet President Gorbachev tried *glasnost* (openness) and *perestroika* (economic restructuring) to save the Soviet system, but the Soviet Union dissolved in 1991. While many in the United States were eager to take credit for the fall of the Soviet Union, most historians agreed that it collapsed due to its own internal weaknesses. Pressure from the United States did play a role but only a secondary one.

Ronald Reagan left office with social welfare liberalism on the defensive. He had changed the political conversation in favor of increased power among conservatives. He was succeeded by his former vice president, George H. W. Bush, a former CIA director and a loyal follower of President Reagan's policies. Bush faced an early crisis in the Middle East when Saddam Hussein of Iraq launched an invasion of neighboring Kuwait in a dispute over access to oil reserves. The United States joined a United Nations-led coalition of countries to liberate Kuwait. The victory of UN troops gave the United States a new standing in the Middle East, though the end of the Soviet Union would result in a **postwar world that would make the Middle East, and the world in general, much more complex for all the players**.

Chapter 31
Confronting Global and National Dilemmas, 1989 to the Present

For Americans, the years between the end of the Cold War and the present have been defined by twin dilemmas: What is the position of the United States in the global arena, and how does the United States manage cultural conflicts and still ensure economic opportunity for all Americans?

By the end of the twentieth century, globalization saw the rapid spread of capitalism around the world, increases in trade and commerce, and the **diffusion of communications technology, including the Internet**. Some nations benefitted while others did not.

The bipolar world of two superpowers was gone, and multiple power centers began to emerge. In 1992, the nations of Western Europe created the European Union (EU), encompassing the third largest population in the world, after China and India. Their currency, the euro, rivaled the dollar and the Japanese yen for supremacy as an international currency. China became the world's fastest-growing economic power, supplying the American market with inexpensive imports. **All of these developments challenged America's global economic position.**

The United States entered a new era of global economics and policy in the 1990s. The world's leading capitalist nations formed a group known as the Group of Eight (G8 — the United States, Britain, Germany, France, Italy, Japan, Canada, and Russia) to oversee major international financial organizations, including the World Bank, the International Monetary Fund (IMF), and the General Agreement on Tariffs and Trade (GATT). In 1995, the GATT evolved into the World Trade Organization (WTO), with over 150 nations participating.

The United States, Canada, and Mexico signed the North American Free Trade Agreement (NAFTA) in 1993 to create a free trade zone in North America. Other similar regional organizations were organized around the world. Multinational corporations became the norm in international trade in the search for new markets all over the globe. Financial deregulation made investment easier and in some cases led to spectacular profits. At the same time, the potential for equally spectacular loss was also a possibility, something that became clear in the financial crisis of 2008. The technology revolution fueled much of this growth. By the 1990s, personal computers and the Internet were no longer just for the few. **The World Wide Web opened the possibilities of the Internet to people around the globe.**

By the 1990s, **the United States had become an increasingly pluralistic society. Millions of new immigrants became part of the electorate, coming from East Asia as well as Latin America since the passage of the Immigration and Nationality Act in 1965.** Many immigrants were here illegally, something that increasingly became part of the national political discourse. **Conservatives and liberals argued over the question of whose values were to be the ones that characterized the American nation.** Some charged that the Great Society's welfare initiatives had weakened the traditional model of the two-parent household. **The abortion debate continued as well, with opposing sides lined up as either "prochoice" or "prolife." The gay rights movement continued to anger conservatives, now with the added push for the legal recognition of same-sex marriages. The Religious Right countered with the Defense of Marriage Act in 1998, allowing states to refuse to recognize gay marriages or civil unions as legal.**

Democrat Bill Clinton was elected to the presidency in 1992 in the midst of all this cultural wrangling. Clinton was president when the world witnessed the breakup of Yugoslavia and sectarian violence in the Balkans, an indication of the **changing nature of U.S. foreign policy.** The United States intervened as a part of a UN force to put a stop to the "ethnic cleansing" that characterized the attempts to form new states in that part of the world. The United States also faced hostility in the Middle East from Arab countries that felt that American foreign policy was too favorable toward Israel. This was also a time of the growth of radical fundamentalism in places like Saudi Arabia and Afghanistan, a movement the U.S. State Department largely underestimated, despite an attempt to bomb the World Trade Center in 1993. Clinton appointees identified a shadowy network of radical Islamists known as Al Qaeda.

The close election of 2000 brought George W. Bush into power, although it took a decision of the Supreme Court to validate the election results. The Bush administration immediately began to call for a return to the Reagan tax cuts, even though economists warned that massive tax cuts would only exacerbate federal debt. They did not heed these warnings, and as the Bush years progressed, the **national debt grew along with it.**

The bombing of the World Trade Center on September 11, 2001, shaped much of the Bush presidency. **The War on Terror, the Patriot Act, and the creation of the Department of Homeland Security were all responses of the Bush administration to the threats posed by Al Qaeda and other Islamic radicals.** The United States invaded both Afghanistan and Iraq in the name of rooting out terrorists and destroying weapons of mass destruction, though many of these justifications proved empty as time went on. The country misread the realities of the countries it had invaded, underestimating the difficulties of imposing Western values and government onto radically different cultures, and the hazards of fighting a war against unknown insurgents.

Bush was reelected in 2004, but his second term became one of crisis management. Hurricane Katrina devastated New Orleans in August 2005, and Bush was faulted for an inadequate response. The wars in Iraq and Afghanistan were increasingly unpopular. Then in 2008, the stock market crashed, taking housing prices and other major industries with it, the worst economic fall since the 1930s. This episode came to be known as the Great Recession.

The 2008 election brought Barack Obama into office, the nation's first African American president. He inherited two wars and an economic recession. He called for a "remaking of America," hoping to offer an optimistic tone to a jittery nation. Obama faced stiff opposition from many Republicans. Many of them responded with anger to his health reform proposal, the Patient Protection and Affordable Care Act. His opponents labeled it "Obamacare" and tried to stop its implementation. The bill passed and was affirmed by the Supreme Court. Obama also ended the "Don't ask, don't tell" policy in the military, and gays and lesbians were allowed to serve openly. He appointed two women to the Supreme Court.

The wars he inherited in Iraq and Afghanistan continued, with Obama determined to end the American presence in both places. The "Arab Spring," a wave of protests across the Middle East in 2011 that toppled a number of old regimes, at first held out promise for being liberating movements that might lead to greater democracy. Those hopes dimmed as many of the new regimes fell into new forms of autocracy, and most were not particularly friendly to U.S. interests. On the home front, Obama continued to try to address the issues of the national debt, immigration reform, America's new place in the global economy, increasing inequality in the United States, and the concerns over climate change, issues that will go well beyond the end of his term in 2016.

Thematic Timeline

THEME	REQUIRED CONTENT	SUPPORTING EXAMPLES
AMERICAN AND NATIONAL IDENTITY	• New immigrants from Latin and America influenced the culture of the United States. • Changing demographics fostered political, economic, and cultural debates over immigration and American identity. • Americans debated the impact of demographic changes on gender, family, and racial and national identity.	• Organizations like the Eagle Forum, Focus on the Family, and the Family Research Council promote Christian activism. • Those who identify themselves as Reagan supporters include wealthy white Protestants, middle-class suburbanites, southern supporters of states' rights, evangelical Protestants, and blue-collar Catholics. • Identity politics play a role in the election of 1988, as Pat Robertson, a Republican and conservative Christian, and Jesse Jackson, a Democratic African American civil rights leader, vie in their parties' primaries. • Many Americans oppose multiculturalism, arguing that it encourages ethnic chauvinism and reverse discrimination. • The Supreme Court limits some aspects of affirmative action plans for college admission. • Bilingual education programs are challenged. • It is expected that the United States will become a "majority-minority" nation by 2050. • In the 1990s, many cities and states ban discrimination on the basis of sexual orientation. • Congress passes the Defense of Marriage Act (1996). • President Obama repeals the military's "Don't ask, don't tell" policy, enabling gay men and lesbians to openly serve in the military (2011). • Obama appoints two women, Sonia Sotomayor and Elena Kagan, to the Supreme Court. Sotomayor becomes the first Latina on the Court.

THEME	REQUIRED CONTENT	SUPPORTING EXAMPLES
WORK, EXCHANGE, AND TECHNOLOGY	• A key goal of conservatives was to reduce taxation and free businesses from government regulation. • As the nation moved into the twenty-first century, the American economy became increasingly linked to the world economy, raising the possibility of economic instability and other challenges. • Economic inequality increased in the United States; manufacturing jobs were lost, union membership shrank, and middle class wages stagnated. • Americans debated free trade agreements, reform of the financial system, and the size and scope of the social safety net. • The use of the Internet and other computer technology increased access to information.	**The Reagan and Bush years** • New Right policies are based on support for low taxes, free markets, and limited government. • Reagan's economic policy, called Reaganomics, is based on supply-side economics. • Under President Reagan, defense spending vastly increases. • The Economic Recovery Tax Act significantly decreases personal and business taxes (1981). • Reagan's 1981 tax cuts, coupled with increases in defense spending, result in an increase in the national debt, which triples during the eight years of the Reagan presidency. • Congress refuses to make cuts to Social Security and Medicare. • Reagan's budget director, David Stockman, comes under fire for his belief in the trickle-down theory of economics. • Reagan expands the deregulation of industry, weakening federal agencies that protect consumers, workers, and the environment. • In 1982, due to a recession, Reagan is forced to negotiate a tax increase with Congress. • The economy rebounds by 1983. • The United States becomes a debtor nation in 1985, although the economy expands from the late 1980s through most of the 1990s. **The Clinton years** • Bill Clinton convinces Congress to pass a budget that mandates a reduction in the federal deficit. • The federal budget is balanced and the debt reduced. • Due to Clinton's economic policies, the economy booms. **The twenty-first century** • The American economy moves increasingly toward a service economy as many manufacturing jobs vanish. • Capitalism spreads throughout the world, and global trade increases. • Protesters attack the symbols of global capitalism in Seattle (1999).

THEME	REQUIRED CONTENT	SUPPORTING EXAMPLES
WORK, EXCHANGE, AND TECHNOLOGY (*continued*)		• Human rights organizations ask how global trade can foster sustainable development and be used for the benefit of all people. • The euro is introduced (2002). • The U.S. economy is challenged by the rise of China as an economic power. • Global financial markets are integrated, and there is an expansion of multinational corporations. • Financial deregulation offers the opportunity for huge profits but also the risk of serious economic downturns. • Congress and President Bush slash tax rates (2001 and 2003). • At the same time, federal expenditures increase, largely due to increased health care costs. • The U.S. economy tumbles as the stock market loses half of its value (2008). • Unemployment rises to over 10 percent. • Shortly before the 2008 election, Congress passes the Emergency Economic Stabilization Act in order to stabilize the banking system. • After the near-collapse of the American economy, President Obama signs the American Recovery and Reinvestment Act. **Technology and the American economy, 1981–2013** • Conservative religious leaders like Jerry Falwell and Pat Robertson use television to advance their agenda. • The computer revolution, led by pioneers like Bill Gates, Steve Wozniak, and Steve Jobs, begins to transform the American economy. • Computer technology, first designed for military and corporate use, becomes accessible to individual consumers in the 1980s. • IBM sells the first personal computers in 1981, and Apple's Macintosh is marketed in 1984. • The World Wide Web appears in 1991. • The Internet links people around the world. • New communication technologies, for example, satellites, fiber optics, and global positioning systems, change the nature of international communications.

THEME	REQUIRED CONTENT	SUPPORTING EXAMPLES
MIGRATION AND SETTLEMENT	• After 1980, population shifted to the South and West, and the political, economic and cultural influence of those areas increased. • Migration from Latin America and Asia contributed to the population growth of the South and West.	• The population of the United States increases from 203 million in 1970 to 280 million in 2000. Immigrants account for 28 million of that increase. • Twenty-five percent of immigrants entering the United States in this period enter the country illegally. • Most of these new immigrants come from Latin American and Asia. • Much of the new immigration is facilitated by the 1965 immigration legislation that permits family members of legal U.S. residents to enter without being subject to numerical limitations. • The Immigration and Control Act, passed in 1986, grants citizenship to many who arrived in the United States illegally. • By the 1990s, social diversity is no longer symbolized by a melting pot but by multiculturalism. • Californians approve Proposition 187, barring illegal immigrants from obtaining education and nonemergency health care (1994). A federal court later declares Proposition 187 unconstitutional.
POLITICS AND POWER	• Conservatism experienced a resurgence because many Americans doubted that government could solve the nation's economic problems and were concerned that political scandals, foreign policy failures, and moral and social decay were harming the nation. • Neoconservatives successfully spread their message to the broader public. • Religious conservatives became more active in politics as they worked to oppose liberal social beliefs and political actions.	**The Reagan and Bush years** • The New Right, built through conservative grassroots activism in the 1960s and 1970s, dominates Republican politics in the 1980s. • The New Right supplants the liberal republicanism of Dwight Eisenhower and holds up William F. Buckley, Barry Goldwater, and Ronald Reagan as its heroes. • The New Right is based on three pillars: anti-communism, free-market economics, and religious moralism. • Events such as the war in Vietnam, *Roe v. Wade* and other Supreme Court decisions, and mandatory school busing fuel conservatives' desire for change. • Taking advantage of President Carter's unpopularity due to continued economic woes at home and the taking of American hostages in Iran, Ronald Reagan is elected president in 1980. • Reagan is considered a master of political rhetoric and changes the dynamics of American politics.

THEME	REQUIRED CONTENT	SUPPORTING EXAMPLES
POLITICS AND POWER (*continued*)	• In the 1980s and into the 1990s, conservatives achieved victories in their efforts to reduce taxation and deregulate industry, but they faced increased opposition when they tried to advance their moral agenda. • The size and scope of the federal government actually increased after 1980, as voters were reluctant to see cutbacks in popular programs. • Americans debated the war on terrorism and its impact on both domestic and foreign policies. • The war on terrorism also led to debates about how to protect civil liberties and human rights while at the same time keeping the nation safe.	• Reagan leaves his mark on the courts by appointing conservative judges; he nominates three new justices to the Supreme Court. • Chief Justice William Rehnquist leads the court in a conservative direction, limiting the power of federal laws, ending court-ordered busing, and protecting property rights. • The Rehnquist Court is unable to overturn *Roe v. Wade*, end affirmative action, or limit the rights of criminal defendants. • Sandra Day O'Connor, appointed by Reagan as the first women on the Supreme Court, proves to be an unreliable conservative. • Reagan is reelected, defeating Walter Mondale (1984). • Due to controversy over homosexuality, Reagan moves slowly to respond to the AIDS/HIV crisis; under pressure from gay activists, he devotes more federal resources to combating this health crisis in his second term. • Despite Reagan's vocal support for limited government, he has not significantly scaled back big government by the end of his presidency. • George H. W. Bush is elected to follow Ronald Reagan into the White House, after defeating Pat Robertson in the Republican primaries (1988). • The Bush campaign and election once again pit conservatives against liberals, a pattern that will repeat in subsequent elections. **The Clinton years** • Bill Clinton promises a middle-class tax cut, universal health insurance, and deficit reduction. He defeats George H. W. Bush and Ross Perot (1992). • Clinton tries to take the middle ground between liberal Democrats and party moderates. • Opposition from small businesses and health insurance companies contributes to the failure of Clinton's health care proposals. • In the 1994 midterm election, Republicans gain control of the House of Representatives for the first time since 1954. • In response to this, Clinton moves to the right, claiming that "the era of big government is over."

THEME	REQUIRED CONTENT	SUPPORTING EXAMPLES
POLITICS AND POWER (*continued*)		• Clinton supports the Personal Responsibility and Work Opportunity Reconciliation Act, which reforms the social welfare system. • Clinton is reelected and shortly afterward becomes the second president to be impeached (1996). • The Senate does not convict Clinton, and he remains in office. **The twenty-first century** • George W. Bush is elected president, despite losing the popular vote (2002). • Bush's disputed election as president is affirmed by the Supreme Court. • Bush is encouraged to move to the right by his vice president, Dick Cheney, and adviser Karl Rove. • In 2002, Republicans gain control of both houses of Congress. • Following the September 11, 2001, attacks, Congress passes the USA Patriot Act, increasing the ability of the government to conduct domestic surveillance. • Bush is reelected in 2004. • Hurricane Katrina strikes New Orleans and the Mississippi coast in 2005. President Bush is severely criticized for his administration's inadequate response to this crisis. • Americans grow war weary as the wars in Iraq and Afghanistan drag on. • In 2008, the United States enters the worst recession since the Great Depression of the 1930s. • Barack Obama is elected the nation's first black president in 2008. • Obama sets out an ambitious domestic agenda, including an economic stimulus program, reform of the health insurance system, and regulation of Wall Street, and he also promises to end the war in Iraq. • Obama's most controversial initiative results in the passage of the Patient Protection and Affordable Care Act, designed to expand health coverage to all Americans (2010). • Opposition to Obama and his policies coalesces in the Tea Party movement. • Republicans gain control of the House of Representatives in 2010. • Obama is elected to a second term; African Americans, Hispanics, Asian Americans, women, and the young form the base of his support (2012).

THEME	REQUIRED CONTENT	SUPPORTING EXAMPLES
AMERICA IN THE WORLD	• Ronald Reagan's policy was anticommunist and interventionist. • Reagan called for increased defense spending and military action, and sometimes used inflammatory rhetoric. • Later, Reagan accepted détente and developed a good relationship with Soviet leader Mikhail Gorbachev. • Reagan and Gorbachev reached agreements that resulted in significant arms reductions. • The end of the Cold War forced the United States to redefine its foreign policy and build new relationships with the international community. • Later presidents used the military in peace-keeping roles in armed conflicts. • Americans debated the role of the United States in world affairs. • After the September 11, 2001, attacks on the World Trade Center and the Pentagon, U.S. foreign policy focused on combatting terrorism, including going to war in Iraq and Afghanistan.	**The Reagan and Bush years** • Reagan enters the White House calling for the defeat, and not merely the containment, of the Soviet Union, breaking with the policies of his predecessors. • Reagan proposes a Strategic Defense Initiative, often called "Star Wars" (1983). • Reagan supports CIA initiatives to support anticommunist movements around the world, sometimes aiding undemocratic governments like those in El Salvador and Nicaragua. • In 1983, Reagan refers to the Soviet Union as an "evil empire." • The Iran-Contra affair, which begins in 1985, becomes the most controversial foreign policy issue of Reagan's presidency. • Soviet leader Mikhail Gorbachev introduces *glasnost* and *perestroika*, policies that will contribute to the fall of the Soviet Union a few years later. • Reagan moves toward détente in his second term; he and Mikhail Gorbachev cooperate to lessen the chance of nuclear war. • Velvet Revolutions spread through Eastern Europe (late 1980s). • The Berlin Wall comes down in 1989. • The USSR is formally dissolved in late 1991, and conservative Republicans claim credit for bringing about the end of communism in Europe. • While still confronting communism in Eastern Europe, the Reagan administration also tries to promote stability in the Middle East. • Following Reagan's support of an Israeli invasion of Lebanon, Lebanese militants kill 241 American Marines (1982). • The United States unsuccessfully attempts to persuade the Palestinian Liberation Organization to recognize the state of Israel and also urges Israel to accept the creation of a Palestinian state. • With the collapse of the Soviet Union, the American Cold War foreign policy is supplanted by concern over regional, religious, and ethnic conflicts, especially in the Middle East. • Iraq invades Kuwait, and UN forces led by the United States drive Saddam Hussein's forces from Kuwait (1990).

THEME	REQUIRED CONTENT	SUPPORTING EXAMPLES
AMERICA IN THE WORLD (*continued*)		• President Bush declines to invade Iraq but convinces the United Nations to impose sanctions on Hussein's government. • The European Union is formed (1992). • By the early 1990s, the world has become a multipolar one, as the economic potential of the European Union, the rise of anti-Western ideology and Arab regionalism, and the emergence of China as a world economic power force the United States to deal with these important post–Cold War developments. **The Clinton years** • The North American Free Trade Agreement is signed (1993). • The World Trade Organization is formed (1995). • International organizations like the Group of Eight (G8), formed in 1997, assume a major role in regulating the world economy through its influence over the World Bank and the International Monetary Fund. • Yugoslavia breaks into smaller countries, and Serbia is accused of undertaking an ethnic cleansing campaign. • The United States supports a NATO-led bombing campaign against the Serbs (1995). • NATO intervenes in Kosovo (1999). • Islamic fundamentalism poses an increasing threat to the United States and its allies. • Al Qaeda leader Osama bin Laden declares a holy war against the United States and its allies (1998). • Terrorists detonate a bomb beneath the World Trade Center (1993) and blow up U.S. embassies in Kenya and Tanzania (1998). **The twenty-first century** • Globalization and America's place in the changing world is one of the great challenges facing the United States in this century. • Between 2000 and 2008, the gross domestic product of China quadruples as the Chinese embrace capitalism. • The Pacific Rim becomes more influential on the world stage. • By 2010, twelve new nations, most in Eastern Europe, are admitted to NATO. • Terrorists bomb the USS *Cole* in in a Yemeni port (2000).

THEME	REQUIRED CONTENT	SUPPORTING EXAMPLES
AMERICA IN THE WORLD (*continued*)		• Terrorists destroy the World Trade Center, killing nearly 3,000 (September 2001). • President Bush declares a war on terror and orders an attack on Afghanistan (October 2001). • Bush orders an invasion of Iraq, causing rifts between the United States and many of its allies and inciting opposition to the United States in the Arab world (2003). • Incidents at the Abu Ghraib prison in Iraq foment further opposition to the U.S. presence in Iraq. • The last U.S. soldiers leave Iraq in 2011, ending the nine-year war there. • The promise of the 2010 "Arab Spring" is questioned as instability plagues the Middle East. • U.S. Special Forces locate and kill Osama bin Laden (2011).
GEOGRAPHY AND THE ENVIRONMENT	• Conflict in the Middle East and worries over climate change led to debates over U.S. energy policy and American reliance on fossil fuels. • Many Americans were concerned about the impact of modern industrial life on the environment.	• Reagan and his secretary of the interior, James Watt, weaken the enforcement powers of the Environmental Protection Agency. • Watt expands the use of public lands by private businesses. • Protests against Reagan's environmental policies increase, prompting Reagan to increase the EPA's budget in his second term. • By the second decade of the twenty-first century, scientists reach consensus on climate change, though it proves difficult to get agreement on policies to address it. • "Cap-and-trade" legislation stalls in Congress.
CULTURE AND SOCIETY	• Conservatives defended traditional social values, rejected liberals' views about the role of government, and often espoused religious fundamentalism. • Evangelical and fundamentalist Christian organizations and churches grew rapidly. • New social networks changed the ways Americans received information and shared their culture.	• Following the lead of Barry Goldwater, many other Republicans support libertarian ideas, especially the importance of limited government and personal liberty. • Intellectuals like William F. Buckley, founder of the *National Review*, and Milton Friedman, a Nobel Prize-winning economist, set forth the foundations of the conservative movement. • A new generation of religiously conservative ministers condemns divorce, abortion, premarital sex, and feminism and urges Christians to become politically active in order to combat what they perceive to be immoral.

Theme	Required Content	Supporting Examples
CULTURE AND SOCIETY (*continued*)		• The antiabortion organization, Operation Rescue, is formed (1987). • The Supreme Court limits access to abortion in decisions such as *Webster v. Reproductive Health Services* (1989) and *Planned Parenthood of Southeastern Pennsylvania v. Casey* (1992). • Pat Buchanan declares the start of a "culture war" (1992). • *Lawrence v. Texas* overturns laws prohibiting homosexual activity (2003). • Twenty-four-hour news outlets like Fox News and MSNBC contribute to bitter partisanship. • American culture celebrates the accumulation of wealth as seen by the public's fascination with men like Donald Trump and Lee Iacocca.

Period 9 Practice Questions

Multiple-Choice Questions

Questions 1–4 refer to the excerpt below.

"These United States are confronted with an economic affliction of great proportions. We suffer from the longest and one of the worst sustained inflations in our national history. It distorts our economic decisions, penalizes thrift, and crushes the struggling young and the fixed-income elderly alike. It threatens to shatter the lives of millions of our people. . . .

"But great as our tax burden is, it has not kept pace with public spending. For decades, we have piled deficit upon deficit, mortgaging our future and our children's future for the temporary convenience of the present. . . .

"In this present crisis, government is not the solution to our problem. . . .

"It is my intention to curb the size and influence of the Federal establishment and to demand recognition of the distinction between the powers granted to the Federal Government and those reserved to the States or to the people. . . .

"It is no coincidence that our present troubles parallel and are proportionate to the intervention and intrusion in our lives that result from unnecessary and excessive growth of government."

Ronald Reagan, First Inaugural Address, January 20, 1981

1. Ronald Reagan's victory in the 1980 election signaled which of the following shifts in political thinking on the part of the American people?
   - (A) A significant shift to the left from Americans fed up with the malaise of the 1970s
   - (B) A massive growth in moderates dissatisfied with the bickering of extreme positions in the 1960s
   - (C) A greater demand that government steer clear of moral issues such as abortion and prayer in schools
   - (D) Movement toward greater conservatism by both major parties

2. The political climate of the 1980s led to which of the following?
   - (A) Organized religion playing a greater role in politics
   - (B) A major splintering of the Republican Party into liberal and conservative wings
   - (C) Major growth in the Socialist Party's strength in presidential elections
   - (D) Entrenchment of the Democratic Party in the "solid South"

3. The following are true of the Reagan administration EXCEPT
   - (A) annual deficits by the federal government were eliminated and the national debt reduced.
   - (B) social welfare programs were cut, leaving the poor in worse conditions than before.
   - (C) environmental regulations on industry were reduced to promote productivity.
   - (D) military appropriations were expanded and most Americans felt a resurgence of patriotic pride.

GO ON TO THE NEXT PAGE.

4. Which is the following happened in the 1980s?

    (A) There was a major defunding of Social Security to balance the budget.
    (B) Prosperity increased for the middle class and up.
    (C) The Equal Rights Amendment was ratified.
    (D) There were massive increases in arms production by both the United States and the Soviet Union by the end of the decade.

Questions 5–7 refer to the excerpt below.

"A return to a missionary foreign policy was clearly evident under President Ronald Reagan. With references to the window of vulnerability and continual emphasis on the expansionist, evil empire of the Soviet Union, the Reagan Doctrine promised not only containment but also the rollback communism worldwide. It also led to a dramatic increase in defense spending and a renewed arms race with the Soviet Union. Central America and the Caribbean became the testing ground for his crusade. Yet, by Reagan's second term, it was becoming evident that this policy could not be sustained. With massive government deficits due to declining revenues and increased spending during his first term, the budget became a constraint on his activist foreign policy. Other factors, including substantive changes in the policies and governing principles of the Soviet Union under Mikhail Gorbachev, the stalemated civil wars in both El Salvador and Nicaragua despite tremendous aid from the United States, the Iran-Contra scandal, and the fact that Reagan and Gorbachev finally met one another and actually liked each other—all these led to yet another swing of the pendulum to a more pragmatic foreign policy."

Cliff Staten, *U.S. Foreign Policy since World War II*, 2005

5. Which of the following is true of U.S. foreign policy between 1990 and 2010?

    (A) The United States expanded its Cold War attempts to contain the spread of communism.
    (B) The United States succeeded in not committing troops to European conflict.
    (C) The United States successfully overthrew communist rule in Cuba.
    (D) The United States expanded attempts to combat terrorism.

6. The Reagan administration initially embraced which of the following attitudes toward the Soviet Union in the early 1980s?

    (A) A continuation of the détente policies of the preceding three presidential administrations
    (B) Negotiation with the Soviet Union to reduce the arms race
    (C) Confrontation designed to force the Soviet Union into economic hardship
    (D) Commitment of U.S. troops to aid Eastern European countries in their attempts to throw off Soviet domination

7. In the years since 2000, U.S. foreign policy has been primarily focused on

    (A) improving relations with its NATO alliances.
    (B) defending South Korea from a North Korean invasion.
    (C) lessening the threat of terrorism.
    (D) improving trade with Latin American countries.

GO ON TO THE NEXT PAGE.

Questions 8–10 refer to the two maps below.

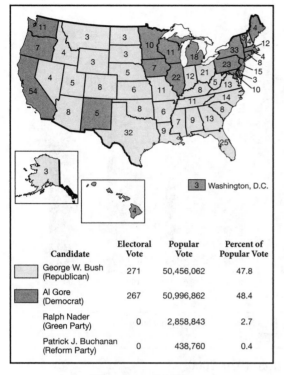

Election of 2000

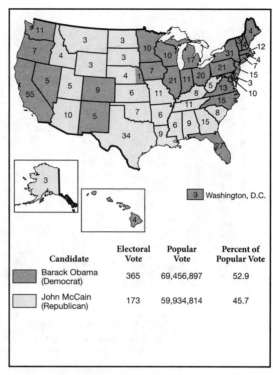

Election of 2008

8. During the Gilded Age a relatively few states generally known as "doubtful" or "swing states" determined the outcome of presidential elections. Based on the maps above which of the following might be considered "doubtful" or "swing states" in the first decade of the twenty-first century?

    (A) California
    (B) Florida
    (C) North Dakota
    (D) New York

9. Which of the following can be determined from the map on the election of 2000?

    (A) All states bordered by oceans voted Democratic.
    (B) The heartland of the country and the South tended to vote Democratic.
    (C) The presidential candidate with the most popular votes wins.
    (D) A presidential candidate could gain the presidency while winning fewer than half of the states.

10. The maps of the elections of 2000 and 2008 support which of the following conclusions?

    (A) Conservative political principles were favored by the majority of Americans.
    (B) Democratic political power tended to be based in the northeastern quarter of the country and on the West Coast.
    (C) Republicans controlled southern votes by increasing their appeal to African Americans.
    (D) States with large rural populations tend to be more liberal than states with large urban populations.

END OF MULTIPLE-CHOICE SECTION

Short-Answer Question

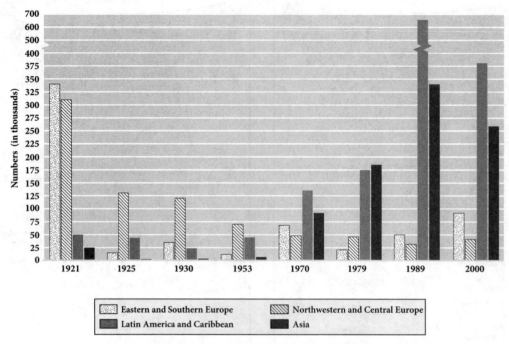

American Immigration, 1920–2000

1. Using the graph above, answer a, b, and c.

   a) Explain the reasons for decreasing immigration between 1925 and 1953.

   b) Explain the reasons for a pronounced increase in Asian immigration in the 1970s.

   c) Explain the factors that pulled immigrants to the United States between 1980 and 2010.

END OF SHORT-ANSWER SECTION

Answer Key to Period 9 Practice Questions

Multiple-Choice Questions

1.
Answer	Learning Objectives	Historical Thinking Skills	Key Concepts in the Curriculum Framework
D	POL-1.0	Patterns of Continuity and Change over Time	9.1

Explanation: During the 1980s, there was a major shift to more conservative thinking by a majority of Americans. The Reagan Revolution of 1980 resulted in a significant swing to the right by both major parties. Much of this was fueled by high interest rates and a stagnant economy during the 1970s. As prosperity increased, many American stopped supporting social welfare legislation that didn't benefit them.

2.
Answer	Learning Objectives	Historical Thinking Skills	Key Concepts in the Curriculum Framework
A	POL-2.0	Patterns of Continuity and Change over Time	9.1

Explanation: Moral social issues began to enter the political arena in the 1980s. Religious groups such as the Moral Majority and the Christian Coalition organized their followers to become active in politics. Strong pressure was brought to bear from these groups to pass constitutional amendments that would ban abortion, allow prayer in public schools, and balance the federal budget.

3.
Answer	Learning Objectives	Historical Thinking Skills	Key Concepts in the Curriculum Framework
A	WXT-2.0	Patterns of Continuity and Change over Time	9.2

Explanation: Despite rhetoric to the contrary, budget deficits reached record proportions and the national debt skyrocketed during the 1980s. Tax cuts and significantly increased military spending failed to be offset by cuts in social welfare program. Programs such as the Strategic Defense Initiative were particularly expensive, though they did translate to technology development in consumer goods as well.

4.
Answer	Learning Objectives	Historical Thinking Skills	Key Concepts in the Curriculum Framework
B	WXT-2.0	Patterns of Continuity and Change over Time	9.2

Explanation: Reaganomics, or "supply-side" economics, tended to economically benefit the middle class and up. Those in the lowest socioeconomic classes tended to suffer, and homelessness increased. Social Security was too entrenched to be attacked, and the Equal Rights Amendment was never ratified. While the beginning of the decade saw Reagan referring to the Soviet Union as the "evil empire," accommodation was reached with the Soviet Union by the end of the decade that reduced nuclear arms.

5.

Answer	Learning Objectives	Historical Thinking Skills	Key Concepts in the Curriculum Framework
D	WOR-2.0	Patterns of Continuity and Change over Time	9.3

Explanation: The United States greatly expanded its effort to combat terrorism following September 11. The Cold War diminished in importance after the breakup of the Soviet Union and ushered in a significant change in the focus of U.S. foreign policy. In the 1990s, the United States committed troops to conflict in Bosnia. Continued economic sanctions against communist-controlled Cuba failed to bring about the downfall of the communist regime there.

6.

Answer	Learning Objectives	Historical Thinking Skills	Key Concepts in the Curriculum Framework
C	WOR-2.0	Patterns of Continuity and Change over Time	9.3

Explanation: Reagan characterized the Soviet Union as the "evil empire" and pursued a policy of massive arms buildup designed to put pressure on the Soviet economy to keep pace with the United States. Later in the decade, the United States and the Soviet Union entered into agreements for the reduction of arms. Initially, therefore, Reagan rejected the notion of détente with the Soviet Union and pursued a much more confrontational stance. The United States never committed troops to aid Eastern European countries to overthrow communist regimes.

7.

Answer	Learning Objectives	Historical Thinking Skills	Key Concepts in the Curriculum Framework
C	WOR-2.0	Patterns of Continuity and Change over Time	9.3

Explanation: Since September 11, the focus of U.S. foreign policy has been reduction of the threat of terrorism worldwide. The United States has been at war in Afghanistan and Iraq, as well as pursuing a policy design to take out Al Qaeda leadership whenever the opportunity presents itself. The war on terror has also had a domestic component that has raised questions concerning the constitutional rights of U.S. citizens.

8.

Answer	Learning Objectives	Historical Thinking Skills	Key Concepts in the Curriculum Framework
B	NAT-4.0	Patterns of Continuity and Change over Time	9.2

Explanation: Florida is the only state of the four that went from one party in 2000 (Republican) to another in 2008 (Democrat).

9.

Answer	Learning Objectives	Historical Thinking Skills	Key Concepts in the Curriculum Framework
D	POL-3.0	Interpretation	9.2

Explanation: The map demonstrates that if Al Gore won states such as Texas or Florida, his electoral votes total would have surpassed that of George W. Bush. To be elected president, a candidate must win a majority of electoral votes regardless of how the popular vote may fall. There have been several instances in U.S. history where the candidate with the most popular votes lost the election.

10.

Answer	Learning Objectives	Historical Thinking Skills	Key Concepts in the Curriculum Framework
B	NAT-4.0	Interpretation	9.2

Explanation: In both of the elections shown, the Democratic Party dominated the northeastern quarter of the country and the West Coast. The maps do not indicate whether conservative or liberal tendencies were at work in which states. The Republican Party continued to have problems attracting African American votes. The map also fails to show which states are dominated by urban or rural populations.

Short-Answer Question

1.

Learning Objectives	Historical Thinking Skills	Key Concepts in the Curriculum Framework
MIG-2.0	Causation Contextualization	7.2 8.3 9.2

What a good response might include

a) A good response would describe one of several possible strong reasons for decreasing immigration to the United States between 1925 and 1953. Possible examples include the following:
  ✦ Congress passes several pieces of legislation specifically limiting the numbers of people who could come to the United States from foreign countries in the early 1920s.
  ✦ The Emergency Quota Act of 1921 and the National Origins Act of 1924 may be cited as congressional actions that limited immigration.
  ✦ While immigration dropped overall, the numbers of those coming from Southern and Eastern Europe showed the greatest percentage of decline.
  ✦ The impact of the Great Depression further limited willingness to accept immigrants as they represented job competition.
  ✦ World War II further limited the number of people who were either able to or allowed to immigrate to the United States.

b) A good response for the increase in Asian immigration in the 1970s would include one of the following:
  ✦ In 1965, Congress passed the Immigration Act of 1965, which abolished the national quota system that previously set limits on the numbers of immigrants who could come from a country in a given year.

✦ The 1965 Immigration Act made it easier for close relatives of legal residents in the United States to immigrate. This particularly benefitted Asian and Latin American immigrants.

c) A good answer that explains factors that pulled immigrants to the United States between 1990 and 2010 might include the following:

✦ The Latino population grew dramatically as economic and political troubles in their countries of origin led many to come to the United States for jobs and political freedom.

✦ Asian immigration jumped over 100 percent from 1980 to 1990 due to a search for better jobs and political stability.

✦ Many immigrants believed the United States offered more generous public services than actually existed, and they hoped for that support after they arrived.

✦ Wars, political unrest, and economic hardships continued to be a factor encouraging new waves of immigrants to come to the United States, now from the Middle East as well as other countries of origin.

✦ In 1986, President Reagan signed the sweeping Immigration Reform and Control Act that offered amnesty to anyone who was in the country illegally prior to 1982. This bill encouraged many to come forward and apply for citizenship, leading to a spike in new citizens in the late 1980s.

SECTION 3
Practice Tests

PRACTICE TEST 1

SECTION I

Part A: Multiple-Choice Questions

Questions 1–3 refer to the 1893 political cartoon below.

LOOKING BACKWARD.

1. The above political cartoon most reflects commentary on the rise of nativist sentiment as a result of

   (A) the Red Scare of 1919 and 1920.
   (B) massive Irish immigration during the 1840s.
   (C) waves of new immigrants entering the country after 1890.
   (D) anti-Chinese sentiment present on the West Coast in the 1880s.

2. The cartoonist's view reflects a reaction to attempts to

   (A) restrict immigration.
   (B) repeal the quota system.
   (C) exclude a literacy test for immigrants as a condition of admission.
   (D) expand a more positive foreign policy toward Latin American nations.

GO ON TO THE NEXT PAGE.

3. Which of the following was true of immigration policy during the 1920s?

    (A) The United States developed a more restrictive policy for Southern and Eastern European immigrants.
    (B) The influx of massive numbers of Irish led the United States to exclude Ireland from the quota system.
    (C) The United States did away with quotas for Northern and Western Europeans, but not for Southern and Eastern Europeans.
    (D) Labor shortages called for the relaxation of immigration restrictions.

Questions 4–6 refer to the graph below.

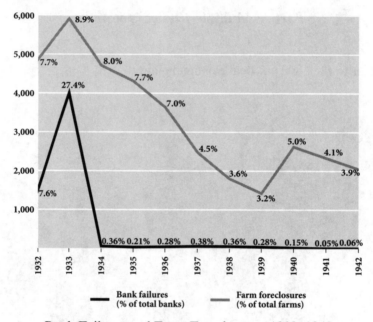

Bank Failures and Farm Foreclosures, 1932–1942

4. Which of the following statements is best supported by the graph above?

    (A) Farm foreclosures remained the same throughout the New Deal.
    (B) The rates at which banks failed and farms were foreclosed were about the same.
    (C) Banks recovered quickly in the early years of the New Deal.
    (D) Farm foreclosures went down steadily throughout the New Deal.

5. Which of the following represent the greatest change in government policy ushered in by the New Deal?

    (A) The government was responsible for the economic well-being of the country.
    (B) The government should steadfastly retain a laissez-faire approach to economic recessions.
    (C) The government's primary role should be to defend the United States from foreign invasion.
    (D) Quack remedies would not put an end to the Great Depression.

GO ON TO THE NEXT PAGE.

6. The Great Depression was ended by
    (A) New Deal relief programs like the Federal Emergency Relief Administration.
    (B) work programs such as the Civilian Conservation Corps and Works Progress Administration.
    (C) industrial expansion fueled by acts like the Lend-Lease Act.
    (D) the Court-packing scheme to uphold critical New Deal programs.

Questions 7–10 refer to the 1900 political cartoon below.

7. The above cartoon best reflects a growing call for
    (A) eliminating the capitalist system.
    (B) reducing the power of the central government.
    (C) regulating big business by the federal government.
    (D) taking a more laissez-faire approach toward monopolies.

8. The supporters of which of the following concepts would be most likely to support the opinion expressed by the political cartoonist?
    (A) Believers in new imperialism
    (B) Believers in the concept of Social Darwinism
    (C) Believers in the principles of the Populist Party
    (D) Believers in the principles of boss control

9. The above political cartoon best foreshadows the development of all of the following EXCEPT
    (A) the growth of social welfare legislation during the Progressive Era.
    (B) calls for government intervention in the economy during the Great Depression.
    (C) the Great Society of the 1960s.
    (D) calls for the deregulation of industry in the 1980s.

GO ON TO THE NEXT PAGE.

10. The above political cartoon best reflects concerns that emerged during which of the following time periods?

   (A) 1844–1877
   (B) 1865–1900
   (C) 1945–1980
   (D) 1980–present

Questions 11–13 refer to the excerpt below.

"But what do we mean by the American Revolution? Do we mean the American war? The Revolution was effected before the war commenced. The Revolution was in the minds and hearts of the people; a change in their religious sentiments of their duties and obligations. While the king, and all in authority under him, were believed to govern in justice and mercy, according to the laws and constitution derived to them from the God of nature and transmitted to them by their ancestors, they thought themselves bound to pray for the king and queen and all the royal family, and all in authority under them, as ministers ordained of God for their good; but when they saw those powers renouncing all the principles of authority, and bent upon the destruction of all the securities of their lives, liberties, and properties, they thought it their duty to pray for the continental congress and all the thirteen State congresses."

John Adams to Hezekiah Niles, February 13, 1818

11. Prior to 1754, the British North American colonies demonstrated

   (A) a strong desire to form an intercolonial government.
   (B) an unwillingness to form any coalitions between colonies.
   (C) a greater sense of colonial identity than American identity.
   (D) respect for the fact that resources were not renewable.

12. By 1763, the British North American colonists showed

   (A) majority sentiment for revolution against British rule.
   (B) a strong desire to form a powerful intercolonial central government.
   (C) a tendency to view slavery as a positive good.
   (D) tendencies to challenge British authority.

13. Between 1754 and 1775, the British North American colonists

   (A) formed organizational structures to combat British attempts to increase control over the colonies.
   (B) violated the provisions of the Trade and Navigation Acts for the first time.
   (C) formed alliances with European countries that sought to diminish British power.
   (D) refrained from using violent tactics against British rule.

Questions 14–16 refer to the excerpt below.

"We have become great in a material sense because of the lavish use of our resources, and we have just reason to be proud of our growth. But the time has come to inquire seriously what will happen when our forests are gone, when the coal, the iron, the oil, and the gas are exhausted, when the soils shall have been still further impoverished and washed into the streams, polluting the rivers, denuding the fields, and obstructing navigation."

Theodore Roosevelt, 1908

GO ON TO THE NEXT PAGE.

14. In the late nineteenth and early twentieth centuries, environmental concerns focused primarily around

    (A) growing concerns over the safety of nuclear power.
    (B) growing recognition that the nation's resources were not inexhaustible.
    (C) growing concerns about the effects of pesticides on the environment.
    (D) growing concern over the negative environmental impact of massive swamp drainage projects.

15. In the late 1950s and early 1960s, environment concerns focused primarily around

    (A) growing concerns over the disposal of toxic wastes.
    (B) concerns over the safety of nuclear power because of the meltdown at Three Mile Island.
    (C) recognition that dwindling coal resources would eventually cripple the economy.
    (D) growing concerns about the effects of pesticides on the environment.

16. In the late twentieth and early twenty-first centuries, environmental concerns focused primarily around

    (A) destruction of the national park system.
    (B) fear of a new Ice Age.
    (C) safe destruction of chemical weapons.
    (D) greater use of renewable resources.

Questions 17–19 refer to the excerpt below.

"There was a time in Wisconsin when the boss and representatives of the railroads nominated the candidates for both parties. How? By intervening between the voter and the nomination and 'getting' the delegates. . . .

"There was a time in Wisconsin when the railroads ruled and ruled supreme. They openly boasted of their power. For more than thirty years no law was enacted except by consent of the railroads. . . .

"La Follette secured the anti-lobby law. . . .

"La Follette secured the anti-pass law and thus did away with the common and wholesale bribery of public officials.

"La Follette secured the corrupt practices acts. . . .

"La Follette, with a clear vision, saw then what Roosevelt and Hughes see now—that the people must be freed from boss rule.

"La Follette secured the primary election law. . . .

"This great movement in Wisconsin has given Wisconsin a reputation throughout the nation. It is the Wisconsin Idea and other states are following in its wake. . . .

"But La Follette has done more than to save your dollars. He has made it possible in Wisconsin for you, the people, to rule, to govern yourselves, to be represented by men you choose."
     Campaign pamphlet for Robert La Follette, candidate for U.S. Senate, 1906

17. Progressives supported legislation between 1900 and 1920 that accomplished which of the following?

    (A) An easing of racial tensions through a policy of eugenics and sterilization
    (B) Major environmental legislation such as the Clean Water Act and establishment of the Environmental Protection Agency
    (C) Elimination of the income tax, making the protective tariff the chief source of government income
    (D) Democratized the political process through initiatives such as the Seventeenth and Nineteenth amendments

GO ON TO THE NEXT PAGE.

18. Progressive-supported legislation between 1930 and 1940 accomplished which of the following?

   (A) The elimination of subsidies to farmers
   (B) Suppression of the power of railroads through nationalization
   (C) Legislation that established a minimum wage and maximum hours of work
   (D) Establishment of a system of national health insurance

19. Progressives supported legislation between 1960 and 1968 that accomplished which of the following?

   (A) A successful war that eliminated poverty in Appalachia
   (B) Eliminated conflict with the Soviet Union, ending the Cold War
   (C) A ban on the construction of nuclear power plants in light of Three Mile Island and Chernobyl
   (D) Social welfare legislation such as Medicare and Head Start designed to provide a safety net for the poor

Questions 20–22 refer to the excerpt below.

"The recent alarming development and aggression of aggregated wealth, which . . . will inevitably lead to the pauperization and hopeless degradation of the toiling masses, render it imperative, if we desire to enjoy the blessings of the government bequeathed to us by the founders of the republic, that a check should be placed upon its power and unjust accumulation, and a system adopted which will secure to the laborer the fruits of his toil."

Terence V. Powderly, *Thirty Years of Labor*, 1889

20. In the last half of the nineteenth century, which of the following changes in organized labor occurred?

   (A) It moved from vague, idealistic goals to concrete goals seeking higher wages and shorter hours.
   (B) The major unions were taken over by radical socialists bent on overthrowing the capitalistic system.
   (C) Organized labor unions were outlawed by the Supreme Court.
   (D) Support for labor unions from the federal government increased.

21. Which of the following was true of labor unions between 1877 and 1900?

   (A) They achieved remarkable success in securing a national minimum wage and maximum hours.
   (B) Their actions encountered significant negative reaction from mainstream newspapers.
   (C) They achieved their goals because of the shortage of unskilled labor, which kept wages high.
   (D) They increasingly shunned violent confrontation with big business.

22. In which of the following periods did the federal government show its strongest support for organized labor?

   (A) 1980–present
   (B) 1890–1945
   (C) 1865–1890
   (D) 1800–1844

GO ON TO THE NEXT PAGE.

Questions 23–25 refer to the map below.

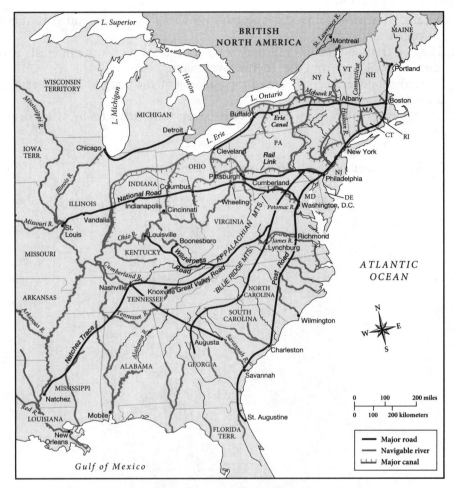

Roads and Canals to 1837

23. The transportation revolution of the period between 1800 and 1830 saw all of the following EXCEPT
   (A) the completion of significant railroad links between the Northeast and Northwest.
   (B) the growth of river cities in the West due to the proliferation of shallow-draft steamboats.
   (C) calls for the federal government to finance internal improvement projects.
   (D) a canal-building era that lowered the price of transporting bulk commodities.

24. The transportation revolution in the first half of the nineteenth century resulted in
   (A) suppression of western economic interests by leaving the section unconnected to eastern interests.
   (B) reduced sectional tension by tying the Northeast and Southeast together through canals and railroads.
   (C) the completion of a transcontinental railroad, opening Asian markets for eastern manufacturers.
   (D) movement toward a national market economy by establishing transportation links between various regions.

GO ON TO THE NEXT PAGE.

25. Which of the following is true about the development of transportation in the United States between 1800 and 1844?

(A) A canal system was financed and built primarily by the federal government to improve coastal defenses.

(B) The first transcontinental railroads were completed by private interests with significant financial help from the federal government.

(C) The federal government financed the building of the Oregon Trail to facilitate westward expansion.

(D) The majority of transportation improvement were financed by states or private enterprise.

Questions 26–28 are based on the 1786 illustration below.

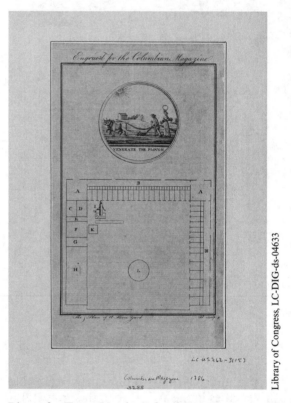

The Plan of a Farm Yard, *Columbian Magazine,* 1786

26. The above political cartoon best demonstrates that in the post–American Revolution time period,

(A) the federal government discouraged westward expansion.

(B) the role of women was significantly expanded.

(C) an agrarian lifestyle was viewed as promoting democratic principles.

(D) serious environmental concerns over soil depletion encouraged farmers to be more progressive in cultivation practices.

GO ON TO THE NEXT PAGE.

27. The scene depicted above best suggests which of the following future conflicts the United States would face?

    (A) The existence of slavery
    (B) The division of powers between the state and federal governments
    (C) White encroachment on the lands of American Indians
    (D) The acquisition of Florida from Spain

28. The above scene foreshadows which of the following disagreements in the new republic?

    (A) Debate over the future of the United States as an agrarian or commercial industrial nation
    (B) Debate over federal funding of internal improvements
    (C) Debate over whether future states should be added as equal states to existing states
    (D) Whether states should give up western land claims to the national government

Questions 29–31 refer to the excerpt below.

"I am tired of fighting. Our chiefs are killed. Looking-glass is dead. Too-hul-hul-suit is dead. The old men are all dead. It is the young men, now, who say yes or no. He who led on the young men is dead. It is cold, and we have no blankets. The little children are freezing to death. My people—some of them—have run away to the hills, and have no blankets, no food. No one knows where they are—perhaps freezing to death. I want to have time to look for my children, and to see how many of them I can find; may be I shall find them among the dead. Hear me, my chiefs; my heart is sick and sad. From where the sun now stands, I will fight no more forever!"
                    Surrender Speech by Chief Joseph of the Nez Perce, October 5, 1877

29. The above surrender speech by Chief Joseph reflects the success of which of the following government policies regarding American Indians following the Civil War?

    (A) Movement of American Indian tribes to one large reservation on the Great American Desert
    (B) Assimilation of American Indians into American culture
    (C) Movement of American Indian tribes to small, scattered reservations
    (D) The granting of 160 acres of land to every tribal member

30. Which of the following represents the primary attempt by American Indian advocates to provide native populations with a viable existence in the late nineteenth century?

    (A) "Kill the Indian, save the man."
    (B) "The only good Indian is a dead Indian."
    (C) "There is no human right to the state of barbarism."
    (D) "The conquest . . . by the whites of the Indian."

31. All of the following contributed to the decline of American Indian society EXCEPT

    (A) American Indian society's treatment of women as equals.
    (B) continued white encroachment on American Indian lands.
    (C) American Indians tribes failed to form unified alliances to prevent the advance of white settlement.
    (D) the completion of transcontinental railroads.

GO ON TO THE NEXT PAGE.

Questions 32–34 refer to the excerpt below.

"There is on the globe one single spot, the possessor of which is our natural and habitual enemy. It is New Orleans, through which the produce of three eighths of our territory must pass to market, and from its fertility it will ere long yield more than half of our whole produce and contain more than half our inhabitants. . . . Not so can it ever be in the hands of France: the impetuosity of her temper, the energy and restlessness of her character, placed in a point of eternal friction with us, . . . render it impossible that France and the U.S. can continue long friends, when they meet in so irritable a position. . . . The day that France takes possession of New Orleans . . . we must marry ourselves to the British fleet and nation."

Thomas Jefferson, 1802

32.   The problem related in the above excerpt was permanently resolved through the
    (A)   purchase of Florida in 1819.
    (B)   formation of a perpetual alliance with Great Britain.
    (C)   the Louisiana Purchase of 1803.
    (D)   the Treaty of San Lorenzo granting the United States the right of deposit at New Orleans.

33.   In order to effect control of New Orleans, Jefferson had to
    (A)   loosen his interpretation of the Constitution.
    (B)   institute the first personal income tax in U.S. history.
    (C)   stop his proposed expansion of the navy to make funds available.
    (D)   agree to move the national capital to Washington, D.C.

34.   The strongest support for gaining control of New Orleans came from
    (A)   northeastern merchants, who wanted to gain access to new markets.
    (B)   the British, who were anxious to remove the French presence from North America.
    (C)   western farmers, who wanted control of New Orleans to provide an outlet for their produce.
    (D)   Federalists, who saw control of New Orleans as a way to support the expansion of the power of the national government.

Questions 35–37 are based on the following Supreme Court decision.

"Prior to any questioning, the person must be warned that he has a right to remain silent, that any statement he does make may be used as evidence against him, and that he has a right to the presence of an attorney, either retained or appointed. The defendant may waive effectuation of these rights, provided the waiver is made voluntarily, knowingly and intelligently. If, however, he indicates in any manner and at any stage of the process that he wishes to consult with an attorney before speaking, there can be no questioning. Likewise, if the individual is alone and indicates in any manner that he does not wish to be interrogated, the police may not question him. The mere fact that he may have answered some questions or volunteered some statements on his own does not deprive him of the right to refrain from answering any further inquiries until he has consulted with an attorney and thereafter consents to be questioned."

U.S. Supreme Court majority opinion, *Miranda v. Arizona*, 1966

GO ON TO THE NEXT PAGE.

35. The primary focus of Supreme Court decisions in the 1960s revolved around the

(A) regulatory power of the federal government versus the private enterprise system.
(B) power of the federal government versus the power of state government.
(C) rights of the individual versus the regulatory power of government.
(D) the constitutionality of government regulations concerning the environment.

36. By 1968, backlash against a liberal Supreme Court could be seen in

(A) the overturning of the precedent established in *Brown v. Board of Education*.
(B) the 1968 law-and-order campaigns of Richard Nixon and George Wallace.
(C) antiwar demonstrations against the Supreme Court's upholding the constitutionality of the war in Vietnam.
(D) Congress's decision to impeach three Supreme Court judges.

37. The nation moved toward a more conservative political posture between 1960 and 1970 for all of the following reasons EXCEPT

(A) the increased militancy of the civil rights movement.
(B) antiwar protests that sometimes turned violent.
(C) the spiraling costs of social welfare legislation initiated by the Great Society.
(D) the 50 percent unilateral reduction in U.S. nuclear arms undertaken during Democratic administrations.

Questions 38–39 refer to the map below.

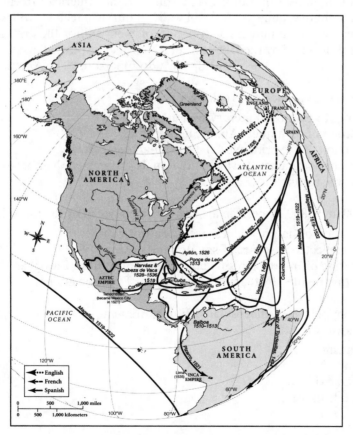

European Exploration in the Americas, 1492–1536

GO ON TO THE NEXT PAGE.

38. Prior to 1600, the dominant European colonizer of the Western Hemisphere was

    (A) Spain.
    (B) Portugal.
    (C) England.
    (D) France.

39. The most devastating effect of the Columbian Exchange on American Indians was

    (A) the introduction of horses, which destroyed the nomadic lifestyle of the Plains Indians.
    (B) superior firearms that gave the invaders a decided advantage in military struggles.
    (C) the introduction of diseases for which American Indians had little immunity.
    (D) the introduction of European crops that devastated native species and reshaped the environment.

Questions 40–43 refer to the following below.

"Another sign of our times, also marked by an analogous political movement, is the new importance given to the single person. . . .

"The scholar is that man who must take up into himself all the ability of the time, all the contributions of the past, all the hopes of the future. He must be a university of knowledges. . . . The world is nothing, the man is all; in yourself is the law of all nature, and you know not yet how a globule of sap ascends; in yourself slumbers the whole of Reason. . . . We have listened too long to the courtly muses of Europe. The spirit of the American freeman is already suspected to be timid, imitative, tame. . . . We will walk on our own feet; we will work with our own hands; we will speak our own minds. . . . A nation of men will for the first time exist, because each believes himself inspired by the Divine Soul which also inspires all men."
Ralph Waldo Emerson, "The American Scholar," 1837

40. In the above passage, Emerson is calling for

    (A) adherence to European literary standards.
    (B) the creation of a uniquely American literature.
    (C) the rejection of the principles of Jacksonian democracy.
    (D) support for communes in which individuals suppressed their personal desires for the good of the community.

41. Between 1800 and 1860, American art best reflected which of the following trends?

    (A) Glorification of nature and a sense of patriotic pride
    (B) Realism reflected in scenes of squalor and poverty
    (C) A mirroring of impressionism and expressionism from European models
    (D) Portraiture painted by the untrained hands of house painters

42. The philosophy that best encapsulated Emerson's view of the role of the individual and intuition was known as

    (A) pragmatism.
    (B) nihilism.
    (C) Social Darwinism.
    (D) transcendentalism.

GO ON TO THE NEXT PAGE.

43. Emerson's glorification of the individual fits most closely with which of the following political trends of the time period 1800 to 1840?

 (A) Jeffersonian democracy's belief in rule by the educated common man
 (B) Federalist notions of rule by the educated elite
 (C) Whig insistence on a powerful national government
 (D) Jacksonian democracy's belief in rule by the common man

Questions 44–46 refer to the graphs below.

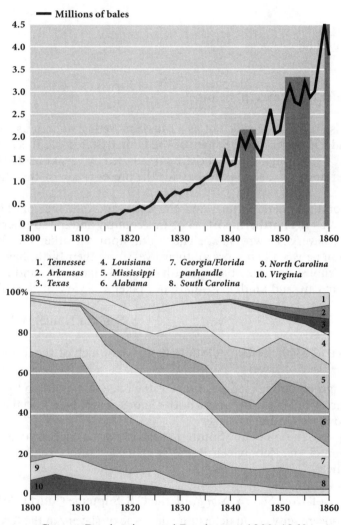

1. Tennessee   4. Louisiana   7. Georgia/Florida   9. North Carolina
2. Arkansas   5. Mississippi   panhandle   10. Virginia
3. Texas   6. Alabama   8. South Carolina

Cotton Production and Producers, 1800–1860

44. Which of the following is directly supported by one or both of the above graphs?

 (A) Cotton production showed a massive decline as a result of economic depressions such as the Panics of 1837 and 1857.
 (B) Cotton represented more than 50 percent of U.S. exports by 1860.
 (C) The massive increase in cotton production between 1855 and 1860 was the result of the invention of the cotton gin in 1847.
 (D) Cotton production continued to increase in the late 1850s despite increased sectional tension.

GO ON TO THE NEXT PAGE.

45. Which of the following statements is directly supported by one or both of the above graphs?

    (A) Cotton production was increasing more rapidly in western sections of the country than in eastern sections.
    (B) Cotton production was primarily moving north into states like Arkansas and Texas.
    (C) By 1860, Virginia no longer had any need for slaves.
    (D) The abolitionist movement was most successful in reducing slavery in eastern states.

46. Which state saw the most significant decrease in cotton production between 1800 and 1860?

    (A) Virginia
    (B) North Carolina
    (C) South Carolina
    (D) Texas

Questions 47–49 refer to the excerpt below.

"Mr. President, I wish to speak to-day, not as a Massachusetts man, nor as a northern man, but as an American, and a member of the Senate of the United States. . . . It is not to be denied that we live in the midst of strong agitations, and are surrounded by very considerable dangers to our institutions of government. . . . I speak to-day for the preservation of the Union. 'Hear me for my cause.' . . .

"Now, sir, upon the general nature, and character, and influence of slavery there exists a wide difference between the northern portion of this country and the southern. It is said, on the one side . . . that . . . slavery is a wrong; . . . The South, upon the other side, having been accustomed to this relation between two races all their lives, from their birth, having been taught, in general, to treat the subjects of this bondage with care and kindness—and I believe, in general, feeling for them great care and kindness—have not taken the view of the subject which I have mentioned."

U.S. Senator Daniel Webster, March 7, 1850

47. Between 1844 and 1860, the United States witnessed which of the following regarding the debate over the issue of slavery?

    (A) Increasingly emotionalized positions of the issue that made compromise less likely
    (B) A temporary lull in the debate as both regions savored territorial acquisition without regard to the extension of slavery
    (C) Growing recognition by the South that slavery was a "necessary evil"
    (D) Formation of the Republican Party by radical abolitionists bent on ending slavery immediately

48. In the 1857 case of *Dred Scott v. Sandford,* the U.S. Supreme Court ruled that

    (A) popular sovereignty could determine the issue of slavery in the territories.
    (B) the Fugitive Slave Law was unconstitutional.
    (C) Congress lacked the power to regulate slavery in the territories.
    (D) slavery could not exist north of 36°30" North latitude.

GO ON TO THE NEXT PAGE.

49. Which of the following is true of the 1854 Kansas-Nebraska Act?

    (A) It set the eastern terminus of the transcontinental railroad at St. Louis.
    (B) It demonstrated that popular sovereignty was a viable option in determining the issue of slavery in the territories.
    (C) It effectively undermined the Missouri Compromise.
    (D) It allowed Kansas to enter the Union as a slave state and California to enter as a free state.

Questions 50–52 refer to the excerpt below.

"We are people of this generation, bred in at least modest comfort, housed now in universities, looking uncomfortably to the world we inherit.

"The search for truly democratic alternatives to the present, and a commitment to social experimentation with them, is a worthy and fulfilling human enterprise, one which moves us and, we hope, others today."

Students for a Democratic Society, The Port Huron Statement, 1962

50. Which of the following best reflects the major reason for the discontent of out of the mainstream youth of the 1960s?

    (A) The growth of suburbs
    (B) The shallowness, superficiality, and conformity of society
    (C) The discontent of baby boomers with their lack of affluence
    (D) The failure of American education to meet the challenges of the Cold War

51. Which of the following groups most challenged the societal conformity alluded to in the above excerpt in the early 1960s?

    (A) The silent majority
    (B) The Southern Christian Leadership Conference
    (C) The Ku Klux Klan
    (D) The counterculture

52. Spurred on by challenges to the status quo by the civil rights movement's call for social justice and criticism of the regimentation of society, many other groups sought to overcome traditional obstacles to full rights in the 1960s. These groups included all of the following EXCEPT

    (A) women's rights groups that sought an Equal Rights Amendment to the Constitution.
    (B) migrant workers who sought to improve working conditions in agricultural fields.
    (C) gays and lesbians who sought less discrimination and a more open society.
    (D) the moral majority who sought to increase religious participation in politics.

GO ON TO THE NEXT PAGE.

Questions 53–55 refer to the image below.

Sculpture of Mary Dyer on Boston Common

53. Which of the following was true of religious freedom in the British North American colonies between 1607 and 1754?

(A) Religious freedom was promoted in Massachusetts Bay by the doctrine of intellectual freedom of the Puritan church.

(B) Religious freedom was advanced by the open immigration policy that led divergent groups to settle in the colonies.

(C) The Church of England was the dominant church in all thirteen colonies.

(D) Colonists unanimously rejected the notion of a state church supported by tax dollars.

54. The diversity of religious denominations in the colonies led to

(A) major religious wars in New England that resulted in the death of more than four thousand people.

(B) advances in higher education as different denominations set up colleges to train ministers.

(C) Parliament allowing only Anglican Englishmen to settle in the colonies after 1700.

(D) English trade restrictions on colonial trade with Catholic nations.

55. The greatest religious diversity in the British North American colonies prior to 1754 existed in which of the following sections?

(A) Canada

(B) The southern colonies

(C) The middle colonies

(D) New England

GO ON TO THE NEXT PAGE.

Part B: Short-Answer Questions

"Whoever, when the United States is at war, shall willfully make or convey false reports or false statements . . . or incite or attempt to incite, insubordination, disloyalty, mutiny, or refusal of duty, in the military or naval forces of the United States, or shall willfully obstruct . . . the recruiting or enlistment service of the United States, or . . . shall willfully utter, print, write, or publish any disloyal, profane, scurrilous, or abusive language about the form of government of the United States, or the Constitution of the United States, or the military or naval forces of the United States . . . . shall be punished by a fine of not more than $10,000 or imprisonment for not more than twenty years, or both."

Sedition Act, 1918

1. Using the excerpt above, answer a, b, and c.

    a) Cite and explain one specific example of the suppression of constitutional rights during World War I.

    b) Cite and explain one example of the suppression of constitutional rights during wartime for the period 1844 to 1877.

    c) Cite and explain one example of the suppression of constitutional rights during wartime for the period 1980 to the present.

2. Answer a, b, and c.

    a) Identify one group or individual who was a primary focus of authorities in the first Red Scare following World War I, and explain why the group or individual was a primary focus.

    b) Identify one group or individual who was a primary focus of authorities in the second Red Scare following World War II, and explain why the group or individual was a primary focus.

    c) Explain which Red Scare constituted a more severe threat to the United States, and explain why.

3. Answer a, b, and c.

    a) Explain how urban transportation systems changed residential patterns in the late nineteenth century.

    b) Explain how cities with limited geographic space continued to expand in the late nineteenth century.

    c) Explain one specific effort to accommodate the needs of poor migrants to American cities in the late nineteenth century.

GO ON TO THE NEXT PAGE.

4. Answer a, b, and c.

   a) Explain one major compromise of the Constitutional Convention, and explain how it satisfied differing opinions.

   b) Explain one postratification accommodation made by those supporting the Constitution to appease concerns of those who had opposed ratification.

   c) Explain how debates over constitutional interpretation led to the development of the First American Party System.

STOP

END OF SECTION I

SECTION II

Part A: Document-Based Question

Directions: The following question in based on the accompanying documents. The documents have been edited for this exercise. Spend approximately 15 minutes planning and 45 minutes writing your answer.

Write an essay that does the following:

- ✦ States an appropriate thesis that directly addresses all parts of the question.
- ✦ Supports the thesis or argument with evidence from all or all but one of the documents AND your knowledge of U.S. history beyond the documents.
- ✦ Analyzes all or all but one of the documents.
- ✦ Places each document into at least one of the following categories: intended audience, purpose, historical context, and/or point of view.
- ✦ Uses historical evidence beyond the documents to support your argument.
- ✦ Places the argument in the context of broader regional, national, or global processes.
- ✦ Incorporates all of the elements above into a convincing essay.

Question: Evaluate how and why American society was divided in the 1920s.

Document 1

Source: Cartoonist Billy Ireland, 1919

Document 2

Source: F. Scott Fitzgerald, *This Side of Paradise*, 1920

Long after midnight the towers and spires of Princeton were visible, with here and there a late-burning light—and suddenly out of the clear darkness the sound of bells. As an endless dream it went on; the spirit of the past brooding over a new generation, the chosen youth from the muddled, unchastened world, still fed romantically on the mistakes and half-forgotten dreams of dead statesmen and poets. Here was a new generation, shouting the old cries, learning the old creeds, through a revery of long days and nights; destined finally to go out into that dirty gray turmoil to follow love and pride; a new generation dedicated more than the last to the fear of poverty and the worship of success; grown up to find all Gods dead, all wars fought, all faiths in man shaken.

Document 3

Source: H. L. Mencken, *Baltimore Sun*, July 26, 1920

When a candidate for public office faces the voters he does not face men of sense; he faces a mob of men whose chief distinguishing mark is the fact that they are quite incapable of weighing ideas, or even of comprehending any save the most elemental—men whose whole thinking is done in terms of emotion, and whose dominant emotion is dread of what they cannot understand. So confronted, the candidate must either bark with the pack or be lost. . . . All the odds are on the man who is, intrinsically, the most devious and mediocre—the man who can most adeptly disperse the notion that his mind is a virtual vacuum. The Presidency tends, year by year, to go to such men. As democracy is perfected, the office represents, more and more closely, the inner soul of the people. We move toward a lofty ideal. On some great and glorious day the plain folks of the land will reach their heart's desire at last, and the White House will be adorned by a downright moron.

Document 4

Source: President Warren G. Harding, c. 1921

I talk to the other side and they seem just as right, and here I am where I started. I know somewhere there is a book that will give me the truth, but, hell, I couldn't read the book. I know somewhere there is an economist who knows the truth, but I don't know where to find him and haven't the sense to know him and trust him when I find him. God! what a job!

GO ON TO THE NEXT PAGE.

Document 5

Source: "The Creeping Shadow," *The Afro-American*, October 3, 1925. Cartoonist: Fred B. Watson.

Used with permission from the Afro-American Newspapers Archives and Research Center.

Document 6

Source: "The Descent of the Modernists," cartoon by E. J. Pace, in William Jennings Bryan, *Seven Questions in Dispute*, 1924.

Document 7

Source: William Jennings Bryan, undelivered closing statement prepared for the Scopes trial, 1925

Christianity welcomes truth from whatever source it comes and is not afraid that any real truth from any source can interfere with the divine truth that comes by inspiration from God Himself. It is not scientific truth to which Christians object, for true science is classified knowledge, and nothing therefore can be scientific unless it is true.

Evolution is not truth: it is merely an hypothesis—it is millions of guesses strung together. It had not been proven in the days of Darwin; he expressed astonishment that with two or three million species it had been impossible to trace any species to any other species. It had not been proven in the days of [Thomas Henry] Huxley, and it has not been proven up to today.

Part B: Long Essay Questions

Choose between one of the following two questions. You will have 35 minutes to complete your answer.

Question 1: Historians often disagree about turning points in U.S. history. Analyze the reasons that a historian might choose the year 1890 as a turning point in U.S. history.

Question 2: Historians often disagree about turning points in U.S. history. Analyze the reasons that a historian might choose the year 1968 as a turning point in U.S. history.

STOP

END OF EXAM

ANSWER KEY TO PRACTICE TEST 1

Multiple-Choice Questions

1.

Answer	Learning Objectives	Historical Thinking Skills	Key Concepts in the Curriculum Framework
C	MIG-2.0	Patterns of Continuity and Change over Time Analyzing Evidence: Content and Sourcing	6.2

Explanation: Southern and Eastern European immigration increased dramatically after 1890, leading to a strong nativist response. Groups such as the Immigration Restriction League, the American Protective Association, and the KKK sought to restrict immigration. Differences in culture, religion, and politics made the assimilation process more difficult for new immigrants.

2.

Answer	Learning Objectives	Historical Thinking Skills	Key Concepts in the Curriculum Framework
A	NAT-4.0	Patterns of Continuity and Change over Time Analyzing Evidence: Content and Sourcing	6.2

Explanation: The cartoonist attempts to point out the hypocrisy of nativists whose ancestors had immigrated to the United States. The caption is, "They would close to the new-comer the bridge that carried them and their fathers over." The cartoonist's view was that America was a nation of immigrants. The quota system and literacy test were not established until later in the twentieth century.

3.

Answer	Learning Objectives	Historical Thinking Skills	Key Concepts in the Curriculum Framework
A	CUL-4.0	Patterns of Continuity and Change over Time Analyzing Evidence: Content and Sourcing	7.2

Explanation: The quota system was established in the 1920s as a result of the Emergency Quota Act of 1921 and the National Origins Act of 1924. Both acts had as their purpose a reduction of overall immigration. However, the laws were specifically designed to discriminate against Southern and Eastern Europeans. Quotas for these groups were much lower than current immigration warranted.

4.

Answer	Learning Objectives	Historical Thinking Skills	Key Concepts in the Curriculum Framework
C	WXT-2.0	Analyzing Evidence: Content and Sourcing Patterns of Continuity and Change over Time	7.1

Explanation: The graph most clearly illustrates that banks recovered quickly in the early years of the New Deal. Farm foreclosures declined for the most part throughout the New Deal, although there was an upsurge in foreclosures in the late 1930s. The rate at which farms were foreclosed was clearly higher than the rate at which banks failed.

5.

Answer	Learning Objectives	Historical Thinking Skills	Key Concepts in the Curriculum Framework
A	POL-3.0	Patterns of Continuity and Change over Time	7.1

Explanation: The New Deal assumed government responsibility in helping to maintain a stable economy. This notion rejected the idea of rugged individualism and the Social Darwinist theory that economic depressions weed out the unfit. Acceptance of the New Deal by the American public was extremely quick as it was codified into law in the Employment Act of 1946.

6.

Answer	Learning Objectives	Historical Thinking Skills	Key Concepts in the Curriculum Framework
C	WOR-2.0	Causation	7.3

Explanation: Roosevelt's belief that the United States would inevitably be drawn into European conflict led him to pursue a policy in which the United States would supply war material to "keep England fighting" while making the United States the "great arsenal of democracy." Programs like "cash and carry" and the Lend-Lease Act geared up U.S. industry toward wartime production, providing jobs and income that ultimately ended the Great Depression.

7.

Answer	Learning Objectives	Historical Thinking Skills	Key Concepts in the Curriculum Framework
C	POL-2.0	Patterns of Continuity and Change over Time Analyzing Evidence: Content and Sourcing	7.1

Explanation: The Progressive movement of the early twentieth century sought the regulation of business in order to increase the power of labor. Progressives wanted to tweak the capitalistic system rather than replace it. One historian has noted that the single cry of Progressives was "strengthen the state."

8.

Answer	Learning Objectives	Historical Thinking Skills	Key Concepts in the Curriculum Framework
C	POL-3.0	Contextualization Analyzing Evidence: Content and Sourcing	7.1

Explanation: The Progressive movement was an outgrowth of the Populist movement of the 1880s and 1890s. Populists sought government ownership of utilities and increased regulation of big business, particularly railroads. Whereas the Populist movement was largely an agrarian movement, the Progressive movement was primarily an urban one leading to greater demands for the regulation of manufacturing industries and social welfare legislation for industrial workers.

9.

Answer	Learning Objectives	Historical Thinking Skills	Key Concepts in the Curriculum Framework
D	WXT-2.0	Patterns of Continuity and Change over Time Analyzing Evidence: Content and Sourcing	9.1

Explanation: The cartoon does not reflect support for the deregulation in industry that was undertaken under the Reagan administration. Reagan's belief was that excessive regulation, particularly environmental regulation, made American industry less competitive with countries that did not impose such regulations. The Progressive movement, the New Deal, and the Great Society all saw government as a leveling agent of social welfare.

10.

Answer	Learning Objectives	Historical Thinking Skills	Key Concepts in the Curriculum Framework
B	POL-2.0	Periodization Analyzing Evidence: Content and Sourcing	6.3

Explanation: The expansion of big business during the Gilded Age produced great disparities in wealth. The power of big business to influence government and control the lives of workers led disadvantaged groups to look to regulation by the federal government. Labor unions and agrarian organizations such as the Farmers' Alliance and the Grange organized in an attempt to influence politics at the state and local level. This agenda was crystallized in the Populist Platform (Omaha Platform) of 1892.

11.

Answer	Learning Objectives	Historical Thinking Skills	Key Concepts in the Curriculum Framework
C	NAT-1.0	Patterns of Continuity and Change over Time Analyzing Evidence: Content and Sourcing	2.2

Explanation: Prior to 1754, British North American colonists had shown a reluctance to create an intercolonial government through such actions as the rejection of the Albany Plan of Union. At the same time, the colonists had shown the ability to form necessary coalitions for specific problems, such as the New England Confederation. What the colonists did demonstrate was a greater attachment to their specific colony rather than a sense of American identity.

12.

Answer	Learning Objectives	Historical Thinking Skills	Key Concepts in the Curriculum Framework
D	NAT-1.0	Patterns of Continuity and Change over Time Analyzing Evidence: Content and Sourcing	3.1

Explanation: The French and Indian War combined with the First Great Awakening emboldened the colonists to challenge established authority. Although the colonists showed an emerging identity through collective actions such as the Sons of Liberty and the Stamp Act Congress, these were temporary associations designed to confront specific circumstances rather than a strong desire to unite. Even at the time of the American Revolution, majority sentiment was not for revolution against Great Britain. Slavery still tended to be viewed as a "necessary evil" rather than as a positive good until 1837.

13.

Answer	Learning Objectives	Historical Thinking Skills	Key Concepts in the Curriculum Framework
A	NAT-1.0	Patterns of Continuity and Change over Time	3.1

Explanation: Between the end of the French and Indian War and the beginning of the Revolutionary War, colonists established organized structures such as circular letters, committees of correspondence, nonimportation agreements, and the First Continental Congress to combat Britain's assertion of power over them. The Trade and Navigation Acts had been violated throughout their existence. Sons of Liberty engaged in violent (if not necessarily deadly) acts through destruction of property and tarring and feathering, among others. European countries were reluctant to aid the United States prior to a demonstration that the revolution stood a legitimate chance of success.

14.

Answer	Learning Objectives	Historical Thinking Skills	Key Concepts in the Curriculum Framework
B	GEO-1.0	Periodization Analyzing Evidence: Content and Sourcing	7.1

Explanation: With the closing of the frontier in 1890 and the Panic of 1893, the United States awakened to the realization that the nation's natural resources were finite. As a result, conservation movements took on added importance, and the United States began to look outward for both additional markets and resources. Issues such as the safety of nuclear power, the effect of pesticides on the environment, and the destruction of natural habitat through swamp drainage were issues that arose later in the twentieth century.

15.

Answer	Learning Objectives	Historical Thinking Skills	Key Concepts in the Curriculum Framework
D	GEO-1.0	Periodization	8.2

Explanation: Rachel Carson's *Silent Spring*, published in 1962, focused attention on the negative impact of pesticides on the environment. Ultimately this increased awareness of the impact of chemicals on the environment and greater environmental consciousness generally. Although there was concern over the environmental impact of strip mining for coal, the development of nuclear power was heralded as the energy of the future. Concern over the disposal of toxic waste markedly increased in the 1970s, as did concern over the safety of nuclear power after the Three Mile Island incident.

16.

Answer	Learning Objectives	Historical Thinking Skills	Key Concepts in the Curriculum Framework
D	GEO-1.0	Periodization	9.3

Explanation: Since at least the Carter administration, the United States has focused on achieving energy self-sufficiency, and renewable sources of energy have come to the forefront. Destruction of chemical weapons has been a limited concern that has not overshadowed concerns over global warming and renewable resources. While national parks have been closed temporarily because of government shutdowns, the country continues to support their existence and integrity.

17.

Answer	Learning Objectives	Historical Thinking Skills	Key Concepts in the Curriculum Framework
D	POL-2.0	Causation Analyzing Evidence: Content and Sourcing	7.1

Explanation: The Progressive movement achieved its greatest lasting accomplishment in the area of making government more responsive to the will of the people. This was accomplished on the national level through the establishment of the direct election of senators and the granting of women's suffrage. On the state level, the political system became more democratic through the introduction of the secret ballot, initiative, referendum, and recall, as well as attempts to limit boss rule. Progressives did little to advance racial equality and were generally much more concerned with social welfare than environmental issues.

18.

Answer	Learning Objectives	Historical Thinking Skills	Key Concepts in the Curriculum Framework
C	POL-3.0	Periodization	7.1

Explanation: The Roosevelt administration enacted significant prolabor legislation, including the National Labor Relations Act legalizing collective bargaining and the Fair Employment Practices Act establishing a minimum wage and maximum hours. Railroads that had been nationalized during World War I were returned to private ownership in the early 1920s. The Agricultural Adjustment Administration provided aid to farmers, and national health insurance did not become an issue until the Truman administration.

19.

Answer	Learning Objectives	Historical Thinking Skills	Key Concepts in the Curriculum Framework
D	POL-3.0	Periodization	8.2

Explanation: The Great Society of the Lyndon Johnson administration was designed to realize the original Progressive goal of establishing a safety net for average Americans. While the War on Poverty was a failure, the lasting legacy of the administration is reflected in programs like Medicare and Head Start. A thawing of relations with the Soviet Union did not occur until the Nixon administration, and concerns over nuclear safety did not intensify until the 1970s.

20.

Answer	Learning Objectives	Historical Thinking Skills	Key Concepts in the Curriculum Framework
A	WXT-2.0	Patterns of Continuity and Change over Time	7.1

Explanation: In the late nineteenth century, organized labor moved from the lofty goals of establishing "a just and harmonious society" to the "bread-and-butter" unionism of the American Federation of Labor, which sought higher wages, shorter hours, and better working conditions. Mainstream organized labor sought reform rather than elimination of the capitalistic system. Throughout the period, the federal government tended to side with big business by the issuing of injunctions and use of federal troops to quell labor disputes. The Supreme Court did not outlaw labor unions in the last half of the nineteenth century.

21.

Answer	Learning Objectives	Historical Thinking Skills	Key Concepts in the Curriculum Framework
B	WXT-1.0	Periodization Analyzing Evidence: Content and Sourcing	6.1

Explanation: Newspapers, as part of the business establishment, portrayed unions and strikes as socialistic or anarchistic attempts to threaten the public good. Minimum wages and maximum hour goals were not achieved until later in the twentieth century. As the nineteenth century progressed, violence in labor disputes increased in instances such as the Railway Strike of 1877, the Haymarket Square incident, and the Homestead and Pullman strikes. Increased immigration from Southern and Eastern Europe swelled the supply of unskilled labor during the period.

22.

Answer	Learning Objectives	Historical Thinking Skills	Key Concepts in the Curriculum Framework
B	WXT-2.0	Periodization	7.1

Explanation: Franklin Roosevelt's New Deal represented the first time a presidential administration took a dominantly prolabor position. Enactment of the National Labor Relations (Wagner) Act and the Fair Labor Standards Act benefitted organized labor to a degree unseen prior to that period. Organized labor was weak and labor strife muted during the period from 1800 to 1844. The Gilded Age, 1865–1890, was dominated by big business ideology during which the federal government did little to assist organized labor. Between 1980 and the present, the clout of labor unions has diminished as the economy moved from a dominantly manufacturing economy to a dominantly service-based economy.

23.

Answer	Learning Objectives	Historical Thinking Skills	Key Concepts in the Curriculum Framework
A	WXT-3.0	Periodization	4.2

Explanation: Railway links between the Northeast and Northwest were not begun until well after 1830. The period 1800 to 1830 saw the tremendous expansion of a canal system that tied the Northwest and the Northeast more closely together economically, politically, and socially. That system, particularly the Erie Canal, dramatically lowered the cost of shipping bulk commodities. Henry Clay's call for federally funded internal improvements went largely unheeded.

24.

Answer	Learning Objectives	Historical Thinking Skills	Key Concepts in the Curriculum Framework
D	WXT-3.0	Causation	4.2

Explanation: The transportation revolution of the first half of the nineteenth century greatly increased the connective links between various regions, resulting in the creation of a national market economy. Particularly important were the canal and railroad links between the Northeast and Northwest. The transcontinental railroad was not completed in this time period. The connective links between the Northeast and Northwest arguably left the South out and likely intensified sectional conflict.

25.

Answer	Learning Objectives	Historical Thinking Skills	Key Concepts in the Curriculum Framework
D	WXT-2.0	Patterns of Continuity and Change over Time	4.2

Explanation: State and private enterprise ventures created the majority of internal improvement in the United States prior to 1850. While Henry Clay's American System called for federally funded internal improvements, that call was largely ignored. Although the first transcontinental railroad was completed by private interests with federal assistance in the form of land grants and subsidies, it was initiated well after 1844. The federal government did not play a role in building the Oregon Trail.

26.

Answer	Learning Objectives	Historical Thinking Skills	Key Concepts in the Curriculum Framework
C	CUL-4.0	Patterns of Continuity and Change over Time Analyzing Evidence: Content and Sourcing	3.3

Explanation: Following the American Revolution, many saw the ideal of the small farmer, tilling his own land, as a stabilizing and democratic force in society. In the cartoon, the farmer is aided by Miss Liberty, representing American democracy. America's vast area of free or cheap land made the ideal a real possibility. The image does not speak to the role of women, and concerns over soil depletion were not yet an issue. The government consistently pursued policies that encouraged westward expansion.

27.

Answer	Learning Objectives	Historical Thinking Skills	Key Concepts in the Curriculum Framework
C	MIG-2.0	Patterns of Continuity and Change over Time Analyzing Evidence: Content and Sourcing	3.3

Explanation: Continued population increases led Americans to expand settlement westward. The need for new and fertile land led to conflicts with American Indians. A continuing tension could be felt between the eastern elite and the backcountry over adequate protection from American Indians.

28.

Answer	Learning Objectives	Historical Thinking Skills	Key Concepts in the Curriculum Framework
A	POL-3.0	Comparison Analyzing Evidence: Content and Sourcing	3.2

Explanation: In the early republic, two views of government emerged that coincided with beliefs about what the future of the United States should be. Alexander Hamilton believed the future of the country lay in commerce and industry, which would need a powerful national government to support and defend it. Thomas Jefferson believed the United States should be a nation of small farmers, which would reduce the need for a powerful national government and eliminating the fear of tyranny.

29.

Answer	Learning Objectives	Historical Thinking Skills	Key Concepts in the Curriculum Framework
C	WOR-1.0	Contextualization Analyzing Evidence: Content and Sourcing	6.2

Explanation: Following the Civil War, the federal government abandoned its policies of the assimilation of American Indians into white society or movement to one large reservation west of the Mississippi. The opening of the Great Plains to cultivation meant continued white encroachment on native lands. Thus, the government adopted a policy of moving tribes to small, scattered reservations to make them easier to control and to open up additional acres for agriculture.

30.

Answer	Learning Objectives	Historical Thinking Skills	Key Concepts in the Curriculum Framework
A	MIG-2.0	Argumentation	6.2

Explanation: Indian advocates such as Helen Hunt Jackson believed the only hope for American Indians was to assimilate into white American society. Thus, they supported acts like the Dawes Severalty Act that was designed to break down tribal loyalty by offering free homesteads to heads of households, establishing Indian schools, and not recognizing the tribe as a political unit. Thus, the "Indians" had to be killed so they might become "white."

31.

Answer	Learning Objectives	Historical Thinking Skills	Key Concepts in the Curriculum Framework
A	WOR-1.0	Causation	6.2

Explanation: The social structure of American Indian society had little influence on decline. Continued expansion of whites onto native lands provoked hostile conflict throughout U.S. history. American Indians were unable to unite in a significant enough alliance to pose a major threat to continued expansion, despite the effort of leaders like Tecumseh. The completion of transcontinental railroad accelerated the intrusion on to native lands.

32.

Answer	Learning Objectives	Historical Thinking Skills	Key Concepts in the Curriculum Framework
C	WOR-2.0	Causation Analyzing Evidence: Content and Sourcing	4.3

Explanation: While the Treaty of San Lorenzo granted the United States the right of deposit at New Orleans in the 1790s, cession of Louisiana by Spain to France negated the agreement. Through the purchase of Louisiana from the French, Jefferson was able to accomplish both his goal of perpetual U.S. control of New Orleans and expansion of U.S. territory to allow the establishment of an agrarian society. Jefferson tended to be pro-French in outlook and would not have favored a permanent alliance with Great Britain.

33.

Answer	Learning Objectives	Historical Thinking Skills	Key Concepts in the Curriculum Framework
A	WOR-1.0	Analyzing Evidence: Content and Sourcing	4.3

Explanation: Jefferson's strict constructionist view of constitutional interpretation meant that he had to loosen his interpretation in order to purchase Louisiana. Although he favored a constitutional amendment to allow the purchase, his advisors cautioned him that the delay might cause Napoleon to change his mind and negate the purchase. Jefferson, seeking to pursue a policy that best benefitted the United States, agreed to swallow his concerns and complete the purchase.

34.

Answer	Learning Objectives	Historical Thinking Skills	Key Concepts in the Curriculum Framework
C	CUL-4.0	Argumentation	4.3

Explanation: Western farmers favored securing the right of deposit at New Orleans to provide an outlet for their produce. Water transportation provided a much cheaper form of transportation for the bulk commodities than overland transportation. Many Federalists opposed the purchase because it would result in expanded political power for Jeffersonian Democrats.

35.

Answer	Learning Objectives	Historical Thinking Skills	Key Concepts in the Curriculum Framework
C	POL-3.0	Periodization Analyzing Evidence: Content and Sourcing	8.2

Explanation: Since the New Deal, the Supreme Court's major focus has been on protecting the rights of the individual from the power of the state and national government. In the 1960s, that focus was accentuated by decisions on free speech, prayer, and Bible reading in public schools and, particularly, rights of those accused of committing a crime. The Gilded Age saw the primary focus of the Court on the regulatory power of the government over private enterprise. Early in the nineteenth century, the Court focused primarily on the power of the federal government versus the power of states.

36.

Answer	Learning Objectives	Historical Thinking Skills	Key Concepts in the Curriculum Framework
B	POL-1.0	Contextualization Analyzing Evidence: Content and Sourcing	8.2

Explanation: The 1960s witnessed an early surge of liberalism followed by an erosion of support for social welfare programs. Part of that backlash was focused on liberal Supreme Court decisions, particularly in the area of the rights of the accused. Increasing militancy in the civil rights movement and increasing public protests over the war in Vietnam left many Americans concerned over civil disobedience. This led to the "law-and-order" campaigns of Richard Nixon and George Wallace in the election of 1968.

37.

Answer	Learning Objectives	Historical Thinking Skills	Key Concepts in the Curriculum Framework
D	POL-3.0	Patterns of Continuity and Change over Time Analyzing Evidence: Content and Sourcing	8.2

Explanation: The increased militancy of the civil rights movement as well as protests against the war in Vietnam helped fuel the resurgence of conservatism by the late 1960s. As well, the spiraling costs of social welfare programs and expenditures for the war in Vietnam convinced many in the silent majority of the need for cutbacks. Increasingly middle-class Americans did not see social welfare programs as beneficial to themselves.

38.

Answer	Learning Objectives	Historical Thinking Skills	Key Concepts in the Curriculum Framework
A	WOR-1.0	Contextualization Analyzing Evidence: Content and Sourcing	1.2

Explanation: The Spanish explored and settled far more Western Hemisphere territory than England, France, or Portugal. The dominance of the Spanish navy made colonization by other European countries a precarious venture. Substantial colonizing on the part of England and France did not occur until after 1600. The defeat of the Spanish Armada made the success of colonization much more likely.

39.

Answer	Learning Objectives	Historical Thinking Skills	Key Concepts in the Curriculum Framework
C	WOR-1.0	Analyzing Evidence: Content and Sourcing	1.2

Explanation: While the Columbian Exchange did reshape the environment of the Western Hemisphere, disease was its most devastating aspect. The lack of immunity to European diseases, particularly smallpox, had a catastrophic effect on tribes throughout the Western Hemisphere. The introduction of the horse altered the lifestyle of plains Indians in a positive way. Firearms accounted for far fewer deaths than did disease.

40.

Answer	Learning Objectives	Historical Thinking Skills	Key Concepts in the Curriculum Framework
B	CUL-2.0	Analyzing Evidence: Content and Sourcing	4.1

Explanation: Emerson espoused the development of a uniquely American literature rather than a parroting of European standards and themes. In Emerson's mind, the role of the individual and personal experience led the way to new American literary formats. The elevation of the role of the individual corresponds with the rise of the common man during the era of Jacksonian democracy. Emerson would not support subjugation of the individual to the community at large.

41.

Answer	Learning Objectives	Historical Thinking Skills	Key Concepts in the Curriculum Framework
A	CUL-2.0	Analyzing Evidence: Content and Sourcing	4.1

Explanation: Patriotic paintings such as of the signing of the Declaration of Independence and famous military battles of the American Revolution and the War of 1812 abounded in the first third of the nineteenth century. That was followed by the glorification of nature in the Hudson River School of art in the 1840s and 1850s. Portraiture painting, while still prevalent, was more associated with the colonial period and with untrained artists. Realism and impressionism/expressionism are associated with the last half of the nineteenth century.

42.

Answer	Learning Objectives	Historical Thinking Skills	Key Concepts in the Curriculum Framework
D	CUL-2.0	Analyzing Evidence: Content and Sourcing	4.1

Explanation: The role of conscience and intuition were primary components of the transcendental philosophy. Under this philosophy, one could not understand truth, only know that it exists. In order to accomplish that, one must become a transparent eyeball that sees all things and is seen by all things. Pragmatism, nihilism, and Social Darwinism emerged later in the nineteenth century.

43.

Answer	Learning Objectives	Historical Thinking Skills	Key Concepts in the Curriculum Framework
D	CUL-2.0	Analyzing Evidence: Content and Sourcing	4.1

Explanation: Glorification of the individual dovetailed nicely with the rising participation of Jacksonian democracy. While Jeffersonian democracy touted the benefits of an educated common man, transcendentalism placed more emphasis on conscience and personal experience than formal education. Rule by the educated elite would thwart individual participation in government.

44.

Answer	Learning Objectives	Historical Thinking Skills	Key Concepts in the Curriculum Framework
D	WXT-1.0	Patterns of Continuity and Change over Time Analyzing Evidence: Content and Sourcing	5.2

Explanation: Despite increasing sectional tension over the extension of slavery into the territories, cotton production continued to increase throughout the 1850s. While cotton exports did exceed 50 percent of U.S. exports by 1860, neither of the graphs demonstrates that. The cotton gin was invented in 1793 and was instrumental in increasing cotton production during the entire period, though that is not reflected in either document.

45.

Answer	Learning Objectives	Historical Thinking Skills	Key Concepts in the Curriculum Framework
A	WXT-1.0	Analyzing Evidence: Content and Sourcing	5.2

Explanation: Soil overuse reduced the fertility of eastern cotton-growing lands. As a result, cotton production expanded westward into the Black Belt of Alabama and Mississippi and beyond. Neither source speaks to the reason for the reduction in cotton production in the East. While cotton production did increase in Arkansas and Texas, that did not constitute movement north. Virginia by 1860 was still a slave state.

46.

Answer	Learning Objectives	Historical Thinking Skills	Key Concepts in the Curriculum Framework
C	WXT-1.0	Analyzing Evidence: Content and Sourcing	5.2

Explanation: Although both North Carolina and Virginia experienced large decreases in cotton production, the most significant decrease occurred in South Carolina. Some historians contend that this drop in economic dominance and diminished political clout led South Carolina to become the most adamant state in challenging the authority of the federal government and, in fact, South Carolina was the first state to secede.

47.

Answer	Learning Objectives	Historical Thinking Skills	Key Concepts in the Curriculum Framework
A	NAT-1.0	Contextualization Analyzing Evidence: Content and Sourcing	5.2

Explanation: Increasingly emotional debates over the issue of the extension of slavery into the territories were characteristic of the 1850s. The South rejected the notion that slavery was a necessary evil as apologists characterized it as a positive good. Debate over slavery in California, the Mexican cession, Kansas, and Nebraska all moved the two sides further away from compromise. The Republican Party, formed in reaction to the Kansas-Nebraska Act, was initially a free-soil party that opposed the extension of slavery into the territories rather than its complete abolition.

48.

Answer	Learning Objectives	Historical Thinking Skills	Key Concepts in the Curriculum Framework
C	NAT-2.0	Contextualization Analyzing Evidence: Content and Sourcing	5.2

Explanation: The *Dred Scott* decision ruled the Compromise of 1820 unconstitutional despite the fact it had been repealed by the Kansas-Nebraska Act. In doing so, the Supreme Court ruled that Congress lacked the authority to regulate slavery in the territories. The Taney Court said that slaves were property under the meaning of the Constitution and property could not be taken away without due process. Popular sovereignty, shown to be an unviable option in "bleeding Kansas," did not constitute due process.

49.

Answer	Learning Objectives	Historical Thinking Skills	Key Concepts in the Curriculum Framework
C	NAT-2.0	Causation	5.2

Explanation: The Kansas-Nebraska Act repealed the Missouri Compromise and allowed popular sovereignty to determine the issue of slavery in the two territories. Stephen Douglass originally proposed to divide the territories of Kansas and Nebraska to increase the possibility of Chicago becoming the eastern terminus of the transcontinental railroad. In order to gain southern support for his idea of popular sovereignty, he gave the South hope that slavery could be extended north of the 36°30" North latitude established by the Missouri Compromise of 1820.

50.

Answer	Learning Objectives	Historical Thinking Skills	Key Concepts in the Curriculum Framework
B	CUL-4.0	Argumentation Analyzing Evidence: Content and Sourcing	8.2

Explanation: Many members of the New Left and counterculture of the 1960s criticized the shallowness and superficiality of American society, as the topical songwriters and the Beat generation of the late 1950s and early 1960s had. While all of the other three answer choices may have been concerns of young people, they do not represent the basic idea contained in the goals of the Port Huron Statement.

51.

Answer	Learning Objectives	Historical Thinking Skills	Key Concepts in the Curriculum Framework
D	CUL-4.0	Periodization	8.2

Explanation: The counterculture challenged the traditional American family stereotype. As a group, they tended to reject the American dream of getting ahead financially. The counterculture also promoted communal existence to replace the "dog-eat-dog" competition prevalent in traditional American individualism. The silent majority represented a traditional conservative constituency put off by the hedonistic behavior of the counterculture.

52.

Answer	Learning Objectives	Historical Thinking Skills	Key Concepts in the Curriculum Framework
D	NAT-1.0	Periodization Patterns of Continuity and Change over Time	8.2

Explanation: The success of the civil rights movement led other disadvantaged groups to more actively protest their positions in society. A new women's rights movement led to formation of the National Organization for Women and called for an Equal Rights Amendment. Cesar Chavez organized migrant workers and led a national grape boycott. The Stonewall riots brought attention to discrimination over sexual orientation. The moral majority became active in the 1980s and didn't represent a discriminated-against group.

53.

Answer	Learning Objectives	Historical Thinking Skills	Key Concepts in the Curriculum Framework
B	MIG-1.0	Causation Analyzing Evidence: Content and Sourcing	2.3

Explanation: The lack of restriction on who could immigrate to the British North American colonies meant that many diverse ethnic and religious groups settled in the colonies. This religious diversity resulted in increased religious freedom as each group accepted the other religions in exchange for being able to practice its own religion freely. Massachusetts Bay did not initially welcome dissenters and in fact initially banished them. Several different churches were tax supported in the colonial era. Although the Church of England was the state church in many colonies, it was not dominant in all.

54.

Answer	Learning Objectives	Historical Thinking Skills	Key Concepts in the Curriculum Framework
B	CUL-1.0	Patterns of Continuity and Change over Time Periodization	2.2

Explanation: As new denominations arose, they found the need to establish colleges and universities to train ministers. Early on, Harvard College was formed to train Puritan ministers necessary for the expansion of Massachusetts Bay. The First Great Awakening split denominations into "new light" and "old light" factions, which advanced the proliferation of educational facilities. No major religious wars occurred in New England, nor did Parliament restrict either immigration or trade on the basis of religion.

55.

Answer	Learning Objectives	Historical Thinking Skills	Key Concepts in the Curriculum Framework
C	CUL-4.0	Analyzing Evidence: Content and Sourcing	2.2

Explanation: The middle colonies displayed the greatest ethnic and religious diversity in the colonial period. New England, despite the existence of Rhode Island, had a homogeneous population, dominantly English and Puritan. The southern colonies were dominantly Anglican, and Canada did not become a British possession until 1763.

Short-Answer Questions

1.

Learning Objectives	Historical Thinking Skills	Key Concepts in the Curriculum Framework
NAT-2.0	Patterns of Continuity and Change over Time	5.2 6.3 7.2 9.3

What a good response might include

a) A good response will note that during World War I, the United States took an active interest in suppressing dissent as exemplified in the Sedition Act of 1918. Specific examples and explanations might include one of the following:

 ✦ The Committee on Public Information, a government propaganda agency, specifically targeted German Americans and encouraged vigilante groups such as the American Protective League (APL) to spy on neighbors and coworkers. They targeted both German Americans and those who opposed the war or the draft. Members of the APL, who were issued badges by the U.S. Justice Department, led violent raids against all three of these groups.

 ✦ Targets for suppression were socialists, in particular, Socialist Party leader Eugene V. Debs, who was sentenced to a ten-year jail term for making an antiwar speech. Debs's and other socialists' convictions were upheld by the U.S. Supreme Court as constituting a "clear and present danger."

 ✦ A less obvious but nonetheless valid example of the suppression of constitutional rights during World War I involved the arrest and imprisonment of dozens of members of the National Women's Party (NWP) who picketed the White House for women's voting rights during the war. Arrested for obstructing traffic, a number of women, including party leader Alice Paul, were sentenced to long jail terms and force-fed when they went on hunger strikes. This suppression backfired as public opinion rallied around the suffragists and led President Woodrow Wilson to finally urge national support for women's suffrage as a "war measure."

b) Specific examples and explanations might include one of the following:

 ✦ The most obvious answer from 1844 to 1877 is the suspension of habeas corpus by President Abraham Lincoln during the Civil War, in violation of the Fifth Amendment to the Constitution. During the war, the Union jailed some 15,000 southern sympathizers, mostly from border states, and held them without indictment or trial (the latter a violation of Sixth Amendment rights). Lincoln justified these arrests without trial as a necessary war measure.

 ✦ A less obvious example from the period 1844 to 1877 is the U.S. violation of numerous treaties with American Indians during and immediately following the Civil War. In 1864, during the Civil War, a Colorado militia led by Colonel John Chivington slaughtered a camp of unarmed Cheyennes, most of them women and children, in the Sand Creek Massacre.

c)   The best example from the period since 1980 is only arguably a violation of constitutional rights. In the aftermath of the September 11, 2001, attacks on the World Trade Center and the Pentagon, the USA Patriot Act of 2001 granted the president sweeping power to monitor private citizens and arrest suspected terrorists.

2.

Learning Objectives	Historical Thinking Skills	Key Concepts in the Curriculum Framework
NAT-2.0	Patterns of Continuity and Change over Time Comparison Contextualization Analyzing Evidence: Content and Sourcing	7.2 8.1

What a good response might include

a)   A good response will note that the Russian Revolution of 1917 spread the fear of communism and radical political ideology. Examples of a group or individual who was a primary target of authorities during the first Red Scare include the following:

   ✦ Recent Southern and Eastern European immigrants, some of whom had radical or socialist views, were targeted in part because they were not citizens, and many were deported.

   ✦ Two individuals who were targeted were Nicola Sacco and Bartolomeo Vanzetti, two Italian immigrants who were also socialists who were charged with the murder of two men during a robbery. Although there was no evidence to link them to the robbery, they were tried, convicted, and executed.

b)   A good response will note that in the aftermath of World War II, a Cold War began between the United States and the Soviet Union that, once again, heightened the fear of communism and radical ideas. Examples of a group or individual who was a primary target of authorities during the second Red Scare include the following:

   ✦ In the late 1940s, the House Un-American Activities Committee targeted alleged Communists within the film industry. A group of writers known as the Hollywood Ten were jailed for refusing to testify about past associations with Communists.

   ✦ Senator Joseph McCarthy alleged that there was mass Communist infiltration in the U.S. State Department. McCarthy, a Republican, targeted members of Democratic President Harry Truman's administration.

   ✦ An individual who was targeted was Alger Hiss, a former official of the State Department who had advised President Franklin Roosevelt during World War II.

   ✦ Also targeted were Julius and Ethel Rosenberg, who were charged with passing atomic secrets to the Soviet Union. The husband and wife were executed in 1953.

c) A good response will take a position on which of the Red Scares posed a greater actual threat to the United States and support that position with relevant evidence. Arguments in favor of one or the other Red Scare as constituting the greater threat might include the following:

+ You could argue that the Soviet Union posed a much greater threat to the United States following World War II because of its increased power and eventual possession of the atomic bomb. You might further explain that in 1919, Communists were focused on consolidation of power within the Soviet Union.

+ On the other side, you might argue that Communists and anarchists were well established in the United States by 1919 and posed a real threat to the security of the United States. You might note that the United States was militarily and psychologically weaker following World War I with a more apathetic populace that was more naive and unsuspecting than following World War II.

+ A somewhat different approach might argue that the two Red Scares posed real threats to civil liberties and individual rights and argue that the 1920s or the 1950s posed a greater threat to American freedom because of the tactics used by officials.

3.

Learning Objectives	Historical Thinking Skills	Key Concepts in the Curriculum Framework
WXT-3.0	Causation	6.1
MIG-2.0	Patterns of Continuity and Change over Time	7.1 7.2

What a good response might include

a) A strong response will explain the development of stream-driven cable cars, electric trolleys, streetcars, and subways in the late nineteenth century. Examples of how urban transportation systems changed residents patterns include the following:

+ These transportation innovations led to residential patterns that saw the poor remain in the inner city while more affluent middle and upper classes moved outside the inner city and took advantage of the new public transportation. You might also indicate that this pattern of settlement broke down the idea of "walking cities."

b) Examples of how cities with limited geographic space continued to expand in the late nineteenth century include the following:

+ Cities built upward, developing skyscrapers that allowed cities to expand up because of steel infrastructures, elevators, and central heating.
+ Some cities expanded by reclaiming land, particularly in the Back Bay area of Boston.

c) Examples of a specific effort to accommodate the needs of poor migrants to American cities in the late nineteenth century include the following:

+ Private charities and organization such as the Salvation Army and the YMCA attempted to assist immigrants.
+ The settlement house movement emerged to ease the assimilation of immigrants into American society.
+ Patterns of settlement within cities sometimes helped poor immigrants as they settled in neighborhoods with people from their home regions or countries.

4.

Learning Objectives	Historical Thinking Skills	Key Concepts in the Curriculum Framework
POL-1.0	Causation	3.2
NAT-2.0	Contextualization	4.1

What a good response might include

a) A good response will note the many diverse opinions of representatives from the various states. Examples of a major compromise at the Constitutional Convention include the following:

+ The Great Compromise (sometimes known as the Connecticut Plan) attempted to appease those who favored the Virginia Plan, which called for a strong national government and rejected state sovereignty, and those who favored the New Jersey plan, which preserved state control over their own laws and guaranteed the equal power of states, large and small, in the national government. The Great Compromise, accepted after long and bitter debate, created a bicameral legislature. One branch, the Senate, gave states equal power by providing for two senators for each state, regardless of size; the other branch, the House of Representatives, apportioned representation by population, giving more populous states more power.

+ Another major compromise was the inclusion of the three-fifths clause in which delegates agreed that each slave would count as three-fifths of a person for purposes of representation and taxation. This compromise also included a fugitive clause and called for the abolition of the international slave trade after 1808.

b) Examples of postratification accommodations made by those supporting the Constitution to appease concerns of those who had opposed ratification include the following:

+ The promise and then passage of the Bill of Rights to accommodate those who feared the new government might pose a threat to individual liberty.

+ The postratification compromise to build a new national capital along the Potomac River, to satisfy the concerns of the southern states over the potential power of populous northern states. This new capital was Washington, D.C.

c) A good response will note that debates over interpretation of the Constitution began almost immediately after ratification and center around strict construction—the belief that only the national government had the power that was fully articulated in the Constitution—and loose construction—the belief that the Constitution carried within it an implied powers clause that gave the federal government some leeway in asserting power not enumerated in the Constitution. Specific issues that led to the First American Party system include the following:

+ Thomas Jefferson believed in a strict interpretation of the Constitution and opposed the national bank and the national debt.

+ Alexander Hamilton advocated for a loose interpretation of the Constitution and proposed a national bank and supported the Judiciary Act of 1789, which called for an extensive federal court system. Hamilton also supported the federal government's assumption of state debts accrued during the era of the American Revolution and the Articles of Confederation.

Document-Based Question

Learning Objectives	Historical Thinking Skills	Key Concepts in the Curriculum Framework
MIG-2.0 CUL-4.0	Analyzing Evidence: Content and Sourcing Contextualization Argumentation Synthesis	7.1 7.2

This question asks you to consider the cultural conflicts that defined the 1920s. You should thus craft a thesis based on the historical thinking skill of **contextualization** in which you place these conflicts into the context of emerging modernity and traditional religious, cultural, and social values. You will also need to incorporate other historical thinking skills, including **historical argumentation** and **appropriate use of relevant historical evidence**. Your thesis must do more than simply repeat the prompt. Strong essays will deal with all four parts of the question: challenges to traditional values of optimism, American identity, religious beliefs, and how religious beliefs divided society in the 1920s. You must also explicate and evaluate the documents and place them in proper historical context.

In order to earn the maximum for 3 points for documents use, you must analyze *all* or *all but one* of the documents (that is, at least six in this DBQ) and address how these documents provide evidence of division in American society in the 1920s. Do not forget the requirement to address one of these points for each document you use: audience, purpose, historical context, or point of view. If you are not certain how to do this, ask your teacher to show you some examples. You cannot merely name the intended audience or simply state the speaker's or artist's point of view. Instead, you must link this discussion to the question at hand: how and why there were cultural divisions in the 1920s. Analysis of the documents must provide evidence to support the thesis **AND** explain how and why the evidence supports the thesis.

You are also required to bring in outside information not included in the documents. The political cartoon by Billy Ireland (Document 1) laments the state of the U.S. melting pot and the cultural expectation that new immigrants would assimilate to American culture and values and give up the values and habits of their home countries. Ireland is clearly skeptical that this is possible, viewing the newest wave of immigrants as "scum." He identifies them as radical unionists, anarchists, and communists (or Bolsheviks, as they were called in the new Soviet Union). This cartoon speaks clearly to the Red Scare of the 1920s, which resulted in the Palmer Raids of 1920, the trial and subsequent executive of Sacco and Vanzetti, and the passage of strict immigration laws designed to halt the flow of immigrations from Eastern Europe.

The excerpt from acclaimed writer F. Scott Fitzgerald (Document 2) expresses a different kind of disillusionment. Fitzgerald, one of the "lost generation of writers" from the 1920s, articulates a kind of hopelessness at the shallowness and superficiality of modern society as well as the disappointment that many Americans felt after the end of World War I and the U.S. failure to join the League of Nations or ratify the Treaty of Versailles.

The excerpt from noted journalist and social critical H. L. Mencken (Document 3) expresses disillusionment with American politics, in particular, the American voting public. Predicting that the "White House will be adorned by a downright moron" on some day in the future, Mencken argues that elections are increasingly won by the men who are "the most devious and mediocre." Mencken was perhaps best known for his satirical articles on the 1925 Scopes trial, which he dubbed the "monkey trial," a nickname that stuck long after the trial ended.

President Warren G. Harding (Document 4) bemoans his position and his seeming inability to know what to do and whom to trust in his job as president. Given Harding's record as president, mired as it was in endless scandal, one might argue that Mencken was right.

The image from *The Afro-American* (Document 5), an African American newspaper, speaks to the resurgence of the Ku Klux Klan (KKK) in the 1920s. Originally founded in the late 1860s, the KKK functioned as a terror group that forced southern African Americans to fear exercising their civil and political rights during Reconstruction. The group's revival in the 1920s was in response to increased immigration, the Red Scare, and the migration from the South of large numbers of African Americans. The KKK of the 1920s spread from the South into the Midwest. The black press was among a handful of Americans who spoke out against the KKK in the 1920s.

The image "The Descent of the Modernists" (Document 6) perfectly illustrates the conflict between modernists and antimodernists in the 1920s. Many Americans at that time embraced scientific methods and the theory of evolution to explain human life. This cartoon by E. J. Pace, published in an antimodern volume by William Jennings Bryan, sees modernism on an inexorable path to atheism.

William Jennings Bryan was the special prosecutor in the Scopes trial of 1925, in which a Tennessee science teacher was arrested and charged with teaching evolution in his classroom, a violation of Tennessee state law. Bryan had prepared the closing argument excerpted in document 7, but he never had a chance to deliver it, as the defense asked the jury to find the defendant guilty so that they could test the constitutionality of the Tennessee law.

Good responses will incorporate an in-depth analysis of a majority of the documents that examines point of view, intended audience, purpose, or other features specified in the directions. For example, a strong essay might note the cynicism and disillusionment that resulted from the failure of World War I to realize its idealistic goals and divided society into optimistic and pessimistic camps. A strong essay might also note that the Red Scare increased nativism and called into question what it meant to be an American.

Strong essays must link similar documents together to make a convincing argument. For example, the essay might link together documents that illustrate a decline of optimism. Other documents illustrate changing or contested ideas about American identity and/or the use of disadvantages groups as scapegoats.

A strong essay also will demonstrate awareness of the broader historical processes and issues. In your discussion of the cultural divisions of the 1920s, for example, you might refer to the "culture wars" of the 1980s or to earlier antinative activity in the 1850s.

Do not refer to the documents as "Document 1" or "Document 6." Instead, refer to the type of document (painting, address to Congress . . .) and its context, and reference the author, the title of the work, and his purpose audience, or point of view. Be certain to link the document to your thesis. One of the worst errors you can make is to do what is called "laundry listing" the documents.

When you finish writing, look over your essay. Be certain that you have included all of the required elements. If you do not already have a generic rubric, ask your teacher to give you a copy of one so you will be absolutely certain that you understand what the person who scores your essay is looking for. The rubric is a sort of map for your essay. Remember that if you go on a journey without a map, you might never know when you arrive at your destination. So commit that rubric to memory and pay attention to your destination and what it takes to get there.

Long Essay Questions

1.

Learning Objectives	Historical Thinking Skills	Key Concepts in the Curriculum Framework
WXT-3.0 POL-2.0 CUL-2.0 WXT-2.0	Patterns of Continuity and Change over Time Contextualization Argumentation	6.1 6.2 6.3

A solid essay demonstrates mastery of several historical thinking skills. Most important for this essay is **historical argumentation, contextualization,** and **continuity and change over time**. In this essay, you must analyze why a historian would choose the year 1890 as an important turning point (or watershed) in U.S. history. You must develop a thoughtful thesis that clearly states the argument you will craft. Your essay must synthesize a significant body of evidence and must support your thesis. Remember not to rush through your essays; rather, take the time to make sure that you are answering the question and not merely summarizing events and ideas but rather analyzing them. After you write your introductory paragraph, put down your pen and carefully read what you have just written. It is far easier to make changes in your essay at the beginning rather than trying to correct your mistakes as time expires. Also, occasionally stop writing as you work on the rest of your essay and examine your work to ensure that you are saying just what you want to say.

Look at the prompt carefully and make sure you understand the meaning of every word in it. Take this opportunity to craft a more sophisticated analysis. A good response might see 1890 as a watershed year by explaining factors that set up a before-and-after picture.

Here are some examples to consider in crafting your essay:

Social/Cultural

+ The year 1890 marked a turning point in immigration. The 1890s was the first decade in which new immigration (Southern and Eastern European immigration) surpassed old immigration (Northern and Western European immigration). These new immigrants had more difficulty assimilating into American society, causing a rise in anti-immigrant sentiment (nativism) to increase substantially, as it had in the 1840s and 1850s.
+ With this new immigration and the culmination of changes in business practices as a result of corporate mergers and trusts, the United States witnessed an explosive growth in its cities and a shift from a largely rural society to a more urban one.
+ The technological innovations that emerged after 1890 helped facilitate urban growth and expansion. These innovations included transmission of electricity, the development of skyscrapers, and the advent of mass transit.
+ The Progressive movement got its start around 1890 with the advent of settlement houses and calls from middle-class Americans for reforms in the working and living conditions of America's poor. Settlement houses in particular gave educated women a chance to use their skills to pioneer the field of social work.
+ The 1890s also saw a breaking down of the rigid confines of separate spheres for men (public) and women (private). Society now heralded a "new woman" who was athletic, educated, and, to some extent, independent—a significant departure from cultural norms prior to 1890.

Political

+ The Populist movement, a forerunner of the Progressive Era, had its greatest success after 1890. Throughout the 1890s, particularly during the economic crisis of 1893–1894, there were calls for the federal government to take a more active role in reform.

+ After languishing for several decades after the Civil War and the heated debates over women's suffrage when Congress considered the Fifteenth Amendment to the Constitution, the women's rights moved reemerged with the formation of the National American Woman's Suffrage Association in 1890. That year, the women's rights movement began its long, final push toward full enfranchisement for women.

+ The years after 1890 saw a rapid erosion of African American rights as Jim Crow laws became commonplace throughout the South and in many other parts of the country as well. During the 1890s, the U.S. Supreme Court consistently upheld both Jim Crow laws (for example, in its ruling in *Plessy v. Ferguson* in 1896) and state laws that required citizens to take literacy tests and pay poll taxes, designed to further disenfranchise African Americans.

America in the World

+ In 1890 the historian Frederick Jackson Turner, speaking at a meeting in Chicago, declared the American frontier "closed." As a result of this perception—that after 1890, all the habitable land within the continental United States had been settled—the United States became more involved in overseas imperialism, for both economic and political reasons.

+ For example, in 1892, the United States overthrew the queen of Hawaii and a few years later, annexed Hawaii.

+ In the 1890s, the United States also became involved in the War of 1898 in which the Spanish were ousted from Cuba, Puerto Rico, and the Philippines. In the aftermath, the United States gained possession of Puerto Rico and the Philippines.

+ The closing of the frontier came at a great cost to American Indians, who were forcibly removed to reservations throughout the West.

Environment

+ The so-called closing of the frontier also led to more conversations and concern that America's resources were not inexhaustible, ushering in an era of environment awareness not previously seen in U.S. history.

2.

Learning Objectives	Historical Thinking Skills	Key Concepts in the Curriculum Framework
WOR-2.0 POL-2.0 CUL-2.0	Patterns of Continuity and Change over Time Contextualization Argumentation	8.1 8.2 8.3

A solid essay demonstrates mastery of several historical thinking skills. Most important for this essay is **historical argumentation, contextualization,** and **continuity and change over time.** In this essay, you must analyze why a historian would choose the year 1968 as an important turning point (or watershed) in U.S. history. You must develop a thoughtful thesis that clearly states the argument you will craft. Your essay must synthesize a significant body of evidence and must support your thesis. Remember not to rush through your essays; rather, take the time to make sure that you are answering the question and that you are not merely summarizing events and ideas but rather analyzing them. After you write your introductory paragraph, put down your pen and carefully read what you have just written. It is far easier to make changes in your essay at the beginning rather than trying to correct your mistakes as time expires. Also, occasionally stop writing as you work on the rest of your essay and examine your work to ensure that you are saying just what you want to say.

Look at the prompt carefully, and make sure you understand the meaning of every word in it. Take this opportunity to craft a more sophisticated analysis. A good response might see 1968 as a watershed year by explaining factors that set up a before and after picture.

Here are some examples to consider in crafting your essay:

Social/Cultural

- In many ways, the year 1968 marks the culmination of the "rights" movements that gained strength in the aftermath of World War II. The struggle for black civil rights, which had been ongoing since the Civil War, gained considerable momentum in the 1950s and saw a number of significant gains in the early 1960s, including the Civil Rights Act of 1964 and the Voting Rights Act of 1965. By 1968, however, the civil rights movement had begun to splinter. In addition, in 1968, its leader, Martin Luther King Jr., was assassinated.
- Other rights movements gained considerable momentum in the early 1960s. Notable among them was the movement for women's liberation.
- An emerging student movement had emerged to protest U.S. involvement in the war in Vietnam beginning about 1965; by 1968, public sentiment increasingly had come to oppose the war.
- Growing numbers of Americans, however, were disaffected with the protest movements and began to make their views known both through the ballot box and by counter-demonstrations.

Political

- The election of 1968 was a watershed in that it marked a departure from the liberalism of the early 1960s growing conservative sentiment of the late 1960s and 1970s. Richard Nixon, the successful Republican candidate, had run on a platform promising a return to "law and order," claiming that he spoke for the "silent majority" who did not protest.
- In 1968, the Democratic Party imploded, torn by the war in Vietnam and the civil rights movement.
- In April 1968, the incumbent Democratic president, Lyndon Johnson, announced that he would not seek reelection, changing the race dramatically. In the aftermath of Johnson's announcement, New York senator Robert Kennedy became the frontrunner for the Democratic nomination.
- In June 1968, Robert Kennedy was assassinated, which dealt a blow to the party and the antiwar movement.
- The South, a stronghold of the Democratic Party since the end of Reconstruction, moved toward the Republican Party. In 1968, a number of southern Democrats voted for former Democrat George Wallace of Alabama, who ran as an independent candidate.
- The Democratic leadership endorsed Vice President Hubert Humphrey for the nomination, a move that led antiwar protesters to come to the Democratic National Convention in Chicago to protest. In response, Chicago police, on orders from the city's mayor, unleashed a barrage of violence against the protesters on the night of the nomination, tainting Humphrey's reputation.

America in the World

- ✦ The year was a turning point in support for the war in Vietnam. After the Tet Offensive in early 1968, international support for the United States declined. The disastrous effects of U.S. defeats in Vietnam set the stage for the election of Republican Richard Nixon.
- ✦ With Nixon's election, U.S. foreign policy began to shift in significant ways. Nixon's efforts to open diplomatic relations with China and ease tensions with the Soviet Union marked a turning point for the United States.

PRACTICE TEST 2

SECTION I

Part A: Multiple-Choice Questions

Questions 1–3 refer to the excerpt below.

"Each public officer who takes an oath to support the Constitution swears that he will support it as he understands it, and not as it is understood by others. It is as much the duty of the House of Representatives, of the Senate, and of the President, to decide upon the constitutionality of any bill or resolution which may be presented to them for passage or approval, as it is of the Supreme Judges when it may be brought before them for judicial decision. The opinion of the Judges has no more authority over Congress than the opinion of Congress has over the Judges; and, on that point, the President is independent of both. The authority of the Supreme Court must not, therefore, be permitted to control the Congress or the Executive when acting in their legislative capacities, but to have only such influence as the force of their reasoning may deserve."

Andrew Jackson, veto message, July 10, 1832

1. Jackson's message seems to be challenging which of the following constitutional principles?
   - (A) Division of powers between the states and the federal government
   - (B) The principle of judicial review established in Article I of the Constitution
   - (C) Separation of powers among the three branches of government
   - (D) Congressional authority to legislate

2. The Jackson presidency is most noted for which of the following?
   - (A) The creation of a civil service system based on merit
   - (B) Increasing the power of the presidency
   - (C) Its firm stance against the extension of slavery into the territories
   - (D) Staunch opposition to the expansion of voting rights for unpropertied classes

3. During the era of Jacksonian Democracy, the United States saw
   - (A) an accelerated movement toward universal white male suffrage.
   - (B) the direct election of senators become a reality with the ratification of the Seventeenth Amendment.
   - (C) Andrew Jackson strongly support federally funded internal improvements.
   - (D) the elimination of the Second American Party System.

GO ON TO THE NEXT PAGE.

Questions 4–6 refer to the political cartoon below.

Conrad Collection, The Huntington Library, Art Collections, and Botanical Gardens, January–June 1972.

"I'm Hijacking This Bus! . . . Take us Back to 1954!"

4. The political cartoon pictured above is most reflective of which of the following changes occurring in the late 1960s?

   (A)   Blue-collar reaction against antiwar protests at colleges and universities
   (B)   Silent majority opposition to federal funding for public education
   (C)   Republican movement toward a southern strategy
   (D)   The failure of the Great Society Head Start program

5. In the election of 1968, Republicans attempted to increase their appeal to

   (A)   southern African American voters by sponsoring Freedom Summer.
   (B)   northern liberals by endorsing a dramatic expansion of the Great Society.
   (C)   cold war conservatives by direct challenges to the Soviet Union and China.
   (D)   conservative southern Democrats.

6. Which of the following happened in the 1960s?

   (A)   The Supreme Court ruled in *Brown v. Board of Education* that schools must be desegregated.
   (B)   Cold War tension increased when the Soviet Union launched *Sputnik*.
   (C)   African Americans gained greater access to public accommodations.
   (D)   Gas prices spiraled upward as a result of the Arab oil embargo.

GO ON TO THE NEXT PAGE.

Questions 7–10 refer to the excerpt below.

"For the encouraging and increasing of shipping and navigation . . . no goods or commodities whatsoever shall be imported into, or exported out of, any lands, islands, plantations or territories to his Majesty belonging, or in his possession . . . in any other ship or ships, vessel or vessels whatsoever, but such ships and vessels as did truly and without fraud belong only to the people of England."

British Parliament, Navigation Act of 1660

7. What was a major goal of the legislation cited above?
    (A) To subdue increasing unrest in the British North American colonies
    (B) To undermine the increasing power of the Spanish monarchy
    (C) To more tightly control the British textile industry
    (D) To combat international economic competition

8. Which best describes the policy behind the Navigation Act of 1660?
    (A) Mercantilism
    (B) Capitalism
    (C) Imperialism
    (D) Market revolution

9. What happened following this action by the British government?
    (A) The American colonists agreed that this was a reasonable assertion of imperial power.
    (B) For several decades, the British government largely allowed the colonists to govern their own affairs.
    (C) France declared war on England.
    (D) Britain's alliances with North American Indian tribes forced the American colonists to call for closer ties with Britain.

10. What event in the eighteenth century was most responsible for forcing the British to consolidate further control over its American colonies?
    (A) The spread of Enlightenment ideas
    (B) The invention of new navigational technologies
    (C) Increasing conflicts between the New England and Chesapeake colonies
    (D) The Seven Years' War

Questions 11–13 refer to the excerpts below.

"Here individuals of all nations are melted into a new race of men, whose labors and posterity will one day cause great changes in the world. Americans are the western pilgrims, who are carrying along with them that great mass of arts, sciences, vigour, and industry which began long since in the east; they will finish the great circle."

J. Hector St. John de Crèvecoeur "What Is an American?"
in *Letters from an American Farmer*, 1782

"The notorious ignorance in which the great mass of these emigrants have been all their lives sunk, until their minds are dead, makes them but senseless machines; they obey orders mechanically, for it is the habit of their education, in the despotic countries of their birth. And can it be for a moment supposed by any one that by the act of coming to this country, and being natural-

GO ON TO THE NEXT PAGE.

ized, their darkened intellects can suddenly be illuminated to discern the nice boundary where their ecclesiastical obedience. . . . ends, and their civil independence . . . begins?"

Samuel F. B. Morse, *Imminent Dangers to the United States through Foreign Immigration*, 1835

11. What did de Crèvecoeur mean when he referred to Americans as "western pilgrims"?
     (A) Americans came to the New World in search of religious freedom.
     (B) Immigrants arrived on the East Coast of the United States but soon moved across the Mississippi River, carrying American ideals with them.
     (C) Most early immigrants came to the shores of Massachusetts.
     (D) Europeans came across the Atlantic in search of a new life.

12. What do these two passages have in common?
     (A) The immigrants described in both passages came primarily from Western and Central Europe.
     (B) Both authors voiced concerns that too many immigrants were maintaining their old traditions.
     (C) Crèvecoeur and Morse agreed that immigrants were able to successfully overcome obstacles and would eventually improve American society.
     (D) Both authors urged the U.S. government to adopt policies regulating immigration.

13. What best accounts for increased opposition to immigration in the first half of the nineteenth century?
     (A) Thousands of Chinese arrived in the United States as the railroad industry expanded.
     (B) Immigrants from Southern and Eastern Europe arrived in huge numbers.
     (C) Union members and their leadership feared that immigrants would take jobs from American workers.
     (D) Protestants opposed the influx of large numbers of Roman Catholics into urban areas in the eastern United States.

Questions 14–15 refer to the excerpt below.

"The primary cause of the buffalo's extermination, and the one which embraced all others, was the descent of civilization, with all its elements of destructiveness, upon the whole of the country inhabited by that animal.

"The secondary causes of the extermination of the buffalo may be catalogued as follows: (1) Man's reckless greed, his wanton destructiveness, and improvidence in not husbanding such resources as come to him from the hand of nature ready made. (2) The total and utterly inexcusable absence of protective measures and agencies on the part of the National Government and of the Western States and Territories. (3) The fatal preference on the part of hunters generally, both white and red, for the robe and flesh of the cow over that furnished by the bull, (4) The phenomenal stupidity of the animals themselves, and their indifference to man. (5) The perfection of modern breech-loading rifles and other sporting fire-arms in general. "

William T. Hornaday, The Extermination of the American Bison, 1889

14. The above account reflects a growing sentiment in the late nineteenth century that
     (A) natural resources were not inexhaustible.
     (B) the surest way to end Indian resistance was by government-sponsored decimation of the buffalo herds.
     (C) Indians must be confined to small, scattered reservations.
     (D) the advancement of civilization took precedence over the preservation of the environment.

GO ON TO THE NEXT PAGE.

15. In the late nineteenth century, efforts to assimilate Indian populations into white culture

  (A) largely destroyed Indian culture.
  (B) were strongly opposed by Indian advocates.
  (C) Indian suffrage becoming a reality by 1900.
  (D) were largely unsuccessful.

Questions 16–18 refer to the image below.

Broadside of Baptist Minister William Miller, 1843

16. The event above reflected the enthusiasm that was an essential part of

  (A) Protestant evangelism in colonial America.
  (B) Enlightenment belief in progress.
  (C) the Second Great Awakening.
  (D) Romanticism.

GO ON TO THE NEXT PAGE.

17. Utopian reformers in America at the time portrayed in the broadsheet believed most fervently in
    (A) progressivism.
    (B) romanticism.
    (C) perfectionism.
    (D) rationalism.

18. The beliefs of the Millerites would best be reflected later in American history by which of these groups?
    (A) Populists
    (B) Progressives
    (C) Charles Darwin
    (D) Twentieth-century evangelists

Questions 19–21 refer to the excerpt below.

"America is the one country in the world that has taken most care over time to lay out clearly separate paths for the two sexes and also to ensure that the two walk as equals but always on separate paths."

Alexis de Tocqueville, *Democracy in America,* 1848

19. Which of these best accounts for the phenomenon that Tocqueville described in the 1830s?
    (A) The market revolution was changing the nature of work and the relationship between home and the workplace.
    (B) Women, both rich and poor, decided that it was better for them to stay home and care for their families.
    (C) Slavery in the South and the influx of European immigrants into the North made it possible for women to focus their attention on the home.
    (D) In an effort to protect women as the nation became more industrialized, state legislatures began to regulate women's work.

20. Which of these was most responsible for bringing women more fully into the public sphere in the mid-nineteenth century?
    (A) As the nation became more divided and the Civil War approached, factories in the North needed more workers.
    (B) As a result of the Second Great Awakening, women increasingly were involved in antebellum reform movements.
    (C) The expansion of suffrage and the democratization of American society brought women further into the mainstream of American economic life.
    (D) As education for women became more accessible, women gained the knowledge and skills that enabled them to enter the workplace.

21. What impact did Manifest Destiny have on women's roles?
    (A) The expansion of slavery into western territories reinforced the "clearly separate paths" for men and women.
    (B) Rapid industrialization and the growth of cities like Chicago and St. Louis reinforced the view that women belonged in the home.
    (C) The gap between middle- and working-class women increased.
    (D) Women in the West were more likely to participate as equal partners in the economic life of their family.

GO ON TO THE NEXT PAGE.

Questions 22–24 refer to the excerpt below.

"If we call one the natural method, we must call the other the artificial method. If nature's process is rightly named natural selection, man's process is artificial selection. The survival of the fittest is simply the survival of the strong, which implies, and might as well be called, the destruction of the weak. And if nature progresses through the destruction of the weak, man progresses through the *protection* of the weak."

Lester Frank Ward, *Glimpses of the Cosmos*, 1913–1918

22. Based on his views expressed in the passage above, which of these would Ward have been most likely to support?

    (A) Legislation limiting the number of Eastern Europeans who could immigrate to the United States
    (B) The application of Social Darwinism to public policy
    (C) Progressives' efforts to relieve poverty in American cities
    (D) The Chinese Exclusion Act

23. Who would have been most likely to oppose Ward's position?

    (A) Nativists
    (B) Leaders of the Roman Catholic Church
    (C) Settlement house workers
    (D) Political machine bosses

24. In the decades leading to World War I, which of these did NOT fuel the debate between the "natural" and the "artificial" processes that Ward addressed in this passage?

    (A) Conflicts between Native Americans and the U.S. government
    (B) Increased migration of Asians into the United States
    (C) The activism of religious reformers who espoused the Social Gospel
    (D) Passage of legislation that established a quota system to regulate immigration

Questions 25–27 refer to the excerpt below.

"Neither slavery nor involuntary servitude, except as a punishment for a crime whereof the party shall have been duly convicted, shall exist within the United States, or any place subject to their jurisdiction."

Thirteenth Amendment to the U.S. Constitution, 1865

25. This amendment to the Constitution was passed by Congress and ratified in 1865 for which of the following reasons?

    (A) The states of the defeated Confederacy were determined to keep the institution of slavery even after the war ended.
    (B) This addition to the Constitution was necessary to banish slavery from states not covered by the Emancipation Proclamation.
    (C) Slavery was a common and widespread practice in most of the overseas territories controlled by the United States at this time.
    (D) Republicans in Congress were still reluctant to ban slavery in places where it had traditionally existed.

GO ON TO THE NEXT PAGE.

26. Southern states attempted to restore some of the restrictions on newly freed African Americans by which of the following tactics?

    (A) Some states were able to reestablish slavery through elaborate contracts that the federal Justice Department was unable to have declared illegal.

    (B) Former slaves were prevented by law from working on any property that was owned by their former masters.

    (C) Southern states devised systems of local laws that restricted social, political, and economic freedoms for African Americans for the next century.

    (D) Southern legislatures tried to restrict the rights of African Americans, but their efforts were overturned by the Supreme Court in the 1890s.

27. Which of the following represents the first real success in overturning laws and customs mandating second-class citizenship for American Americans?

    (A) The Civil Rights Act of 1964

    (B) *Brown v. Board of Education of Topeka, Kansas*

    (C) *Plessy v. Ferguson*

    (D) The economic programs of Johnson's Great Society

Questions 28–30 refer to the excerpt below.

"GROCERY cart and harness for sale—In good order, and one chestnut horse, 8 years old, an excellent saddle horse; can be ridden by a lady. Also, one young man wanted, from 16–18 years of age, able to write. No Irish need apply. Cluff & Tunis, No. 270 Washington-st., corner of Myrtle-av., Brooklyn."

New York Daily Times, March 25, 1854

28. The advertisement above appeared in a New York City newspaper in 1854. What do these employment notices indicate about American society in the middle of the nineteenth century?

    (A) Nativist sentiment continued to be a problem for immigrants coming to the United States.

    (B) Equal employment opportunities were available for both men and women during this era.

    (C) A strong economy meant employment was available for anyone who was looking for a job.

    (D) Few immigrants who arrived in the United States in the first half of the nineteenth century were literate.

29. What might explain the attitudes represented by the advertisement above?

    (A) Many immigrants arriving in the United States in the early nineteenth century were discriminated against because they were Catholic and might take jobs from those already here.

    (B) There was little land available on the frontier for the huge numbers of immigrants who were coming at this time, so they were flooding urban job markets.

    (C) Federal regulations limited immigration, and those who came anyway were in the country illegally.

    (D) Most new immigrants refused to live in ethnic communities once they came to the United States, and they threatened the property values of established urban neighborhoods.

GO ON TO THE NEXT PAGE.

30. How is the sentiment in this advertisement illustrated by decisions made by Congress in the early twentieth century?

(A) Attempts were made to reverse what was known as the Great Migration, a movement of southern African Americans from the Deep South to other parts of the country in search of better jobs.

(B) The government passed a series of laws establishing highly restrictive immigration quotas to reduce the numbers of people moving to this country.

(C) Overseas expansion was discouraged by Congress out of fear that it would create new waves of immigrants, particularly to the West Coast.

(D) Congress refused to sign the Treaty of Versailles or participate in the League of Nations primarily out of fear of encouraging new waves of immigration to this country.

Questions 31–33 refer to the map below.

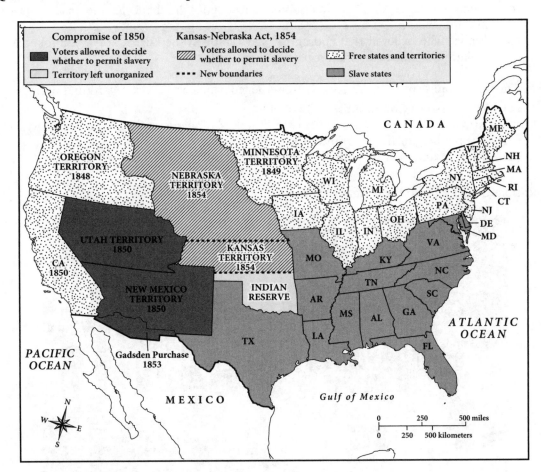

The Compromise of 1850

31. Which of the following provisions of the Compromise of 1850 caused the most negative reaction among citizens of the northern states?

   (A) The use of popular sovereignty to determine the status of slave and free states in the unorganized territory

   (B) The end of the slave trade in Washington, D.C.

   (C) The new Fugitive Slave Law

   (D) A reduction in the size of Texas in exchange for a payment to the state of $10 million

32. Northern objections to the Compromise of 1850 came from

   (A) free-soilers, who were opposed to the extension of slavery into any new states or territories.

   (B) Republicans, who insisted that the Compromise of 1850 include the immediate abolition of slavery.

   (C) Know-Nothings, who believed popular sovereignty should decide the issue of slavery in California.

   (D) Whigs, who believed that ending the slave trade in the District of Columbia was a violation of constitutional property guarantees.

33. The Compromise of 1850 effectively strengthened which earlier act regarding slavery?

   (A) The Missouri Compromise of 1820

   (B) Article IV, Section II, of the Constitution regarding the return of runaway slaves

   (C) The banning of the slave trade after 1808

   (D) The guarantees of individual freedoms in the Bill of Rights

Questions 34–35 refer to the images below.

Cliff Palace at Mesa Verde

GO ON TO THE NEXT PAGE.

Cahokia Mounds Reconstruction

34. The two civilizations above, which existed in the Southwest and the Mississippi Valley, respectively, before the arrival of Europeans to North America, indicate which of the following about native populations?

(A) These societies were complex and exhibited diverse economic development and social diversification.

(B) Like most other native societies, these two groups depended on hunting and gathering for subsistence.

(C) These societies were largely mobile due to a scarcity of natural resources.

(D) Large-scale agriculture was favored instead of trade with other villages to support these communities.

35. These two civilizations, along with many others of native populations, began to disintegrate after the arrival of Europeans in part because of which of the following conditions?

(A) Native populations chose to move to areas dominated by Europeans because there were more jobs available in those places.

(B) Europeans brought epidemic diseases that took a heavy toll on native populations and weakened social and political structures in their communities.

(C) Rapid climate change made most of the areas previously settled by native populations unsuitable for traditional agriculture.

(D) The decline of the great buffalo herds made traditional ways of life impossible in the Southwest and the Mississippi Valley.

GO ON TO THE NEXT PAGE.

Questions 36–37 refer to the map below.

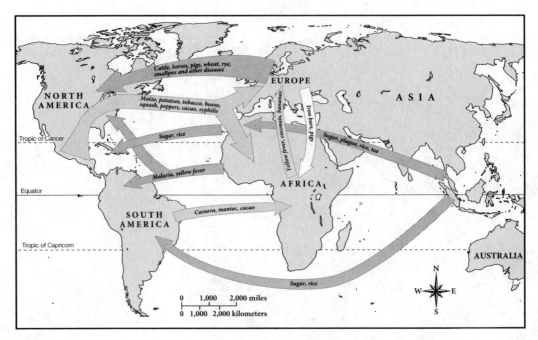

The Columbian Exchange

36. The exchange of goods and the interactions of societies across the Atlantic known as the Columbian Exchange resulted in which of the following?

   (A) Changes occurred on both sides of the Atlantic as the introduction of new agricultural products and animals created new markets and altered lifestyles.

   (B) Changes occurred in diets and agriculture, but little in other areas of life for the two regions.

   (C) Changes occurred that could ultimately be regarded only as positive, in that both areas benefitted from the introduction of new foods.

   (D) There was tremendous population growth on both sides of the Atlantic due to improvements in nutrition.

37. What else was an important part of the Columbian Exchange going from Africa to the Western Hemisphere that is not represented on this chart?

   (A) Silver
   (B) Slaves
   (C) Iron weapons
   (D) Maize

Questions 38–39 refer to the quotation below.

"This political year features the 'compassionate conservatism' espoused by presidential candidate George W. Bush. Some question whether it is a political slogan or a philosophy. I would submit that it is a coherent principled philosophy that organizes and explains a superior approach to domestic policy. . . . Compassionate conservatives believe that government should have a limited role in people's lives and that competition in the marketplace is the most effective

GO ON TO THE NEXT PAGE.

means of producing social and economic progress. Consequently compassionate conservatives believe in low taxes, limited government regulation, and the vast power of the free enterprise system. . . . Government has a responsibility not to redistribute the wealth of citizens but to provide the underprivileged with skills and opportunities to create their own wealth."

Stephen Goldsmith, "What Compassionate Conservatism Is—and Is Not,"

Hoover Digest, 2000

38. The source above was an attempt to explain which of the following trends in American politics in the last decades of the twentieth century?

   (A) A general movement away from the principles and policies of Lyndon Johnson's Great Society
   (B) The shift in political power from major urban centers to more rural voters
   (C) The elimination of all trade barriers with foreign nations
   (D) A shift from concentrating on U.S. power abroad to a more limited role for the military in general

39. Which of the following examples from earlier U.S. history represents a similar call for individuals to handle their own problems rather than look to the government or the charity of individuals for relief and support?

   (A) Late nineteenth-century support for the principles of Social Darwinism
   (B) Southern leaders who called for a "New South" in the years following Reconstruction
   (C) Reformers who supported such efforts as the settlement house movement
   (D) Labor leaders who lobbied for better pay and safer working conditions for factory workers

Questions 40–41 refer to the excerpt below.

"Our nation has been put on notice: We are not immune from attack. We will take defensive measures against terrorism to protect Americans. . . .

   "These measures are essential. But the only way to defeat terrorism as a threat to our way of life is to stop it, eliminate it, and destroy it where it grows."

President George W. Bush, September 20, 2011

40. The aftermath of the attack on the World Trade Center and the Pentagon in September 2001 led the U.S. government to do which of the following?

   (A) Concentrate on security at home rather than taking on challenges to U.S. power abroad
   (B) Pass a series of laws aimed at increasing domestic security, which have subsequently come under criticism for threatening individual rights
   (C) Reduce the numbers of women and minorities allowed to serve in the military
   (D) Renew national efforts at finally winning the Cold War with the former Soviet Union

41. What missions undertaken by the United States grew directly out of the World Trade Center and Pentagon attacks in the name of increasing homeland security?

   (A) Attacks on Afghanistan and Iraq
   (B) Efforts to shut down Central American drug cartels
   (C) Tighter immigration controls along the borders of Texas and Mexico
   (D) Tighter quality controls over goods coming in from China and East Asia

GO ON TO THE NEXT PAGE.

Questions 42-43 refer to the photograph below.

The My Lai Massacre, 1970

42. The above photograph led to which of the following in the 1970s?
    (A) Increased calls for gun control in the United States
    (B) Dramatically increased support for immigration restriction
    (C) Eroding support for the war in Vietnam
    (D) Increasing support for Supreme Court rulings protecting the rights of the accused

43. In 1968, support for the U.S. war effort in Vietnam
    (A) increased dramatically as the United States launched major offensives.
    (B) decreased as a result of increased support for the Great Society.
    (C) decreased significantly because of a perceived lack of progress against the Vietcong.
    (D) decreased because of the energy crisis brought on by the Arab oil embargo.

Questions 44–46 refer to the following quotation.

"But the motor age changed advertising to a series of prestigious urges to spend and buy; a bigger car than your neighbor's; a luxury cruise, an all-electric kitchen, a mink coat and diamonds for Mother. . . .

"Advertising also promoted the revolution of rising expectations . . . . Advertisers had taught them it was 'un-American' to be without."

Samuel Eliot Morison, *The Oxford History of the American People,* 1965

GO ON TO THE NEXT PAGE.

44. The growth of consumerism in the 1920s was most fueled by which of the following?

   (A) The widespread introduction of credit cards

   (B) An unparalleled rise in the prices of agricultural commodities

   (C) The introduction of television advertising

   (D) Installment buying

45. The rising expectations that Morison alludes to were most characterized by which of the following in the 1920s?

   (A) The belief that nuclear power would provide cheap energy and make America energy independent

   (B) Rising stock prices

   (C) The optimism brought on by the success of making the world "safe for democracy"

   (D) Immigration restriction

46. Politically the 1920s saw the United States

   (A) return to the progressivism of the prewar era.

   (B) assume leadership of newly created international organizations.

   (C) dominated by conservative leadership.

   (D) play a major role as an international peacekeeper in the Middle East.

Questions 47–49 refer to the following quotation.

"I am convinced that the fifth-column activities of our enemy call for the participation of people who are in fact American citizens.

"... We believe that any delay in the adoption of necessary protective measures is to invite... a Pearl Harbor incident.

"... We have had no sabotage and no fifth column activities in this state.... But I take the view that we are just being lulled into a false sense of security and that the only reason we haven't had a disaster in California is because it has been timed for a different date.

"... I want to say that the consensus among the law enforcement officers of this State is that there is more potential danger among the group of Japanese who are born in this country than from the alien Japanese."

California Attorney General Earl Warren testifying before a U.S. Congressional Committee on Japanese Internment, 1942

47. Ultimately fear of Japanese citizens during World War II led to

   (A) the execution of forty-three Japanese American citizens for sabotage and espionage.

   (B) the deportation of Japanese American citizens from the United States.

   (C) internment of Japanese American citizens in closely guarded camps.

   (D) Japanese American citizens being forced to labor on white-owned farms due to the shortage of agricultural labor.

48. African Americans also suffered discrimination during World War II. Which of the following represents progress made by African Americans prior to the end of the war?

   (A) Racial segregation in the armed forces was ended.

   (B) A federal agency was formed to prevent racial discrimination in hiring for defense plants.

   (C) Schools were integrated.

   (D) African American troops were no longer assigned to the Pacific theater of the war.

GO ON TO THE NEXT PAGE.

49. During World War II, American women
   (A) found new employment opportunities in traditionally male industrial jobs.
   (B) served in front-line combat roles with men.
   (C) achieved equal pay for equal work in defense industries.
   (D) were given the right to vote in return for their support of the war effort.

Questions 50–52 refer to the image and excerpt below.

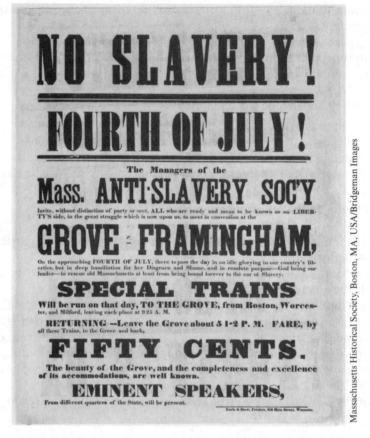

Anti-Slavery Rally in Framingham, Massachusetts, July 4, 1854

"Our slaves are black, of another and inferior race. The *status* in which we have placed them is an elevation. They are elevated from the condition in which God first created them, by being made our slaves."

James Henry Hammond, speech before the U.S. Senate, March 4, 1858

50. What do these two sources tell you about the debate over slavery in the 1850s?
   (A) The issue of slavery played little role in sectional tensions after the passage of the Compromise of 1850.
   (B) Attitudes toward slavery became more hardened and less open to any compromise during the 1850s.
   (C) Southerners were generally able to stop the spread of abolitionist literature by controlling the activities of the antislavery press.
   (D) People on both sides of the abolitionist arguments felt the government was working in support on their side.

GO ON TO THE NEXT PAGE.

51. Among the arguments used by those opposing the activities of abolitionists was which of the following?

    (A) Slaves were generally better farmworkers than white laborers.
    (B) Slaves were considered to have benefitted from conversion to Christianity, something they would not have known in Africa.
    (C) The northern economy would not be able to survive without the work of slaves in southern cotton and tobacco fields.
    (D) Slaves were critical labor to southern manufacturing and ironworks.

52. Which of the following proved to be a major source of disagreement among northern abolitionists in the decade leading up to the Civil War?

    (A) Some abolitionist groups were determined to use nonviolent means to achieve their goal, while others felt slaves should use whatever means necessary to gain freedom.
    (B) The groups argued over whether Congress had the power to issue the Fugitive Slave Law that was part of the Compromise of 1850.
    (C) Some wanted to shut down efforts to help slaves escape, as they felt it was too dangerous.
    (D) They disagreed over whether former slaves would be able to obtain employment in northern manufacturing once they made an escape to freedom.

Questions 53–55 refer to the image below.

David G. Houser/Corbis

Marble House, The Vanderbilt Mansion in Newport, Rhode Island, Built 1892

53. The Marble House mansion represents the tremendous wealth accumulated by robber barons, or captains of industry, during the Gilded Age. Thorstein Veblen criticized such displays of wealth in *The Theory of the Leisure Class* as

    (A) ostentatious opulence.
    (B) conspicuous consumption.
    (C) scientific management
    (D) utilitarianism.

GO ON TO THE NEXT PAGE.

54. By the late 1800s, the increasing disparity of wealth between the rich and poor led for successful calls to

   (A) place a cap on the maximum income one could attain in a single year.
   (B) nationalize major industries such as steel, oil, and banking.
   (C) impose government regulations on private industry.
   (D) redistribute income by lowering tariffs.

55. In the late nineteenth century, efforts to help the poor came primarily from

   (A) private organizations designed to meet their basic needs.
   (B) the federal government in the form of welfare payments.
   (C) railroad companies who offered free transportation to the west.
   (D) state welfare agencies that provided free housing and food for the needy.

Part B: Short-Answer Questions

"Apprehension seems to exist among the people of the Southern States that by the accession of a Republican Administration their property and their peace and personal security are to be endangered. There has never been any reasonable cause for such apprehension. . . .

"I have no purpose directly or indirectly, to interfere with the institution of slavery in the States where it exists. I believe I have no lawful right to do so, and I have no inclination to do so."
                                  Abraham Lincoln, First Inaugural Address, March 1861

"On the occasion corresponding to this four years ago . . . One eighth of the whole population were colored slaves, not distributed generally over the Union, but localized in the Southern part of it. These slaves constituted a peculiar and powerful interest. . . . To strengthen, perpetuate, and extend this interest was the object for which the insurgents would rend the Union, even by war; while the government claimed no right to do more than to restrict the territorial enlargement of it. . . . The prayers of both could not be answered."
                                  Abraham Lincoln, Second Inaugural Address, March 1865

1. Using the excerpts above, answer a, b, and c.

   a) Briefly explain Lincoln's main point in the passage from his First Inaugural Address.

   b) Briefly explain Lincoln's main point in the passage from his Second Inaugural Address.

   c) Explain how and why the two addresses differ, citing at least two specific pieces of evidence to support your answer.

2. Answer a, b, and c.

   a) There were significant political, social, cultural, and economic conflicts in the United States during both the 1920s and 1950s, as Americans debated the institutions and the ideas that would move the nation forward. Discuss two examples of conflicts that occurred in the 1920s.

GO ON TO THE NEXT PAGE.

b) Discuss two examples of conflicts that occurred in the 1950s.

c) Explain one way that these conflicts were similar in the 1920s and 1950s and one way that they differed.

"All children born in this country shall be held bond or free only according to the condition of the mother; and that if any Christian shall commit fornication with a Negro man or woman, he or she so offending shall pay double the fines imposed by the former act." (December 1662)

"The conferring of baptism does not alter the condition of the person as to his bondage or freedom." (September 1667)

"Moderate corporal punishment inflicted by master or magistrate upon a runaway servant shall not deprive the master of the satisfaction allowed by the law." (September 1668)

"If any slave resists his master . . . and by the extremity of the correction should chance to die, that his death shall not be accounted a felony, but the master . . . be acquitted." (October 1669)

Virginia Slave Laws, 1660s

3. Using the excerpts above, answer a, b, and c.

a) Explain why slavery was viewed as necessary in Virginia despite the existence of an indentured servant system.

b) Explain one event from the period 1670 to 1754 that would lead to harsher restrictions on slaves.

c) Explain one significant difference between the way the English colonies viewed slaves and the way either the French or Spanish viewed slaves.

"The principal attention has been to the stamp bill that has been preparing to lay before Parliament for taxing America.

"I beg leave to give you a Summary of the Arguments which are made in favor of such authority. The House of Commons, say they, is a branch of the supreme legislature of the nation, and which in its nature is supposed to represent, or rather to stand in the place of . . . the great body of the people who are below the dignity of peers. . . . They further urge that the only reason why America has not been heretofore taxed in the fullest manner has been merely on account of their infancy and inability; . . . in short, they say a power to tax is a necessary part of every supreme legislative authority, and that if they have not that power over America. they have none, and then America is at once a kingdom of itself.

"On the other hand, those who oppose the bill say it is true the Parliament have a supreme unlimited authority over every part and branch of the king's dominions, . . . yet we believe a British Parliament will never think it prudent to tax Ireland. . . . 'Tis true they say that the commons of England and of the British Empire are all represented in and by the House of Commons, but this representation is confessedly on all hands by construction and virtually only as to those who have no hand in choosing the representatives, and that the effects of this implied representation here and in America must be infinitely different in the article of taxation. . . . We think, say they, that it will be only to lay a foundation of great jealousy and continual uneasiness, and that to no purpose, as we already by the regulations upon their trade draw from the Americans all that they can spare. At least they say this step should not take place until or unless the Americans are allowed to send members to Parliament."

Jared Ingersoll, *Report on the Debates in Parliament*, 1765

GO ON TO THE NEXT PAGE.

4. Using the excerpt above, answer a, b, and c.

 a) Explain why Great Britain found it necessary to tax the colonies in 1765.

 b) Explain the arguments of the American colonists who opposed taxation of this kind.

 c) Explain what British action was taken and the American response to that action.

STOP

END OF SECTION I

SECTION II

Part A: Document-Based Question

Directions: The following question in based on the accompanying documents. The documents have been edited for this exercise. Spend approximately 15 minutes planning and 45 minutes writing your answer.

Write an essay that does the following:

+ States an appropriate thesis that directly addresses all parts of the question.
+ Supports the thesis or argument with evidence from all or all but one of the documents AND your knowledge of U.S. history beyond the documents.
+ Analyzes all or all but one of the documents.
+ Places each document into at least one of the following categories: intended audience, purpose, historical context, and/or point of view.
+ Uses historical evidence beyond the documents to support your argument.
+ Places the argument in the context of broader regional, national, or global processes.
+ Incorporates all of the elements above into a convincing essay.

Question: Following the American Revolution, the United States faced a number of political and diplomatic problems. Analyze those problems and assess the degree to which the new nation successfully resolved those issues between 1783 and 1801.

Document 1

Source: Alexander Hamilton, Constitutional Convention debate, June 18, 1787

All communities divide themselves into the few and the many. The first are the rich and well-born, the other the mass of the people. . . . The people are turbulent and changing; they seldom judge or determine right. Give, therefore, to the first class a distinct, permanent share in the government. They will check the unsteadiness of the second, and, as they cannot receive any advantage by a change, they therefore will ever maintain good government.

GO ON TO THE NEXT PAGE.

Document 2

Source: An Ordinance for the government of the Territory of the United States northwest of the River Ohio, July 13, 1787

Sec. 9. So soon as there shall be five thousand free male inhabitants of full age in the district, upon giving proof thereof to the governor, they shall receive authority, with time and place, to elect a representative from their counties or townships to represent them in the general assembly.

Art. 5. There shall be formed in the said territory, not less than three nor more than five States.

Art. 6. There shall be neither slavery nor involuntary servitude in the said territory, otherwise than in the punishment of crimes whereof the party shall have been duly convicted: *Provided, always*, That any person escaping into the same, from whom labor or service is lawfully claimed in any one of the original States, such fugitive may be lawfully reclaimed and conveyed to the person claiming his or her labor or service as aforesaid.

Document 3

Source: The Anti-federalist Papers, No. 46 "Where Then Is the Restraint?" *Maryland Gazette and Baltimore Advertiser,* November 2, 1788.

My object is to consider that undefined, unbounded and immense power which is comprised in the following clause—"And to make all laws which shall be necessary and proper for carrying into execution the foregoing powers, and all other powers vested by this constitution in the government of the United States; or in any department or offices thereof." Under such a clause as this, can anything be said to be reserved and kept back from Congress? Can it be said that the Congress have no power but what is expressed? "To make all laws which shall be necessary and proper"—or, in other words, to make all such laws which the Congress shall think necessary and proper—or who shalt judge for the legislature what is necessary and proper?

GO ON TO THE NEXT PAGE.

Document 4

Source: Tarring & Feathering an Excise Officer, 1794

Art Resource, NY

Document 5

Source: Treaty of Amity Commerce and Navigation (also known as Jay's Treaty) between the United States and Great Britain, November, 1794

ARTICLE 2. His Majesty will withdraw all His Troops and Garrisons from all Posts and Places within the Boundary Lines assigned by the Treaty of Peace to the United States. This Evacuation shall take place on or before the first Day of June One thousand seven hundred and ninety six, and all the proper Measures shall in the interval be taken by concert between the Government of the United States, and His Majesty's Governor General in America, for settling the previous arrangements which may be necessary respecting the delivery of the said Posts: . . .

ARTICLE 12. His Majesty Consents that it shall and may be lawful, during the time hereinafter Limited, for the Citizens of the United States, to carry to any of His Majesty's Islands and Ports in the West Indies from the United States in their own Vessels, not being above the burthen of Seventy Tons, any Goods or Merchandizes.

GO ON TO THE NEXT PAGE.

Document 6

Source: Map of New Orleans, Louisiana, 1798

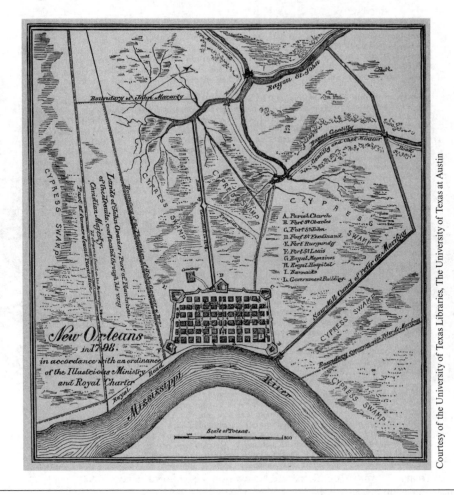

Courtesy of the University of Texas Libraries, The University of Texas at Austin

Document 7

Source: Thomas Jefferson, First Inaugural Address, March 4, 1801

Still one thing more, fellow-citizens—a wise and frugal Government, which shall restrain men from injuring one another, shall leave them otherwise free to regulate their own pursuits of industry and improvement, and shall not take from the mouth of labor the bread it has earned. This is the sum of good government, and this is necessary to close the circle of our felicities.

GO ON TO THE NEXT PAGE.

Part B: Long Essay Questions

Choose between one of the following two questions. You will have 35 minutes to complete your answer.

Question 1: To what degree did the U.S. government adopt a strict laissez-faire policy during the Gilded Age, and to what degree did it vary from a strict laissez-faire policy?

Question 2: To what degree did the U.S. government adopt a strict laissez-faire policy during the 1920s, and to what degree did it vary from a strict laissez-faire policy?

STOP

END OF EXAM

ANSWER KEY TO PRACTICE TEST 2

Multiple-Choice Questions

1.

Answer	Learning Objectives	Historical Thinking Skills	Key Concepts in the Curriculum Framework
C	NAT-2.0	Analyzing Evidence: Content and Sourcing	4.1

Explanation: The Constitution established a system of checks and balances to make certain no one branch of government abused its power. Jackson challenged the notion of separation of powers by asserting that all branches of government could judge the constitutionality of laws, not just the Supreme Court. Jackson further demonstrated this by ignoring the Supreme Court decision in *Worcester v. Georgia,* which ruled that the Cherokees could not be forcibly removed to Indian Territory. Division of powers refers to power being divided between the states and the national government. Judicial review was established in the case of *Marbury v. Madison,* not in Article I of the Constitution.

2.

Answer	Learning Objectives	Historical Thinking Skills	Key Concepts in the Curriculum Framework
B	NAT-2.0	Analyzing Evidence: Content and Sourcing Patterns of Continuity and Change over Time	4.1

Explanation: Jackson significantly increased the power of the presidency, taking actions that sometimes challenged constitutionality. This was demonstrated in his removal of deposits from the Second Bank of the United States, his threat to invade South Carolina during the nullification crisis, and his use of the spoils system and rotation in office, to name a few. The civil service system was not created until 1883. Jackson's tenure saw significant movement toward universal white male suffrage. Jackson was uncharacteristically timid in the Texas revolution because of the issue of slavery.

3.

Answer	Learning Objectives	Historical Thinking Skills	Key Concepts in the Curriculum Framework
A	NAT-2.0	Patterns of Continuity and Change over Time	4.1

Explanation: Jacksonian democracy saw the elimination of property qualifications for voting, moving the United States much closer to universal white male suffrage. The direct election of senators was not accomplished until 1913, and the Second American Party System actually emerged during the era of Jacksonian Democracy. Jackson was not supportive of federally funded internal improvements, as witnessed by his veto of the Maysville Road bill.

4.

Answer	Learning Objectives	Historical Thinking Skills	Key Concepts in the Curriculum Framework
C	POL-1.0	Analyzing Evidence: Content and Sourcing	8.3

Explanation : The southern strategy of the Republican Party was to appeal to conservative southern Democrats by taking a less-than-enthusiastic stand on enforcing court-ordered desegregation. In doing so, the Republican Party fundamentally abandoned the idea that attracting the votes of southern African Americans was a viable option. The political cartoon really has nothing to do with antiwar protests, federal funding for public education, or the Head Start program.

5.

Answer	Learning Objectives	Historical Thinking Skills	Key Concepts in the Curriculum Framework
D	POL-1.0	Analyzing Evidence: Content and Sourcing	8.3

Explanation: The southern strategy of the Republican Party included a less rigorous enforcement of laws regarding civil rights for African Americans, which the party believed would bring conservative southern Democrats to the Republicans. This strategy was foreshadowed by the inroads Barry Goldwater had made into the solidly Democratic South in the election of 1964. The Republican Party did not sponsor Freedom Summer or support expansion of social welfare programs initiated by the Great Society. Nixon worked to defuse Cold War hostilities through détente.

6.

Answer	Learning Objectives	Historical Thinking Skills	Key Concepts in the Curriculum Framework
C	NAT-2.0	Periodization	8.2

Explanation: The Civil Rights Act of 1964 guaranteed equal access to public accommodations regardless of race or gender. Southern congressmen believed that adding gender to the bill would ensure its defeat, a strategy that clearly backfired. *Brown v. Board of Education* and the launching of *Sputnik* both occurred in the 1950s. Spiraling gas prices were the result of the Arab oil embargo in the 1970s.

7.

Answer	Learning Objectives	Historical Thinking Skills	Key Concepts in the Curriculum Framework
D	WOR-2.0	Analyzing Evidence: Content and Sourcing	2.2

Explanation: The late seventeenth century witnessed increased competition among the European powers for raw materials and markets. This, coupled with the expansion of the economy of the British North American colonies, led the British government to issue the Navigation Acts in an effort to control colonial production and trade so that Britain, rather than colonial rivals, would reap the profits the British believed were rightly theirs.

8.

Answer	Learning Objectives	Historical Thinking Skills	Key Concepts in the Curriculum Framework
A	WOR-1.0	Causation	2.2

Explanation: Mercantilism is an economic system based on government regulation. Although the other choices here are terms important to the study of economics, the Navigation Acts were clearly an effort to regulate colonial trade.

9.

Answer	Learning Objectives	Historical Thinking Skills	Key Concepts in the Curriculum Framework
B	WOR-1.0	Causation	2.2

Explanation: The colonists largely ignored mercantilist laws. After the Glorious Revolution and well into the eighteenth century, the British made few efforts to strictly regulate the North American colonies. This relatively benign approach to colonial governance is often called "salutary neglect."

10.

Answer	Learning Objectives	Historical Thinking Skills	Key Concepts in the Curriculum Framework
D	WOR-1.0	Causation	3.1

Explanation: Beginning in 1754, the British fought a costly war in North America against the French and their Indian allies. The French and Indian War, known in Europe as the Seven Years' War, forced Britain to reassess its policies toward the American colonies. In order to pay its war debt and maintain control over the border between the British colonies and French territory, Parliament abandoned salutary neglect and attempted to reassert its authority over the American colonists.

11.

Answer	Learning Objectives	Historical Thinking Skills	Key Concepts in the Curriculum Framework
D	NAT-3.0	Contextualization Analyzing Evidence: Content and Sourcing	3.3

Explanation: When Crèvecoeur wrote *Letters from an American Farmer*, the mass movement of Americans across the Mississippi River had not yet begun. Crèvecoeur, writing in the aftermath of the American Revolution, described how and why Europeans who came to the British colonies had transformed into something new, "Americans."

12.

Answer	Learning Objectives	Historical Thinking Skills	Key Concepts in the Curriculum Framework
A	MIG-1.0	Comparison Analyzing Evidence: Content and Sourcing	3.3

Explanation: Prior to the Civil War, most immigrants to the United States came from Western and Central Europe, especially England, Ireland, Scandinavia, and Germany.

Crèvecoeur believed that immigrants had become truly "American," while Morse questioned whether immigrants, especially those who were Roman Catholic, could ever be fully assimilated.

13.
Answer	Learning Objectives	Historical Thinking Skills	Key Concepts in the Curriculum Framework
D	NAT-4.0	Causation	5.1

Explanation: Irish and German Catholics came to America in increasing numbers in the mid-1800s. Many settled in urban areas. Protestant opposition to Catholicism led to overt discrimination against Catholic immigrants.

14.
Answer	Learning Objectives	Historical Thinking Skills	Key Concepts in the Curriculum Framework
A	GEO-1.0	Analyzing Evidence: Content and Sourcing Periodization	6.2

Explanation: The closing of the frontier in 1890 and the Panic of 1893 demonstrated to Americans that resources were not inexhaustible. There is no indication that Hornaday favored government annihilation of buffalo herds or that Indians should be confined to small, scattered reservations, although they were. Hornaday is critical of the impact of civilization on the environment.

15.
Answer	Learning Objectives	Historical Thinking Skills	Key Concepts in the Curriculum Framework
D	NAT-4.0	Patterns of Continuity and Change over Time	6.2

Explanation: While initiatives like the Dawes Act were designed to assimilate American Indians into white society by breaking down tribal loyalty, they were largely unsuccessful. Attempts to promote private, rather than tribal, ownership of land also failed. Indian advocates like Helen Hunt Jackson believed assimilation was the best hope for American Indians. Indian suffrage did not become a reality until the Indian Citizenship Act of 1924.

16.
Answer	Learning Objectives	Historical Thinking Skills	Key Concepts in the Curriculum Framework
C	CUL-1.0	Contextualization Analyzing Evidence: Content and Sourcing	4.1

Explanation: The Second Great Awakening of the first half of the nineteenth century witnessed the emergence of many new religious groups, among them, the Mormons, the Oneida Community, the Shakers, and the Millerites. This period of religious reform also was characterized by the spread of evangelical enthusiasm and the growing influence of the Methodists and Baptists.

17.

Answer	Learning Objectives	Historical Thinking Skills	Key Concepts in the Curriculum Framework
C	CUL-1.0	Contextualization	4.1

Explanation: In the first half of the nineteenth century, many utopian experiments, both secular and religious, reflected the optimism of the Second Great Awakening and the belief that humans could be made perfect or at least much better, given the right environment.

18.

Answer	Learning Objectives	Historical Thinking Skills	Key Concepts in the Curriculum Framework
D	CUL-1.0	Patterns of Continuity and Change over Time Analyzing Evidence: Content and Sourcing	4.1

Explanation: The Millerites were part of a religious reform movement, as was the growth of the evangelical movement in the twentieth century. Populism, progressivism, and Social Darwinism were largely secular.

19.

Answer	Learning Objectives	Historical Thinking Skills	Key Concepts in the Curriculum Framework
A	CUL-3.0	Analyzing Evidence: Content and Sourcing	4.2

Explanation: The market revolution of the 1820s to 1850s resulted in a greater separation between the home and the workplace as production moved from the home to the factory. Roles for middle-class women whose economic role in the family was diminished were now defined by the "cult of true womanhood," which clearly reinforced women's role as wife and mother.

20.

Answer	Learning Objectives	Historical Thinking Skills	Key Concepts in the Curriculum Framework
B	CUL-3.0	Patterns of Continuity and Change over Time	4.1

Explanation: Women, regarded as the keepers of morality and rectitude in the mid-nineteenth century, assumed important roles in their churches during the Second Great Awakening. The skills they developed helped propel middle-class women into other reform movements: education, abolitionism, prison reform, and women's rights.

21.

Answer	Learning Objectives	Historical Thinking Skills	Key Concepts in the Curriculum Framework
D	CUL-4.0	Causation	5.1

Explanation: The challenges of moving west and establishing homes and communities in a harsh new environment required all family members to contribute to the welfare of their families. This was a democratizing process, and it was no coincidence that western states often granted more rights to women than they had had in the East.

22.

Answer	Learning Objectives	Historical Thinking Skills	Key Concepts in the Curriculum Framework
C	CUL-2.0	Comparison Analyzing Evidence: Content and Sourcing	6.3

Explanation: Ward argued that while Darwin's theories applied to the physical evolution of species, they did not apply to human behavior. He agreed with the Progressives who advocated efforts to improve the lot of the poor.

23.

Answer	Learning Objectives	Historical Thinking Skills	Key Concepts in the Curriculum Framework
A	NAT-4.0	Contextualization	6.2

Explanation: Nativists were opposed to immigration and generally opposed efforts to help the working poor, many of whom were recent immigrants. Nativists viewed immigrants as dregs of society. All of the other choices strongly indicate support for helping the poor.

24.

Answer	Learning Objectives	Historical Thinking Skills	Key Concepts in the Curriculum Framework
D	CUL-2.0	Causation	6.2

Explanation: It was not until the 1920s that Congress passed laws that established quotas and restricted immigration.

25.

Answer	Learning Objectives	Historical Thinking Skills	Key Concepts in the Curriculum Framework
B	NAT-1.0	Patterns of Continuity and Change over Time Analyzing Evidence: Content and Sourcing	5.3

Explanation: The Emancipation Proclamation issued in January 1863 freed only slaves living in states currently in rebellion against the United States. When the war ended in April 1865, Congress proposed the Thirteenth Amendment, to be ratified by all the states, to complete the process of emancipation throughout the nation.

26.

Answer	Learning Objectives	Historical Thinking Skills	Key Concepts in the Curriculum Framework
C	NAT-2.0	Patterns of Continuity and Change over Time	5.3

Explanation: Southern states ratified the Thirteenth, Fourteenth and Fifteenth amendments as a requirement to rejoin the Union at the end of the Civil War, but most were determined to prevent African Americans from enjoying the full rights of citizens. The states passed a series of restrictive laws, known collectively as Jim Crow laws, to restrict full access to citizenship rights and retain a system of social segregation in the southern states. Attempts to have such laws overturned by the federal court system were generally unsuccessful in the nineteenth and early twentieth centuries.

27.

Answer	Learning Objectives	Historical Thinking Skills	Key Concepts in the Curriculum Framework
B	NAT-2.0	Contextualization	8.2

Explanation: The 1954 Supreme Court decision, *Brown v. Board of Education of Topeka, Kansas*, was the first time the Court overturned a Jim Crow law that had claimed the right to establish "separate-but-equal" facilities for different races. The Court ruled that by requiring separation, the assumption was that there was no equality. The earlier case, *Plessy v. Ferguson*, had established the separate-but-equal justification in the 1890s.

28.

Answer	Learning Objectives	Historical Thinking Skills	Key Concepts in the Curriculum Framework
A	NAT-4.0	Causation Analyzing Evidence: Content and Sourcing	5.1

Explanation: These advertisements are representative of the discrimination faced by Irish immigrants who came to the United States in the 1840s and 1850s. They were singled out because they were Catholic and were willing to take whatever jobs were available at whatever wage was offered. They were perceived as a threat to many laboring class Americans.

29.

Answer	Learning Objectives	Historical Thinking Skills	Key Concepts in the Curriculum Framework
A	NAT-4.0	Contextualization	5.1

Explanation: Many working-class Americans feared Irish immigrants would replace them in their jobs as they were willing to work for lower wages. Most of the Irish who came in the 1840s and 1850s were impoverished and could not afford land out west, so they settled in urban areas where jobs were available for those with minimal skills and education. There were no federal government limits on immigration in this period of U.S. history. Immigrant neighborhoods became a common feature in many U.S. cities during the nineteenth century.

30.

Answer	Learning Objectives	Historical Thinking Skills	Key Concepts in the Curriculum Framework
B	CUL-4.0	Contextualization	7.2

Explanation: The U.S. Congress passed a series of restrictive immigration laws in the years immediately following World War I in an effort to protect jobs for those already in the country and out of a fear that immigrants, particularly those coming from parts of the world where communism and socialism were influential, might bring radical political ideas with them. These laws did not affect the movements within the country of other ethnic groups and was not directly related to concerns over the terms of the Treaty of Versailles.

31.

Answer	Learning Objectives	Historical Thinking Skills	Key Concepts in the Curriculum Framework
C	NAT-2.0	Causation	5.2

Explanation: The Compromise of 1850, which temporarily settled the issue of the extension of slavery into the territories gained from Mexico in the Mexican War, also laid the groundwork for new conflicts that ultimately resulted in the Civil War. The new Fugitive Slave Law, which allowed runaways to be recaptured in the North and returned to southern owners, radicalized many in the North who had previously been insulated from the real horrors of slavery. The public capture and return of some who had lived for years as free in the North received wide publicity and created strong opposition to slavery where feeling had not been so strong before the passage of this law. Abolitionist groups gained strength in both Congress and in the feelings of the general public.

32.

Answer	Learning Objectives	Historical Thinking Skills	Key Concepts in the Curriculum Framework
A	NAT-1.0	Causation	5.2

Explanation: Northern free-soilers were opposed to the extension of slavery into any new territories or states. The Compromise of 1850 left the question of the extension of slavery open to decisions made on the basis of popular sovereignty in the unorganized territories, two areas that were expected to be divided into Kansas and Nebraska. Many felt Kansas was likely to be open to slavery, while Nebraska would most likely be a free territory.

33.

Answer	Learning Objectives	Historical Thinking Skills	Key Concepts in the Curriculum Framework
A	NAT-2.0	Patterns of Continuity and Change over Time	5.2

Explanation: A stronger fugitive slave law was enacted as part of the Compromise of 1850. The Missouri Compromise was repealed by the Kansas-Nebraska Act in 1854 and was later ruled unconstitutional in the U.S. Supreme Court decision in *Dred Scott v. Sandford* (1857). Despite the 1808 banning of the slave trade, slaves continued to be imported into the United States. The compromise did nothing to gaurantee individual freedoms provided in the Bill of Rights.

34.

Answer	Learning Objectives	Historical Thinking Skills	Key Concepts in the Curriculum Framework
A	GEO-1.0	Contextualization Comparison Analyzing Evidence: Content and Sourcing	1.1

Explanation: These two societies were established and permanent, sustained by the cultivation of maize, trade, and a mixture of foraging and hunting as well as agriculture. They are examples of such settlements that developed in very different environments.

35.

Answer	Learning Objectives	Historical Thinking Skills	Key Concepts in the Curriculum Framework
B	MIG-1.0	Causation	1.2

Explanation: The introduction of European diseases played a major role in the destruction of native populations in both the Southwest and the Ohio Valley. While many native people ultimately worked for European colonists, it was rarely by choice and more often by force. Buffalo herds were not an essential part of the economies of the native populations in the areas represented by the photographs.

36.	Answer	Learning Objectives	Historical Thinking Skills	Key Concepts in the Curriculum Framework
	A	WOR-1.0	Causation Analyzing Evidence: Content and Sourcing	1.2

Explanation: The Columbian Exchange introduced new agricultural products, animals, and diseases into both the Americas and Europe, leading to changes in diet, lifestyles, and ultimately social structures. While many positive benefits came with the addition of new foods and farm animals, the exchange of diseases caused massive numbers of deaths in the Western Hemisphere. The introduction of a new form of syphilis to Europe was also devastating, though not in the numbers associated with smallpox, measles, and other European diseases that ravaged the native populations.

37.	Answer	Learning Objectives	Historical Thinking Skills	Key Concepts in the Curriculum Framework
	B	MIG-1.0	Causation Analyzing Evidence: Content and Sourcing	1.2

Explanation: European colonizers quickly began to import African slaves to the Western Hemisphere when native populations were not sufficient to do the work of the newly established plantations and mining ventures.

38.	Answer	Learning Objectives	Historical Thinking Skills	Key Concepts in the Curriculum Framework
	A	POL-3.0	Contextualization Analyzing Evidence: Content and Sourcing	9.1

Explanation: The last decades of the twentieth century saw the rise of neoconservatism and a general disdain for the broad social welfare programs of midcentury. Politicians supporting this position called for smaller government, lower taxes, and a pulling back from programs they felt created a welfare state. Citizens were called on to be responsible for their own well-being and stop relying on government support.

39.	Answer	Learning Objectives	Historical Thinking Skills	Key Concepts in the Curriculum Framework
	A	POL-1.0	Contextualization Patterns of Continuity and Change over Time	9.1

Explanation: In the late nineteenth century, many promoted "Social Darwinism," the idea that those who possessed energy and initiative would work their way to success. If one failed to succeed at what one attempted, then the fault was entirely his or her own. There was no belief that it was the place of the government to provide any social or economic safety net.

40.

Answer	Learning Objectives	Historical Thinking Skills	Key Concepts in the Curriculum Framework
B	WOR-2.0	Analyzing Evidence: Content and Sourcing Causation	9.3

Explanation: The attack on the World Trade Center and the Pentagon led the U.S. Congress to pass a number of laws aimed at increasing domestic security. Some, like the Patriot Act, included clauses than many have felt compromised some of the liberties guaranteed in the Bill of Rights.

41.

Answer	Learning Objectives	Historical Thinking Skills	Key Concepts in the Curriculum Framework
A	WOR-2.0	Causation	9.3

Explanation: The United States launched an attack on the strongholds of Al Qaeda in northern Afghanistan immediately after the attacks on the World Trade Center. An invasion of Iraq took place later when the Bush administration claimed the regime of Saddam Hussein was giving aid to America's enemies and stockpiling weapons of mass destruction that it could use against the United States and its allies in the future.

42.

Answer	Learning Objectives	Historical Thinking Skills	Key Concepts in the Curriculum Framework
C	WOR-2.0	Causation Analyzing Evidence: Content and Sourcing	8.1

Explanation: The war in Vietnam was extensively covered by the media, which brought the conflict into the living rooms of Americans nightly. Photos and videos showing the police chief of Saigon shooting a man suspected of being a Vietcong, naked children running from a napalm attack, and bodies lined up along a roadside after the My Lai massacre led Americans to question the values the United States was fighting for in Vietnam. Inroads made by the Vietcong in the Tet Offensive of 1968 also helped fuel the antiwar movement.

43.

Answer	Learning Objectives	Historical Thinking Skills	Key Concepts in the Curriculum Framework
C	WOR-2.0	Patterns of Continuity and Change over Time	8.1

Explanation: In the Tet Offensive, Communist forces won back most of the territory the United States and its allies had gained since 1963. This eroded support for the war as there seemed to be no end in sight to it. There was a large increase in the percentage of people who considered themselves doves (those who opposed the war) and a decrease in those who considered themselves hawks (those who favored continuing the war). The energy crisis did not come about until the 1970s.

44.

Answer	Learning Objectives	Historical Thinking Skills	Key Concepts in the Curriculum Framework
D	WXT-3.0	Periodization Interpretation	7.2

Explanation: Installment buying came into vogue in the 1920s. This allowed people to blur the distinction between needs and wants and purchase goods they might not otherwise afford. The introduction of credit cards is more closely tied to the 1950s. Radio and print media were the largest outlets for advertising as television did not become commonly available until after World War II. Prices for agricultural commodities decreased in the 1920s, and farmers did not enjoy the same prosperity as other Americans.

45.

Answer	Learning Objectives	Historical Thinking Skills	Key Concepts in the Curriculum Framework
B	WXT-3.0	Periodization	7.2

Explanation: The "big bull market" of the 1920s created a sense of optimism in the United States. The prices of consumer goods, like the Model T, enabled more people to feel that the quality of life was improving. Nuclear energy was a product of the post–World War II era, and immigration, while restricted, had little to do with the rising expectations of Americans. The failure of the United States to realize its goals in World War I actually led to increased cynicism and disillusionment.

46.

Answer	Learning Objectives	Historical Thinking Skills	Key Concepts in the Curriculum Framework
C	NAT-3.0	Patterns of Continuity and Change over Time	7.3

Explanation: In 1920, Warren G. Harding called for a "return to normalcy." That meant returning to the Gilded Age prior to the progressive reforms of the pre–World War I era. Republican presidents and conservative ideas dominated the political landscape during the 1920s. The United States refused to join the League of Nations or the World Court. The United States did not play the role of international peacekeeper in the Middle East.

47.

Answer	Learning Objectives	Historical Thinking Skills	Key Concepts in the Curriculum Framework
C	NAT-3.0	Historical Causation Analyzing Evidence: Content and Sourcing	7.3

Explanation: The fear of the concentration of Japanese American citizens on the West Coast led to the issuing of Executive Order 9066 by President Roosevelt, which ultimately set up internment camps in the interior of the country. While Japanese Americans did work in agricultural fields, they were not forced labor. Japanese American citizens could not be deported because of constitutional guarantees. Although there were some violent deaths in the camps, there were no executions for espionage or sabotage.

48.

Answer	Learning Objectives	Historical Thinking Skills	Key Concepts in the Curriculum Framework
B	NAT-4.0	Periodization	7.3

Explanation: A. Philip Randolph threatened a march on Washington if President Roosevelt did not establish a commission to investigate and prevent racial discrimination in hiring defense workers. Ultimately this led to the establishment of the Fair Employment Practices Commission. Racial segregation in the armed forces was not ended until the Truman administration. Schools remained segregated in much of the United States until long after the *Brown v. Board of Education* decision in 1954. African American troops served in both the European and Pacific theaters of the war until the war ended in 1945.

49.

Answer	Learning Objectives	Historical Thinking Skills	Key Concepts in the Curriculum Framework
A	CUL-3.0	Patterns of Continuity and Change over Time	7.3

Explanation: The classic example of Rosie the Riveter demonstrated that labor shortages opened opportunities for women and minorities. Women succeeded in jobs traditionally reserved for men.. However, they earned significantly less than men in the same positions. While women served in various branches of the military, they were not assigned combat roles. Women won the right to vote with the ratification of the Nineteenth Amendment in 1920, well before World War II.

50.

Answer	Learning Objectives	Historical Thinking Skills	Key Concepts in the Curriculum Framework
B	NAT-2.0	Comparison	5.2

Explanation: After the passage of the Compromise of 1850, attitudes toward slavery and abolition became more polarized in both the North and the South, with both sides increasingly unwilling to work for a middle ground. Southerners felt their entire economy and way of life was threatened, while northerners increasingly came to see slavery as an intolerable immoral practice.

51.

Answer	Learning Objectives	Historical Thinking Skills	Key Concepts in the Curriculum Framework
B	WXT-1.0	Causation	5.2

Explanation: Southern slaveholders made many different arguments to justify the slave system, among them the belief that had Africans not been taken into slavery, they would have never been exposed to Christianity and could not have hoped to be allowed into heaven after they died. While slaves may have been more efficient at some types of farmwork, the argument that they were better than white workers was not generally made. There was very little southern manufacturing before the Civil War. Most slaves were used in agricultural work or as house slaves. There was some urban slavery in the South, but not in factories.

52.

Answer	Learning Objectives	Historical Thinking Skills	Key Concepts in the Curriculum Framework
A	POL-2.0	Comparison	5.2

Explanation: Many abolitionist groups argued over which tactics were appropriate to use to try to bring about the end of slavery. Some advocated nonviolence, hoping slave owners could be persuaded to give up their chattel through appeals to logic and religious principles. Others, particularly those who had former slaves among their membership, believed that slaves had the right to do whatever was necessary to gain their freedom.

53.

Answer	Learning Objectives	Historical Thinking Skills	Key Concepts in the Curriculum Framework
B	CUL-2.0	Periodization	6.3

Explanation: Veblen criticized the rich for excessive displays that flaunted their wealth for no other reason than they could. He referred to that as "conspicuous consumption." Robber barons like the Vanderbilts and the Bradley Martins built ornate mansions and threw lavish parties that cost far more than many factory workers would earn in a lifetime. While scientific management and the philosophy of utilitarianism were associated with the time period, they didn't deal with such excessive displays of spending.

54.

Answer	Learning Objectives	Historical Thinking Skills	Key Concepts in the Curriculum Framework
C	POL-3.0	Periodization	7.1

Explanation: Abuses of power by big business led to increased calls for government regulation of business at both the national and state levels. Legislation such as the Interstate Commerce Act and the Sherman Antitrust Act, though weak and fairly ineffective, set the precedent for government regulation of business. While a graduated income tax was proposed, passed, and subsequently ruled unconstitutional, there were no calls for a cap on income. While the Populist Party supported government ownership of utilities and railroads, that call was not realized.

55.

Answer	Learning Objectives	Historical Thinking Skills	Key Concepts in the Curriculum Framework
A	POL-3.0	Periodization	6.3

Explanation: Both the state and federal governments took a laissez-faire (hands-off) attitude toward social welfare in the time period. Private movements like the settlement house movement, the Salvation Army, and the YMCA took up the slack to try to alleviate suffering among the poor. Railroad companies did not offer free transportation to the west.

Short-Answer Questions

1.

Learning Objectives	Historical Thinking Skills	Key Concepts in the Curriculum Framework
MIG-1.0 WOR-2.0	Analyzing Evidence: Content and Sourcing Patterns of Continuity and Change over Time	5.2 5.3

What a good response might include

a) A good response might include the following: It will note that in his First Inaugural Address, Lincoln states that he has no intention or right to interfere with slavery where it exists; it will note that Lincoln was a free-soiler and that his primary objective early on in the sectional crisis was to preserve the Union.

b) A good response might include the following: It might explain that Lincoln's Second Inaugural Address attempted to place the blame for the Civil War on the South; it might explain that this inaugural address offered hope for a lenient reconstruction.

c) A good response might note the following: Lincoln's first address was given before the Upper South had seceded and before the Civil War had begun. Thus, his objective was to placate the southern states and preserve the Union. In contrast, by the time of the Second Inaugural Address, Lincoln had already issued the Emancipation Proclamation, which had freed the slaves in the areas of the Confederacy still in rebellion in 1863. Lincoln's objective in issuing the Emancipation Proclamation was to clarify the status of runaway slaves and slaves in areas that were conquered. He also hoped to prevent any European alliances with the Confederacy by making the Civil War more clearly about slavery.

2.

Learning Objectives	Historical Thinking Skills	Key Concepts in the Curriculum Framework
CUL-2.0 NAT-2.0 POL-2.0	Contextualization Comparison	7.2 7.3 8.2

What a good response might include

a) A good response might include one or more of the following examples of conflicts: the conflict over the Eighteenth Amendment, which prohibited alcohol within the United States; the conflict over immigration and the quota system devised in the 1920s; the debate between fundamentalism and scientific modernism; concepts of Victorian womanhood versus modern womanhood (private versus public spheres).

b) A good response might include one or more of the following examples of conflicts: conflicts over segregation and civil rights; the liberalism of the legislative branch and the conservatism of the executive branch; disagreements over how to combat the threat of Soviet expansion; the growing generation gap between youth and adults, especially among the middle class.

c)   A good response might include one or more of the following examples of similarities: both periods were times of economic growth and prosperity; both periods also witnessed an expansion of consumerism and the suburbanization of American society; both periods also saw the emergence of a youth culture that challenged the prevailing morals of the established generation. Examples of differences might include the following: whereas the 1920s was a time of activism in women's rights, the 1950s were relatively dormant in this regard; the 1950s saw a much more active expansion of the civil rights movement during the 1950s, including the movement toward nonviolent civil disobedience, than had existed in the 1920s; there were also significantly different challenges in terms of foreign policy, with the 1920s marked by a spirit of isolationism while the 1950s was a time of tremendous international focus, in large part a product of the Cold War.

3.

Learning Objectives	Historical Thinking Skills	Key Concepts in the Curriculum Framework
WXT-1.0 WXT-2.0	Analyzing Evidence: Content and Sourcing Patterns of Continuity and Change over Time	2.1 2.2

What a good response might include

a)   A good response might include the following: Because of improvements in the English economy after the restoration in 1660, the supply of indentured servants from there declined; increasingly colonial authorities felt threatened by freed indentured servants, especially after Bacon's Rebellion in 1676; there was also a high mortality rate among indentured servants.

b)   A good response might include the following: Bacon's Rebellion in 1676 increased colonial authorities' fear of the "landless rabble"; slave rebellions, particularly the Stono Rebellion, along with work slowdowns and sabotage, led colonial assemblies to enact laws that restricted the movement of slaves; plantation owners feared that there would be a labor shortage, thus leading them to advocate that African Americans "servants" and their offspring should be slaves for life.

c)   A good response might include the following: the French in North America had little need for slaves in their North American colonies because their economy was not based on plantation labor; however, slavery was prominent in the French West Indies; in both Spanish and French colonies, slaves and native populations were more likely to intermarry than in the British colonies; the Spanish and French had fewer restrictive laws governing the movement of slaves.

4.

Learning Objectives	Historical Thinking Skills	Key Concepts in the Curriculum Framework
CUL-2.0 NAT-1.0	Analyzing Evidence: Content and Sourcing Patterns of Continuity and Change over Time	3.1 3.2

What a good response might include

a)   A good response might include the following: Great Britain was saddled with debt following the French and Indian War and needed to raise money; the colonists and British disagreed on the contribution of each to victory over the French and who should assume the cost of the victory; the British believed the colonies were undertaxed and were reluctant to raise taxes on citizens in Britain.

b)   A good response might include the following: many Americans believed Britain had the right to regulate trade but lacked the power to impose direct internal taxes on the colonies; many colonists believed that they were being taxed despite not having representatives in Parliament; many colonists rejected the notion of virtual representation in favor, ostensibly, of direct representation.

c)   A good response might include the following: Great Britain attempted to tax the colonies through acts such as the Sugar Act, the Stamp Act, the Townshend Acts, the Quartering Act; colonial resistance including organized protests under the auspicious of the Sons and Daughters of Liberty and included events such as the Stamp Act Congress, nonimportation agreements and boycotts, and the Boston Tea Party.

Document-Based Question

Learning Objectives	Historical Thinking Skills	Key Concepts in the Curriculum Framework
POL-1.0 NAT-2.0 WOR-1.0	Analyzing Evidence: Content and Sourcing Patterns of Continuity and Change over Time Synthesis	3.1 3.2

What a good response might include

This question asks you to consider the domestic and diplomatic problems that the new United States faced between the end of the American Revolution to the beginning of the nineteenth century. You will use primarily the historical thinking skill of **patterns of continuity and change over time**, as well as the skills of **synthesis**, and the **appropriate use of relevant historical evidence**. Begin by crafting a thesis that articulates the major issues revealed by the documents and by fully explaining what you will argue about the relative success of the United States in dealing with these issues. Your thesis must do more than simply repeat the prompt. Strong essays will discuss the origins and outcomes of both the domestic and diplomatic (or foreign policy) issues that the United States faced in the 1780s and 1790s. It will make a case for why these issues were problematic and the degree to which they were successfully resolved by 1801. You must also explicate and evaluate the documents and place them in proper historical context.

In order to earn the maximum of 3 points for document use, in this case you must analyze *all* or *all but one* of the documents (that is, at least six in this DBQ) and address how these documents provide evidence of domestic or diplomatic problems the United States encountered. Do not forget the requirement to address one of these points for each document you use: audience, purpose, historical context, or point of view. If you are not certain how to do this, ask your teacher to show you some examples. You cannot merely name the intended audience or simply state the speaker's point of view. Instead, you must link this discussion to the directive at hand: to analyze the domestic and diplomatic problems that the United States faced and to evaluate the extent to which the new nation succeeded in solving those problems.

Before you even begin writing—and remember to make good use of the 15-minute planning period that you are given—make a list of relevant information that you know about this period. You may remember, for example, that in 1783, the year the United States signed the Treaty of Paris with Great Britain officially ending the American Revolution, the new nation was governed under the Articles of Confederation—the Constitution was still seven years from ratification. The Articles of Confederation failed for a number of reasons, including the ability of the new government to raise revenue or levy taxes. You will likely remember that there was a bitter three-year fight over ratification between people calling themselves Federalists and a group calling themselves Antifederalists. On the diplomatic front, you would do well to recall that the French Revolution, whose effects were felt around the world, began in 1789 and that the various factions within the federal government disagreed about what position the United States should take toward that conflict and the subsequent wars that it engendered. You might also remember that in 1783, the United States held only the eastern part of the North American continent and that the British in Canada and the Spanish to the South and West remained formidable presences on the continent, sometimes threatening U.S. sovereignty.

You should also remember that you are required to link documents together to make a convincing argument. For example, you could use Alexander Hamilton's statement at the Constitutional Convention (Document 1) along with the document from the Antifederalist papers (Document 4) and Thomas Jefferson's first inaugural address (Document 7) to illustrate the ongoing debate throughout this era about how much power the federal government should have. On the diplomatic front, you might connect the Northwest Ordinance (Document 2) with Jay's Treaty (Document 5) to illustrate ongoing problems with British occupation of the Northwest forts. Similarly, both Jay's Treaty (Document 5) and the map of the port of New Orleans (Document 6) expose issues that the United States faced with powerful foreign nations on the North American continent.

Do not refer to the documents as "Document 1" or "Document 6." Instead, refer to the type of document (painting, address to Congress . . .) and its context, and reference the author, the title of the work, and his purpose audience, or point of view. Be certain to link the document to your thesis. One of the worst errors you can make is to do what is called "laundry listing" the documents.

When you finish writing, look over your essay. Be certain that you have included all of the required elements. If you do not have already have a generic rubric, ask your teacher to give you a copy of one so you will be absolutely certain that you understand what the person who scores your essay is looking for. The rubric is a sort of map for your essay. Remember that if you go on a journey without a map, you might never know when you arrive at your destination. So commit that rubric to memory and pay attention to your destination and what it takes to get there.

Long Essay Questions

1.

Learning Objectives	Historical Thinking Skills	Key Concepts in the Curriculum Framework
WXT-2.0 POL-3.0	Analyzing Evidence: Content and Sourcing Contextualization Argumentation Patterns of Continuity and Change over Time	6.1

What a good response might include

This is a clear and straightforward question, and good responses will explicitly address the degree to which the U.S. government adopted a strict laissez-faire policy during the Gilded Age. The essay calls for the historical thinking skills of the **use of relevant historical evidence, contextualization, historical argumentation,** and **continuity and change over time**. You must develop a thoughtful thesis that clearly states the argument you will craft. It is important that you make it clear in your opening statement that you understand what "strict laissez-faire policy" means. The term *laissez-faire*, coined in the nineteenth century, means a complete hands-off approach, with no interference. You might make an argument that laissez-faire as a policy can apply to more than just economics—it can also be applied to social issues.

Your essay must synthesize a significant body of evidence and must support your thesis. Remember not to rush through your essay; rather, take the time to make sure that you are answering the question and that you are not merely summarizing events and ideas but rather analyzing them. After you write your introductory paragraph, put down your pen and carefully read what you have just written. It is far easier to make changes in your essay at the beginning rather than trying to correct your mistakes as time expires. Also, occasionally stop writing as you work on the rest of your essay and examine your work to ensure that you are saying just what you want to say.

You might explain that during the Gilded Age, the federal government pursued a probusiness policy in that it provided land grants and subsidies to railroads. You might also explain that the federal government pursued tight money, high protective tariff policies that aided big business. The federal government also intervened in labor disputes on the side of big business through the issuing of injunctions and commitment of troops, and it encouraged westward expansion through the granting of homesteads and the removal of American Indians. Your essay must cite specific examples to support the thesis and explain how and why those examples do so. All of these policies suggest that the United States did not pursue a strict laissez-faire policy toward the economy.

At the same time, you should consider that the federal government did pursue a strict laissez-faire policy when it came to the regulation of big business. A number of reformers called on the government to end its laissez-faire approach to regulating big business. Early attempts to convince the government to regulate big business were largely unsuccessful. However, over time, Congress passed—and the president signed—legislation that marked the beginning of business regulation. Examples include the Interstate Commerce Act (1887) and the Sherman Antitrust Act (1882). Essays must cite and explain how specific examples such as these support the thesis.

Typically the best responses show an understanding of the fact that things are seldom all one thing or all the other. Thus, essays that acknowledge a more complex analysis would tend to receive higher scores.

2.

Learning Objectives	Historical Thinking Skills	Key Concepts in the Curriculum Framework
WXT-2.0 POL-2.0	Analyzing Evidence: Content and Sourcing Contextualization Argumentation Patterns of Continuity and Change over Time	7.1

What a good response might include

This is a clear and straightforward question, and good responses will explicitly address the degree to which the U.S. government adopted a strict laissez-faire policy during the 1920s. The essay calls for the historical thinking skills of the **use of relevant historical evidence**, **contextualization**, **historical argumentation**, and **continuity and change over time**. You must develop a thoughtful thesis that clearly states the argument you will craft. It is important that you make it clear in your opening statement that you understand what a "strict laissez-faire policy" means. The term *laissez-faire*, coined in the nineteenth century, means a complete hands-off approach with no interference. You might make an argument that laissez-faire as a policy can apply to more than just economics—it can also be applied to social issues.

Your essay must synthesize a significant body of evidence and must support your thesis. Remember not to rush through your essay; rather, take the time to make sure that you are answering the question and not merely summarizing events and ideas but rather analyzing them. After you write your introductory paragraph, put down your pen and carefully read what you have just written. It is far easier to make changes in your essay at the beginning rather than trying to correct your mistakes as time expires. Also, occasionally stop writing as you work on the rest of your essay and examine your work to ensure that you are saying just what you want to say.

You might explain that during the 1920s, the federal government pursued a probusiness policy in an attempt to return to the policies of the Gilded Age. Just as during the Gilded Age, the federal government in the 1920s pursued tight money and high protective tariff policies that aided big business. The 1920s also witnessed the implementation of the "trickle-down" theory of economics that theorizes that the more that big businesses make, the better the economy will thrive because business leaders will reinvest their profits into the economy, thus creating jobs and expanding the gross domestic product. In the 1920s, the federal government appointed to various regulatory agencies leaders who were probusiness advocates and used those agencies to aid rather than regulate big business. Thus, in terms of aiding big business, the 1920s clearly did not witness a strict laissez-faire policy on the part of the federal government. You might also explain that the government quickly ended government control of businesses after World War I and also cite the federal government's lack of regulation of the stock market that led to the "bull market" of the 1920s that ultimately led to the stock market crash and the Great Depression.

Typically the best responses show an understanding of the fact that things are seldom all one thing or all the other. Thus, essays that acknowledge a more complex analysis would tend to receive higher scores.

Text Credits

Page 213, Short-Answer Question 2. "Immigration into the United States, 1861–2010." Courtesy of the Progressives for Immigration Reform.

Page 292, Multiple-Choice Questions 5–7. Cliff Staten, *U.S. Foreign Policy since World War II*, 2005. Courtesy of American Diplomacy Publishers.

Page 313, Multiple-Choice Questions 44–46. "Cotton Production and Producers, 1800–1860." From *Time on the Cross: The Economics of American Negro Slavery* by Robert William Fogel and Stanley L. Engerman. Copyright © 1974 by Robert William Fogel and Stanley L. Engerman. Used by permission of W.W. Norton and Company, Inc.